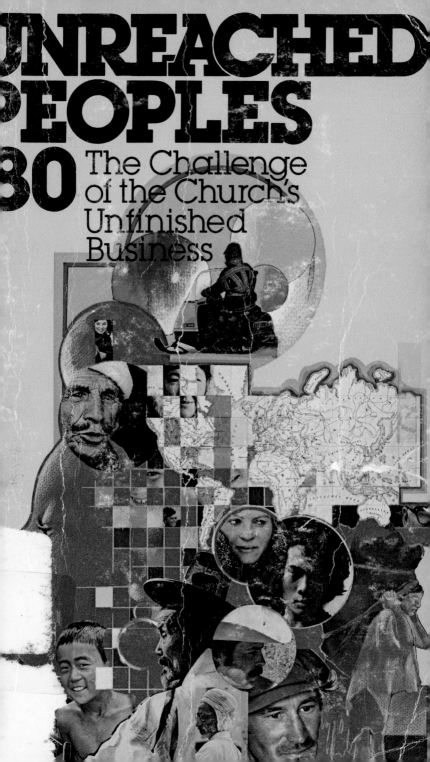

UNREACHED PEOPLES

'80

The Challenge of the Church's Unfinished Business

UNREACHED PEOPLES '80

Also in this series:
UNREACHED PEOPLES '79

UNREACHED PEOPLES '80

'80 C. Peter Wagner and
Edward R. Dayton, editors

David C. Cook Publishing Co.
ELGIN, ILLINOIS—WESTON, ONTARIO

CONTENTS

Introduction   7

Lausanne Committee for World Evangelization as of 1979 14

Part 1 The Unreached and How to Reach Them   17
    Planning Strategies for Evangelism   19
    Muslim Evangelism in the 1980s   38
    The Challenge of Reaching Muslims for Christ   51

Part 2 Case Studies   65
    Responsive Somali Peoples in Kenya   67
    The Sundanese of Indonesia   75
    Reaching the Baranada People of Barunda   85
    Muslim Evangelism in Suranya   95
    A Unique Effort to Reach Jammu-Kashmir for Christ 105

Part 3 Unreached Peoples—Expanded Descriptions   115

Part 4 Registry of the Unreached   205
    Explanation   207
    Index by Group Name   209
    Index by Receptivity   259
    Index by Religion   277
    Index by Language   295
    Index by Country   325

Appendixes   355
    Appendix A   357
    Appendix B   367
    Appendix C: Recommended Bibliography   373
    Notes   377

CONTENTS

Introduction

Part 1 Approach and Overview: General Framework

Part 2 Case Studies

Part 3 Unrealized Trade—Expanded Possibilities

Part 4 Prospect of Transformation

Appendices
  Appendix A
  Appendix B
  Appendix C
  Notes

Introduction

Rarely in recent history have God's people been so acutely aware of the urgency of the task of reaching the people of the world who do not know Jesus Christ with the message of his Gospel. A sense of excitement and anticipation is in the air. Our knowledge about the missionary task has exploded. New missionary agencies have emerged. Third World Christians have responded enthusiastically to the missionary challenge. There have been new political shifts on the international scene. All of this indicates that an unprecedented era of ingathering may have begun. Certainly the current multiplication of churches in region after region of the world may be seen as the first indication of a trend. Every day of the year there are an estimated sixty thousand new Christians. Every week about sixteen hundred new churches are started.

The *Unreached Peoples* series, of which this is the second annual volume, seems to have come at a most opportune time. *Unreached Peoples '79* has been very favorably received. Many church leaders, mission executives, professors of mission, laypeople on church mission committees, and field missionaries have responded positively to the information and challenge presented in that book. It was selected by *The Occasional Bulletin of Missionary Research* as one of the fifteen outstanding mission-related books of the year.

But it was only a start, and a small one at that. In *Unreached Peoples '79,* Ralph D. Winter focused our attention on the fact that the world contains approximately 16,750 cultural groups and sub-groups within a world population of 4.2 billion people. Among this 4.2 billion there are approximately 3 billion people who are not Christians. But 2.5 billion of these non-Christians are found in about 11,300 groups that can only be reached by cross-cultural evangelism. They are the "hidden people." *Unreached Peoples '79* identified and described 666 of them. This volume adds 1,316 more groups. The remaining task, therefore, is tremendous, but the prospects are exhilarating. Instead of thinking about reaching 3 billion non-Christians we can see the missionary task of the church worldwide as planting a viable church among each of these 11,300 hidden groups.

TWENTY PERCENT PRACTICING CHRISTIANS?

A significant number of readers of *Unreached Peoples '79* have asked why we mentioned "twenty percent practicing Christians" as the upper limit for our definition of "unreached peoples." Twenty percent seemed too high to some. Cannot a people be considered reached even if it has less than twenty percent of the population as practicing Christians?

The answer to that question is obviously yes. Twenty percent is on the high side. Social interaction theory has revealed that when an innovation is proposed to a given society, the "early adopters" will constitute somewhere between ten and twenty percent of the people. Until they adopt it, the innovation spreads very slowly. If they do not adopt it, the movement may be arrested and limited to a very small segment of the population. But when the early adoption stage is over and the innovation takes root, the subsequent spread accelerates rapidly.

How does this apply to the spread of the Gospel?

By definition, each of the 11,300 hidden peoples requires E-2 or E-3 evangelism[1] if it is to be reached. Someone has to move out of one culture and into another in order for that to happen, since there is no one presently in that particular culture who constitutes an adequate force for evangelism. But it is equally true that before the evangelism process is finished, most of the individuals in that new culture will be won by monocultural or E-1 evangelism, not by the cross-cultural workers. Perhaps only 1 or 2 percent of the individuals in the new culture will actually accept Christ as Lord and Savior under the direct evangelistic ministry of the cross-cultural missionaries. Perhaps even fewer.

But the initial E-2 and E-3 evangelism is not usually the end of the missionary task. A certain amount of Christian nurture is called for. The new converts are babes in Christ. They need to be taught the Word of God. They need to learn to pray. They need to discover their spiritual gifts. They need to be introduced to the Christian ethical code. They need to begin to sing and to worship God in a way that is properly contextualized for their culture. All this demands the attention of cross-cultural missionaries. It is initially an E-2 or E-3 task. The missionaries should avoid the all-too-common mistake of prolonging this nurture process and thereby supporting a distasteful paternalism. But adequate nurture is always necessary for beginning a strong church that has the evangelistic momentum to complete the task by E-1 methods.

When should the missionary consider his or her task accomplished? When E-2 or E-3 ministry is no longer called for and when the E-1 form can take over and effectively spread the Gospel.

And how does the missionary know when this stage has occurred? What we are saying is that the critical point is reached when about 10 to 20 percent of the people are practicing Christians. From one point of view, the number is somewhat arbitrary. But from another, it reflects a degree of realism. More research is needed, and as new information is available we may well decide to alter the figure accordingly.

THE 1980 FOCUS: MUSLIMS

While *Unreached Peoples '79* was not focused on any particular category of peoples, the current volume emphasizes Muslims. After the initial chapter by Edward R. Dayton, which explains the general approach that the Lausanne Strategy Working Group is taking toward evangelistic and missionary strategies, all subsequent chapters deal with some aspect of Muslim peoples. Michael Youssef provides an overview of worldwide Muslim evangelism. Don M. McCurry writes an informative article on some recent developments in Muslim evangelism from a North American perspective.

McCurry, a seasoned Presbyterian missionary to Pakistan, has answered a new call from God in his life and become the director of the new Samuel Zwemer Institute in Pasadena, California. He has functioned as the third member of the editorial team of this volume along with Edward Dayton and myself. He worked with us in the planning process, the arrangements that had to be made for the case studies, and the polishing of the copy. This volume reflects to a very significant degree the genius of Don McCurry, and we are grateful to him.

The Muslim world is over seven hundred million strong. Muslims are found on every continent of the world. Although they are concentrated in North Africa and the Middle East, and across Southern Asia to Indonesia, very important and growing pockets of Muslims are to be found in all the traditionally non-Muslim areas of the world. It is estimated, for example, that twenty-four million Muslims live in Europe, with eight million in western Europe alone. Two million are in France, one million in West Germany, and one million in Great Britain. In the Western Hemisphere, one million are found in Latin America, two million in the United States, and three hundred thousand in Canada.[2]

In the Soviet Union alone there are between thirty and forty million Muslims. The five republics of Soviet Central Asia—Uzbekistan, Kirgiziya, Tadzhikistan, Turkmenistan, and Kazakhstan—have twenty-three million Muslims. Some observers feel that the long-term experience of living under an atheistic Soviet regime has weakened the religious hold of Islam on those peoples, although cultural ties to the Muslim way of life seem to have remained strong. If this conclusion is correct, it is likely that Soviet Muslims will be more receptive to the Gospel than those in Muslim-dominated lands.[3]

Receptivity to the Christian message, however, is only one qualification for evangelizing Muslims. Another equally important condition is that they perceive the presentation of the message as culturally relevant. The most formidable barriers to becoming Christian are more frequently social than theological, as Donald McGavran observed years ago. Increasingly, missionaries to Muslims are asking each other whether one reason for the relative

11

lack of results may have been that the presentation of the Gospel has been much too Western, and that it has therefore not received a fair consideration. As missionaries ask new questions, older strategies are being reevaluated. Here are some examples of issues raised some time ago by missiologists Charles Kraft and Ralph Winter:

1. Is there any way for Muslims to become Christians without first becoming Europeans?
2. Do we even need to use the label "Christian" to designate Muslim followers of Jesus?
3. Do we have the right to deemphasize (not deny) aspects of traditional Christian teaching such as the Son of God or the death of Jesus or the Trinity or water baptism as we initially present the message to them?
4. Can we start with the Muslim understanding of God (and call him Allah), or must Muslims convert to our understanding of God as a *precondition* of salvation?
5. Can we start with the Koran's understanding of Jesus, or must Muslims convert to our understanding as a *precondition* of salvation?

Questions like these are somewhat mindboggling, especially when one knows that they and others like them come from individuals who are firmly planted in mainstream evangelical Christianity. They are not being raised by those who have accepted a modernistic theology that denies the inerrancy of Scripture, or doubts the reality of heaven and hell, or questions the deity of Christ. In order to give a thorough airing to such questions, the North American Lausanne Committee for World Evangelism convened a special high-level Consultation on Muslim Evangelism, held in Glen Eyrie, Colorado, October 15 to 21, 1978. Don McCurry, the special consultant for this volume, was the general coordinator of that conference, and he tells more about it in his chapter. The report of the Glen Eyrie Consultation[4] and the compendium of papers presented at the conference entitled *The Gospel and Islam*[5] are essential documents for Christian workers interested in understanding new developments in Muslim evangelism.

LOOKING AHEAD

It is important to see that each volume of *Unreached Peoples* is part of a larger whole. Each contains a set of expanded descriptions of sixty to eighty unreached groups of people. Each has basic information needed to see the on-going picture of attempts to proclaim Christ to all peoples everywhere. To adequately understand *Unreached Peoples '80* you should also have *Unreached Peoples '79*.

The next two volumes in this series will concentrate on two highly significant regions of the world. *Unreached Peoples '81* will focus on Asia, and *Unreached Peoples '82* will emphasize urban groups. Work on them has already begun, and they promise to be valuable additions to this growing library of information on the church's unfinished task.

The entire staff of the MARC division of World Vision International merits recognition for the essential part it has played in compiling this book. Particularly important were David Fraser, James Griffith, and Boyd Johnson.

Ed Dayton and I would also like to salute the David C. Cook Publishing Company for the extraordinary help it has given to get this information to the Christian public. We thank God for the vision He has given them to use their resources effectively for the worldwide spread of the Gospel.

—C. Peter Wagner, Chairman
LCWE Strategy Working Group and
Associate Professor of Church Growth,
Fuller Seminary School of World Mission

LAUSANNE COMMITTEE FOR WORLD EVANGELIZATION AS OF 1979

One of the outcomes of the International Congress on World Evangelization held in Lausanne, Switzerland, in the summer of 1974 was a mandate from the 2,400 participants to form an ongoing committee. The "Spirit of Lausanne" was a powerful new thrust for completing the task of world evangelization. It was not to die.

The Lausanne Committee for World Evangelization was born at a meeting in Mexico City, January 20-23, 1975. The committee drew up a constitution, named forty-eight charter members, and elected Leighton Ford president and Gottfried Osei-Mensah executive secretary.

The central offices of the LCWE are located in Nairobi, Kenya (P.O. Box 21225). Four working groups carry out its basic ministries—intercession, theology/education, strategy, and communications. The current listing of committee members follows:

Francisco Anabalon, Chile
Ramez Atallah, Canada
*Saphir Athyal, India, *Deputy Chairman*
 Peter Beyerhaus, West Germany
 Henri Blocher, France
 Vonette Bright, U.S.A.
 Michael Cassidy, South Africa
 Chongnahm Cho, Korea

*Executive Committee member

14

Robert Coleman, U.S.A.
Mariano DiGangi, Canada
Nilson Fanini, Brazil
Ajith Fernado, Sri Lanka
*Leighton Ford, U.S.A., *Chairman*
*Bruno Frigoli, Bolivia
* Andrew Furuyama, Japan
Emmy Gichinga, Kenya
Geziel Nunes Gomes, Brazil
Billy Graham, U.S.A. *(ex officio)*
Edward Hill, U.S.A.
Fritz Hoffmann, East Germany
C. B. Hogue, U.S.A.
*Donald Hoke, U.S.A., *Treasurer*
*Armin Hoppler, Switzerland
Abd-el Masih Istafanous, Egypt
Festo Kivengere, Uganda
A. T. Victor Koh, Philippines
Gordon Landreth, England
Lamuel Libert, Argentina
Branco Lovrec, Yugoslavia
Billy Melvin, U.S.A.
Stanley Mooneyham, U.S.A.
Agne Norlander, Sweden
Petrus Octavianus, Indonesia
*Samuel Odunaike, Nigeria
*Gottfried Osi-Mensah, Kenya, *Executive Secretary*
Pablo Perez, Mexico
Ted Raedeke, U.S.A.
*John Reid, Australia, *Intercession Working Group
    Chairman*
John Richard, India
Subhas Sangma, Bangladesh
Peter Schneider, Germany
*John Stott, England, *Theology and Education Working*

Group Chairman
*C. Peter Wagner, U.S.A., *Strategy Working Group Chairman*
Ben Wati, India
Warren Webster, U.S.A.
James Wong, Singapore
*Thomas Zimmerman, U.S.A., *Communications Working Group Chairman*
Isaac Zokoue, Ivory Coast

Strategy Working Group
The Strategy Working Group of the Lausanne Congress on World Evangelism has the task of discovering unreached groups of people and helping to design strategies to reach them.
C. Peter Wagner, U.S.A., *Chairman*
Fouad Accad, Arabian Gulf
Edward R. Dayton, U.S.A.
David Gitari, Kenya
Tom Houston, England
John Y. Masuda, Japan
George Samuel, India
Douglas Smith, Bolivia
James Wong, Singapore

PART 1
The Unreached and How to Reach Them

PLANNING STRATEGIES FOR EVANGELISM

Edward R. Dayton

Introduction

There are an estimated three billion non-Christians in the world. They are found in settings as different as the countries in which they live. Some of these groups are relatively large and homogeneous, for example, the sixty million rural Javanese. Others are quite small. In a very real sense each group is unique and exists within certain national boundaries, a given cultural milieu, a specific history, and a particular set of immediate circumstances.

Groups that are less than 20 percent Christian may be called "unreached peoples." Though they may be unreached in varying degrees, each group has its own set of distinctive attributes, those things that make it a group.

The Lausanne Committee for World Evangelization has defined a "people group" as "a significantly large sociological grouping of individuals who perceive themselves to have a common affinity for one another." The basis of this definition, on which *Unreached Peoples '80* rests, is found in the Lausanne/MARC publication *To Reach the Unreached*[1] and in the chapter of that same title found in *Unreached Peoples '79*.

It follows that there is no one evangelistic method that will be useful to all of these many groups. Nor can there be one evangelistic strategy for reaching them. We should not be surprised by this. Evangelical Christian theology is based on the belief that God sees every individual as unique. He has a specific concern and "plan" for each person's life. When unique individuals are placed together in groups, the group by implication is also unique.

This is not to say that we cannot learn a great deal from observing the effectiveness of various methods. It does say that we need to do our homework before we begin. There are no standard answers to evangelization. However, there is a set of questions that may be very useful as we think about planning strategies for reaching a particular group.

Since the historic Lausanne Conference in 1974, the Strategy Working Group and the Missions Advanced Research and Communications Center (MARC) have been attempting to discover the questions that appear to be universally applicable to reaching any group of people. These questions have been put together in a workbook entitled *Planning Strategies for Evangelism,* now in its seventh edition.[2] This workbook has been used in hundreds of situations around the world. The questions it has asked have greatly assisted the evangelist in uncovering God's strategy for the evangelism of a particular group of people. In this chapter we attempt to describe the questions the workbook used and to explain their usefulness.[3]

A Circular Model

This is a plan for planning. What is represented in Figure 1 are not the *steps* that a person might take to reach a people, but rather the questions that he should ask to decide what people should be reached, and how effective previous efforts have been. The workbook describes this as a ten-step circular process. The steps need not necessarily follow one after the other but, since any written description is restricted to "linear thinking," for ease of understanding the diagram lays them out in the form of a circle that turns back on itself.

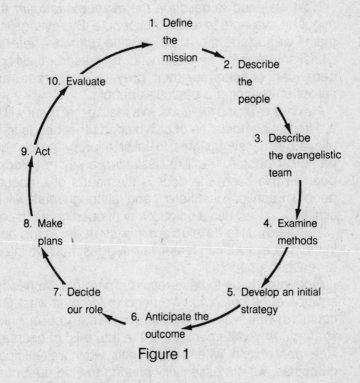

1. Define the mission
2. Describe the people
3. Describe the evangelistic team
4. Examine methods
5. Develop an initial strategy
6. Anticipate the outcome
7. Decide our role
8. Make plans
9. Act
10. Evaluate

Figure 1

We begin by *defining our mission*. What is it that God wants us to do? We obviously cannot reach everyone. What specific group of people does he want *us* to reach with the good news of Jesus Christ?

The next step is to *describe the people* as best we can. We need to see them within the context of their spiritual and other needs before we make plans to reach them. We call this "inside out" planning. Rather than start with a *method* or a program, we first try to understand the need. We have to sense that these are people God loves, and we have to count on the fact that God has a special plan for reaching them.

Next we need to *describe the evangelistic team* that might be available to reach this people. By "evangelistic team" we include the entire existing church. There are Christians all over the world who, because of their concern, can concentrate their prayers, resources, and selves on reaching a particular people.

Next we examine *methods*. We realize that there will be a different combination of old methods that needs to be alloyed with new insights to tailor a program for each particular people. It is like designing a key to unlock a door. In this case, the door is the hearts of a specific people. Each lock is different and, although there will be similarities, God has a unique way of opening each one.

This leads us to develop an *initial strategy*. At this point in the process we can tentatively suggest how we intend to reach the people.

God intends us to have results. Therefore we need to *anticipate the outcome*. We need to forecast what God could do in the lives of the people as we carry out our initial strategy. Any statement about the future is, of course, a statement of faith. When we set goals, when we anticipate outcomes, we are essentially offering to God our understanding of what he wants us to do.

Too often we automatically assume that, because we have a concern for a particular people, we are the ones who should be directly involved in reaching them. This is not always the case. Some of us are gifted in one way, others have different gifts. We need to *decide our role,* either as individuals or as an agency, before we move ahead.

Assuming that we have decided to move ahead, we need to *make plans.* In faith we need to decide how we are going to reach the goals we believe God has set for us. Once again, any statement about the future is a statement of faith. The larger our faith, the greater our plans.

We then *act* to carry out our plans, gather resources, set in motion what we believe God wants us to do.

But as we act we need to *evaluate.* Things seldom go as we anticipate. Plans will go awry. Situations will change. The Holy Spirit will lead in new paths. We do not need to follow plans too slavishly. We need to stay tuned to God. When we have carried out all our plans and modified them as we go, we need to begin the cycle again, and *redefine the mission.* We may have discovered entirely new insights.

This process may take a week or it may take ten years. Steps 1 through 8 may move very rapidly, and many of them may be taken at the same time. A better model might look like Figure 2.

If the rather convoluted, strange-looking drawing in Figure 2 seems to picture a confusing process, we have made our point. The human mind has a marvelous ability to take into account a tremendous number of things at the same time. It is almost impossible to think about "defining the mission" without thinking about a people, an evangelistic team, the means and methods that might be used, the approach we might take, and the outcome we expect, as well as our role in it.

So we view the task of planning strategies as a repetitive process, one that is useful for thinking about reaching any group. It is not tied down to any particular means or method. It does not make any assumptions about the

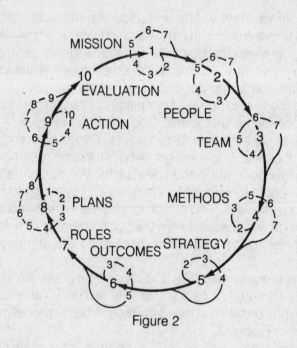

Figure 2

people we are trying to reach. Rather it attempts to keep us tuned to what the Holy Spirit is saying to us by leading us through a thought process.

The following questions, based on the above model, lead us through the process. The reader who takes a quick look at them may say, "We could never get all those answers!" True. Seldom would any individual have all the information needed. But the significant thing is not necessarily the answers but rather the attempt to answer the questions. The questions themselves will make us think more specifically about the particular group we are trying to reach. Experience with groups in many parts of the world has demonstrated that just asking a group of knowledgeable people the questions activates ideas that become God's strategy for reaching them.

1. DEFINE THE MISSION

Our mission may be the family living next door. It may be a particular group of people within our city or neighborhood. It may be a group living in a distant land. But it should be a *specific* group of people. Too often our strategies go awry because we have tried to cover too many people with one approach. We must first ask:
1. To what people has God called us?

2. DESCRIBE THE PEOPLE

By a "people group" we mean "a significantly large sociological grouping of people who perceive themselves to have a common affinity for one another." This affinity may be the result of a shared language, religion, ethnicity, residence, occupation, class or caste, or situation, or a combination of these factors and others.

The important thing is to put "boundaries" around a particular people. It is just as important to define the people we are *not* trying to reach when we design a strategy. Most of us are used to thinking about a "people group" as being synonymous with an ethnic or tribal group. However, there are many other ways of defining them. Here are some of the questions that should be answered (see Appendix B for a detailed unreached-people questionnaire).

1. What is the name of these people—what do they call themselves?
2. Where do they live?
3. What is their population and what is the population of the larger group(s) of which they are a part?
4. What language(s) do they speak?
5. What makes them identifiable as a special group of people (language, location, class, religion, etc.)?
6. How many can and do read?
7. What are their major religious and philosophical beliefs?
8. How do you think these people see *themselves*? What do you think *they* would say are their important spiritual, physical, and emotional needs?
9. Which of these needs seem to be already adequately met? What needs have not been met?
10. How do *you* see them? What would you say their important spiritual, physical, and emotional needs are?
11. How do you know the answers to these questions? Where did you get your information about the people?
12. Who else might have accurate information about them? How might you go about discovering what they know?
13. What other information peculiar to this people do you need to know to understand them?

What Do They Know About the Gospel?

The previous questions have dealt with the people group within their milieu. But we also need to view them from a Christian perspective. What is their relationship to Christ? One of the most valuable methods of answering this question for evangelistic purposes is the decision-process scale developed by Dr. James Engel and Viggo Søgaard.[4]

The questions that result from the Engel scale are:

1. What percentage (approximately) of the group has no awareness of Christ?
2. What percentage has an awareness of the existence of Christ but has moved no further?
3. What percentage knows something about Jesus Christ but does not understand who he is?
4. What percentage understands who Christ is or what the Gospel says about him?
5. What percentage has grasped the personal implications of what it knows?
6. What percentage recognize a need in their own lives that Christ could meet?
7. What percentage is at the point of making a decision to receive Christ?

While it is not too difficult to answer questions 1, 2, and 3, questions 4, 5, 6, and 7 are intimately entwined, and answers to them will vary from group to group. In most cases they can only be inferred from answers to the other questions. We are, however, looking for estimates rather than precise data. The intent of the questions is to help us select the right means and methods (see below).

Assuming that there are some who have decided to make Christ their Lord, we need to ask the following questions:

8. What percentage is evaluating its decision and has not yet joined a local fellowship?
9. What percentage is now incorporated into a fellowship of Christians?
10. What percentage have become active propagators of the Gospel?

Because there are so often those who have become incorporated into some Christian fellowship but show

none of the marks of a Christian, we ask the question:
11. What percentage appears to be Christian in name only?

Their General Receptivity

The scale helps indicate whether people have faith in Jesus Christ and whether they have become his disciples, but it does not tell us anything about their *movement* toward or away from him. Some groups may be very stable but others may be changing rather quickly. So we ask the following questions:
1. How open is the group to religious change of any kind?
2. Why? Give specific evidence.
3. What is its attitude toward the Gospel and/or Christianity?
4. Why? Give specific evidence.
5. Is the group becoming more or less open to the Gospel, or is there no noticeable change?

Their Cultural Practices and Receptivity to the Gospel

The present culture of a group will always have a bearing on its openness to the Gospel.[5] The following questions will help us understand how to approach a particular culture:
1. What cultural values, beliefs, and practices might be significant in the group's understanding of the Gospel and a favorable attitude toward it?
2. What cultural values, beliefs, and practices might produce a negative attitude toward the Gospel?
3. Are there common cultural practices that seem to be clearly prohibited by Scripture? If so, what are they?

4. Are there some important cultural values or practices that could be reinterpreted and incorporated into a Christian lifestyle? If so, what are they?
5. Are the people satisfied with their traditional religious or magical understanding of disease, sickness, and death? Why?

The Resulting Church

The last set of questions focuses on the kind of a church that should result if the Gospel is widely accepted by the group:
1. If the members of the group become Christians, what kind of biblical, worshiping fellowship would be most likely to attract other members of the same group?
2. How should they worship?
3. How should they show their concern for others?
4. How should they witness to others?
5. How should they relate to other Christian groups?

3. DESCRIBE THE EVANGELISTIC TEAM

There are many ways of discovering what other Christian groups are doing among the people a mission may have chosen to reach. It is important to remember that the church is described as a *body*. We need to work together.
1. What churches, agencies, or other groups of Christians are already working with these people?
2. What are they doing?
3. How effective have they been?
4. Which groups or agencies appear to understand the needs of the group?
5. If there are already established churches, which, if

any, have shown a 50 percent increase or more in the last five years? Why?
6. Are the established churches accepted as an integral part of the cultural group? Why or why not?
7. What role should the evangelist or evangelizing group adopt in the culture to be effective?
8. Which Christians or Christian groups are most likely to reach these people?
9. Where can we get more accurate information about the group's openness to evangelism?

Questions 8 and 9 are important because we need to listen to what the Spirit is saying to others in the Christian community.

Forces Opposed to Evangelism

It is good to know who our friends are, but we must also be aware of those who may oppose us.
1. What organized groups or agencies would be opposed to the proclamation of the Gospel to this group?
2. What forces, spiritual and secular, appear to be arrayed against the Gospel? What forces hinder individuals or family groups from committing themselves to Christ in an open, active way?
3. If some became Christians but later turned away from the Lord, what seemed to draw them away from God?
4. If Christians are present in this group, what, if anything, prevents them from having an active and effective witness?

4. EXAMINE METHODS

Each individual who comes to know Jesus Christ has a

personal experience when our Lord meets him in a one-to-one relationship. However, different methods of communicating the Gospel have been found effective in different cultures, societies, and situations. Christians are often tempted to adopt one method and believe that it is uniformly applicable to all peoples in all situations. But we have an infinite God who can use an infinite variety of methods to reach people. We need to be open to this tremendous diversity. We have learned a great deal from church history about how people have come to know Christ. Methods vary greatly from age to age. We should still expect variety today.

1. In the light of what the people need, where they seem to be as a group in their understanding of the Gospel, and the available evangelistic team, what methods are most likely to be most effective?
2. What methods would move individuals in the group toward Christ?
3. Are these methods compatible with biblical principles? Are they ethical?
4. Where could you learn more about possible methods?
5. What organizations or individuals would probably cooperate with you?

Preconceptions

How easy it is to move ahead without understanding our own motivations or the motivations of others. We all plan for the future on the basis of our assumptions about the present and the past, both spoken and unspoken.

1. What are your preconceptions about yourself?
2. What are your preconceptions about your organization?
3. What are your preconceptions about other churches or

missions?

4. What are your preconceptions about the country in which the people you hope to reach live?
5. What are your assumptions about their culture?
6. Do you have any other preconceptions?

5. DEVELOP AN INITIAL STRATEGY

The answers to the above questions will give us an understanding of the people we are trying to reach, identify the forces that might be available to reach them, and suggest various methods that God might lead us to use. Now we are ready to develop an initial strategy to reach them. We need to consider where to begin and what we might expect God to do with them. We need broad overall goals. We also need to plan constructive programs to meet the people's needs and at the same time tell them about the saving power of Jesus Christ.

1. Will you try to reach the entire group or only a subgroup? If the latter, which subgroup?
2. What need of the group will you tackle first?
3. Who should be asked to reach this particular group?
4. What methods should be used?

6. ANTICIPATE THE OUTCOME

We also need to anticipate what will happen as a result of our initial strategy. No one can predict the future, of course. But God is still in control of the universe, and his will will be done. He expects us to ask him in faith what he wants us to be, where he wants us to go, and what he wants us to do. He expects us to think about our goals and the probable *outcome* of our strategy:

1. If your approach is successful, what do you expect God to do through the evangelistic team?
2. What kind of response to Christ do you expect the group to make?
3. How will you *know* whether they have responded to Christ? (You can't build on the results unless you know how individuals have responded.)
4. What problems do you expect to encounter? Can you minimize or overcome them?
5. Are the anticipated outcomes satisfactory? Could they be improved?

7. DECIDE OUR ROLE

Because an individual Christian or a local body of Christians is concerned about another individual or group, it does not mean *they* will be the most effective in reaching those people. We need to understand where we fit in the total task of evangelization. Those with a gift for planning are not necessarily gifted in leadership. Evangelists are not always good coordinators. In one situation we may be leaders but in another we should only be members.

1. What role, if any, can you and/or your agency best play in carrying out the projected mission?
2. How will you and your agency have to change in order to carry it out?

8. MAKE PLANS

God's strategy is made up of a people to be evangelized, an evangelist, a means of evangelism, and possible outcomes. We need to understand God's will for the people we want to reach. Evangelists need to use the best methods so the Lord will produce the greatest harvest. We need to pray, believe, and act if we believe we are God's instruments of love. Action should be based on specific plans.

1. What do you believe God wants to see happen in the lives of the group you hope to reach for Christ?
2. What steps should be taken to reach this goal?
3. When do these steps need to be taken, and who should be responsible for each one?

9. ACT

Gather Resources

The best plans are useless unless we have adequate resources to implement them:

1. How many people and what specific types of personnel will you need to carry out the above plans?
2. How much will it cost to carry out these plans? Where will the money come from?
3. What facilities and equipment will be needed?

Action will require a great investment of time and energy. We have identified the people God has called us to reach for Christ. We have tried to discover those God might use to reach them. We have tried to find our own role in God's plan. We have made plans to reach them. We have tried to determine where they are in their relationship to Christ, and we have analyzed the resources we will probably need. Now is the time to ask some final prayerful questions:

1. Is the plan practical? If not, how should it be modified?
2. If the plan looks like God's best, what is your first step?

10. EVALUATE

Many programs of evangelism fail because no effort is made to evaluate progress early enough. We need to evaluate in order to determine how we are progressing toward our stated goals. Will the series of steps we are following take us to the goal God wants us to reach? Evaluation enables us to be accountable and to hold others involved in evangelism accountable to God and to each other for carrying out the steps we believe God wants us to take. Evangelism makes us aware of areas in which our goals need to be changed, our methods rethought, and our resources and time redistributed so they will be more effective for Christ:

1. How will you check your progress during the carrying out of your strategy?
2. When will you first review your strategy and the effectiveness of your efforts to reach your goals? Who will be involved in the review?
3. What information will you need to determine how effective your strategy has been?

REDEFINING THE MISSION

This closes the circle and brings us back to where we began: We need to redefine our mission in the light of our evaluation.

Conclusion

Copies of "Planning Strategies for Evangelism: A Workbook" and *That Everyone May Hear* are available from MARC, 919 West Huntington Drive, Monrovia, CA

91016, U.S.A. The basic approach is being used by the Strategy Working Group of the Lausanne Committee for World Evangelization. It should be seen as a "work in process." As you look through the balance of this year's Unreached Peoples Directory, you may want to consider how the questions from this workbook might help you in your attempt to understand God's strategy and become a part of communicating the Gospel to the thousands of unreached people around the world.

EDWARD R. DAYTON is the founder and director of the Missions Advanced Research and Communications Center (MARC) of World Vision International. He previously worked for sixteen years in various engineering and management positions within the field of aircraft and space electronics. After receiving an M.Div. degree from Fuller Theological Seminary in 1967, he devoted himself to helping the church develop more effective strategies for evangelization. He has written books in the area of management and missions. The most recent include *Tools for Time Management, Strategy for Living,* and *The Art of Management for Christian Leaders*. He was the editor of the eleventh edition of the *Mission Handbook*. He is currently the director of the Evangelism and Research Division of World Vision International.

MUSLIM EVANGELISM IN THE 1980s

Michael Youssef

In any attempt to evangelize Muslims today, we can hardly afford the mistakes of the past. One of our greatest mistakes has been that of not sufficiently taking into account cultural, linguistic, ethnic, and sociological factors in the background of the people. Nor can we afford the luxury of ancient but erroneous prejudices against the Muslim world.

Perhaps the most damaging mistake of all has been our neglect of Muslims. Hiding behind excuses such as "monolithic Islam," and "Muslims are resistant to the Gospel," we have invested less than 2 percent of North American Protestant missionaries in reaching Muslims. There has been little sowing; there has been little reaping.

The Muslim world, however, has been subjected to the secularizing influences of the West. Past Western domination of present-day independent Muslim nations has not helped the Christian mission, but it did transmit Western ideas and values to a whole generation of Muslim elite.

Some observers felt that these secularizing influences, which have eroded the faith of many in the West in Christ, might well erode Islamic beliefs, too. Little did they suspect the opposite reaction, a revival within Islam in reaction to the secularizing influence of the West.

And yet, in the midst of our miscalculations, prejudices, and neglect, I believe God has made this the hour for Muslim evangelism. Surprising stories from Muslim countries tell us of unprecedented events in the evangelization of Muslims. They reveal that the Muslim world is not everywhere resistant. They give hope to the church to redeem her neglect, to erase her prejudices, and to turn back from former mistakes.

THE IDEOLOGICAL STRUGGLE IN THE MUSLIM WORLD—GOD'S OPPORTUNITY

We have observed an increase in Islamic militancy in the past ten years. In Pakistan, Iran, Iraq, Egypt, Libya, and Indonesia, militant movements are spreading, some more extensively than others. Ironically, even though most Muslim nations are signatories of the U.N.'s Declaration on Human Rights, they interpret that declaration in a distinctive way. They reason that, since Islam is a total way of life, the people of a given nation are free under Islam, and since God's law is above human laws and declarations, whatever Islam says is right.

I believe the problem is complicated by more than Islamic militancy. In many cases, Muslim countries that are suspicious of Western influence and Western missions are also susceptible to association with the Russian communist regime. This is illustrated by countries such as Libya, Afghanistan, Algeria, Syria, and Iraq. And although some other countries, such as Indonesia, Egypt, Sudan, and the United Arab Emirates, have not yet opened their doors to missionaries, they are at least allowing them in.

Secularization, both capitalistic and communistic, contributes to the ideological struggle going on in some Muslim countries. The current situation in Iran is a good illustration of this struggle.

In the midst of this kind of struggle and anxiety, the Christian Gospel can be very attractive. We should be watching for stress points in the ideological struggles of the Muslim world. Rather than pulling our people out of such situations, we need to persevere as witnesses. In Iran, for example, a young believer recently led twenty people to Christ in a period of six months! In America, where many Iranians have been stranded by the present government, there are Iranian converts to Christ in almost every major city. Stress produces openness. Restless hearts in search of meaning and peace are finding their rest in Christ.

Another place to watch in the coming days is Afghanistan. Conservative Muslim tribals are up in arms against the Marxist-oriented government of Taraki. After the uprising in Heerat, Russian planes strafed the city for two days, leaving a thousand dead. The general populace, terribly offended by both their own Muslim leaders and their allies, the Russians, have recently shown an uncommon friendliness to Christians passing through the area. There is some sense in which such tragedies can become God's opportunities.

THE USE OF THE KORAN AS A BRIDGE

It is of particular relevance to Muslim evangelism to examine the Scriptures and what they show about culturally sensitive approaches to other people. Jesus' approach is especially suggestive. He did not come to preach Judaism, nor did he come to preach salvation through the Law. Yet he never attacks the Law. Rather he shows the Jews that the Law was in fact pointing to him.

Is there a similar way in which we can use the Koran with Muslims? Before I answer, I must make it clear that in no way do I equate the Koran with the Old Testament. I am merely making an analogy. The vast majority of Muslims take the Koran to be the direct word of God. We should meet them where they are.

The Koran contains some magnificent verses about Jesus. So exhilarating and glorifying are these stories that from its pages we see Jesus as the greatest prophet and in a special way close to God. This could not be called the "Gospel in the Koran" but it nevertheless gives the Christian an excellent opportunity to talk to Muslims about Christ.

I am personally convinced that the prophet Muhammad was confused in his understanding of who Jesus was. On the one hand he denied his deity and crucifixion. On the other hand Jesus is called *Kalamet Allah,* "the Word of God" (4:171), and *Rouh Allah,* "the Spirit of God" (2:87). Jesus is significantly quoted as saying, "His (God's) blessing is upon me wherever I go" (19:30). A better translation would be "He (God) has made me blessed wherever I may be." Also, in the Koran Jesus is the only prophet who raises the dead. There is also mention of his miracles and healings and his miraculous virgin birth.

I believe the Koran can be used to bring Muslims to the feet of Jesus. Virtually all converts from Islam say that the God they knew distantly in the Koran they now know more fully in Jesus Christ. As Jesus and his apostles were able to point to the Gospel from the Old Testament, so we can point our Muslim friends to Jesus from the Koran.

I know someone will say, "But Muslim teachers and leaders do not believe that in the Koran Jesus is elevated

41

to deity." This is true. But back in the first century, neither did the Pharisees and other Jewish religious leaders accept Jesus as the fulfillment of Old Testament prophecies. Yet the Gospel nevertheless spread among those who responded to Christian preaching. Using the Koran as a bridge, we can reach Muslims who have been prepared by God to see Jesus as the one he has sent for their redemption.

CULTURAL SENSITIVITY AND THE ADVANCEMENT OF THE GOSPEL

A related question has to do with Islamic culture. What percent of his Islamic culture can a new believer in Christ retain without compromising the Gospel?

One of the most exciting parts of the Lausanne-sponsored Conference on Muslim Evangelism (Colorado Springs, October, 1978) was the presentation of a field situation from a certain Muslim country. This case study was presented by a veteran missionary who had experimented with new approaches more congenial to converts from Islam. In this field situation the author described the changes in the thinking of his mission through the years:

> Our goal was to evangelize, using the traditional methodology of the local church. Our activities and zeal, however, did not produce fruit. Almost no one was won to faith in Christ until 1975. And then miracles began to happen.
>
> Now there are two worshiping groups of believers. Each fellowship is made up of fifteen Muslim converts. The reason for success, first of all, is the Spirit of God at work in the hearts of the

people. Humanly speaking, while remaining faithful to the Word of God in their preaching, they demonstrated a new sensitivity to the cultural context of the new believers.

The missionaries identified closely with the lifestyle of the local people in dress, food, and customs. The form of worship was similar to that practiced in the mosque where the worshipers wash before prayer, sit on the floor, and take off their shoes. Occasionally they would put Greek and Hebrew Testaments on the lectern along with the Bible in the language of the worshipers. In prayer, they would lift up their hands Muslim style and use Muslim tunes to words of the Scripture in singing. The Gospel spread along family and friendship lines.

The author was very careful, however, to explain that this was not a well-tested situation; it was merely a beginning. He was keenly aware of the deep theological problems that attended this innovative approach. But it did constitute a breakthrough, and it was a first step, opening the door to other Muslim friends who could come to the faith with little or no cultural or linguistic hindrances.

THE ISLAMIC MONOLITH: FACT OR FANCY?

Underlying our concern for culturally sensitive models is the awareness of the rich diversity within Islam. Muslims are divided into hundreds of "homogeneous units" that differ from each other geographically, ethically, ideologically, culturally, and often theologically. Iran, for example, cannot be called a monolithic society. Ethnic Persians make up only 48 percent of the population. Eight percent of Iran's population is Kurdish, 19 percent Turkish-speaking, 18 percent tribal Gulani, Baluchi, and Luri, and the remaining are divided among many smaller groups. Religiously, Iran's Muslims are divided into Shias, Sunnis, Bahais, Ismailis, Ahl-i-Haqq, Yezidis, communists, secularists, and both progressive and conservative Muslims. This kind of diversity can be observed in dozens of Muslim countries.

Other examples of surprising diversity are the 20,000 Chinese Muslims who have migrated and presently live in Saudi Arabia, 145,000 Kurds living in Kuwait, and 20,000 Circassian Muslims living in Jordan. The 720 million Muslims of the world speak at least five hundred different languages and are subdivided into probably 3,500 different homogeneous units.

A SPECIFIC APPROACH FOR EACH ETHNIC GROUP

One of the assumptions held in the past by those working with Muslims was that the same approach would work anywhere. This was based on the observation that, no matter where the approach was used, a handful came to Christ.

What was not noticed was that more than 99 percent of all Muslims were left untouched by this approach. Recently it has been discovered that, when well-thought-out approaches are developed that are tailor-made for a particular situation, there is a far more encouraging response. This leads to the idea that we need as many different strategies as there are differing kinds of Muslims. These approaches must come to terms with the peculiar mix of cultural, linguistic, political, sociological, ideological, and even theological varieties in Islam. Having said this, I would add that neither this nor any other approach guarantees results either with Muslims or with any other group of people.

DIFFERING KINDS OF SOILS—A CLUE

Dr. Peter Wagner believes that, just as in the Parable of the Sower the seeds that fell upon different soils produced different results, so it is in the area of evangelism. We cannot expect the same response when the Word is preached to diverse groups of people. We will find varying degrees of responsiveness and resistance. Wagner asks, "What was the factor that made only one out of four fields produce fruit?"[1] His answer is that the secret is in neither the sower nor the method nor the seed, but rather in the soil.

What does this mean in terms of Muslim evangelism? Should we neglect resistant Muslims because they have proven to be hard to reach? This brings me back to my earlier question about strategy.

Just as there were different kinds of soil in Jesus' parable, so we are likely to find many different kinds of Muslim peoples. Several are described in this book. Unfortunately, some people treat the whole Muslim world as if it were a single type of soil and erroneously attempt to use only one method on it. It is not, as many who are currently involved in a ministry to Muslims can testify.

Indonesia, for example, is the largest Muslim country in the world, with 121 million Muslims, over 87 percent of the population. Yet Indonesia is not an Islamic state. The number of responsive Muslims to the Christian faith in Indonesia is quite astounding. The Sundanese of Java, for

45

example, long considered resistant to the Gospel, are of varying levels in their commitment to Islam. Some areas are highly orthodox and resistant to Christianity. Others are far less Islamicized. House churches have been successfully planted in nonresistant areas.

The point is that we can find responsive people (good soil) even in the world's most populous Muslim nation. This does not mean we should neglect the unresponsive segment of the population. But it does mean that we should invest our greatest efforts on the fruitful ground and encourage our converts, who appreciate the reasons for resistance to the Gospel, to evangelize the less responsive areas. And we must simultaneously experiment with new strategies.

OPPORTUNITIES FOR CROSS-CULTURAL WORKERS OF ALL NATIONALITIES

Sometimes we can learn from our Muslim friends. For example, there is a growing effort by Saudi Arabia and other Mideastern countries to strengthen the growth of orthodox Islam within Indonesia. Most of the missionaries in that movement are Cairo-trained Arabs sent to Indonesia to teach the Arabic language and Islamic theology.

A suggested strategy, in this case, would be to send Arab Christians as missionaries to these heavily populated Muslim islands of Indonesia. They, too, can teach Arabic, and preach the Gospel. They will be very acceptable because it is prestigious to be an Arabic-speaking person.

Korean Christians are making a far greater impact upon the Muslims in Saudi Arabia than any other group. Saudis expect the adherents of the Greek, Coptic, and Syrian orthodox churches along with the Armenians to be Christians. They expect the Americans, Germans, and British to be at least nominally Christians. But what is baffling to them is how the Koreans, having no Christian background or history can be dedicated believers in Christ. What could be more significant than a Korean mission in Saudi Arabia, in the form of technical advisors, laborers, doctors, engineers, etc.?

In a recent article, Norman Horner gives some excellent statistical information concerning the Arabian Gulf states. His conviction is that, while these are "arid and sparsely populated regions where the economic and cultural character has undergone more rapid and far-reaching change in the last ten years than has happened almost anywhere else on earth, yet they look to be the promised land for so many foreigners."[2] Of course, the reason for this is obviously the production of oil and all the economic prosperity that accompanies this product. Cultural, economic, and sociological change should be viewed very seriously by missionary-minded people. I believe that cultural distortion and disorientation often provide fertile ground for the Christian advocate and a culturally-relevant evangelism.

However, this is not the only good news about prospects of evangelism in the Gulf area in the eighties. Horner explains that a large influx of foreigners, primarily from India, Pakistan, Iran, Egypt, Syria, Lebanon, Europe, and America, now vastly exceeds the population of the natives. Among these people are a sizable number of Christians. In Kuwait, for example, it is estimated that 5 percent of the population is Christian. In Bahrein, about 2 percent of the population are Christians; in Qatar, over 2 percent; in Abu Dhabi, about 4 percent; in Dubai, a little over 3 percent. Mind you, the vast majority of these Christians are foreigners. There are very few native Christians, if any.

The largest Christian community by far in the Arabian Gulf area is the Indian Christian community. It is estimated that over 30 percent of all Indians living in the Arabian Gulf are Christians.

This is, in my judgment, one of the greatest opportunities for Indian missionaries. That is, Indian missionaries, preferably converts from Islam themselves, should be prepared to work in this area of the world where relative freedom is enjoyed, and there witness for Christ and build his church.

CONCLUSION

Seven hundred and twenty million Muslims cannot be forgotten by the church. We must not spare any effort to make the Gospel relevant to Islam's various ethnic units.

When Jesus was asked "Which is the greatest commandment of the law?" he replied by quoting Deuteronomy 6:5: "You shall love the Lord your God with all your heart, and with all your soul, and with all your might."

But Jesus added a highly significant clause not found in Deuteronomy, "with all your mind." For full Christian missionary commitment it is necessary not only to dedicate ourselves to evangelism; it is also necessary to think through the most effective ways in which we can carry out Christ's command.

The apostle Paul planned and thought out the best way to allow the Gospel to make its maximum impact. We need to plan Muslim evangelism in the eighties with the same thoroughness. Let us adopt the appropriate means to produce a rich harvest in the Muslim world in our day.

Michael Youssef is special assistant to the president,

Haggai Institute for Advanced Leadership Training, in Atlanta, Georgia. He researches and lectures on Muslim evangelism and cross-cultural communications. He is also involved in personal diplomacy with world leaders. Youssef was born in Assuit, Egypt. At the age of twenty he immigrated to Sydney, Australia, where he received his Th.L. degree and was ordained to the Anglican ministry (Sydney Diocese). He served as a curate under the leadership of the Most Reverend Sir Marcus Loane, Archbishop of Sydney. In 1978 Youssef graduated from the Fuller Theological Seminary School of World Mission with the Th.M. in missiology. The subject of his thesis was "Jesus in the Koran and Muslim Evangelism." He is currently a doctoral candidate at Fuller's School of World Mission. He is married and has three children.

THE CHALLENGE OF REACHING MUSLIMS FOR CHRIST

Don M. McCurry

As though God wanted to get our attention on our unfinished task, he has given the Muslims of our day unprecedented power through oil and money. Whether it is banks in Atlanta, farmlands in Iowa, or mansions in Beverly Hills, the presence of wealthy Muslims is inescapable for a North American. I am sure the same is true for those watching the mosque go up in Regent's Square in London, or for the Pope looking out of his window at the Vatican to see what Muslims are building in Rome to rival St. Peter's. It is as though the old invasion patterns are reasserting themselves, except that this time the conquest is economic instead of military. The squeeze is on, a strategy is at work, and the old Muslim dreams of empire are unmistakably on the verge of becoming a reality in our times.

Contemporary Christians have apparently learned very little from the past. At the time of the advent of Islam, Christian policy erred by either the neglect or the abuse of those who were soon to become Muslim. Then it was the errant and abortive efforts of the Abyssinian Christians to invade and conquer Arabia, the cruel use by the Christian Byzantines of Arabs as mercenaries, and the deviations of the Nestorian monastic system that set the stage for the rise of an Arab prophet with an Arabic book for the Arabic people to rise and become "the sword of Allah" to bring judgment on unrepentant Christians. Through the intervening centuries, the pendulum of history has swung with an inexorable rhythm from Christian to Islamic to Christian dominance, and it appears that we are at the apex of a swing toward possible Islamic dominance once again. Glorious or fearful consequences teeter in the balance. How will we approach our opportunities? Will the shift be as an occasion to advance the Gospel or to perpetuate animosities and invite a fresh stroke of judgment?

Christianity has lost its innocency. We come with a history, and a sordid one at that. Centuries of bloodshed and rivalry have heaped up enormous legacies of ill will between Christians and Muslims. A closer look at some of our earlier heroes reveals only another page of horrors. Raimon Lull, the "fool of love," turned in his latter years to agitating with the popes for fresh crusades. Fortunately the age of military crusades had ended. But warfare of other types was to follow. Each succeeding century bore its own stigma. And like it or not, when Christians go forth to share their faith with Muslims, there is a credibility gap. More often than not, the message is rejected, not because of its essential content, but because of anti-Christian sensitivities of the Muslim who has learned through a great deal of pain to beware of Christians.

Think for a moment of just the last thirty years. Western nations assisted in the creation of a Zionistic State in Palestine—at the expense of the Palestinians, the majority of whom were Muslims. The present powder-keg atmosphere of the Middle East, which has all world powers intensely interested and involves the rights of Muslims to their land, touches every Christian on the face of the earth. What is the Christian understanding of the "end times" and the subsequent lineup or nonalignment with certain schools of Christian eschatology with regard to the modern State of Israel? This theological choice affects our understanding of the proper approach to Muslim evangelism.

Not unrelated is the bloody war in Lebanon. In spite of all disclaimers to the contrary, it shapes up in the last analysis as Christian against Muslim.

Out in the Mediterranean, Cyprus bears brutal witness to just another case of Christians trying to take over Muslims by force. Small wonder that the Muslim Turkish army invaded and expanded Turkish areas when the Greek Cypriots sought union with Greece.

Formerly Christian Ethiopia, with its decades-long war with the Muslim countries of Somalia and Eritrea, also demonstrates that Christians have not been slow to take up the sword in their own cause. Sub-Saharan Africa, too, illustrates this ancient rivalry, with the Christian ruler of Chad trying to put down Muslim guerrilla movements in opposition to him. Moving across the subcontinent to the only Christian nation in Asia, the Philippines, one finds again that Muslim guerrillas are at war with the ruling Christian government.

This unhappy record, so seldom thought about in the West, is part of the unavoidable and unpleasant liabilities faced by the Christian missionary who seeks to work among the Muslims in Africa, the Middle East, or Asia. There is a sense in which Christianity has lost its right to a clear conscience in carrying the Gospel to them. And for those who do go, the above heritage of ill will may be what has contributed to the heavy load of prejudice that many missionaries take with them into their assignments in Muslim lands. These factors, plus the innate resistance of much of Islam to any change or receptivity to the Gospel, may explain why the North American Protestant missionary force has invested only 2 percent of its personnel in evangelizing Muslims.

TIME FOR A TURNAROUND IN
MISSIONS TO MUSLIMS

There are many reasons why it is fitting to reconsider our commitment to the evangelization of the Muslim world. First of all, the Lord himself has commanded it. We are to disciple *ta ethne,* the New Testament phrase for "all the ethnic groups of people in the world." This includes the estimated thirty-five hundred ethnic varieties of Muslims. We have not even begun to take the Great Commission seriously in discipling this vast multitude of unreached people.

This book is a good beginning in bringing before the reader a sampling of some of these Muslim ethnic groups. You will note that quite a few are listed as being somewhat receptive. This conclusion corresponds with what many field workers are saying. The sale of Bibles in Muslim countries is unprecedented. Christian radio programs are eliciting a surprising number of inquiries and a significant increase in enrollments in Bible correspondence courses. And many of the field missionaries are reporting a greater degree of receptivity than in previous years. There is no denying that there is a larger number of conversions among Muslims, some of which are reported in this volume. In some cases, we even know of Muslim groups asking Christian workers to come and teach them.

A third reason for considering a renewed effort to win Muslims to Christ is that we are learning a lot more about how they think, how change occurs, and how to discover receptive groups of Muslims. Much of this new insight comes from the contributions of anthropologists and sociologists to the field of cross-cultural communication. Much comes from the Church Growth Movement. These new insights call for new applications, or at least for an attempt to make new applications, in the cross-cultural communication of the Gospel to Muslims. A major effort to begin this process was launched in October 1978 with the North American Conference on Muslim Evangelization.

THE SIGNIFICANCE OF THE NORTH AMERICAN CONFERENCE ON MUSLIM EVANGELIZATION

In October 1978, a unique kind of conference was held, the first major conference on Muslim evangelization in the last seventy years. Initiated and sponsored by the North American Committee of the Lausanne Committee for World Evangelization, it brought together an unusual mixture of talented people from twenty-six countries. Among them were outstanding Christian leaders from African and Asian countries, North American mission executives and missionaries, professors of missions, heads of research institutes, Christian anthropologists and Islamists, experts in cross-cultural media, and Bible translators, as well as a few theologians conversant with the issues between Islam and Christianity.

Preconference preparation was a prerequisite for obtaining an invitation to participate. This preparation involved responding in writing to forty foundation papers sent out at the rate of two a week in the six months preceding the conference. It gave the authors of the papers a chance to interact with the participants. The significance of the papers and the responses and rejoinders is in direct relation to their place in the stream of recent developments in mission thinking.

Two major spheres of research converged in the papers. The earlier research was initiated by the International Congress on World Evangelization in Lausanne, Switzerland, in 1974. Thousands of evangelical leaders from churches and missions all over the world were suddenly and dramatically confronted with a demographic picture of how far from finished the task of evangelizing the unreached still is. They learned that the 720 million Muslims of the world, one-sixth of the human race, are the second-largest bloc of unreached people in the world, surpassed only by the enormous Chinese bloc. As startling as this picture was, it was no more surprising than to learn that forty-four countries, about one-fifth of the world's nations, call themselves Muslim countries. Even that does not tell the whole story. Each of the forty-four countries is a mosaic of ethno-linguistic units. A rough estimate is that there are thirty-five hundred such groups comprising Islam. If we are to accept the thinking of those who met during the Pasadena Consultation on the Homogeneous Unit principle, these groups need to be further subdivided into easily identifiable units. If the ideal mode of working is to have teams of expert cross-cultural communicators working in the midst of each unit of Muslim peoples, it is apparent that we who are inside the kingdom of God have hardly scratched the surface in terms of manning these fields of unreached Muslim peoples.

The second sphere of research has to do with a conglomerate of ideas concerning the structures of societies, principles of communication, the understanding of how people perceive, the phenomena of cultural change, the search for a better understanding of indigenization, and, beyond that, contextualization and its meaning for cross-cultural communicators of the Gospel. None of these subjects is new in and of itself. But the good news is that the Christian movement is beginning to apply these concepts to developing more effective approaches to Muslim people groups.

Topics that opened up new vistas for new approaches can be seen in the following titles of the conference foundation papers: "The Gospel and Culture," "The Cross-Cultural Communication of the Gospel to Muslims," "The Incarnational Witness to the Muslim Heart," "The Muslim Convert and His Culture," "Dynamic Equivalence Churches in Muslim Society," "Power Encounter in Conversion from Islam," "Contextualization: Indigenization and/or Transformation?" "New Theological Approaches in Muslim Evangelization," "An 'Engel Scale' for Muslim Work?" "Resistance/Receptivity Analysis of Muslim Peoples," "Islamic Theology: Limits and Bridges," "Popular Islam: The Hunger of the Heart," "An Overview of Missions to Muslims," "The Development of New Tools to Aid in Muslim Evangelism," "Levels, Styles and Locations of Training Programs," "The Value and Methodology of Planning Strategies," "Tentmaking Ministries in Muslim Countries," "North American Ties to Third World Missions," "The Role of Local Churches in God's Redemptive Plan for the Muslim World," and "The Christian Approach to the Muslim Woman and Family."

This list is not exhaustive, but it does demonstrate the breadth and perimeters of what was broached in the foundation papers. These and twenty other papers, along with responses and rejoinders, can be found in the volume the author edited, *The Gospel and Islam: A 1978 Compendium,* available from MARC. The above-mentioned topics only open up the issues needing tc be investigated; they do not solve the problem of how tc be more effective. That will take a vigorous amount of hard thinking and persuading and experimentation.

Among the topics listed, one that requires special mention is planning. In my own visits with Christian workers in many Muslim countries, the appalling absence of good solid planning stood out as requiring serious attention. The conference in Colorado devoted a good deal of time to planning approaches to specific people groups.

Such planning did not come easily to those unaccustomed to it. But afterward many of the participants expressed gratitude for the experience. We learned that specific approaches need to be developed for specific peoples.

One of the great delights and benefits of the Colorado conference was that men and women from so many disciplines and cultures learned to draw from one another's experiences and expertise as they worked through plans for reaching unreached Muslims. This interaction happened especially in the sessions devoted to planning and was carried over into the resolutions developed by the various task forces set up toward the end of the week.

Growing out of the task-force mandates drafted at the end of the conference was a wide range of activities, including the formation of theological study groups; survey efforts to discover where all the North American Muslims are; methods to develop culturally attuned approaches to Muslim women; and the organization of a coordinating hub, a training center for North America in southern California. The latter has already come into being and is known as the Samuel Zwemer Institute, located in Pasadena. This institute has developed several levels of training programs for both residential and seminar participants from across North America. The staff is also involved in research here and abroad to discover unreached Muslim people groups that are receptive to the Gospel and develop new approaches to bringing Muslims to the saving knowledge of Christ.

THE VALUE OF CASE STUDIES

Included in this volume are five case studies from several major Muslim countries. Two of the studies have been disguised in order to protect the authors and the local believers involved. Would that Islam were more tolerant of Muslims who find new life in Jesus Christ and choose to follow him openly. Since that is not the case, care needs to be taken to protect those involved from undue publicity.

These studies are interesting in that they illustrate a variety of principles in operation. Some, of course, are common to two or more of them; others are quite unique, being creative adaptations to local customs or situations.

In the Jammu-Kashmir area, for example, a deliberate challenge to the existing religions is made in a kind of "power encounter" approach by the annual parade of Christians. To everyone's surprise, it has led to heightened excitement in the community and has built a sense of expectancy that actually makes conversions easier. However, this approach would not work in many other countries.

In another Muslim country a combination of persistence, preaching before giving medical treatment, and home-to-home visitation by women missionaries led to a steady number of converts over a period of two decades. What is highly significant is that hostility gave way to curiosity and then acceptance.

Common to both of the above and subsequent studies was the use of local folk music to which the Christian workers put Christian words.

In situations where there was some kind of caste structure, it was discovered that when the Christian hospital workers treated all patients and their Muslim friends equally, it was the poor who responded to the Gospel. In the attitude of the Christian workers they felt a dignity and equality they had never before experienced.

The responsiveness of the Somali immigrants to Kenya, free from the tremendous pressure to conform to their community in Somalia, resulted from methods we might apply to Muslim migrants wherever we find them.

In the work in "Baranada" we have, perhaps for the first time, a deliberate attempt to incorporate patterns of worship for converts from Islam that borrow heavily from Islamic religious and cultural forms. Since this work is quite young, it is still too soon to evaluate its effectiveness. The interesting thing is that with the help of both missionaries and older Muslim converts the local groups of believers are working things out for themselves. It is of equal interest that one of the missionaries involved in this project is now surveying fellow missionaries from many other Muslim countries to see what kind of consensus there is concerning thirty to forty different Islamic forms that could be borrowed and used in Christian worship. Much will be learned from following this case.

Surveys have revealed that among the twenty-four million Sundanese of Java, Indonesia, a people previously considered quite resistant to Christianity, there is a great deal of heterogeneity. In this large block of people there are receptive groups as well as resistant groups. Only by probing can we determine whether a people is receptive to the Gospel. Very few people are trying to work among the Sundanese, but those who are there are seeing results.

SUMMARY THOUGHTS

The Need to Discover Unreached Muslim People Groups

We have very little knowledge of the approximately

thirty-five hundred different Muslim ethnic groups scattered across the globe. Furthermore, we have no idea how many of them actually might be receptive to the Gospel, for the simple reason that we have never gone there to find out. This volume, excellent as it is, only scratches the surface of the massive effort that needs to be made. Even though many Muslim countries are closed to missionaries, or at least to Western missionaries, it does not necessarily mean that there is no way to enter, or find out what the picture is, or minister. Our God is the God of the impossible. The one who came to seek and save that which was lost now sends us in his place. He will make a way.

The Need to Understand How God Relates to Cultures

Cultures have been developed by people living in a particular community. The Word of God has very little to say explicitly about most of the world's cultures. Each one has elements that reflect the fact that we were all made in God's image. Each has elements that demonstrate the demonic, and elements that are apparently more or less neutral. Islamic cultures are no exception. They have elements that need to be judged, elements that reflect the divine image in human beings and elements that are morally neutral.

Our attitude needs to be shaped by this kind of thinking. God loves to invade and transform each culture if believers are willing to be his leaven and light and salt. Let us be as generous to Islamic cultures as we have been to our own, albeit under the light of God's Word.

The Need to Overcome Old Patterns of Prejudice

No relationship has been more marred by hatred and

bloodshed and exploitation than that between Muslims and Christians. And there have been 1,350 years of it. In spite of the grievous memories, Christ asks us to go out as sheep among wolves, and to love—yes, love—even our enemies, if that is what they are. We cannot refuse to love Muslims. The Scriptures tell us that the sons of Ishmael are to come with acceptance to God's altar (Isa. 60). We need a new objectivity here, a willingness to start over and to go among Muslims with the message of Christ. Perhaps we need to say, *only* with the message of Christ, not with all of the cultural baggage we so often confuse with that message. Let's ask a new question: How much of his or her culture can a Muslim retain and also say with integrity "Christ is Lord of my life"?

The Need to Complete Our Obedience to Christ in Reaching Muslims

The tragedy of our day is that we have allowed bad memories to frighten us out of our obedience. We need to repent for our past mistakes. We need to open unopened doors and enter yielding ones. Christ has never withdrawn his command for us to disciple all the ethnic groups, all the nations of the world. It is time for new efforts among those 720 million Muslims who have never really learned about the love of God in Christ. They will only learn as we make ourselves willing and available to go. Jesus said, "As the Father has sent me, even so I send you" (John 20: 21 RSV). Trusting in his power and filled with his love, let us rededicate ourselves to reaching the unreached Muslims of our world with the only thing really worth having—Jesus Christ.

DON M. McCURRY is a native of Washington, D.C., and a graduate of the University of Maryland (B.S.) and Pittsburgh Theological Seminary (M.Div.). He also holds an M.Ed. from Temple University and has done special studies in Urdu literature at the Hartford Seminary Foundation and doctoral studies at the School of World Mission, Fuller Theological Seminary. He served in Pakistan for eighteen years with the United Presbyterian Church, primarily at the Forman Christian College and the Gujranwala Theological Seminary. McCurry is the editor of *The Gospel and Islam* (World Vision, 1979). He has also published articles on missions to Islm in several Christian periodicals. Currently he is director of the Samuel Zwemer Institute in Pasadena, California.

PART 2
Case
Studies

RESPONSIVE SOMALI PEOPLES IN KENYA

Earl Andersen with David Cashin

Stretching across the northern third of Kenya is an arid region formerly known as Jubaland. Best suited to animal husbandry, this northern province is sparsely populated with seminomadic peoples representing at least eight different ethnic groups. Together they account for only 6 percent of the population of Kenya. An ethnic distribution map (page 68) gives a rough idea of the location of these groups.

The largest of these pastoral groups is the Somali. The Somali are the most recent in a stream of nomadic groups that have moved through the open terrain of northern Kenya. They first began to push into Jubaland from their homeland to the north and west in the late nineteenth century. More militant than their southern neighbors, the Somali had gained ascendance in the eastern area around Wajir by the early twentieth century. Initially Jubaland was administered by the British as a separate political entity. However, in the 1930s it was incorporated as the northernmost province of Kenya. This incorporation sowed the seeds of later conflict.

KENYA: MAP OF TRIBAL DISTRIBUTION IN THE NORTH

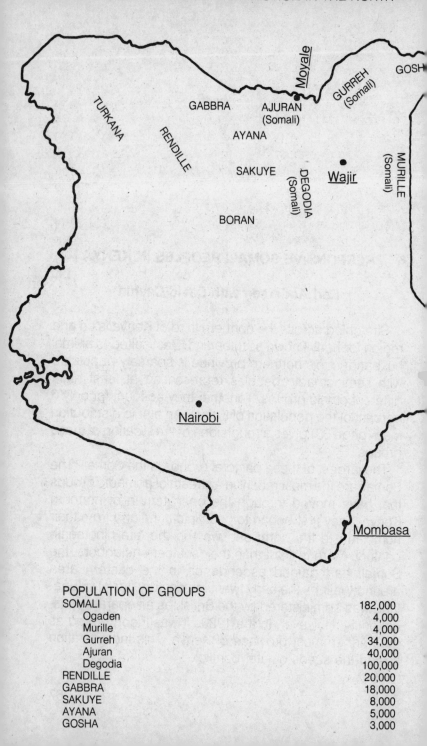

POPULATION OF GROUPS

SOMALI	182,000
Ogaden	4,000
Murille	4,000
Gurreh	34,000
Ajuran	40,000
Degodia	100,000
RENDILLE	20,000
GABBRA	18,000
SAKUYE	8,000
AYANA	5,000
GOSHA	3,000

The total Somali population has been variously estimated at 200,000 and 472,000 (both 1978 estimates).
There are many problems in trying to estimate the population of nomadic groups, especially when some may be
illegal aliens. However, field missionaries are inclined to
accept the more conservative figure. The ethnic Somali
are further divided into five subgroups or clans: the
Murille, Gurreh, Degodia, Ajuran, and Ogaden. This
further breakdown is particularly significant, as we shall
see. Population estimates for these five groups are very
rough. The Ogaden and Murille are the smallest and are
dispersed among the three larger groups; they probably
number no more than 4,000 each. The Gurreh number up
to 30,000 but this estimate is complicated by the fact that
they intermarry freely with the Boran, a non-Somali Islamic
group. The Gurreh make up the largest proportion of the
Shifta, or bandits, of the northern region. The Ajuran and
Degodia are the largest Somali groups, with populations
of up to 40,000 and 100,000 respectively. Although there
are slight dialectal differences between them, they can all
understand each other.

All the Somali groups are Sunni Muslims of the Shafi
school, with the exception of a few who belong to the
Ahmadiyya school. A significant offshoot from Sunni Islam
is known as the Ayana or demon worshipers. This group
represents a reaction against the dry orthodoxy of the
Sunnis, and they have been the source of much demon
possession, particularly among the Gabbra tribe. Islamic
structures in northern Kenya are divided along tribal lines.
Thus in the city of Godoma there are four mosques, one for
the Boran, one for the Gurreh, one for the Ajuran, and one
for the Ayana (although the Ayana are not a single ethnic
group).

THE STATUS OF CHRISTIANITY AMONG THE SOMALI

Until recently the Somali were very resistant to the Gospel, and there were few converts from among them. This resistance has changed radically as a result of recent political changes. At present there are three groups of believers among them, numbering about forty converts. Fourteen are at Korondille, eight to ten at El Das, and thirteen at Giriftu. Almost all are from the Degodia. Three have been baptized. These converts are the result of tapes of Christian messages recorded in Somali that were distributed in the area. The Somali are over 90 percent illiterate. The tragedy of the situation is that there are no workers to work with those who have said openly, "We wish to become Christians." Although the total number of converts is quite small in proportion to the population, in the light of the small amount of personnel and material invested they are indicative of high receptivity to the Gospel.

REASONS FOR RECEPTIVITY: GOD'S POLITICAL PROVIDENCE

Since the time of the Somali incursion into northern Kenya, the eastern region of Jubaland has been considered part of greater Somalia. With Somali independence in 1960 there has been a continual movement to subvert this region and bring it under Somali control. A quasi-guerilla movement, known as the Shifta, emerged, but the Degodia refused to aid them in their efforts at reunification with Somalia. This rejection, a major breach with their Muslim brothers across the border, was made for two reasons. First, the Degodia are slightly different, ethnically speaking, from the Somali in Somalia, and they were afraid of the likelihood of second-class status. Second, the Degodia are the wealthiest of the Somali groups in Kenya; they have the largest flocks of animals. They were afraid of losing their flocks if they united with a socialist government. Their resistance to the Shifta has virtually guaranteed such a loss were they now to be incorporated. Moreover, retribution of a more violent nature would also be likely.

For political reasons the Degodia feel they will be better protected by the government in Nairobi if they become Christians. It is a situation startlingly like that of Indonesia in 1965. However you react to such motives for becoming Christian, it presents a major opportunity for the discipling of the Degodia.

There are other reasons for the present openness, too. Like all Sunni Muslims, the Degodia believe that Jesus is coming back. And, they believe he is coming back to judge the world! They are unusually receptive to Christianity because they believe one day they will all bow the knee to Jesus Christ. As one missionary put it, "Why put off bowing the knee?"

Since the Somali failed to win over the Ogaden, they have been talking about subverting northeast Kenya. This has heightened concern among the Degodia and led to the present conversions.

POSSIBLE FORCES FOR EVANGELISM

One of the great tragedies of the opportunites in northern Kenya is the lack of Christian workers. At present there are only about twenty workers in this northern third of the country. Most of them are working with other receptive ethnic groups, and only three are currently concentrating on the Degodia. They are hindered by the poor terrain and the lack of funds to cover gasoline costs for traveling to the widely dispersed Degodia groups. They could use five full-time church-planting evangelists *right now!*

Two groups of workers are particularly qualified to evangelize the Degodia. The first are missionaries expelled from Somalia. Many of them feel frustrated that they have not been restationed in northern Kenya, since they already speak the language of the people. A concerted effort should be made to find those who already know the Somali language and might be available for this work. The second group are those Degodia who have been educated. Degodia, as well as other Somali groups, have gradually filtered down in great numbers into southern Kenya, so that there are no major towns and cities in Kenya today without a Somali community. About two hundred Degodia have been educated to the high school level, and several have been won to Christ through local Christians. They could comprise a leadership group to go back and reach the other Degodia for Christ. Church planting should be pursued among the urban Somali in the south and among the larger groups in the north. By way of strategy, Christian tape cassettes have already proven to be highly effective among the Degodia. Fulltime church planters should also be sent into those camps where interest in the Gospel has been shown.

Somali converts still face considerable persecution in some cases. In response, a twofold strategy has been pursued to incorporate converts into the church and develop them economically. First, wherever possible, whole families have been baptized together. The fourteen converts in Korondille are all male heads of families. Before the man is baptized, he is told to bring his wife to Christ. When she has become a Christian, they focus upon the oldest son. In this way they try to insure as little family dislocation as possible at the time of baptism. Forty converts among the Muslim Boran are following this pattern.

Some converts have lost their means of livelihood as a result of their conversion. Many of them have gone on to establish Christian villages. Missionaries have used water-development skills to aid these new Christians. Dams on infrequently running watercourses, as well as deep-well drilling, have helped numbers of Muslim converts to become economically reestablished.

There is also a tremendous need for culturally sensitive workers. There has been much breaking of traditional taboos by Christians in the area. For example, dogs are kept in the home and pork is eaten. Particularly among the missionaries, there is much violation of proper dress customs. Especially cited were women who wear shorts because of the heat. On a positive note, there is much power in being able to quote from the Koran. The Somali will respect and listen to those who respect their customs and understand their holy book. Their understanding of Jesus can provide a tremendous bridge for the expression of the Gospel. As one missionary put it, "The Degodia are extraordinarily open for a Muslim group." The need of the hour is for harvesters.

EARL ANDERSEN is a missionary with forty-five years' experience in Kenya with the African Inland Mission. He is the son of missionaries and was raised in Kenya. He holds a Th.B. from Burton Seminary and engineering degrees in aircraft maintenance and training and water technology. He has translated the New Testament into Kipsigi and has been involved in various tribal language projects. Three sons are third-generation missionaries in Kenya.

DAVID CASHIN is a research associate in the Samuel Zwemer Institute in Pasadena, California.

THE SUNDANESE OF INDONESIA

THE SUNDANESE OF INDONESIA

William N. McElrath

The Sundanese of West Java, Indonesia, are one of the largest groups of people as yet unreached for Christ. *Unreached Peoples '79* lists only five other groups with as great or a greater total population. Of these six peoples numbering twenty-five million or more, only the Sundanese and one other group are starred in the "Unreached People Register" as being "receptive" to the Gospel.[1] Another recent source states: "Among Islamic groups, only six ethnic identities form a larger population than the twenty-one million Sundanese."[2]

Yet the Sundanese are perhaps as little known to Westerners as any major ethnic group in the world today. Neither the *Encyclopedia Americana* (1973 edition), *World Book* (1978), *Compton's* (1971), nor the *New Columbia Encyclopedia* (1975) contains an article on the Sundanese tribe—only on "Sunda" as a geographical term in the Indies. The last-mentioned reference work, in a more general article, even commits the all-too-common error of misprinting "Sundanese" as "Sudanese."

DESCRIPTION OF THE PEOPLE

The vast majority of the world's twenty-one to twenty-five million Sundanese live in West Java—generally speaking the most fertile and most scenic one-third of that tropical island. Many other Indonesian tribes tend to scatter to other parts of the archipelago; the Sundanese are stay-at-homes. They speak Sundanese, a much more subtle and complicated Malay language than Indonesian, the national language to which it is akin. (About half the Sundanese speak both languages.)[3]

Physically, the Sundanese closely resemble their nearest tribal cousins, the Javanese and Balinese: small and graceful of form, tan or pale brown in color, delicate of features. They also share many of the same traditions with those better-known peoples: age-old dances performed to the metallic tones of the *gamelan* or percussion orchestra; fondness for the *wayang* or puppet play; and basic styles of dress, such as the *sarong* for men, and the closely fitted long-sleeved bodice, tight waistband, and ankle-length skirt for women. (Of course many Sundanese, especially in cities, have adopted Western clothing.)

In disposition the Sundanese are more like the Balinese than the Javanese: They smile readily, engage in chatter easily, and seem accommodating and eager to oblige. They are "polite, friendly, spontaneous, cheerful, and avoid flatly saying 'no.' "[4] Yet this surface manner—quite different from the comparatively shy or dour impression often given by Javanese—hides an inner citadel that has thus far proved almost impervious to the Gospel.

The majority of Sundanese today are wet-rice farmers, as their forefathers have been ever since coming over from the Asian continent before the time of Christ. Their flooded paddies make stairsteps that mirror the sky all up and down the volcanic slopes of West Java. Tea is also a major crop, mainly on vast plantations in the higher mountains. Other food crops, garden vegetables, fruits, rubber, lumber, ore from the hills, fish from the ponds and coasts—these are the principal natural products of *Pasundan,* the land of the Sundanese.

In the midst of this pastoral landscape are set two of Indonesia's three largest cities. Jakarta, the sprawling megalopolis and national capital, has an official population of more than six million. Nobody knows how many people actually walk its broad prestigious thoroughfares and unbelievably crowded back streets. Bandung's population is listed as a million and a quarter, but everybody knows it is really more than that.

These cities, like urban areas everywhere, attract a mixed population. There is considerable industry to draw people from the countryside: great textile mills in Bandung, all sorts of factories in Jakarta. Geographical proximity supports the conclusion that a large percentage of these city dwellers, too, are Sundanese.

Islam entered Java through its northern coast in the thirteenth through sixteenth centuries.[5] East and Central Java had powerful royal centers that tended to preserve the Hindu religion and Hindu culture as well as the older tribal traditions that underlay them. West Java had no such bastion against the inroads of the new monotheistic faith. The Dutch conquered West Java long before East or Central Java; throughout Indonesian history, Dutch colonial rule tended to hasten Islamization, precisely because Islam gave a rallying point against the proud white men who came from "Christian" lands.[6]

Because the gentle, pleasure-loving Sundanese set great store by family and village connections, Islam's emphasis on brotherly solidarity struck a responsive chord. Other elements of Islam also seemed made to order for the Sundanese and so were readily worked into their lifestyle. For example, the Sundanese were already circumcising their sons and sacrificing animals before the coming of Islam.[7] Statistics indicate that 95 to 98 percent of all inhabitants of West Java (including non-Sundanese as well) now claim to be Muslims.[8]

Yet Hendrik Kraemer, perhaps the most perceptive student of the Sundanese whose works have appeared in English, goes so far as to say that, contrary to general opinion, the Sundanese are not strong Muslims. Fanatic Muslim tribes in Indonesia would agree; they consider the Sundanese lax in their observance of the faith. Rather, Islam fitted into a ready-made niche in Sundanese tradition and so gained wide acceptance more as a matter of culture than of conscience.[9] "Though the life of the Sundanese is permeated by many customs with a strong Mohammedan tinge, yet most of them are quite indifferent to religion."[10] Thus Kraemer summarizes the distinction.

A more recent observer of this contradictory phenomenon writes: "Sundanese people are strongly Islamic, but the attraction is more cultural than religious. Islamic leaders admit that 40 percent do not attend the mosques or pray. Probably more than 60 percent do not follow any Islamic religious practices except those connected with the formalized cultural life of the villages. . . . All Sundanese consider themselves Muslim even though they know little or nothing about the religion. In fact, they are strongly influenced by animism (spirit worship). Every detail of their daily lives is related to spirit beliefs."[11]

STATUS OF CHRISTIANITY

For two centuries the Dutch did nearly nothing to share Christianity with the Sundanese. The first missionaries to

West Java arrived in 1863, and they met what seemed to be a stone wall.

It cannot be said that they failed to try. They used a variety of classic mission approaches, and as a result West Java today is heavily dotted with Christian schools, hospitals, student hostels, and children's homes. The missionaries even tried establishing new Christian villages as a way of breaking the rigid mold of Sundanese law and custom. But again and again they found themselves sidetracked into working among Chinese, Javanese, Moluccans, Menadonese, and other transplanted minorities. Those who responded from the indigenous population of West Java were pitifully few. In Bandung, seven years' hard work produced twenty-five Christians. It took ten years to reach that many in Sukabumi. In Bogor, after fourteen years there were six believers—but two of them were Chinese. In Cianjur, forty years' labor gathered a congregation of little more than seventy.[12] Perhaps it is no accident that the Sundanese word for law and custom is *kukuh,* which also means "stout, strong, impregnable"!

The Pasundan Christian Church is the spiritual heir of that earlier scattering precious seed with weeping. By 1932 it had reached a membership of 4,092.[13] This number nearly doubled to 8,234 by 1953, and nearly doubled again to 15,500 by 1967.[14]

The 82 percent increase from 1953 to 1967 is perhaps deceptively encouraging. Political and social upheavals in Indonesia during those years were used by God to cause growth among almost all Christian groups—spectacular growth among some.[15] Furthermore, as many as two-thirds of the present twenty thousand members of the Pasundan Christian Church are Chinese, Javanese, and others—not ethnic Sundanese.[16]

Perhaps as many as two thousand other Sundanese

converts are sprinkled among other denominations: Catholics, Baptists, Pentecostals, Adventists, Christian and Missionary Alliance, and others.[17] Such scattered individuals seem in some ways to be deracinated, cut off from true Sundanese traditions. Some of them tend to be loners; some are married to spouses from other tribes. Nothing remotely resembling a people movement has yet appeared among the Sundanese.

INDICATORS OF RECEPTIVITY

Yet it cannot be said that Pasundan presents a Muslim monolith against efforts at evangelization. A Sundanese evangelist told me in the early 1970s that hardness toward the Gospel in West Java was spotty, not solid. One village might hear him gladly, while a few miles away the people might stone him out of town. He soon learned to listen for barking dogs as an early indicator of hope—truly devout Muslims do not keep these "unclean" animals.

A Western-trained scholar who is also a pastor and the son of a pastor in the Pasundan Church recently said to a friend (here paraphrased in English): "Sundanese are not closed to the Gospel, . . . but they have their unique . . . customs. . . . In reality, they like something new, so they are open to the Gospel. There is a future for Christianity because the Muslim people are empty. They claim to have love and mercy, but in actuality they don't love their neighbors. What they reject is not the believing, but customs. To drop their own traditions is unthinkable— impossible."[18]

One factor that offers encouragement is the above-mentioned movement of Sundanese into the cities and larger towns (although some 80 percent of them are still rural). Here they inevitably rub shoulders with those whose lifestyles and beliefs are different from their own. Youthful rebellion against the norms set by elders may also help Sundanese young people become more open to change.

In fact, it is rather misleading to list only one category of Sundanese among the unreached peoples of the world. At least three large subgroups immediately come to mind: (1) Sundanese in urban areas; (2) rural Sundanese who speak Indonesian, and thus are exposed to broader cultural influences; and (3) Sundanese in the more remote villages, whose lives have been touched but little by the outside world.

The foreign missionary who has been most active among the Sundanese in the 1970s summarizes the current situation as follows: "On the basis of work done in the last ten years—touching several thousands, involving four hundred baptisms, I would classify them as having at least several million who are receptive. . . . Millions of Sundanese adults have never heard the name of Jesus and have no idea who he is. . . . This unreached people is unreached because no one is trying to reach them."[19]

POSSIBLE FORCES FOR EVANGELISM

The most immediate force for evangelism to which we might logically turn would be the Pasundan Christian Church, in which are found the vast majority of the less than one-fourth of 1 percent of all Sundanese who name the name of Christ. This denomination boasts a long-established presence in West Java, highly visible churches and institutions, and considerable use of Sundanese, the people's true "soul language."

Recent years have seen a modest increase in church-supported evangelistic activity. But the Pasundan Church in general seems to be living in a stained-glass ghetto. It "ministers only to Christian families and takes no responsibility for Muslim Sundanese."[20] It is one of those encapsulated Christian minorities we find throughout the world. In a harsh Muslim environment, "don't rock the boat" becomes an article of faith.

In 1971 one of the Sundanese Christian villages (which have declined in size and importance during this century) brought a religious drama to Bandung. I joined many Sundanese friends and neighbors in the party-like atmosphere that overflowed a large high school auditorium. The play presented its message with Sundanese dialogue, singing, dancing, instrumental music, even styles of clowning. All of this was good, yet I could not help noticing that the Christian minister—a Sundanese like everyone else in the cast—was portrayed in costume and manner as a Dutch Calvinist dominie of the past century!

Perhaps more hopeful is the recent rise of the Tent of David Foundation, an independent group headquartered in Bandung that has the avowed intent of reaching the Sundanese.[21] I have heard people in this group—nearly all of them members of other Indonesian tribes—speak feelingly of their desire to reach the Sundanese and of the great difficulties they have faced in trying to do so. Hindrances to these local cross-cultural efforts parallel in many respects obstacles encountered by those of us usually designated as foreign missionaries.

The Sundanese Missionary Fellowship (American headquarters in Lynchburg, Virginia) seeks to channel and correlate the efforts of others as well as do direct evangelism. One result has been a considerable enlargement in the body of hymns using Sundanese melody and meter. Audio-visual materials, evangelical literacy materials, and theological education by extension are among other ministries of this group.[22]

The overall lack of forces committed to reaching Sundanese Muslims is truly staggering: no denomination, no major mission agency, less than five foreign missionaries, less than fifty evangelical Indonesians, no Indonesian ordained ministers, no Indonesian full-time evangelists.[23]

STRATEGY SUGGESTIONS

In 1978 the Indonesian Bible Society published a New Testament in a common-language Sundanese version, similar to the English *Good News Bible* (Today's English Version). Previously the only translation in print had been hard to find and hopelessly literary for most readers. But only seventy-five hundred common-language Testaments were printed, and the Old Testament will not become available till 1980.[24] Increased distribution of Sundanese Scriptures that make sense should certainly claim a priority in any evangelistic strategy.

The establishment at Bandung in 1975 of the Inter-Mission Center of Language Learning and Cross-Cultural Communication (IMLAC) has opened new avenues of contact. Its major thrust is teaching the Indonesian language and some of the more general aspects of Indonesian culture; but IMLAC has also developed a vigorous program for studying the Sundanese language and culture. Both expatriates and Indonesians have begun to use this course as an entree into the world of Pasundan. Further in-depth studies are needed.

There should be much more use of mass media: shortwave broadcasts in Sundanese, other radio work, a widened cassette ministry. More Bible teaching and congregational leadership training are also needed.[25]

Christians from other backgrounds might seek opportunities to train members of the Pasundan Christian

83

Church in cultural self-awareness and evangelistic approaches. Even so simple a matter as practicing circumcision might make the Christian lifestyle seem less foreign.[26] This denomination's great potential for outreach among its own people is as yet largely unrealized.

And, as is the case in so many places, there is still a great need for Christians, wherever they may come from, who are willing to plant their lives among the Sundanese and serve sacrificially, while praying and waiting for the harvest. Hendrik Kraemer's words, first written for West Java in the 1930s, are just as applicable to West Java in the 1980s:

> It is of primary importance that, through their training, missionaries acquire the attitude that everything they learn serve as an *impetus to penetrate* into the indigenous world. The aim should certainly be that a missionary, upon his arrival, is someone who considers it quite natural and obvious that, while making the most of the little knowledge he has gained, he penetrates slowly but steadily into this world which will be the subject of his work and love.[27]

WILLIAM N. McELRATH has served since 1965 as a missionary in Indonesia with major responsibilities at the Baptist Publishing House in Bandung, West Java. He has written more than thirty books in both English and Indonesian, including biographies, biblical reference works, and programmed instruction texts for theological education by extension. Other published works deal with missions, music, drama, and children's curriculum. McElrath holds the B.A. degree from Murray State University and the M.Div. and Th.M. degrees from Southern Baptist Theological Seminary.

REACHING THE BARANADA PEOPLE OF BARUNDA

Paul Pearlman

Introduction

This is a case study of a contemporary effort to reach Muslims for Christ. It is a "live" study in that it describes an actual situation. Names and locations (including the name of the author and the country, here called "Barunda") have been changed to protect those involved. However, all significant data relating to cultural practices, the method of ministry, and the history of the work are accurate.

Nestled between Maluwa, Batu, and the blue ocean, Barunda is a tropical nation of fifteen million people. In the past twenty-one years, the country has gone through considerable upheaval. Innumerable governments have come and gone—vividly portraying Barunda's most famous poet's characterization of political leadership rising and falling like the scorching East African sun. Tragedy has buffeted this resilient people in the form of tornadoes, drought, and famine. The "ultimate" in suffering occurred in the bloody two-year civil war of 1971-73. A total of one-and-one-half million citizens migrated to Maluwa, while the remaining populace endured the hell of murder, rape, looting, and burning. Emerging from such a nightmare of violence has been a continuing process. The past three years have been relatively calm and have resulted in a climate conducive to economic progress. There is room for an optimistic short-range prognosis for the good of the Baranada people.

There are some twenty-eight million Baranada; they are the second-largest Muslim ethnic group in Africa. About 60 percent of the ethnic Baranada are Muslims; the remainder are animists. Present-day Barunda is the ancestral homeland of the Baranada people, who are distinct from the surrounding animistic tribes. Barunda, which is unusual for its ethnic homogeneity, is 90 percent Muslim with a 10 percent animist population, mostly of ethnic Baranada background. Eighty-five percent of the ethnic Baranada outside of Barunda are animists, the remainder being Muslims.

The vast majority of the Baranada, both Muslim and animist alike, are subsistence grain farmers. The low-lying terrain of Barunda is ideally suited to such agriculture, but it has been subject to severe weather, including both flooding and droughts. Population is quite dense in areas where cultivatable land is at a premium.

The countryside is socially divided along patrilineal kinship lines. Kinship, which includes the widest possible range of people "related" by blood or marriage, is reckoned in several complex ways and is ingeniously expandable to include close social relationships. The basic community structure is the village, within which there is considerable interrelationship. Households are divided into "eating groups," which are communally run. This household unit symbolizes its mutual interdependence through the preparation and sharing of common food and living quarters. The concept of "community" is a cultural norm traceable well into the animistic past of the Baranada. A person's family membership and place of residence are thus the focal points for all of his activities in the world.

Social hierarchy is highly structured in Baranada society, reflecting the influence of animism and slave trade in the past. Marriage always takes place within one's own social group. Curiously, however, the Baranada seem to prefer marriage across kinship lines in order to expand the kinship matrix. Among subsistence farmers, who make up the bulk of the Baranada, a fairly egalitarian structure exists. Butchers, weavers, and itinerant traders are classed lowest on the social scale. Farmers are next, followed by local clergy and government officials.

Islam came to the Baranada during the fourteenth century and experienced a rapid growth under the influence of Sufi sheikhs, whose egalitarianism was very appealing during the period of slave trading. The Baranada are Sunni Muslims, for whom the five pillars of Islam are deeply embedded in daily life. The custom of female seclusion is quite strong. Sufi orders also continue to flourish in the rural areas. There are, however, a number of animistic practices the Baranada maintain, one of which is saint worship, as witnessed by the widespread participation in *natu,* "commemorative gatherings," at the tombs of their saints.

Urbanization has been slow in Barunda. The influence of Westernization and secularization is hard to determine since the metropolitan and industrial classes are, in most cases, only a generation or two removed from the countryside. Though there has been some departure from Islamic customs in the urban areas, the bedrock of Baranada society remains Islamic. Outside Barunda, the Muslim minorities of Maluwa and Batu struggle to keep their Islamic flavor and practice.

THE STATUS OF CHRISTIANITY IN BARUNDA

Christians number some thirty thousand—equally divided between Protestants and Catholics—and comprise less than 1 percent of the population. The church is derived entirely from Baranada people who have had an animistic background. Despite their common racial background, animists have no dealings with Muslims. The various denominations are almost entirely dependent financially on Western Christian assistance. This applies to church budgetary needs as well as to job opportunities in mission institutions and Western developmental organizations. As pressures continue to increase for the establishment of *shariat,* or Islamic sacred law, in Barunda, the church has been concerned with the growing instances of persecution and social second-class status.

The church, a small, introspective, and often insecure body of believers, has been growing slowly. Twenty-five Protestant mission societies have some 250 missionaries working throughout Barunda, and Catholics 169. There are twelve denominations in the country. Most missionaries work within the established church or are attached to mission-operated institutions. There is a definite trend to place more missionaries in full-time evangelistic outreach.

NEW EFFORTS TO REACH THE BARANADA IN THE MAWASA AREA

Despite the Baranada's seeming resistance to the Gospel, some recent breakthroughs have occurred among them under the leadership of the Overseas Christian Missionary Fellowship (OCMF). In 1959, the OCMF entered the town of Mawasa, which has a population of eight thousand in a district of two hundred thousand. Between one and three missionary couples have resided in the town up to the present. Until 1975, their efforts proved fruitless; no church was established and almost no one was led to Christ. Mawasa appeared to be barren and resistant. The OCMF field council determined that it would be expedient to withdraw from that area unless a breakthrough occurred in the ensuing twelve months. Then, the miraculous began to unfold. Through the influence of two Muslim converts, Tabbar and Sadig, the OCMF began to adopt Baranada Muslim forms in their work of communicating the Gospel. Presently there are two worshiping groups of believers in the Mawasa area. Each fellowship is made up of fifteen Muslim converts, almost all of whom are male heads of families. Numerous factors have played a part in the new responsiveness. For example, the response of Christian agencies during natural catastrophe has built up an attitude of goodwill. However, the vast majority of converts cite the Baranada-like quality of the message as being the main reason for their conversion. The Baranada have a highly developed culture and sense of historical tradition. Thus, adapting the forms of the message of the Gospel to fit their patterns and to speak to the needs of their society has been the key factor in establishing the fellowships. The following descriptions of these groups illustrate this point.

DESCRIPTION OF CONVERTS

The majority of converts are farmers who, on the average, are barely literate; economically they are self-supporting; and they are close enough sociologically to be able to intermarry. Those who have grown most rapidly spiritually were formerly devout Muslims. Almost all converts are reading the Bible (or having it read to them), praying, and meeting together informally in their village homes for worship—without the presence of a foreign missionary. Witnessing to their neighbors and extended families began on the day of their conversion and has been the major cause of reproduction. Until now, it has not been the missionary who has won these men to the Lord, with a very few exceptions. His role is basically to give spiritual encouragement and biblical teaching. The believers have shown initiative and vision. After a study of 1 Corinthians 12, one group on their own appointed an evangelist, an administrator, a prayer coordinator, and a pastor. A few of the wives and children have accepted Christ, but this area of evangelism still remains an obstacle. There has been an appreciation of the supernatural on a practical level, with visions and dreams of spiritual significance occurring fairly frequently. There is a simple faith that prayer is an instrument of change. Crying out to God and fasting are utilized to effect release from difficulty as well as to bring healing to the afflicted.

FORM ADAPTATIONS

The apostle Paul in 1 Corinthians 9:19-23 set down some practical theological guidelines for his involvement in the cross-cultural communication of the Gospel. In Barunda, we are seeking to minister within the same liberties and restrictions that Paul experienced. The offense of the nature of God and the atonement of the cross will and must remain. However, there are innumerable peripheral areas that can be subject to alteration without violation of scriptural command or principle. A list of implemented form adaptations follows:

The Missionary

1. Our men wear the clothing of the target group, which is the village farmer. Our women wear the local dress and at times have worn the veil covering, which has been very much appreciated by the Muslim and convert community.
2. Several of our men have full beards, which is part of the appearance of a Muslim religious man.
3. Lifestyles are simple.
4. Eating style corresponds to Muslims. No pork is eaten
5. Time is regarded as more "event oriented" than the traditional time absolutes of the West. Some have adopted the 8 P.M. Barunda suppertime and thus have entered into the social visitation pattern of the society, which takes place each evening between 6 and 8 P.M.

The National

1. A place for washing before prayer is provided for optional use. It is explained that there is no merit attached to such ceremonial washing.
2. Shoes are removed before entering the worship center.
3. All worshipers sit on the floor.
4. Bibles are placed on folding stands such as are used for the Koran.
5. Occasionally, Greek and Hebrew Bibles are placed in a prominent position in front of the worshipers, thus demonstrating our regard for the "original" Bible, such as Muslims feel toward the Arabic Koran.
6. Hands are lifted up Muslim style during prayer times. Prostration is frequently done in Muslim fashion. Some pray with their eyes open, wearing traditional prayer hats.
7. Muslim tunes with Christian words are utilized. Scripture is chanted, as are personal testimonies.

8. The local Muslim dialect, rather than the animist dialect of the Christian church, is spoken and read in the services.
9. Embracing is done in Muslim fashion.
10. Days and times of worship are pragmatically regulated.
11. Fasting is an area of liberty, but is scripturally explained.
12. A Muslim-convert, homogeneous church has developed rather than one of a heterogeneous character.
13. Informal church organization is promoted, basically along the lines of the mosque.
14. The Muslim names of converts are retained.
15. The word *Christian* is avoided because of negative connotations. Presently Christians are called "followers of Isa" (Jesus).
16. Bible study, prayer, and fasting are emphasized. A higher profile of religious observance is encouraged because Muslims feel Christians are spiritually lazy when they are never seen praying.
17. The converts have chosen their own leadership.
18. The church grows along family and friendship lines.

FINANCIAL CONSIDERATIONS

Gifts and employment opportunities from the West have created a horizontal dependence syndrome within the Barunda Christian community. There is little motivation to give sacrifically or to pray about church needs when one is assured budgets will be met with foreign assistance. Christians are given preferential treatment at mission hospitals and schools. A select few are granted theological scholarships abroad. Comparison of lifestyles between nationals and missionaries convinces Barunda Christians that personal sacrifice is not particularly relevant to the "dedicated life." In my view, all of this points to a basic failure on the part of missionaries to live, teach, and administer sound indigenous financial policy in relationship to the national church. The crashing wave of a forced missionary evacuation, which was only barely averted last December, would most likely reduce our practicing Christian community by a minimum of 50 percent.

In Mawasa there is a fresh slate. No traditional Christians reside in the area. The emerging Muslim convert church is the only worshiping group present. Our approach has been as follows:

Missionary adjustments

OCMF possesses no compounds or purchased property. This assures mobility as well as a lower financial profile. Missionaries live on as low a lifestyle as emotional and physical health permit. One family presently lives in a small bamboo hut with a mud floor. Others are in simple cement houses rented from Muslim landlords.

Financial relationships with nationals

OCMF aims to preserve the financial autonomy of the convert in relationship to himself, his family, and his peers. Existing economic structures should, at all costs, be preserved. The convert is told from the start that Christianity will only be credible among his Muslim friends if he stands without foreign financial assistance. No option for flight from his village is offered. Jobs, scholarships, and relief are not part and parcel of the Gospel. New believers must learn to stand on their own resources from the commencement of their pilgrimage of faith. OCMF has not been involved in institution or relief work. We have no national evangelists, although we have used Sadiq Jabbar occasionally as volunteer help. The emphasis is on lay witness and ministry.

THE EXISTING EVANGELISTIC TEAM

At present six foreign missionaries and the forty national believers from among the converted Muslims comprise the major functioning evangelistic team. Other Muslim converts have and will continue to be involved on an itinerant basis. At present, the Baranada church with its animistic background has been very wary of this Islamic-flavored movement. Those Christians are a potential team to assist with evangelism, as are the missionaries of other societies. However, for the time being they have adopted a wait-and-see attitude and are uninvolved in this work.

PAUL PEARLMAN (a pseudonym) is a native of the southeastern United States and a graduate of Tennessee Temple College and Trinity Evangelical Divinity School. Additional training has included the Missionary Internship program in Detroit and courses at Moody Bible Institute. He has served for seventeen years in Barunda, the last twelve as mission field director. He has also served as the principal of a Bible correspondence school. The writer is the author of a well-known book on missions to Muslims and is currently doing advanced degree work in the United States prior to returning to the field.

MUSLIM EVANGELISM IN SURANYA

Robert Borden

Introduction

This is also a case study of a contemporary effort to reach Muslims for Christ. It is a "live" study in that it describes an actual situation. Names and locations (including the name of the author and the country, here called "Suranya") have been changed to protect those involved. However, all significant data relating to cultural practices, the method of ministry, and the history of the work are accurate.

The region of Suranya is an ethnically diverse crossroads near the traditional invasion route to central Bangui in the Philippines. Nearly ten million people live in the region, representing a dozen ethnic groups. There is, however, a considerable amount of homogeneity because of the common lifestyle of the people.

The majority of the Surani, as the local population is sometimes called, are farmers on some of the richest farmland in Asia. They are suffering from a considerable overpopulation problem, which has led to extensive subdivision of lands and property. The local dialect is a variant of the national tongue and is spoken by most of the population. Suranya is divided into eighteen subdistricts each with a major, centrally located town. The countryside is dotted with regional towns linked to major centers by railways or roads. These regional towns in turn feed a network of smaller villages grouped around them.

Society is divided into three classes. The highest class are former major landholders, ruling-class families and rich merchants. This class has been established for some time and assumes that it carries a privileged status. There is a small middle class of merchants in the larger towns and cities. The majority of the population are farmers and landless laborers. There are far greater cultural differences between the poor and the rich than between the various ethnic groups of the Surani.

The peoples of Suranya are less militaristic than the other members of the region who make up 70 percent of the national army of Bangui. Honor, face-saving, and lavish hospitality are ingrained cultural norms. Social structure is highly patrilineal, and those who are economically well off seek to place their women in seclusion as a matter of social status. Marriages are usually within the local clan with cousin marriage considered ideal.

There has been considerable dissatisfaction among Surani youth in recent years. Those who migrate to the cities and become educated are unwilling to return to the rural areas. Jobs are scarce in the cities, however, and unemployed intellectuals form a large, often Communist-leaning class in the cities. Suranya is 80 percent rural and is only gradually becoming more urbanized.

Eighty-eight percent of the Surani are Sunni Muslims of the Hanafi school. The remaining 12 percent are Shia of the Ithni Ishari branch. Sufis and the Sufic orders are very widespread in Suranya. The people of this region are renowned for their devotion to holy men, poetry, and various animistic practices.

The Suranya region is 99 percent Muslim, with a very small population of Christians concentrated in the larger cities. The region this case study will be focusing on is a rural area that is virtually 100 percent Muslim. The nearest Christian group is thirty miles away and consists of only five active Christians. The only evangelistic team is two women workers and a number of Muslim converts they have led to the Lord.

It has always been assumed that the Surani were resistant to the Gospel. The fact remains that so little work has been done that it is difficult to evaluate receptivity. If receptivity were to be judged by the work of these two women workers then the Surani would be judged to be somewhat receptive.

CASE STUDY: A UNIQUE WORK AMONG THE SURANI

Two single women missionaries teamed up because of their common conviction that Muslims can and must be won to Christ. They began their team effort among women and children in a town of 25,000 that is the center for all the villages in a fifteen-to-twenty-mile radius. All the rest of the population (about 2.5 million) of the district was Muslim.

One of the missionaries is an experienced nurse with a real gift in diagnostic treatment and a thoroughness that probably increases her "cure rate" at least 15 percent over other similarly trained workers. The other missionary has the gift of evangelism together with a concern for people that drives her to constantly try to reach more and more for Christ. These two women carry on a program that would exhaust four men! They have seen approximately 250 people put their trust in Christ and they are in regular contact with 156 of them, discipling them through a full-fledged program.

When they moved into town to begin their work, these missionaries located a building in the middle of town rather than choosing a quieter location on the outskirts. They also set about to learn the local dialect, which is neither written nor read although it is the mother tongue of some ten million people. In this way they were choosing to identify with the common people instead of with the upper middle class as most missionaries do.

Using a dispensary, they presented the Gospel both verbally and in their lifestyle. Early they flew in the face of both culture and religion by insisting that (1) everyone would be treated equally in the order in which they came, and (2) no one would receive medical treatment without also hearing the Gospel. In that culture only the poor masses will stand in line. The upper-class minorities expect to cut in and be waited on first. Of course, as Muslims they objected to being forced to hear the Gospel—at least the upper class did!

The effect of this procedure was that (1) basically only the poor majority came; (2) Christianity was presented as a religion in which the poor man had equal rights, quite in contrast to the prevailing practice of the Muslim society of that area; (3) the Gospel was heard over and over again since most patients came back frequently. Experience over the years shows that initial hostility to the Gospel soon turned into curiosity and finally into understanding; (4) a respect for the Gospel and for the missionaries' convictions about Christ was generated because they did not tolerate any heckling or open opposition to their preaching within the walls of the dispensary. This is consistent with the Muslim cultural pattern of nontolerance of any open attack on Islam; (5) the love of Christ was clearly on display in the care with which medicine was dispensed. In contrast to the local Muslim doctors, these missionaries treated the poor as if their lives really were valuable.

Another part of the initial approach of the two missionaries was the expansion of house-by-house preaching of the Gospel throughout the area on the days that the dispensary was closed. Several significant factors need to be pointed out regarding this: (1) Other missionaries were horrified and strongly objected to two young, unveiled, single women going into remote areas and Muslim homes without any man to protect them. Perhaps they exposed themselves to danger, but by the grace of God no harm came to them; (2) they have demonstrated that women can effectively reach the Muslim family with the Gospel. When a man (missionary or national) goes to visit in a Muslim home, he is received by the men in the front, guest room and has no access to the rest of the house or to the women of the home. Muslim men very much enjoy discussing and arguing religion, and in most cases a presentation of the Gospel by a man is interrupted so frequently with arguments that it is rendered meaningless. In contrast, when these women missionaries enter a Muslim home they are taken into the women's section where all of the women and children are. Since the missionaries do not wear the Muslim veil, the men of the house feel free to enter the room and listen. They do not feel free, however, to enter into too much conversation with a woman. Since Muslim women are not supposed to do much thinking and certainly not much speaking in the presence of their husband or father, they also quietly listen while the Gospel message is clearly presented *to the whole family!* Sometimes during the serving of tea one of the men might ask the usual argumentative question, such as "If Jesus is God's Son, then who is his grandfather?" These two servants of God usually responded to such derogatory remarks by refusing the tea being offered and leaving the house, amidst the pleas of their hosts to please not be offended! A general awareness of the presence of Christians and respect for the basic truths of the Gospel was established in the area through this approach.

As the work continued, other features developed: (1) A separate class for the children of patients was started. (2) The classes for school children, started earlier, began to grow. In recent years attendance has averaged as high as eight hundred different children on a Friday afternoon and as high as twelve hundred on special occasions despite ridicule and occasional beatings. (3) In more recent years a sewing class for teen-age girls has been started. When some strong opposition arose to these young people being "forced" to study the Bible, the missionaries dissolved the class and told all the girls they could come back only if they brought their fathers and had them give their expressed permission for them to study the Bible. The result was eventually an even bigger class! Many of these girls started out in the children's classes and have since accepted the Lord.

Each year a thorough evaluation and report has been made and new goals set for the following year. Many of these goals have to do with attendance at various meetings. The missionaries keep careful records of those who have come to Christ, how and when they came to Christ, their present spiritual condition, and specific prayer requests for them.

The principles behind all these methods seem to be: (1) identify with the poor—the common people—and find out where the people are; (2) find some way to help people with a genuine need; (3) help them in a way that is of higher quality than is available otherwise; (4) have them come to you where you can teach the Gospel freely; (5) *require* the hearing of the Gospel as a part of the program;

(6) plan and evaluate carefully, and set goals.

These women have faced severe opposition on at least three occasions. Their greatest opponents have been the clergy, school teachers, and doctors—for obvious reasons! The loudspeaker of the mosque next door towers over them and constantly booms out Islamic teaching. Although these times have been very trying, they have afforded the missionaries a priceless opportunity to be an example of the believer in Christ. This is desperately needed for new Muslim converts. The women in this area seem stronger in persecution than the men. Not one has left her home. Sometimes they are tolerated as "foolish" women. Yet they often exercise more control in the home than is generally thought. Men seem more bound by their sense of responsibility. In the few cases of husbands and wives that are both believers, it is always the wife that is the stronger and usually the first believer.

A fellowship and worship service has begun, with the men separated from the women by a curtain. This past year the average attendance at both the women's worship service and the joint worship service has been from forty to fifty.

Prayer has been given a significant place in the ministry from the beginning. New believers are taught how to pray and are encouraged to take part in prayer both in the worship services and in prayer meetings. Separate prayer meetings for men and women are well attended, with the same number attending as at the worship services! Seventy percent participate in prayer, and their faith has been strengthened by many answers to prayer.

Baptism and marriage are two sensitive areas that have been handled carefully. Many young people (mostly girls) who have accepted Christ have had to accept marriage arrangements made by their parents, which involves an unsaved Muslim partner. The missionaries have prayed earnestly with and for such young believers and have taught them that they must submit to their parent's authority, trusting God.

In order to avoid creating the impression that young people are being taught to rebel against their parents (an accusation often made), baptism has been given only in the presence of a consenting parent or husband. For this reason, only twelve have been baptized so far. In no case were there group decisions for Christ; in every case they came one by one. In each case there are one or more key believers through whom others in the group have come to the dispensary and then to Christ. The believers may be broken down by age as follows:

11 boys under 14
15 teenage boys age 15-19
11 men over 20

36 girls under age 14
22 teenage girls age 15-19
29 young married women
36 older married women

The group of believers is still a long way from being a church with its own leadership and program, and the greatest weakness at this point is the lack of male leadership.

ROBERT BORDEN (a pseudonym) is an American who grew up on the east coast. He is a graduate of both Wheaton College and the Columbia Bible College Graduate School of Missions. He has served as a missionary in his adopted country off and on for the past twenty-two years. In recent years he has acted as the field director of his mission. Other duties have involved him in itinerant evangelism, Bible translation work, and teaching in a well-known Bible institute. Currently he is in the United States serving as a key person in the administrative head-quarters of his mission. In addition to his duties at the mission office, the author also teaches at a nearby Bible college.

A UNIQUE EFFORT TO REACH JAMMU-KASHMIR FOR CHRIST

P.M. Thomas

Lying on the main invasion route to the Indian subcontinent is the northernmost province of Jammu-Kashmir. A critical point of conflict between India and Pakistan for thirty years, it is the only Indian state with a Muslim majority. In keeping with its invasion-route status, Jammu-Kashmir is populated with a wide variety of peoples representing the groups that have held ascendance over the centuries.

The present population is approximately 5.2 million, of which 65 percent are Muslims. Hindus make up 31.4 percent, Sikhs 2.3 percent, and Buddhists 1.3 percent. Three territorial regions are incorporated in Jammu-Kashmir: Jammu, Ledakh, and Kashmir. As the accompanying literacy chart shows, Muslims comprise the vast majority of Kashmir, Hindus the majority of Jammu, and Buddhists the majority of Ledakh.

The Jammu region is essentially an extension of the Punjab but is less mountainous. The vernacular language is Dogri, now only spoken, with reading and writing done in Urdu, Hindi, and Punjabi.

Kashmir is a land of contrasts containing one of the largest valleys in the world, surrounded by mountains soaring from three thousand to five thousand meters high.

CASE STUDIES

Literacy Chart
Source: Census 1971

Region	Area in square kilometers	Population density per square kilometer	Villages	Percentage of literates to the total population		
				Males	Females	Perso
1	2	3	4	5a	5b	5c
Jammu and Kashmir State	138,992.1	33	6,971	26.75	9.28	18.
Jammu region	26,089.4	72	3,693	28.2	11.4	19.
Kashmir region	15,120.3	161	3,039	23.0	7.2	15.
Ladhakh	97,782.4	1	239	22.17	2.99	12.

POPULATION PERCENTAGES

	MUSLIMS (3.5M)	HINDUS (1.5M)	SIKHS (.110M)	BUDDHISTS (.065M)	OTHERS (9,000)
STATE:	66	30.4	2.2	1.26	.19
JAMMU	33.81	62.06	3.67	.11	.44
KASHMIR	94	4.72	1.2	.05	—
LADAKH	46.66	1.09	—	51.82	—

Kashmiri is the local dialect, with Urdu as the written language of the literate classes.

The entire area of Ledakh lies above three thousand meters and is an extension of the Tibetan plateau. Weather in the region is severe, and so the population is quite sparse. Various Tibetan and tribal dialects are spoken.

Two factors are critical in the understanding of Jammu-Kashmir. The first is the caste system that permeates the region. In spite of Islamic and government policy, both Muslims and Hindus have a strong sense of caste and social grouping. This is not unusual for the subcontinent, as most Muslims were converts from Hinduism. The Hindu caste structure is quite rigid, with dozens of endogamous categories. Muslim caste structure is much more fluid, except in the highest and lowest categories. Syeds and Shaikhs, those who trace their lineage to the prophet or to early Muslim missionaries, are at the top of the social structure. At the bottom are the Hanjis and other laborers in the various "unclean" tasks. The majority of the Muslim population is made up of rural farmers in middle caste groupings. Ninety percent of the Muslim population is rural, while Hindus make up a disproportionate part of the urban population. In Kashmir virtually all Hindus are of the Brahmin (pandit) priestly and ruling class.

This points out the second major factor determining the character of Jammu-Kashmir. Like the Bengali, the Kashmiri Muslims did not have an elite ruling class. The recent history of Kashmir is one of subjugation, first by the Pushtuns of Afghanistan (1752—1819), then by the Sikhs (1819—46), and finally by the Hindu Dogra dynasty (1846—1947). During the course of these periods, an earlier Muslim ruling class died out. This absence of Muslim leadership is conspicuously different from the Muslim

107

leadership in other regions that established Pakistan. This paucity of leadership is being overcome as self-government has been promoted in Kashmir since 1931.

Islam in this region is subdivided into Sunni and Shia sects. Ninety-five percent of the Muslim population is Sunni and five percent is Shia. Sunni Islam is further divided into traditionalists, revivalists, and secularists. The traditional religion was syncretistic, with saint worship and superstitious practices accepted alongside Islamic ritual. The bulk of the Muslims followed these traditions. Revivals of puritan Islam were spearheaded by the Wahabi sect in the past century. Later, the Mama'at-i-Islami carried forward educational programs designed to purge syncretistic practices until its outlawing during the Indian emergency of 1975. The leadership of Jammu-Kashmir has been dominated by secularists seeking to modernize the region. This process has been considerably aided by Indian-subsidized development projects that have been used to gain the loyalty of the Muslim majority. Thus, "An incongruous alliance between traditionalists and secularists has kept the state within the Indian union against the claims and subversive efforts of Pakistan,"[1] which have been fueled by Muslim revivalists.

A BRIEF HISTORY OF CHRISTIAN WORK IN JAMMU-KASHMIR

The first Western missionary group to enter the area was the Central Asian Mission during the first half of the nineteenth century. Virtually nothing remains of their work. The Church Missionary Society (CMS) began work in the Kashmir valley in 1862. It established medical and educational institutions that still service a large portion of the area. Few conversions were recorded through this work, however. With the departure of some CMS missionaries, several of the institutions closed because of a lack of national workers.

The Punjab mission of the Church of Scotland pushed into Jammu from Sialkot in the 1890s and established churches among the sweeper castes. About three thousand were converted through this work, which was an extension of the Punjab mass movement. These churches presently comprise the majority of believers in Jammu-Kashmir.

Moravian Brethren entered the Ledakh area in 1886. Churches were established in Leh, Sheh, and Khalatse from among the Buddhist population. The church grew very slowly but produced some notable Christians such as Joseph Gergan, who translated the Bible into Tibetan. Since the Moravians left in 1950 there has been no Christian worker to care for these churches.

Worldwide Evangelization Crusade (WEC) has been working in the Jammu hills since the 1940s with a series of preaching stations and dispensaries. A number of small groups of believers have resulted from this work.

Roman Catholic activity has focused on institutional work. At present, one hospital, three schools, and one convent are operating.

One further work deserves mention in this context. For the first time in recent history a group of Muslims quite unconnected with any mission were converted and baptized. At the center of this work was a Kashmiri evangelist who was converted while studying to be a *maulvi* (Muslim priest) in Delhi. This work now has ties with the WEC through the Rev. G. Porter. It has established several fellowships in and around Srinagar that are utilizing some of the buildings of the CMS mission that were formerly closed.

Of the non-Roman Catholic foreigners there are at present five CMS missionaries, four WEC missionaries, and two Central Asian Mission missionaries in Jammu-Kashmir.

THE BIRTH OF AN INDIGENOUS MISSIONARY ORGANIZATION

In March 1957 I first visited Jammu-Kashmir as a student and was challenged by the need of the area. After a few more surveys, I moved on faith with my family to the town of Udhampur. WEC missionaries had been working in the area for several years and had four believers who formed the nucleus of the church.

Initially the work progressed very slowly, and there was considerable opposition. I early adopted the principle of an open profile, even instituting a yearly parade by the believers through the town of Udhampur. This parade and other public activities became a point of contention with local authorities and particularly the Muslims. Gradually it also became a gauge of increasing openness as opposition began to decrease. By 1970, thirty-four people had accepted Christ and been baptized. Land was obtained from the government, and a small church building was built.

A second principle that the Kashmir Evangelical Fellowship (KEF), as the mission came to be known, pursued was the multiplication of full-time workers. We were supported through our home churches in South India. Many of the early converts also stepped out on faith to work full time with the KEF. In 1972 Captain A.M. Samuel and P.G. Varghese, who were in the army, were converted through the KEF. Later both resigned from the military and started two new missionary fellowships. As more were converted, particularly out of the army, the number of those offering themselves for full-time service greatly increased. By 1977 there was a total of seventy-seven workers in three missionary fellowships—thirty-two with the KEF, twenty-five with the Vargheses in the India Evangelical Team, and twenty with the Samuels in the Indian Pentecostal Church. Altogether there were twenty-five mission stations, ten churches, and over five hundred converts. By 1979 a total of ninety workers were active and over six hundred converts recorded. These three mission agencies are aiming for a total of one hundred workers by 1980 and eventually for a Gideon's army of three hundred.

Many of the workers are from South India, recruited from Bible schools and seminaries in Kerala and Tamil-Nadu. However, a growing number are native Kashmiri workers. Army converts in particular are from North India, and most of these come from upper caste backgrounds. At present there are no Muslim converts involved in a full-time ministry.

Thus far, about 90 percent of the converts are Hindus. A considerable percentage of them have come from the army, whose presence is quite large due to the border conflict with Pakistan. One worker has been accepted as the official army headquarters chaplain. This has opened tremendous opportunities because the army is widely respected and converts among the soldiers often open new areas for ministry where they are stationed. The majority of the membership of the churches is made up of sweeper caste Hindus. There is also a small number of upper caste Hindu converts. About sixty Muslims, or 10 percent of the total, have been converted through this ministry. All of these diverse groups fellowship together as a demonstration of the unity and equality engendered through the Gospel. Some of the outlying preaching stations and smaller churches are more homogeneous.

The forms of church worship are Indian, not Western.

111

Most of the songs for worship are written by local believers. The believers' faith has grown as they have seen God perform many miracles on behalf of the church in the provision of funds for new buildings and new workers, and in protection in the midst of persecution. About 70 percent of the funds for workers comes from South India and 30 percent from the churches in Kashmir. Considering the large number of workers, this represents considerable liberality in this poverty-stricken area.

The yearly parade of the believers in Udhampur has become a popular and large public function. Resistance has decreased and interest in the Gospel has grown proportionately. Public open-air preaching is a regular aspect of these yearly parades, and at other times as well. The entire program of the churches is highly evangelistically oriented. All funds for the support of workers come from India, and there has been little Western involvement in this movement. All workers from the various fellowships gather for united meetings on planning and outreach to insure that no duplication of efforts occurs. This is particularly needed as workers spread out into the hill country to establish preaching stations.

At present there is no theological school or Bible institute in Jammu-Kashmir. To meet this need, KEF has established a basic missionary training program called the "Alpha course." This includes primarily introduction to the local culture, language study, and practical evangelism training. The KEF plans to expand this training institute to include further training courses, new classrooms, more teaching staff, a larger library, and living accommodations.

One of the weaknesses of Western missionary work is that few have mastered the Dogri or Kashmiri languages. The KEF has translated and published two booklets into Dogri and hopes to expand this publishing work. They also have a Bible correspondence course that has brought conversions and expanded work into new areas.

The state government is now developing hill roads to almost all the interior areas. This improvement has provided opportunities for Christian workers to reach into new areas never before evangelized. The KEF has recently purchased a four-wheel-drive jeep to begin this work.

Three important areas of need have emerged in the past few months. The first is the need to develop a radio ministry in Dogri and Kashmiri. This could have a powerful impact on the five million people of this region. Also, an evangelical Bible school in Urdu would be a great help for the new converts. At present, believers have to leave Jammu-Kashmir in order to get Bible training. Finally, a Christian printing press could help facilitate the publishing of materials for use among the local people.

A government bill against conversion passed recently in one state in India. Other similar bills are being considered, and persecution is beginning in several areas. We need to pray that the door will remain open for a continuing witness to the Good News of Jesus Christ.

FOR FURTHER INFORMATION

Those who want to know more about Jammu-Kashmir may consult the following sources:

Annals of the Church Missionary Society. Available in the library of the Brotherhood of the Ascended Christ, Delhi.
Digest of Statistics, 1975. Jammu-Kashmir Government.
Francke, A. R. *History of Ladakh.* Ed. Gergan and Hussnain. Delhi: Sterling Publishers.
Kaul, G. L. *Kashmir Then and Now—A Historical Survey.*

CASE STUDIES

Lawrence, Walter R. *The Valley of Kashmir.*
The library of the Indian Church History Association at Baring College, Batala, Punjab.
Weekes, Richard V., ed. *Muslim Peoples, A World Ethnographic* Survey. Westport, Conn.: Greenwood Press, 1978.

Rare Old Books

Clark, H. M. *Robert Clark of the Punjab.* London: Andrew Melrose, 1907.
Tyndale-Biscoe, Canon C. E. *Kashmir in Sunlight and Shade.* Reprint. New Delhi: Sagar Publishers. Also see other books by Canon Biscoe and the Neve brothers.
Wilson, Mrs. Camus. *Irene Petrie.* London: Hodder & Stoughton, 1900.

Small Recent Publications

Father Borst. *A Method of Contemplative Prayer.* Bombay: Asia Trading Corporation.
MacMullen and Caleb. *Amritsar Diocese of the CNI.* A sociological study. Batala, Punjab: Christian Institute of Sikh Studies, Baring College.
Purves, Jock. *The Unlisted Legion.* Edinburgh: Banner of Truth Trust, 1976.

P. M. THOMAS started his career as a schoolteacher in Kerala, South India. Later he received a special call from the Lord to become a missionary in North India. For three years he worked with the All Kerala Christian Fellowship, and for another two years he worked as the secretary of the Christian Institute at Aleppey in South India. He graduated from Nagpur University and received his B.D.

from the Union Biblical Seminary, Yoetmal, India. From 1957 on he made several missionary surveys of North India. In 1963 he set out with his wife, Christy, and son for North India and opened a pioneer missionary work at Udhampur in Jammu-Kashmir among the Himalayas. Today the work has grown into three missionary organizations with a total of about ninety full-time missionaries, forty-two of whom are with the Thomases. He is the founder-president of the Kashmir Evangelical Fellowship, has traveled widely, and is a gifted evangelist. The Thomases have two children, a son, Santhosh, 16, and a daughter, Grace, 14.

PART 3
Unreached
Peoples –
Expanded
Descriptions

The following section contains descriptions of seventy-four Muslim people groups in alphabetical order. Each group has a data table printed above the written description, containing information based on questionnaires completed by persons in the same country or otherwise knowledgeable about the people group. (Please see Appendix B for a sample of this questionnaire.)

In the data table, the most common name of the people group is given first, followed by the name of the country in which the group is located. Stars in front of the name indicate receptivity to the gospel; *** = very receptive, ** = receptive and * = indifferent.

The following is a summary of the remaining data categories:

Alternate names: Any alternate names or spellings for the people group.

EXPANDED DESCRIPTIONS

Size of group: Latest population estimate of the group.

MARC ID: An identification number by which information on that particular group is filed. Any correspondence sent to MARC dealing with a group, sending corrections, updates, additions, or requests for further information should refer to that number.

Distinctives: Distinctives that unify this group. Many different things may make a group distinctive or cause them to consider themselves a people. Often several factors give them some kind of affinity toward one another, or make them different from other groups. Respondents to the Unreached Peoples questionnaire were asked to indicate the relative importance of various factors in making the group distinctive. Those factors were: speaking the same language, common political loyalty, similar occupation, racial or ethnic similarity, shared religious customs, common kinship ties, strong sense of unity, similar education level, common residential area, similar social class or caste, similar economic status, shared hobby or special interest, discrimination from other groups, unique health situation, distinctive legal status, similar age, common significant problems, and "other(s)."

Social change: This represents an estimate of the overall rate that cultural and social change is taking place in the group—very rapid, rapid, moderate, slow, and very slow.

Languages: Primary languages. Multilingual communities often use different languages in different situations. They may learn one language in school, another in the market, and yet another in religious ceremonies. Respondents were asked to indicate the major languages used by the group as well as the place or function of each language. These functions are indicated by the following codes:

V—vernacular or common language

T—trade language or lingua franca

S—language used for instruction in schools

W—the language used for any current or past Christian witness

G—the language most suitable for presentation of the gospel

P—the language used in any non-Christian ceremonies

The percentage listed next to the headings *speak* and *read* indicate respectively the percentage of the total group that speak and read the language listed.

Scripture: Indicates the availability of various forms of biblical literature in the languages of the group.

Christian literacy: This indicates the percentage of Christians among the people (if any) over 15 years of age who can and do read in any language.

EXPANDED DESCRIPTIONS

Religion: This indicates the primary religion(s) found among members of the group. The percentage shown next to adherents estimates the percentage of the group who would say that they follow the religion(s) listed. The percentage next to practicing indicates the number who actively practice the religion(s) listed (in the opinion of the researcher or reporter). The determination of the percentage of those adhering to a certain religion versus the percentage that practice their faith is admittedly a subjective judgment. This figure is important, however, when considering Christian populations, because the definition of "unreached" used here is a group that is less than 20 percent *practicing* Christian. -1 percent means less than one percent practicing, and is used when the Christian population is extremely small and difficult to estimate.

Churches and missions: This indicates the primary Christian churches or missions, national or foreign, that are active in the area where the people group is concentrated. The figure under membership is the approximate number of full members of this church or mission denomination from the people group. The figure under community is the approximate number of adherents (including children) to the denomination or mission from the people group. These are not *all* the churches and missions among this group—only the ones that have been reported.

Openness to religious change: This is an estimate of how open the group is to religious change of any kind. Categories are: very open, somewhat open, indifferent, somewhat closed and very closed.

Receptivity to Christianity: This is an estimate of the openness of the group to Christianity in particular. Categories are: very receptive, receptive, indifferent, reluctant and very reluctant.

Evangelism profile: People tend to come to Christ in more or less well-defined steps. This scale (based on a scale developed by Dr. James Engel of the Wheaton Graduate School) indicates the approximate percentage of the group who are at various levels of awareness of the Gospel. The scale ranges from people with no awareness of Christianity to those who are active propagators of the Gospel. A further explanation of this useful tool may be found in Edward Dayton's article, "To Reach the Unreached" in *Unreached Peoples '79.*

Not Reported (nr): Whenever this appears in any category, it indicates that the information has not yet been received by the MARC computers. In future volumes of this series, information will be added as it becomes available.

Validity Code: An estimate of the accuracy and completeness of the data on a scale from one to nine. The code is:

1. The only information available at this point is the group name, country, language, population and primary religion. The percentage listed under practicing Christians is at best a rough estimate.

2. There has been more data collected than the "baseline" information in 1, but it is scanty and/or of poor quality.

3. About one-half of the information on the unreached peoples questionnaire (Appendix B) has been collected, and information on the Christian community, if any, is missing or probably inaccurate.

4. Almost all the data on the unreached peoples questionnaire has been collected *or* the source document has supplied most of the necessary information.

5. Information has been supplied by a completed unreached peoples questionnaire and at least one other document.

6. In addition to 5, there is enough detailed information about the people

group to write an accurate, up-to-date description.

7. There exists an extensive description of the people group in secular or Christian literature.

8. There has been a major research study (thesis or dissertation quality) done on the group which includes detailed information on the Christian community.

9. In addition to 8, the study includes a thorough exploration of evangelism strategy for the particular group, based on firsthand experience.

Following the data table with the basic information about the people group are several paragraphs further detailing the characteristics of the group. A glossary (Appendix A) explains the meaning of unfamiliar words found in the text.

A complete listing of all unreached people groups currently identified in the MARC files can be found in Part 4. For many of these groups there is more information available. To obtain the data on a particular group, just send in the card located in the back of this book.

INDEX OF PEOPLE GROUPS WITH DESCRIPTIONS

Page Number

Achehnese (Indonesia)	129
Afawa (Nigeria)	130
Afo (Nigeria)	131
Albanian Muslims (Albania)	132
Algerian (Arabs) (Algeria)	133
Azerbaijani Turks (Iran)	134
Babur Thali (Nigeria)	135
Bakhtiaris (Iran)	136
Baluchi (Iran)	137
Bariba (Benin)	138
Bashkir (Soviet Russia)	139
Batak, Angkola (Indonesia)	140
Bengali (Bangladesh)	141
Bosnian (Yugoslavia)	142
Bugis (Indonesia)	143
Busa (Nigeria)	144
Bwa (Upper Volta)	145
Cham (Western) (Kampuchea, Democratic)	146
Diola (Guinea—Bissau)	147
Divehi (Maldives)	148
Dyerma (Niger)	149
Gayo (Indonesia)	150
Gbari (Nigeria)	151
Gurage (Ethiopia)	152
Hui (China)	153
Igbira (Nigeria)	154
Jama Mapun (Philippines)	155
Kaffa (Ethiopia)	156
Kambari (Nigeria)	157

Kamuku (Nigeria) 158
Kanuri (Nigeria) 159
Karakalpak (Soviet Russia) 160
Kazakhs (Iran) 161
Kirgiz (Soviet Russia) 162
Kubu (Indonesia) 163
Kurds in Iran (Iran) 164
Lampung (Indonesia) 165
Lors (Iran) 166
Maguindano (Philippines) 167
Melanau of Sarawak (Malaysia) 168
Meos of Rajasthan (India) 169
Minangkabau (Indonesia) 170
Mossi (Upper Volta) 171
Muslim Malays (Malaysia) 172
North Africans in Belgium (Belgium) 173
Nuristani (Afghanistan) 174
Nyamwezi (Tanzania) 175
Pashtuns (Iran) 176
Persians of Iran (Iran) 177
Punjabis (Pakistan) 178
Qashqa'i (Iran) 179
Redjang (Indonesia) 180
Sama Bangingi (Philippines) 181
Sama Pangutaran (Philippines) 182
Sarakole (Senegal) 183
Sasak (Indonesia) 184
Senufo (Ivory Coast) 185
Shahsavans (Iran) 186
Subanen, Sindangan (Philippines) 187
Sundanese (Indonesia) 188
Tajik (Iran) 189
Tatars (Soviet Russia) 190
Tancouleur (Senegal) 191
Tansug (Philippines) 192

EXPANDED DESCRIPTIONS

Teda (Chad)   193
Temne (Sierra Leone)   194
Thai Islam (Malay) (Thailand)   195
Turkish Workers (Belgium)   196
Turkomans (Iran)   197
Uigur (China)   198
Vai (Liberia)   199
Wolof (Senegal)   200
Yakan (Philippines)   201
Yalunka (Sierra Leone)   202

Achehnese (Indonesia)

ALTERNATE NAMES: Atjehnese; Aceh

SIZE OF GROUP: 2,200,000   MARC ID: 97

DISTINCTIVES: language; ethnicity

SOCIAL CHANGE: not reported

LANGUAGES: Achehnese (100% speak; V); Indonesian (T)

SCRIPTURE: portions

CHRISTIAN LITERACY: not reported

RELIGION: Islam (99% adherents); Christianity (1% adherents/1% practicing)

CHURCHES AND MISSIONS	BEGAN	MEMBERSHIP	COMMUNITY
Gereja Batak Karo Protestant	nr	nr	nr
Gereja Methodist Indonesia	nr	nr	nr
Gereja Keristen Protes. Indon.	nr	nr	nr
Huria Kristen Batak Protes.	nr	nr	nr

OPENNESS TO RELIGIOUS CHANGE: somewhat open

RECEPTIVITY TO CHRISTIANITY: very reluctant

EVANGELISM PROFILE: not reported

VALIDITY: 6

Famous for the strength of their loyalty to Islam, the Aceh or Achehnese occupy the northernmost province of Indonesia. They are the product of centuries of interbreeding of many racial stocks and the interaction of trading and warfare. Highly localized, the Aceh are found in only small numbers outside of Sumatra as students and traders and in a settlement of Kedah in Malaysia.

Most Aceh are agriculturalists, wet-rice farmers in the low lands and dry-rice in the interior highlands. Most of the subsistance work is done by women, with men engaging in various types of cash cropping or trading. Marriage patterns follow Islamic law and couples normally live near the family of the bride. Divorce rates are high (upwards of 50% of all marriages).

They experienced a reformist movement in the 1930s that has produced almost all the present-day leadership in religious and civic life. The modernist movement that developed in the 1960s has brought a split in the society. South Aceh found it less appealing because of a strong brotherhood (Naqshabandiya) that spread in the 1950s and it has become the center of resistance to the modernist impulse as well as a base for a political party (PERTI). The Aceh, together with their fellow Sumatrans, the Minankabau, the Gayo and the Redjang represent a tremendous challenge to Christian evangelization. Only among the Batak and the Serawai have there been significant inroads of Christian faith. Most other churches have been built on immigrant stock from previously Christian groups from Java.

129

EXPANDED DESCRIPTIONS

Afawa (Nigeria)

ALTERNATE NAMES: Paawa

SIZE OF GROUP: 10,000   MARC ID: 559

DISTINCTIVES: language; ethnicity

SOCIAL CHANGE: not reported

LANGUAGES: Afawa (Pa'a) (100% speak; V); Afanci (100% speak;
    V); Hausa (100% speak/1% read; T)

SCRIPTURE: none

CHRISTIAN LITERACY: not reported

RELIGION: Animism (80% adherents); Islam-Animist (19%
    adherents); Protestant (1% adherents/1% practicing)

CHURCHES AND MISSIONS   BEGAN MEMBERSHIP COMMUNITY
    Evangelical Church W. Africa   nr   nr   nr

OPENNESS TO RELIGIOUS CHANGE: not reported

RECEPTIVITY TO CHRISTIANITY: indifferent

EVANGELISM PROFILE: not reported

VALIDITY: 6

The Afawa are a subgroup of the Warjawa. Located about 100 miles
southeast of Kano, they live in the Bauchi State of Nigeria.
They are an example of the partial Islamization of African groups
in Central Nigeria.

An agricultural people somewhat isolated by a lack of real
transportation and communication media, they maintain a strong
traditionalism beneath a gradually growing influence of Islam.
The ancestor cult retains its strength. Outside the compounds of
the families is to be found a clump of logs which represents the
chief ancestral spirit. Blood and beer are periodically poured
over them with the appropriate rites performed. Ancestors are
seen as the powerful force creating and maintaining the good of
life.

While the percentage of those considered Muslim is growing, there
also is a disillusionment present under the surface. Ningi, the
administrative center nearest the Afawa, is a strong center of
Islamic influence, but the Afawa show evidence of acting
independently.

The Sudan Interior Mission began work some 40 years ago and it is
continued today by ECWA. Though there have been many families
who professed faith at one time or another, apparently most of
them have been forced to revert by various means used by the
elders of the tribe. It is currently reported that these elders
are now requesting help from the Christians and show some signs
of an openness to change. But as yet only a few are known to
profess faith and there is only one family present under ECWA
engaging in evangelism. Because of the lack of evangelists or
past effort, it is difficult to say what might happen with a more
concerted, culturally sensitive approach.

Afo (Nigeria)

ALTERNATE NAMES: Eloyi

SIZE OF GROUP: 25,000   MARC ID: 558

DISTINCTIVES: language; ethnicity

SOCIAL CHANGE: not reported

LANGUAGES: Eloyi (100% speak; V); Hausa (75% speak/5% read; T)

SCRIPTURE: none

CHRISTIAN LITERACY: not reported

RELIGION: Animism (94% adherents); Islam-Animist (5% adherents); Protestant (1% adherents/1% practicing)

CHURCHES AND MISSIONS   BEGAN   MEMBERSHIP   COMMUNITY
    Evangelical Church W. Africa   1960   nr   100

OPENNESS TO RELIGIOUS CHANGE: not reported

RECEPTIVITY TO CHRISTIANITY: receptive

EVANGELISM PROFILE: not reported

VALIDITY: 6

Fetishes, sacrifices with beer, rituals held in honor of the powerful ancestors and great feasts honoring Adasaji, the father of the Land, are the dynamic context of religious celebration among the Afo. Clan leaders see that the respect to the gods and ancestors is adequate so that their blessing and favor continues on the crops and animals.

The Afo are divided into two segments: the hill and plain Afo. The plain Afo are much more highly affected by education and young people are migrating to the cities. Two dialects differentiate the Afo: Mbeca and Mbamu. Evangelization has been much stronger among the hill Afo while the plains have been largely neglected.

With the surrounding penetration of Islam, it is little wonder that its influence is present. But the influence is still quite low and the desirability for becoming a Muslim is even lower. Those who are followers of Islam practice their faith in a highly animistic fashion. At present the slow growth of the Christian church as well as the inability of Islam to penetrate more than a small minority is indicative of a strong traditional clan system that is effectively "satisfying" the religious appetites. Economic status is improving and there is little felt need for an alternative.

Christian witness has been present since the 1960s. There are seven ECWA churches in the Odeqi area and a small trickle of yearly baptisms. Leadership of an indigenous origin is undergoing training. Translation work is being done by the Brethern. At present there is significant need for help in the evangelization of the plains Afo in their numerous hamlets and villages. It is estimated that about 25% of the whole tribe has had some type of Christian witness, though many may not have understood its significance.

131

EXPANDED DESCRIPTIONS

Albanian Muslims (Albania)

ALTERNATE NAMES: not reported

SIZE OF GROUP: 1,700,000   MARC ID: 4000

DISTINCTIVES: political loyalty; religion; sense of unity; occupation

SOCIAL CHANGE: rapid

LANGUAGES: Albanian Gheg (V); Albanian Tosk (V, S)

SCRIPTURE: New Testament

CHRISTIAN LITERACY: not reported

RELIGION: Islam (99% adherents)

CHURCHES AND MISSIONS: not reported

OPENNESS TO RELIGIOUS CHANGE: indifferent

RECEPTIVITY TO CHRISTIANITY: indifferent

EVANGELISM PROFILE: not reported

VALIDITY: 6

Albanians became Muslims in the 14th century under the hegemony of the Ottoman Turks. The majority of Albanian Muslims are Sunni or non-practicing descendents of Sunni Muslims. Some 200,000 are estimated to be followers of the Bektashi Sufi brotherhood of Shia Islam. But it cannot be said that religious commitment has ever had the same totalistic meaning it does in other parts of the Islamic world. In the past there was a tolerance of different religious groups and a good deal of intermarriage and common customs between Muslim and Christian Albanians.

Albania is divided by the Shkumbi River. Traditionally the Ghegs lived north of the river and spoke a quite different dialect of Albanian. Tosks lived south in a more productive, less mountainous region. Whereas the difference between the two regions incorporated kinship and social organization (the Ghegs maintained a tribal order based on patrilineal clans into the 20th century, the only remaining tribal organization in Europe), the dramatic reordering of society by the Communists after World War II has induced radical changes for both regions.

Albanian Muslims can also be found in large numbers in Yugoslavia (concentrated in Kosovo) and some in Turkey. Only in these emigrant populations is Islam practiced in an open way. Within Albania itself all formal expression of religion, Christian or Muslim, is strictly forbidden by law and all religious properties have been banished. Foreign visitors are strictly limited. Most Albanians who have emigrated to the USA or Greece are from Christian populations.

Evangelization of Albanian Muslims is at present a very difficult, if not humanly impossible task. It is possible that Yugoslavian Christians might be able to evangelize Albanians in Yugoslavia. Any evangelization within Albania itself would have to be by Albanians and be done extremely quietly.

Algerian (Arabs) (Algeria)

ALTERNATE NAMES: not reported

SIZE OF GROUP: 8,000,000   MARC ID: 179

DISTINCTIVES: religion

SOCIAL CHANGE: not reported

LANGUAGES: Arabic (100% speak; V); French (50% speak; T)

SCRIPTURE: Bible

CHRISTIAN LITERACY: 70%

RELIGION: Islam (95% adherents); Christianity (-1% practicing);
     Unknown (4% adherents)

CHURCHES AND MISSIONS	BEGAN	MEMBERSHIP	COMMUNITY
Reformed Church	nr	nr	nr
Methodist Church	nr	nr	nr
Roman Catholic Church	nr	nr	nr

OPENNESS TO RELIGIOUS CHANGE: somewhat open

RECEPTIVITY TO CHRISTIANITY: very reluctant

EVANGELISM PROFILE: not reported

VALIDITY: 6

The Algerian Arabs are concentrated in the Mediterranean zone of
the Tell Atlas, a 100 mile wide strip that is only 725 miles
long. They are found in all the different professions one comes
to associate with a city such as Algiers (1.6 million people) as
well as in more rural and nomadic occupations. Algeria is a
Muslim state, with the majority of both Arab and Berber adhering
to Sunni Islam.

All contact with the Algerian Arab, both in Algeria and in other
areas where they have migrated (such as France and Belgium), is
mediated by the consciousness of the French colonial occupation
that lasted for over one hundred years, ending only in 1962.
Nationalism has been a potent unifying force in recent years and
Algeria's international charter indicates that it "is Muslim and
will remain as such. Islam is the shield for the preservation of
our national identity and will continue to play that role for the
present and the future."

While missionaries are present, they are very few (about 30). A
recent estimate puts the number of believers in Algeria
(non-expatriates) at 200 with only 60 of them meeting in three
churches. Christian organizations are suspect and conversion to
faith is viewed as a traitorous abandonment of one's heritage,
family and nation. Christian success in evangelization of the
Arabs or the Berber peoples is easily viewed as a form of
neo-colonialism.

Evangelization of necessity will have to be extremely discrete,
oriented to the peculair "folk" Islam of North Africa (with its
focus on saints' tombs, fortune tellers, charms etc.), and
willing to be divorced completely from the political
internationalism of Western governments.

EXPANDED DESCRIPTIONS

Azerbaijani Turks (Iran)

ALTERNATE NAMES: Azeri

SIZE OF GROUP: 6,000,000   MARC ID: 2026

DISTINCTIVES: language; ethnicity; religion; economic status

SOCIAL CHANGE: slow

LANGUAGES: Azerbaijani Turkish (100% speak/2% read; V); Farsi
    (T, S)

SCRIPTURE: Bible

CHRISTIAN LITERACY: not reported

RELIGION: Islam (100% adherents)

CHURCHES AND MISSIONS: not reported

OPENNESS TO RELIGIOUS CHANGE: very closed

RECEPTIVITY TO CHRISTIANITY: very reluctant

EVANGELISM PROFILE: not reported

VALIDITY: 5

The Azerias, or Azerbaijani Turks, are the largest ethnic group
in the northwestern part of Iran. Their people extend over into
Russia (5 million) and Iraq (155,000). The Azeris of Iran are
loyal Shia Muslims and have little interest in either reuniting
with the Russian Azeris or in forming an independent nation. In
fact, the distinctive experiences of the separated peoples is
gradually transforming them into quite different cultural groups.
The Russian Azeris have been changed into a more urbanized,
literate and proletarian nation by the large petroleum industry.

The Azerbaijani of Iran speak seven dialects and their language
is written in Arabic script. A Bible which was produced
originally in 1891 is being revised.

An ancient Persian substratum of religious influence is still
present and visible in rural areas. Holy places are revered and
there are various rites such as the cult of fire which indicate
Zoroastrian influences at work. It is all integrated into a Shia
Islamic identity which supports participation in the current
rennaisance of the Islamic culture in Iran. Unlike their
neighboring Azeris in the USSR, where the anti-religious campaign
has had its effect, the Iranian Azeris continue to exhibit
nominal levels of commitment to the expected Muslim way of life.

The 1979 Islamic revolution in Iran will only have a negative
effect on the opportunity for evangelization. Azeris have not
been noted for welcoming Christian witness and there is still no
evidence that the turmoil of 1979 will change that.

134

Babur Thali (Nigeria)

ALTERNATE NAMES: Bura

SIZE OF GROUP: 75,000   MARC ID: 1057

DISTINCTIVES: language; occupation

SOCIAL CHANGE: rapid

LANGUAGES: Bura (Babur) (100% speak/3% read; V); Hausa (T)

SCRIPTURE: New Testament

CHRISTIAN LITERACY: 1%

RELIGION: Animism (60% adherents); Islam (35% adherents);
    Protestant (5% adherents/3% practicing)

CHURCHES AND MISSIONS   BEGAN MEMBERSHIP   COMMUNITY
    Church of Christ Sudan (EKAS)   nr   nr   nr

OPENNESS TO RELIGIOUS CHANGE: somewhat closed

RECEPTIVITY TO CHRISTIANITY: receptive

EVANGELISM PROFILE: not reported

VALIDITY: 6

Located northwest of Bui, the Babur Thali partially embraced
Islam around the turn of the century. Many who were
agriculturalists, living in somewhat isolated villages, were not
favorable to Islam and retained their traditional ancestor
complex. A related group, the Burra, completely rejected
Islamization and have a strong church in their midst.

The Babur Thali are undergoing a period of significant change at
present. The cash economy which has penetrated their area has
lead to a revolution in expectations. The youth of the villages
are not as concerned with the ancestral rites or with Islam,
though it still remains advantageous for a family head to become
Muslim.

Recent evangelistic efforts such as New Life For All in a number
of the villages has indicated an openness to the gospel. Though
mosques are present, Islamic practice is lax, and the people are
anxious to learn about Christ and to receive compassionate
ministry in the forms of agricultural and medical assistance.
The major reality of their situation is that most have not heard
the gospel and will not hear it in the near future without a
significant increase in personnel actually engaging in
evangelization.

Literacy is low so the revised New Testament in Burra will be of
little use to the majority unless it is packaged into a form that
can be understood by non-literates. Hausa is also widely used
and understood. In the midst of the Babur Thali are remnants of
other tribes such as the Maha, Kimba, Ngulde and Shua who also
need evangelization. Churches have been established in the area
but the presence of Christians is still so small that an
awareness of who Christ is remains too marginal to think that
more than a few know enough to make an intelligible choice for or
against Christ.

EXPANDED DESCRIPTIONS

Bakhtiaris (Iran)

ALTERNATE NAMES: not reported

SIZE OF GROUP: 590,000   MARC ID: 2031

DISTINCTIVES: language; occupation; ethnicity

SOCIAL CHANGE: rapid

LANGUAGES: Bakhtiaris (100% speak; V); Farsi (T)

SCRIPTURE: portions

CHRISTIAN LITERACY: not reported

RELIGION: Islam (100% adherents)

CHURCHES AND MISSIONS: not reported

OPENNESS TO RELIGIOUS CHANGE: not reported

RECEPTIVITY TO CHRISTIANITY: not reported

EVANGELISM PROFILE: not reported

VALIDITY: 5

Famous the world over for their yearly 200-300 mile-long migrations, the Bakhtiaris are experiencing major changes in their life-style. Inhabiting an enormous part of the Zagros Mountains in Western Iran near Kuwait, they must move their sheep and goats from the low foothill winter pastures to the high, intermontane valleys of the summer pasture. Transhumance of this sort takes a heavy toll on both animal and human as icey, rushing streams have to be forded and passes as high as 11,000 feet (3,400 meters) have to be crossed.

The government has been forcing change on them during the span of the 20th century. The earliest was the successful reduction of their political power by eliminating the old system of khans, military and administrative leaders who traditionally used force against sedentary farmers and one another to settle greivances and gain advantages. In recent years the Iranian government has been encouraging national integration by giving little or no support to the nomadism of the Bakhtiaris. Instead of seeking to increase the herds and improve their stock as a part of the national economy, the government has been seeking to establish them in a sedentary life style. Success has attended this policy in that the percentage of the tribe involved in transhumance decreases year by year.

The basic unit of the tribe is the family. In nomadic conditions a patrilineally related unit of 15 tents forms the camps that live and migrate together. The Bakhtiaris are divided into many sub-tribes and alliances, and the most important unit is the taifeh, a segment of the sub-tribe. All camps belong to one taifeh or another and pasturage is "owned" by this larger unit. Taifeh heads mediate and fight disputes. Most marriage is endogamous to this unit. More and more are becoming not only farmers but laborers in the cities and adapting to new conditions. Christian evangelization at present has little impact on this changing people.

Baluchi (Iran)

ALTERNATE NAMES: not reported

SIZE OF GROUP: 1,100,000   MARC ID: 2030

DISTINCTIVES: language; ethnicity; religion

SOCIAL CHANGE: slow

LANGUAGES: Baluchi (100% speak; V); Farsi (T, S)

SCRIPTURE: portions

CHRISTIAN LITERACY: not reported

RELIGION: Islam (100% adherents)

CHURCHES AND MISSIONS: not reported

OPENNESS TO RELIGIOUS CHANGE: very closed

RECEPTIVITY TO CHRISTIANITY: very reluctant

EVANGELISM PROFILE: not reported

VALIDITY: 6

Inhospitable, dry--similar adjectives would characterize the homeland of the Baluchi. Occupying a large plain and mountain area, found in Pakistan in large numbers as well as a hundred thousand or so in Afghanistan, they herd their sheep and goats, till a few oases and drainage basins and restively await the changes that modern times are beginning to etch into their character.

So large a group is bound to be diverse, with variations in social and political organization. Some subgroups act like tribal societies, such as the Yarahmadzai. Ordered by a patrilineal charter in which all in the tribe trace descent from a former ancestor and governed by hereditary chiefs, they wander the plateau with their herds in search of the best pasturage. In other parts of the Baluchi, organization is more ordered by a semi-caste system in which there is a heirarchical series of endogamous social strata who relate to one another as patron-clients. In this case only the middle-caste, such as the hakomzat in Iran and the hakim in Pakistan are self-consciously identified as Baluchi. The lower castes are considered separate peoples (such as the tinkers or Loris).

They are a minority sect in Iran, adhering to Sunni Islam (in contrast to the dominant Shiite sect of Iran). Seclusion of women is practiced by the wealthier Baluchi and even among the nomadic a woman will pull a veil across her face if she is approached by a stranger.

The Baluchi speak a variety of highly localized dialects, classified as Western Baluchi in Iran. The New Testament was translated into Baluchi in 1900 and is probably in serious need of revision if it is to be understood by the modern Baluchi. Available information indicates very little evangelization is taking place, even amoung the half who are sedentary.

EXPANDED DESCRIPTIONS

Bariba (Benin)

ALTERNATE NAMES: Bargu; Baatombu

SIZE OF GROUP: 400,000   MARC ID: 246

DISTINCTIVES: language; ethnicity

SOCIAL CHANGE: not reported

LANGUAGES: Bariba (100% speak/5% read; V); Dendi

SCRIPTURE: New Testament

CHRISTIAN LITERACY: 25%

RELIGION: Animism (69% adherents); Islam-Animist (25% adherents); Roman Catholic (5% adherents/3% practicing); Protestant (1% adherents/1% practicing)

CHURCHES AND MISSIONS	BEGAN	MEMBERSHIP	COMMUNITY
Evangelical Church W. Africa	1946	nr	1,200
Assemblies of God	nr	nr	nr
Methodist Church	nr	nr	nr
Southern Baptist Convention	nr	nr	nr
Roman Catholic Church	nr	nr	12,000

OPENNESS TO RELIGIOUS CHANGE: somewhat open

RECEPTIVITY TO CHRISTIANITY: indifferent

EVANGELISM PROFILE: not reported

VALIDITY: 6

The Fulani jihad of the early nineteenth century was a significant factor in many of the peoples of West Africa being penetrated by Islam. The Bariba or Baatombu (as they designate themselves) were one of the groups who successfully defended themselves against this jihad. For generations the Fulani have served the Bariba, caring for their cattle in exchange for grazing rights on Bariba land. Now that they are settling in villages attached to the Bariba village, the relationship is changing, but the two groups still maintain separate identities.

The Bariba are predominantly agriculturalists, and increasingly their economy is being transformed by cash crops. All the families are normally patrilineally related and the oldest man of the families acts as the local chieftan. The ancestor cult is widespread and libations are regularly offered to ensure health and prosperity.

Muslim conversions began only in the colonial era. Almost all who adopt Islam do so only as an addition to the ancestor cult and continue to consult local healers. Very few make the hajj or accept the Quranic teachings in purified form.

The Church is present and translation work is progressing. One major problem at present is the relative lack of coverage in many of the villages and compounds of the Bariba. There is also need for evangelization among the intermixed Fulani. A dynamic growth potential is indicated as the Bariba loosen ties with their traditionally isolated village life.

Bashkir (Soviet Russia)

ALTERNATE NAMES: Bashgurd

SIZE OF GROUP: 1,200,000   MARC ID: 4001

DISTINCTIVES: occupation; ethnicity; residence

SOCIAL CHANGE: moderate

LANGUAGES: Bashkir (60% speak; V, S); Tatar (40% speak; V)

SCRIPTURE: portions

CHRISTIAN LITERACY: not reported

RELIGION: Islam (99% adherents)

CHURCHES AND MISSIONS: not reported

OPENNESS TO RELIGIOUS CHANGE: not reported

RECEPTIVITY TO CHRISTIANITY: not reported

EVANGELISM PROFILE: not reported

VALIDITY: 5

A culture centered on horses and the drinking of fermented mare's
milk (kumyss) is common to a number of Mongol peoples of the
steppes and hills of Central Asia. One of them, the Bashkir, are
located between the Volga River and the Ural Mountains and
beyond. They are very close to the Tatar and nearly 40% will
list Tatar as their primary language.

They are concentrated in the Bashkir Autonomous Republic. The
vast majority are engaged in farming and animal husbandry on 640
collectives and 150 state farms. Only 20% in this homeland live
in the cities where they are seriously outnumbered by the
Russians and the Tatars. They are a minority in their own
republic, mainly because of the vast reserves of oil which have
drawn large numbers of outsiders to work in the oil fields,
petrochemical factories, and to build and run the cities that
have sprung up. Outside their home territory (in Kemerovo
Oblast, Kazakhstan, Uzbekistan and the Ukraine) the Bashkir are
city dwellers and part of the urban proletariat.

Their religious preference is Sunni Islam of the Hanafi school.
Yet many of the younger generation are "forgetting the prayers"
and, at least officially, the only true believers are those of
the older generation. This portrait probably reflects a growing
secularization as the younger generation takes on a more modern,
city-like culture. Fridays are workdays. The women were not
vieled even before Communist rule so that changes for Bashkir
women have not been dramatic. Ufa, the capital of BAR , is one
of the three Sunni Synods in the USSR.

Little is indicated in our sources as to traditional or
contemporary evangelism focused on the Bashkir. Portions of the
Bible were translated in 1902 and there is a definite translation
need. We do not know whether Russian evangelicals are present or
attempting evangelism among this people or whether there are
Bashkir Christians in the USSR.

EXPANDED DESCRIPTIONS

Batak, Angkola (Indonesia)

ALTERNATE NAMES: not reported

SIZE OF GROUP: not reported   MARC ID: 4002

DISTINCTIVES: language; occupation; religion; residence

SOCIAL CHANGE: slow

LANGUAGES: Batak, Angkola (V)

SCRIPTURE: not reported

CHRISTIAN LITERACY: not reported

RELIGION: Protestant (10% adherents/6% practicing); Islam (90%
    adherents)

CHURCHES AND MISSIONS	BEGAN	MEMBERSHIP	COMMUNITY
Batak Nias Zending	nr	nr	nr
Huria Kristen Batak Protestant	nr	nr	nr
Rhenis Missin Society	nr	nr	nr

OPENNESS TO RELIGIOUS CHANGE: somewhat closed

RECEPTIVITY TO CHRISTIANITY: indifferent

EVANGELISM PROFILE: not reported

VALIDITY: 6

The Batak tribes of northern Sumatra stand out as the major place
where large numbers have become Christian, principally among the
dominant Toba (1.6 million) and the Silindung. The Angkola are
one of approximately seven tribal dialect units who see
themselves as a distinctive sub-ethnic people among the Batak.
While sharing a similar kinship system (patrilineal clans and
marriage exchange alliances), similar political organization
(small, kinship organized villages), and ceremonies to mark life
crises, they share a "notorious" characteristic of suspicion of
others outside one's locale which has encouraged divergence
rather than homogenization among the Batak.

They were forcibly converted by Sunni Muslims of the Shafi school
in the early 19th century. Located in the southern area of Batak
residency, they feel themselves most closely allied with the
uniformly Muslim Mandailing, a Batak group converted at the same
time as the Angkola.

Reputedly the relationships between the Muslim majority and the
Christian minority is quite harmonious. New Protestant pastors
to a village will be greeted by the local hajj. Muslims allow
Christians to say grace in their ceremonies and bring them gifts
of cakes on Id al Fitr. Christians do not raise pigs and send
gifts to their Muslim neighbors on New Year's Day. Intermarriage
is frowned on but allowed when one partner or the other converts.
Apparently kinship and common village loyalty overrides any
tendencies toward interreligious conflicts of a serious nature.

The New Testament is rather old, being produced in 1902.
Evangelism is apparently taking place but Muslims and Christians
have adjusted to a status quo situation. More details are needed
to fill out the specifics of what is needed at this point for
evangelization to take strides forward.

Bengali (Bangladesh)

ALTERNATE NAMES: not reported

SIZE OF GROUP: 80,000,000   MARC ID: 4003

DISTINCTIVES: language; political loyalty; ethnicity

SOCIAL CHANGE: slow

LANGUAGES: Bengali (100% speak; V, T, S, G)

SCRIPTURE: Bible

CHRISTIAN LITERACY: not reported

RELIGION: Christianity (-1% practicing); Islam (87% adherents);
    Hinduism (12% adherents)

CHURCHES AND MISSIONS	BEGAN	MEMBERSHIP	COMMUNITY
Asoc. Bap. World Evangelism	nr	nr	nr
Southern Baptists	nr	nr	nr
Intl. Christian Fellowship	nr	nr	75
Assemblies of God	nr	nr	nr
Roman Catholic Church	nr	nr	nr

OPENNESS TO RELIGIOUS CHANGE: not reported

RECEPTIVITY TO CHRISTIANITY: not reported

EVANGELISM PROFILE: not reported

VALIDITY: 6

After the Arab peoples, the 83 million Muslim Bengali are the
largest single ethnic group of Islam. Part of a larger Bengali
group made up of an additional 40 million Hindus, the Muslim
Bengali is split into the nation of Bangladesh and the Indian
state of West Bengal (which includes Calcutta).

The Bengali are overwhelmingly peasant rice cultivators in
Bangladesh. Settled villages are the basis of organized
religious and political life, given expression in the samaj, a
localized association governed loosley by a sort of counsel of
elders. Local households are patrilineally based and may be
either nuclear or extended. Polygamy is found in only about 5%
of all Muslim marriages.

The Bengalis became Muslims in large numbers only after the 6th
century. They are largely Sunni of the Hanafi school, but there
are those who follow the Shafi, Hanbali and even a distinctive
Bengali Ahle Hadith school of interpretation. Saint (pirs)
worship is widespread and an animistic base expresses itself in
various "syncretistic" practices and beliefs such as in jinns.
The five pillars of the faith are regularly followed.

Evangelization of the Muslim Bengali has been taking place for
many generations with very little success compared with the
evangelization of either the Buddhist tribes along the border
with Burma or the Hindu Bengali. The small Christian Church that
is present is not adapted to accept Muslim converts without
requiring of them a radical break with their family and culture.
Only recently a new experiment with a more formally Muslim
approach, has seen an amazing development of two Muslim convert
fellowships and the hope for a new approach that might succeed.

EXPANDED DESCRIPTIONS

Bosnian (Yugoslavia)

ALTERNATE NAMES: Serbo-Croation Muslim

SIZE OF GROUP: 1,740,000   MARC ID: 4004

DISTINCTIVES: language; religion; sense of unity

SOCIAL CHANGE: moderate

LANGUAGES: Serbo-Croation (100% speak; V, T, S, G)

SCRIPTURE: Bible

CHRISTIAN LITERACY: not reported

RELIGION: Christianity (-1% practicing); Islam (99% adherents)

CHURCHES AND MISSIONS	BEGAN	MEMBERSHIP	COMMUNITY
Greek Orthodox	nr	nr	nr
Roman Catholic	nr	nr	nr

OPENNESS TO RELIGIOUS CHANGE: somewhat closed

RECEPTIVITY TO CHRISTIANITY: indifferent

EVANGELISM PROFILE: not reported

VALIDITY: 6

The Bosnians refer to themselves simply as Muslimani (Muslims).
But they are only the largest of a number of Muslim groups in
Yugoslavia, including the Albanians in Kosovo, the Gypsies, and
minorities such as the few Rumeli Turks. The Bosnians are
concentrated in Bosnia-Hercegovina and are more highly
represented in towns and cities than their proportion of the
population (about 40% of that socialist republic).

They became Muslims in large numbers while the area was part of
the Ottoman Empire. They originated out of a three class system
in which the landlords were Muslims, most serfs were Christian
Serbs and Croats, and the free peasantry (given freedom from
serfdom for conversion) were Muslims. At present the Bosnians
tend to live separately from the Roman Catholic Croats and the
Greek Orthodox Serbs, all of whom speak Serbo-Croation. In the
towns and cities, which are still dominated by the Bosnians, they
live in separate wards or neighborhoods.

In the rural areas there is little difference between the
Bosnians and their Christian neighbors -- all engaging in grain
agriculture and livestock herding. Urban Bosnians are
predominant in the artisan occupations and the old landed Muslim
aristocracy has transformed itself into a professional and
bureaucratic elite by its disproportionate access to education.
Islamic institutions show much influence from Turkish models.
Islamic education is permitted but it is in addition to
compulsory secular education.

The Bosnians tend to marry within their own group, though some
intermarriage is occuring in urban areas. Relationships between
the Christians and Muslim community appears to be stable, with
little evangelization taking place at present. Much more must be
known to assess the present status of evangelization.

Bugis (Indonesia)

ALTERNATE NAMES: To Ugi

SIZE OF GROUP: 3,500,000   MARC ID: 7

DISTINCTIVES: language; ethnicity

SOCIAL CHANGE: not reported

LANGUAGES: Bugis (100% speak; V); Indonesian (91% speak; T); Makassarese (60% speak)

SCRIPTURE: portions

CHRISTIAN LITERACY: not reported

RELIGION: Christianity (1% adherents/1% practicing); Islam (45% adherents); Islam-Animist (50% adherents); Unknown (3% adherents); Hindu-Animist (1% adherents)

CHURCHES AND MISSIONS	BEGAN	MEMBERSHIP	COMMUNITY
Roman Catholic Church	nr	nr	nr
Christ. Ch. S. Sulawesi	1933	nr	nr

OPENNESS TO RELIGIOUS CHANGE: not reported

RECEPTIVITY TO CHRISTIANITY: very reluctant

EVANGELISM PROFILE: not reported

VALIDITY: 6

On that broken, pin-wheel shaped island of Sulawesi, the Bugis inhabit the southwest peninsula. Normally classified with their culturally similar neighbors, the Macassarese, they speak their own language and see themselves as a distinct and superior people. The Bugis have been Islamic since the early seventeenth century, and three centuries have been sufficient to forge a strong and militant Sunni Muslim identity. Next to the Aceh, the Bugis and Macassarese are some of the most rigid of Indonesia's Muslims. Ten years were required after independence to restore order in their area, infested as it was by Muslim guerrilla movements advocating an Islamic religious state.

The largest concentrations of Bugis are to be found in the city of Bone and the port of Ujung Pandang. While they have been migrating for centuries as part of their maritime trading and piracy, their homeland is the central highland between the Macassarese on the south and the Christian Toradja on the north. Most are traditional peasants, another of those great peoples nourished by irrigated rice. Hamlets and villages, held together by strong kinship ties, are the focus of community life. Society is highly stratified with prestige and status as paramount concerns.

Civil order and administration is an extension of the old royal families who have been made a part of the civil bureaucracy. Each principality in the region also has its kadhi, a religious official who looks after Islamic law, and a female specialist, a pinati, who manages the remaining pre-Islamic rites and customs.

EXPANDED DESCRIPTIONS

Busa (Nigeria)

ALTERNATE NAMES: not reported

SIZE OF GROUP: 50,000   MARC ID: 1055

DISTINCTIVES: language; ethnicity

SOCIAL CHANGE: very slow

LANGUAGES: Busa (Bokobarn Akiba) (100% speak/2% read; V);
    Hausa (40% speak; T)

SCRIPTURE: portions

CHRISTIAN LITERACY: 1%

RELIGION: Animism (49% adherents); Islam (50% adherents);
    Christianity (1% adherents/1% practicing)

CHURCHES AND MISSIONS   BEGAN   MEMBERSHIP   COMMUNITY
    Methodist Church   1963   nr   544

OPENNESS TO RELIGIOUS CHANGE: somewhat open

RECEPTIVITY TO CHRISTIANITY: reluctant

EVANGELISM PROFILE: not reported

VALIDITY: 6

The Busa are to be found in Kwara State, about 100 miles
northwest of Ilorin. They stretch over into Benin where the
Sudan Interior Mission is at work with them. Some estimates
place the total population at 100,000.

Islamic penetration into this people began long ago but it was
only as recently as 1959 that large numbers of them declared
their allegiance to Allah. They follow many of the same ritual
complexes as their neighbors who participate in fertility
festivals of various types.

Busa live in small isolated villages and are agriculturalists The
main crops are yams and corn, but peanuts and cotton are raised
for cash. At present the Busa appear to be resisting changes in
their life-style and show no major discontent.

The Methodists began evangelization in their region as early as
1939. At present their some 500 plus church members include only
200 of Busa background. There appears to be some inhibiting
inter-ethnic dynamics in that the Yorubas are identified as
"Christians" by the Busa and are poorly thought of. To be a
Yoruba is to be a cheat and a dishonest person, a hard slander
for the Christian to live down.

It appears that the best approach at present is one that combines
health, agricultural extension and the presentation of the
gospel. Where African Christians with a community approach (such
as those from the Faith and Farm movement) can be utilized for
evangelization, the response seems to be far more positive than
has been experienced by other approaches. Translation into the
vernacular is continuing, but it will be some time before the
entire New Testament is ready.

Bwa (Upper Volta)

ALTERNATE NAMES: Bobo Oule; Bobo Rouge

SIZE OF GROUP: 140,000   MARC ID: 468

DISTINCTIVES: language; ethnicity

SOCIAL CHANGE: not reported

LANGUAGES: Buamu (Bobo Wule) (100% speak/10% read; V); Bambara (40% speak; T); French (10% speak)

SCRIPTURE: portions

CHRISTIAN LITERACY: 13%

RELIGION: Animism (85% adherents); Islam (1% adherents); Protestant (6% adherents/4% practicing); Roman Catholic (8% adherents/5% practicing)

CHURCHES AND MISSIONS	BEGAN	MEMBERSHIP	COMMUNITY
Eglise Chretienne Evangelique	1962	1,820	8,902
Christian & Msny. Alliance	nr	nr	nr
Roman Catholic Church	nr	nr	nr

OPENNESS TO RELIGIOUS CHANGE: somewhat open

RECEPTIVITY TO CHRISTIANITY: reluctant

EVANGELISM PROFILE: not reported

VALIDITY: 6

The Bwa or Red Bobo as they are called by the Bambara are a group only marginally touched by Islam. In general, the Bwa are not favorable toward Islam. They dislike the Muslim Jula merchants and Foula cattle herders who are to be found in their midst. They hate the Mossis who are seen as Muslim oppressors, seizing much of the traditional territory claimed by the Bwa.

The result of this inter-tribal tension has meant a great deal of openness to Christian faith. They are in the process of discarding their animism, and at present, give every evidence of embracing Christian faith in its stead. Among the Christian and Missionary Alliance, church growth has been at a rate of about 10% a year from 1968-1977.

The "Eglise Evangelique de l'Alliance" and the CMA have joined hands to greatly increase the rate of growth in the light of the great openness at present. Evangelism and follow-up are being given great emphasis in joint goals. The most serious problem at present appears to be following up converts. Numerous villages are being reached and are responding favorably.

There are four areas of the tribe which at present are unreached and it will take a significant increase in Bwa evangelists and leaders as well as missionary personnel to capitalize on the opportunity. Little information is given in our sources about social and cultural dimensions that might affect evangelization. Also we are not told growth rates or future plans for the Roman Catholic community.

EXPANDED DESCRIPTIONS

Cham (Western) (Kampuchea, Democratic)

ALTERNATE NAMES: Cambodian Cham; Khmer Islam

SIZE OF GROUP: 90,000   MARC ID: 91

DISTINCTIVES: language; ethnicity

SOCIAL CHANGE: not reported

LANGUAGES: Cham (100% speak; V); Khmer (75% speak/35% read;
    T); Vietnamese (10% speak)

SCRIPTURE: not reported

CHRISTIAN LITERACY: not reported

RELIGION: Islam (50% adherents); Islam-Animist (40% adherents);
    Animism (10% adherents)

CHURCHES AND MISSIONS   BEGAN MEMBERSHIP COMMUNITY
    Khmer Evangelical Church   1924   nr   nr
    Roman Catholic Church   1800   nr   nr

OPENNESS TO RELIGIOUS CHANGE: somewhat closed

RECEPTIVITY TO CHRISTIANITY: indifferent

EVANGELISM PROFILE: not reported

VALIDITY: 6

Most Cham, prior to the revolutionary People's Republic of
Kampuchea, were to be found around Tonle Sap in Cambodia and
along the south-central coastal plain of Viet Nam. They are
descendants of the once powerful ancient kingdom of Champa. When
that Kingdom was destroyed in 1471 by the southward migrations of
the Vietnamese, many fled to Cambodia where they were well
received by the Khmer King.

The Western Cham have adopted many of the customs of the
surrounding Khmer peoples. Thus they are similar in many ways to
a poor Cambodian peasant. Traditionally they were engaged in
market gardening agriculture, and a significant number of them
have also been fishermen and traders. How their traditional life
has been affected by the war, revolution and now
counter-revolution remains to be seen.

The Western Cham are Sunni Muslims of the Shafi school. Whereas
the Cham of Viet Nam have been gradually losing their Islamic
characteristics (indeed some are Hindu-animists in the south),
the larger and more concentrated population pocket in Cambodia
has been able to retain its Islamic identity. This has not been
considered incompatible with a social organization based on
strong matrilineal clans. There also have been accommodations to
the traditional ancestral cult, so that much of the practice of
Islam is cradled in an animistic network of concepts and rituals.

It is difficult to assess the present situation in terms of
evangelization. While some work has been done on a translation
of the Bible, such work has been suspended. There are no known
evangelists currently working for the evangelization of this
people.

146

Diola (Guinea—Bissau)

ALTERNATE NAMES: Yola

SIZE OF GROUP: 15,000   MARC ID: 590

DISTINCTIVES: language; ethnicity

SOCIAL CHANGE: not reported

LANGUAGES: Diola (V)

SCRIPTURE: portions

CHRISTIAN LITERACY: not reported

RELIGION: Islam (60% adherents); Animism (35% adherents);
    Roman Catholic (5% adherents/3% practicing)

CHURCHES AND MISSIONS	BEGAN	MEMBERSHIP	COMMUNITY
Roman Catholic Church	nr	nr	nr
Worldwide Evangelization Crus.	nr	nr	nr

OPENNESS TO RELIGIOUS CHANGE: not reported

RECEPTIVITY TO CHRISTIANITY: not reported

EVANGELISM PROFILE: not reported

VALIDITY: 5

The Diola are not a uniform people. Estimates run from
216,000-500,000 total population, centered mainly in Senegal, but
also found in Guinea-Bissau and Gambia. The homeland is the
lower Casamance river area. South of it the Diola remained
somewhat isolated and consequently retained a stronger
traditional way of life including religion. North of the river
in Fogny, Combo and Boulouf, most have become Muslims.

The Diola of Guinea-Bissau are a small offshoot of this larger
ethnic group. They are to be found in villages revolving about
agriculture. Traditionally the Diola were well known for wet
rice agriculture in reclaimed wetlands about the Casamance river.
Now they have also turned to such cash crops as peanuts.

Traditional religion is animistic with a belief in the spiritual
powers of beings that must be placated with libations of palm
wine and blood sacrifice. Fertility, success in war and the
securing of health are all things these forces enable. Even at
present, many of the Islamic Diola retain the habit of consulting
these forces in times of stress. Furthermore the traditional
villagewide initiation ceremony (bukut) continues though
Islamization is gradually displacing the traditionalist elements.

Purification movements are present in the form of the
brotherhoods (most associate with the Qadiriya while the purists
are most strongly found among the Tijaniya brotherhood).
Marabouts are not as influential among the Diola as they are
among other Muslim populations of West Africa.

Translation of the Bible is taking place and there is a Christian
presence. It is reported that the large Catholic community has
not divested itself of traditionalism so that a rather syncretic
situation is to be found.

EXPANDED DESCRIPTIONS

Divehi (Maldives)

ALTERNATE NAMES: Maldivians

SIZE OF GROUP: 120,000   MARC ID: 4005

DISTINCTIVES: language; occupation; religion; residence

SOCIAL CHANGE: very slow

LANGUAGES: Divehi (V, S, G); Arabic (P)

SCRIPTURE: not reported

CHRISTIAN LITERACY: not reported

RELIGION: Islam (100% adherents)

CHURCHES AND MISSIONS: not reported

OPENNESS TO RELIGIOUS CHANGE: very closed

RECEPTIVITY TO CHRISTIANITY: very reluctant

EVANGELISM PROFILE: not reported

VALIDITY: 6

The Maldives are about 2,000 small coral islands that form a chain 764 by 129 kilometers (475 by 80 miles) in the Indian Ocean. Its northernmost tip is 595 kilometers (370 miles) south of India. Only 200 or so of the islands are inhabited. These descendents of Sinhalese from Sri Lanka call themselves Divehi.

Though they were under British protectorate for nearly 80 years (until 1965), colonialism left virtually no mark. The chief occupation is fishing with a little agriculture to supplement the diet. The tourist business and shipping industry are developing but as yet are too small to employ more than a tiny part of the populace.

Islam is strongly entrenched and has been present for over 800 years. The government is officially Islamic and the law of the land is the Sharia, interpreted by religious judges (qadis) according to the Shafi school of interpretation. All are required to observe the Ramadan, the Id festivals, give to charity, and the times of prayer. Divorce is reputedly the highest for any country in the world (85% of all marriages) and there is apparently a casualness about arranging and terminating marriages.

An animistic base evidences itself in the pervasive fear of jinns. Fandita (religious practitioners offering magical help of various kinds) are to be found in all the islands. They sell mantras, charms rituals for illness in order to help the average Divehi cope with the problems of everyday life and love.

As far as is known there are no Christian Divehi in the Maldives. The only other place they can be found is on Minicoy which is officially claimed by India. It may be possible for evangelization to take place there. More information is needed. Our sources do not indicate any Christian witness among the Divehi anywhere.

Dyerma (Niger)

ALTERNATE NAMES: Dyerma; Zaberma

SIZE OF GROUP: 1,000,000   MARC ID: 4014

DISTINCTIVES: language; occupation; kinship

SOCIAL CHANGE: slow

LANGUAGES: Dyerma (100% speak; V)

SCRIPTURE: New Testament

CHRISTIAN LITERACY: not reported

RELIGION: Christianity (1% adherents/1% practicing);
    Islam-Animist (99% adherents)

CHURCHES AND MISSIONS	BEGAN	MEMBERSHIP	COMMUNITY
Evangelical Baptist Mission	nr	nr	nr
Sudan Interior Mission	nr	nr	nr
Roman Catholic	nr	nr	nr

OPENNESS TO RELIGIOUS CHANGE: not reported

RECEPTIVITY TO CHRISTIANITY: not reported

EVANGELISM PROFILE: not reported

VALIDITY: 6

The Songhay peoples have a memory of an illustrious kingdom that
once held sway over a vast area of the central Sahel region,
focused on the Niger river. After the Songhay Kingdom fell, its
various peoples went their separate ways. Today the strongest
subgroup among the heirs of this tradition are the Zerma. They
are located in the western provinces of Niger, on both sides of
the river and in a "wadi" region near Dosso.

They are agriculturalists for the most part, living in over 2,000
villages with less than 800 population and an additional 100
towns with an average of 3,000 population. The village is
organized on the basis that all men can trace their genealogy
back to a common male ancestor. Sublineages divide the village,
each headed by the eldest male in the line. Polygamy is
practiced (about 25% of the families) and women leave their home
village to live in the village of their husband.

Islam has been an offical part of religious life for over 500
years but it is part and parcel of a nature cult. The Muslim
calendar is followed and the Shariah as interpreted by the Maliki
school of Sunni Islam is in force. But it is complemented by a
host of magicians, griots, therapists, and involvements with the
nature spirits of the soil and river. Only the more
sophisticated urban Zerma of the highest status could be said to
practice a purified Islamic style of life.

Churches are present and a small number of the Zerma are being
evangelized. The New Testament has been available since 1954 and
is currently being revised by a native speaker. In the face of
the large number of villages yet to be evangelized and the highly
animistic nature of Islamic practice, we can say a great
opportunity for evangelization exists here.

EXPANDED DESCRIPTIONS

Gayo (Indonesia)

ALTERNATE NAMES: not reported

SIZE OF GROUP: 200,000   MARC ID: 1132

DISTINCTIVES: not reported

SOCIAL CHANGE: not reported

LANGUAGES: Gayo (100% speak); Indonesian

SCRIPTURE: none

CHRISTIAN LITERACY: not reported

RELIGION: Islam-Animist (100% adherents)

CHURCHES AND MISSIONS: not reported

OPENNESS TO RELIGIOUS CHANGE: not reported

RECEPTIVITY TO CHRISTIANITY: not reported

EVANGELISM PROFILE: not reported

VALIDITY: 4

Sumatra represents one of the greatest challenges to
evangelization in the modern era. Because of the strength of
Islam and the basic isolation of the island from extensive
evangelization efforts, there is probably a larger gap to
overcome in Sumatra than in other islands of Indonesia.

The Gayo live in the highlands of the north. Achehnese surround
them on the north, east and west. To the south are the Batak
highlanders, the one bright spot of evangelization in Sumatra.
There nearly 2 million Bataks have become Christians in a large
Christward movement particularly among the Toba.

The Gayo are similar culturally to the Batak. They live in large
multi-family houses of up to 60 persons. Patrilineal kinsmen are
bound together in groups that act as political and economic
units. Irrigated rice and slash and burn fields serve as the
basis for livelihood. More specific details of the social
organization are not available due to their isolation and general
lack of study by any trained observers.

The Gayo are considered Muslim as a result of the conversions
that took place in the seventeenth century when they were
subjugated by the Achehnese. But what little is known of their
contemporary religious piety indicates an amalgam of traditional
animism as the inner core of a dynamic religious life for which
Islam is the outer shell.

We need further information on the current efforts directed
toward the Gayo. It is not clear whether there are expatriates
present or whether the Batak Churches to the south would find a
reception if they were to send forth personnel to share the good
news.

Gbari (Nigeria)

ALTERNATE NAMES: Goale; Gwali

SIZE OF GROUP: 500,000   MARC ID: 158

DISTINCTIVES: language; ethnicity

SOCIAL CHANGE: not reported

LANGUAGES: Gbari (100% speak; V); Hausa

SCRIPTURE: New Testament

CHRISTIAN LITERACY: not reported

RELIGION: Animism (69% adherents); Islam (20% adherents);
    Christianity (3% adherents/2% practicing); Unknown (8%
    adherents)

CHURCHES AND MISSIONS	BEGAN	MEMBERSHIP	COMMUNITY
Church Missionary Society	nr	nr	nr
Sudan Interior Mission	nr	nr	nr
Evangelical Church W. Africa	nr	nr	10,000

OPENNESS TO RELIGIOUS CHANGE: not reported

RECEPTIVITY TO CHRISTIANITY: not reported

EVANGELISM PROFILE: not reported

VALIDITY: 6

The gospel has been present in parts of this tribe since 1910.
Only in the eastern half of the tribe, the Gbari Matai, have
there been any significant inroads. There the ECWA have 100
churches with about 10,000 in attendance. In the western half,
the Gbari Yamma, very few have become Christians and there are
regions where almost no evangelism has taken place at any time.

The Gbari are located north of Minna in the state of Niger. An
approach that deals with their total life, enabling them to
improve crop yeilds and income as well as express Christian love,
would be ideal.

The area is heavily influenced by Islam and Hausa is a prestige
language. While only 20% are Muslims, the percentage is slowly
growing. The animist sector is focused on the worship of a local
diety, Maigiro, who is thought to be important in fertility,
health and witchcraft. The cult of Maigiro is a male cult. Each
person also has a personal spirit who is placated at a private
tree. The ancestors, especially one's grandfather, are part of
this complex.

Three problems face the Church. Among the Gbari Yamma, some of
the early Christian leaders turned to Islam and their memory has
kept others from considering Christian faith. Also, a number of
the churches in their area are predominantly made up of
"strangers", Africans from other tribes. Inviting them to
worship with strangers has not proved a successful strategy. It
is possible that the Gbari Matai Churches, with the large number
of Christians, are the logical ones to send evangelists to their
fellow tribesmen, even though dialect differences would have to
be overcome. There are a number of regions, particularly
inaccessible that remain unevangelized.

EXPANDED DESCRIPTIONS

Gurage (Ethiopia)

ALTERNATE NAMES: not reported

SIZE OF GROUP: 750,000   MARC ID: 274

DISTINCTIVES: language; ethnicity

SOCIAL CHANGE: not reported

LANGUAGES: Gurage Dialects (100% speak; V); Amharic (75% speak/5% read; T)

SCRIPTURE: New Testament

CHRISTIAN LITERACY: 15%

RELIGION: Islam-Animist (60% adherents); Christo-Paganism (23% adherents); Animism (14% adherents); Christianity (1% adherents/1% practicing); Orthodox (2% adherents/2% practicing)

CHURCHES AND MISSIONS	BEGAN	MEMBERSHIP	COMMUNITY
Lutheran Church	1974	nr	nr
Roman Catholic Church	1910	nr	14,000
Sudan Interior Mission	1974	nr	200
Ethiopian Orthodox Church	nr	nr	15,000

OPENNESS TO RELIGIOUS CHANGE: somewhat open

RECEPTIVITY TO CHRISTIANITY: not reported

EVANGELISM PROFILE: not reported

VALIDITY: 6

Within the larger Gurage group, there are at least three major linguistic branches (Eastern, Western and Northern) which are mutually unintelligible. Located in the southwestern Shoa province, they are divided into more than a dozen dialect groups. Estimates of the total population run as high as 2 million.

Beyond language and religion there are no clearly distinct Muslims and Christians are intermixed with Gurage traditionalists. Islam is dominant among the Selti, Walane, Urbareg and Enneqor of the Eastern Gurage and among the Gogot of the Northern Gurage. The principal focus of Muslim life is the shrine of Shaikh Said Budella. A follower of the Tijaniya brotherhood, the Sahikh is attributed to have done a large number of miracles and pilgrims come to his shrine from far beyond the borders of the Gurage.

Mosques are inconspicuous and no formal Islamic education is offered outside of some instruction traditionally given children in the government schools. How the current revolutionary situation has changed this is not clear. Pre-Islamic beliefs and practices remain entrenched. Nature spirits, sacred groves to various gods, the reliance on celestial beings for good fortune and amulets for good health are widespread. This is no less true for many of the Orthodox Christians, who with the Roman Catholics, make up the largest sub-groups of Christians.

Hui (China)

ALTERNATE NAMES: Chinese Muslims

SIZE OF GROUP: 5,200,000   MARC ID: 4006

DISTINCTIVES: ethnicity; religion

SOCIAL CHANGE: not reported

LANGUAGES: Hui-hui-yu (V); Mandarin (T)

SCRIPTURE: not reported

CHRISTIAN LITERACY: not reported

RELIGION: Islam (100% adherents)

CHURCHES AND MISSIONS: not reported

OPENNESS TO RELIGIOUS CHANGE: not reported

RECEPTIVITY TO CHRISTIANITY: not reported

EVANGELISM PROFILE: not reported

VALIDITY: 6

The Hui are descendents of Arab, Persian and Chinese Muslims of
the Tang Dynasty whose mother tongue is now Chinese. Often they
are referred to as "Chinese Muslims" but this is not quite
accurate. There are ten other minority groups (the Uigur,
Kasakh, T'uchia, Tungsiang, Kirqiz, Salar, Tajik, Tatar, Paozn)
in China which are also Islamic. So while there may be about 20
million Muslims in China, the Hui make up only the largest ethnic
sub-group.

Considerable diversity is to be found in the Hui. While they are
largely sedentary agriculturalists in the northwest (concentrated
in Ningshi Hui Autonomous Region) living in ethnically
homogeneous villages, they are also to be found in many of the
large cities of Northern China. Peking was the center of Hui
culture and even today some 67 mosques are to be found in that
city.

Social customs have adjusted to Chinese traditions. The central
core of the family is the patrilineal extended family. Except
for diet and religion, much of their way of life is
indistinguishable from fellow Chinese. Their dialect
incorporates borrowed words from Arabic and Latin, and Hui
restaurants have Arabic as well as Chinese characters advertising
their service.

Islam has been adjusted to Chinese life. Most Hui are Sunni of
the Hanafi school, but local sectarianism is common. Old sects
exhibit local Chinese adaptations, made during Chinese isolation.
New Sects were developed out of 18th century contact with the
Middle East and the desire to "purify" Chinese Islam. Pir
worship is common. There are some 40,000 mosques officially
reported in China and the Hui have received somewhat preferential
treatment by the People's Republic. They are seen as important
in cultivating the Muslim world.

EXPANDED DESCRIPTIONS

Igbira (Nigeria)

ALTERNATE NAMES: not reported

SIZE OF GROUP: 400,000   MARC ID: 543

DISTINCTIVES: language; ethnicity

SOCIAL CHANGE: not reported

LANGUAGES: Igbirra (100% speak/25% read; V); Yoruba

SCRIPTURE: portions

CHRISTIAN LITERACY: not reported

RELIGION: Islam-Animist (70% adherents); Animism (10%
    adherents); Protestant (8% adherents/6% practicing); Roman
    Catholic (12% adherents/8% practicing)

CHURCHES AND MISSIONS	BEGAN	MEMBERSHIP	COMMUNITY
African Independent Church	nr	nr	nr
Church Missionary Society	nr	nr	nr
Roman Catholic Church	nr	nr	nr
Evangelical Church W. Africa	nr	nr	nr
Wycliffe Bible Translators	nr	nr	nr

OPENNESS TO RELIGIOUS CHANGE: not reported

RECEPTIVITY TO CHRISTIANITY: reluctant

EVANGELISM PROFILE: not reported

VALIDITY: 6

The Igbira represent the difficulty of drawing a border line
between a "reached" and an "unreached" people. There are a large
number of Christians and they are relatively active in church
life. Yet a close look suggests that animism is alive and well
even in Christian circles.

The traditional animistic festivals are still held by the men of
the villages. Masquerade and sacrifices to the ancestral spirits
are distinctive marks of these bi-annual events. Recently
interest in traditional religious consciousness and rituals has
increased as African distinctiveness has been stressed.

The Igbira, like any large group, has a diversity that hides
behind a single name. Igbira are to be found in towns in a
variety of places in Nigeria outside their traditional homeland.
They are traders as well as farmers. Education has helped
perhaps as many as 25% of the adults become literate.

At present the largest favorable response is being given to the
gospel Assemblies. Utilizing worship forms that include dancing
and drumming as well as a focus on healing, the pentecostals are
finding Igbira ready to enter into commitment to Christ. Part of
the perception of the Igbira as somewhat resistant or opposed to
Christian faith may be based on the fact that they do not respond
to the more staid, traditional methods of missions who view
drumming and dancing as incompatible with the form of Chrisianity
they are attempting to communicate. Only a Christian approach
that deals with the spirit world and incarnates itself in Igbira
forms will be able to cope with the powerful realities that hold
Igbira in bondage.

154

Jama Mapun (Philippines)

ALTERNATE NAMES: Cagayano

SIZE OF GROUP: 15,000   MARC ID: 1149

DISTINCTIVES: language; occupation; ethnicity; religion

SOCIAL CHANGE: not reported

LANGUAGES: Mapun (100% speak; V); Cagayan (100% speak; V);
    Tausug (5% speak; T); English (T)

SCRIPTURE: portions

CHRISTIAN LITERACY: not reported

RELIGION: Christianity (-1% practicing); Islam-Animist (99%
    adherents)

CHURCHES AND MISSIONS	BEGAN	MEMBERSHIP	COMMUNITY
Roman Catholic Church	nr	nr	nr
Wycliffe Bible Translators	nr	nr	nr

OPENNESS TO RELIGIOUS CHANGE: very closed

RECEPTIVITY TO CHRISTIANITY: reluctant

EVANGELISM PROFILE: not reported

VALIDITY: 5

While the Jama Mapun are scattered throughout the Sulu
Archipelago, they are especially concentrated on the island of
Cagayan Sulu, about 60 miles from the coast of northeastern
Sabah, and on the islands scattered between. Traditionally they
have been controlled alternatively by the Sultanates of Brunei
and Sulu.

In the past they engaged in fairly extensive maritime trade,
acting as middlemen between the Chinese of Borneo (Kalimantan)
and the natives of Palawan. At present they are increasingly
dependent upon subsistance agriculture and copra production.
Fishing is not extensively practiced except in the smaller island
settlements. The majority of the Jama Mapun live in individual
households scattered near permanent fixed fields.

Households are often made up of extended families that do not
separate until the death of the grandfather. Kinship is
bilaterally traced, but nobility status is traditionally
inherited through one's father's kinship line. Divorce and
inheritance in general follows the Shafi interpretation of Sunni
Islamic law.

Islam is the virtually universal religious identity. But it is
combined with a strong base of folkbeliefs and practices without
any self-consious sense that there might be an incompatibility.
Religious leadership is focused on imams who officiate both at
what might be considered "pure" Islamic ceremonies and those
which are derived from indigenous practices.

Missions and evangelization have only very marginally affected
the Jama Mapun. The Summer Institute of Linguistics is presently
involved in Bible translation.

EXPANDED DESCRIPTIONS

Kaffa (Ethiopia)

ALTERNATE NAMES: Mocha; Kefa

SIZE OF GROUP: 320,000   MARC ID: 363

DISTINCTIVES: language; ethnicity

SOCIAL CHANGE: rapid

LANGUAGES: Kaffenya (Kefa) (100% speak; V); Amharic (20%
    speak/6% read; T); Gallenya (5% speak)

SCRIPTURE: portions

CHRISTIAN LITERACY: 50%

RELIGION: Christo-Paganism (94% adherents); Islam (2%
    adherents); Christianity (2% adherents/2% practicing);
    Unknown (2% adherents)

CHURCHES AND MISSIONS	BEGAN	MEMBERSHIP	COMMUNITY
Kale Heywit Church	1964	nr	900
Ethiopian Orthodox Church	1895	5,000	nr
Roman Catholic Church	1944	800	1,200
Weleyta Church	nr	nr	nr

OPENNESS TO RELIGIOUS CHANGE: somewhat open

RECEPTIVITY TO CHRISTIANITY: indifferent

EVANGELISM PROFILE: not reported

VALIDITY: 6

Islamic penetration south of the Sahara has been spotty and
uneven. The Kaffa are an example of a people only marginally
affected by the advance of Islam. Conquered and "christianized",
the Kaffa have retained much of their traditional indigenous
belief and practice. The current Marxist revolution has
seriously challenged that animistic base. Powerful witch doctors
who controlled much of the spiritual and social life have been
dethroned and in some cases liquidated. Revolutionary peoples
councils now run the civic life.

During 1970-77 the Sudan Interior Mission and the American
Presbyterian Mission stimulated an energetic church growth
thrust. The Weleyta Church of South Ethiopia joined hands with
them and sent 20 evangelists and their families to help. Over 30
churches were planted in eight years.

The Marxist revolution has created some turmoil for Christians
with burnings of churches and one evangelist being killed in an
unfortunate incident. All foreign missionary personnel were
expelled in April, 1978, yet evangelism continues. A Bible
school is in session and the Church's perimeters are growing.
Bible translation is advancing with key portions of both the Old
and New Testaments now completed.

The future appears much more hopeful for Christian evangelization
than for any further advance of the tiny community of Islam. A
Church is present and growing. Ethiopian evangelists from the
Weleyta Church have taken responsibility for introducing the
Kaffa to the Christ they so dimly perceive through the
Christo-paganism that has held them for nearly 100 years.

Kambari (Nigeria)

ALTERNATE NAMES: not reported

SIZE OF GROUP: 100,000   MARC ID: 1173

DISTINCTIVES: language; ethnicity

SOCIAL CHANGE: rapid

LANGUAGES: Kambarci (100% speak/15% read; V); Hausa (75%
    speak; T)

SCRIPTURE: portions

CHRISTIAN LITERACY: 25%

RELIGION: Animism (65% adherents); Islam (25% adherents);
    Roman Catholic (5% adherents/3% practicing); Protestant (5%
    adherents/3% practicing)

CHURCHES AND MISSIONS	BEGAN	MEMBERSHIP	COMMUNITY
United Missionary Church	1935	nr	nr
Baptist Church	1950	nr	nr
Roman Catholic Church	nr	nr	nr

OPENNESS TO RELIGIOUS CHANGE: very open

RECEPTIVITY TO CHRISTIANITY: indifferent

EVANGELISM PROFILE: not reported

VALIDITY: 6

The Kambari are agriculturalists, living in villages in an area
about 100 miles northeast of the city of Minna in the state of
Niger. While traditional religious patterns are strong, there is
evidence of a new openness to change. The Maigiro cult (worship
of a god concerned with fertility and health) is widespread but
apparently accompanied with a great deal of local variation.

The Kambari are widely respected in their area and for that
reason are strategic as a people. Islam is present and slowly
growing in influence and formal adherents. But it is apparent
that not all the traditionalists feel Islam is preferable to
Christianity. In 1975, at the traditionalist center of Salka,
Islamic teachers were run off with the observation that
Christianity is superior to Islam. Since that time the number of
Christian professions has risen.

The church is present and growing. But it is also apparent that
the concentration of witness has been in the north and there are
remote areas that have hardly been touched by itinerant or
permanent witness of any type. Nor is translation being done in
the Kambarci language. Portions were done in the 1930s but
little work has followed that time.

There are two crucial needs at present: for a concentration of
efforts on this people at a time when they are giving evidence of
a new openness and leaders of the communities are inviting
witness (the Emir on the Agwarra side of the Niger has invited
Christian preaching); and for house visitation which appears to
be the most fruitful approach. Jerry Swank writes of this
people: "the KAMBARI are the strategic people in this area upon
which to concentrate our efforts in the immediate future."

EXPANDED DESCRIPTIONS

Kamuku (Nigeria)

ALTERNATE NAMES: not reported

SIZE OF GROUP: 20,000   MARC ID: 536

DISTINCTIVES: language; ethnicity

SOCIAL CHANGE: not reported

LANGUAGES: Kamuku (100% speak; V); Hausa (100% speak/10% read; T)

SCRIPTURE: none

CHRISTIAN LITERACY: 50%

RELIGION: Animism (75% adherents); Protestant (5% adherents/3% practicing); Islam-Animist (20% adherents)

CHURCHES AND MISSIONS	BEGAN	MEMBERSHIP	COMMUNITY
Southern Baptist Convention	1959	400	nr
Evangelical Church W. Africa	1960	150	nr

OPENNESS TO RELIGIOUS CHANGE: not reported

RECEPTIVITY TO CHRISTIANITY: indifferent

EVANGELISM PROFILE: not reported

VALIDITY: 6

The Kamuku are found in Kaduna, Sokoto, but principally in Niger State. They are agriculturalists, living in villages generally located between the Kambari and the Gbari (see articles in this book). They are closely related to the Gbari and are included in the Minna division.

The Maigiro cult is found in a very active and vital form. Ritual drinking of beer and festivals incorporating the masked spirits are to be found practiced throughout the agricultural cycle. The ancestor cult is integrated into the Maigiro worship. This animistic base has proved to be a strong and stable barrier against intrusion by other religious commitments.

Islam is present and slowly growing. It is particularly potent at the political level. Becoming a Muslim offers definite social advantages. Hausa is widely used so that contact with more thoroughly Islamized peoples is no problem.

Gospel witness has been present since 1940 (through the efforts of an independent missionary who left no church). The Southern Baptists, present since 1959, have established eight churches and seem to have the most viablity. ECWA with three churches and a hospital has only a third as many members. The Kamuku have been viewed in the past as somewhat resistant, but no churches present appear to utilize a more charismatic or indigenous African form of Christian worship. It may be that a larger response would be given, provided a more spirit-oriented approach were taken.

No scripture translation is currently underway. Hausa is widely used and the Scriptures are available in that language. Consistent visitation and a more widely dispersed effort will be essential if Christians are to raise the percentage of those who have a viable opportunity to learn of Christ.

Kanuri (Nigeria)

ALTERNATE NAMES: not reported

SIZE OF GROUP: 3,000,000   MARC ID: 4007

DISTINCTIVES: sense of unity

SOCIAL CHANGE: moderate

LANGUAGES: Kanuri Dialects (V)

SCRIPTURE: portions

CHRISTIAN LITERACY: not reported

RELIGION: Christianity (1% adherents/1% practicing); Islam 90% adherents)

CHURCHES AND MISSIONS	BEGAN	MEMBERSHIP	COMMUNITY
Sudan Interior Mission	nr	nr	nr
Sudan United Mission	nr	nr	nr

OPENNESS TO RELIGIOUS CHANGE: not reported

RECEPTIVITY TO CHRISTIANITY: not reported

EVANGELISM PROFILE: not reported

VALIDITY: 6

Centuries ago a civil war in the Kanem Empire forced the migration of some of the ruling family, the Saifawa. They settled southwest of Lake Chad. Setting up a new kingdom they set about subduing and incorporating a variety of indigenous peoples. Commerce, intermarriage, politics and time have yielded the present culturally heterogeneous people who call themselves the Kanuri.

Diversity is also apparent in the occupational structure. While most are agriculturalists, living in hamlets of three or four families or villages that grow into towns of several thousands, artisans, merchants, educationalists, religious and political figures are all present. The growing line of distinction between the educated, bureacratic class and the peasants is the strongest emergent trend of the future. Prestige is accorded to those who occupy positions in the civil and religious heirarchy. Those engaged in dirty occupations such as butchers, barbers, and tanners are ranked at the bottom. Patron-client relationships serve as the basic social structure which governs daily social life.

The Kanuri are strongly Islamic. Family life is ordered according to Islamic law with emphasis on the male head of the household. Polygamy is present. Divorce rates are high (nearly 80% of all marriages). The full ritual year cycle is followed. Charms and amulets are utilized but the presence of traditional animistic elements is less among the Kanuri than the Hausa. The Tijaniya appears to be the most popular brotherhood.

While the Sudan Interior Mission and the Sudan United Mission are working in this area, converts from among the Kanuri are still very few. Definite translation need exists and the New Testament is currently in process of being translated. More information is needed to assess the current status of evangelization.

EXPANDED DESCRIPTIONS

Karakalpak (Soviet Russia)

ALTERNATE NAMES: not reported

SIZE OF GROUP: 277,000   MARC ID: 4011

DISTINCTIVES: language; occupation; ethnicity

SOCIAL CHANGE: moderate

LANGUAGES: Karakalpak (100% speak; V)

SCRIPTURE: not reported

CHRISTIAN LITERACY: not reported

RELIGION: Islam (100% adherents)

CHURCHES AND MISSIONS: not reported

OPENNESS TO RELIGIOUS CHANGE: not reported

RECEPTIVITY TO CHRISTIANITY: not reported

EVANGELISM PROFILE: not reported

VALIDITY: 6

The Karakalpak ('Black hats') are concentrated on the southern
shores of the Aral Sea in the Karakalpak Autonomous USSR. They
appear to have become a relatively distinct people in the 18th
century. Even yet their sense of unity is low. The major
difference between them and the Uzbek and Kazakh lies in the
distinctive language which they speak.

Nearly all of them are now farmers. They have been collectivized
on farms that grow that most profitable crop of cotten.
Collective livestock farming is also practiced and some are
fishers in the southern Aral Sea. Of the approximately 30% who
live in cities, most are workers in light industrial concerns
such as cotten crop processing and textile mills.

The importance of kinship has declined and the Soviet Union has
campaigned against polygamy. The position of the woman is rising
in status and a number of changes have been introduced to
counterbalance the traditional tribal patriarchy.

Sunni Islam has been the traditional religious identity. The
number of "clergy" (madrassas) has steadily declined as well as
the number of functioning mosques. Sunday is now the day of rest
and bazaar. Pre-Islamic rites for childbirth, weddings and death
are the most elaborate rituals still practiced. Nonetheless, the
Karakalpak maintain their separateness by almost never marrying
out of their group and by eating at home rather than take
"forbidden" food at the worker cafeterias.

Our sources do not give information on the situation of
evangelization. The ETHNOLOGUE indicates that there is a
definite translation need. It might be possible to do evangelism
among the Karakalpak who live in Iran but there is no indication
that such a possibility has been seized by Christians.

Kazakhs (Iran)

ALTERNATE NAMES: not reported

SIZE OF GROUP: 3,000   MARC ID: 2055

DISTINCTIVES: language; ethnicity; kinship; residence

SOCIAL CHANGE: slow

LANGUAGES: Kazakhi (100% speak; V)

SCRIPTURE: New Testament

CHRISTIAN LITERACY: not reported

RELIGION: Islam (100% adherents)

CHURCHES AND MISSIONS: not reported

OPENNESS TO RELIGIOUS CHANGE: not reported

RECEPTIVITY TO CHRISTIANITY: not reported

EVANGELISM PROFILE: not reported

VALIDITY: 5

The Kazakhs of Iran cannot be seen in isolation from the main
body of Kazakhs. While only a tiny community is to be found in
the northeast of Iran, some 6 million Kazakhs are to be found in
the USSR, 500,000 in China, 20,000 in Afganistan. Any evaluation
of this tiny minority in Iran will have to be placed against the
changes that are affecting the Kazakhs as a whole.

Traditionally they have inhabited the difficult dry steppes of
central Asia. They organized themselves into three hordes
(ordas) in the 15th century and controlled their territory until
the middle of the 19th century. Noted for their fierce
independence, they theoretically have been assimilated into the
way of life of their host countries (even being collectivized in
the USSR). But the traditional patterns of kinship, arranged
marriage, shamamism with a Sunni Islam overlay continue. The
collective in the USSR now tends to act like the traditional
exogamous clan, and is most frequently made up of close
kinspersons.

Most Kazakhs are settled (perhaps no more than 500,000 fulfill
the traditional portrait of horseperson, herdsperson, hunter,
falconer, warrior). The yurt (felt tent suspended on a wooden
frame) and the diet of Kumyss (fermented mare's milk) remain as
symbols of the tradition of a great people. The combination of
folk religion and Islam remains strong and women are not secluded
or veiled. The Kazakh shaman (bagsha) is widely respected as one
who can cure serious diseases.

The New Testament is available in Cyrillic script and the use of
the Arabic script is dying out. There is some effort at revision
of this old (1910) translation. There is no indication in our
current information that there is any Christian outreach among
the Kazakhs of Iran and one can only suppose that the 1979
revolution will only result in less opportunity for witness.

EXPANDED DESCRIPTIONS

Kirgiz (Soviet Russia)

ALTERNATE NAMES: Kik-kum

SIZE OF GROUP: 1,700,000   MARC ID: 4016

DISTINCTIVES: language; occupation; religion

SOCIAL CHANGE: moderate

LANGUAGES: Kirgiz (100% speak; V)

SCRIPTURE: not reported

CHRISTIAN LITERACY: not reported

RELIGION: Islam-Animist (70% adherents); Secularism (30% adherents)

CHURCHES AND MISSIONS: not reported

OPENNESS TO RELIGIOUS CHANGE: not reported

RECEPTIVITY TO CHRISTIANITY: not reported

EVANGELISM PROFILE: not reported

VALIDITY: 6

Traditionally the Kirgiz were nomadic herders of horses and
sheep. For many years the USSR attempted to revise this reality,
only to admit defeat in the late 1960s. It has become apparent
that the pastoralism which evolved in this region over centuries
is the best form of land management. The Kirgiz extended
families have been organized as work "brigades" and their
activity labelled "herding" instead of nomadism, and presto the
new soviet worker has emerged!

The Kirgiz are distinguished from neighboring herders on the
basis of the mountain pastures they inhabit. The largest part of
the pastoral production is now focused on sheep (in contrast with
the traditional premium placed on horses and the potential they
gave for raiding neighboring peoples).

Perhaps 18% are not engaged in agriculture or pastoral herding.
They are found in the cities that have sprung up, populated
principally by Russian and Ukrainian elements. Their labor is
given primarily to the lower levels of skill and position. They
occupy only one-fifth of the technical and professional jobs in
their own region. The sedentary agriculturalists are for the
most part organized into collectives which act much like the
tribes traditionally did.

Islamic practice and belief has traditionally been strongly
interpenetrated by animistic strands of a shamanistic type. Even
today the "mullah" takes part in such non-Islamic rites as are
associated with death. But there is evidence of a
secularization, especially in urban areas. While only 33 mosques
remain open, there are unoffical mosques in most villages, served
by illegal itinerant "mullahs". Saint worship is still
influential.

Kubu (Indonesia)

ALTERNATE NAMES: Koeboe; Orang Darat

SIZE OF GROUP: 6,000   MARC ID: 1093

DISTINCTIVES: ethnicity; discrimination; economic status

SOCIAL CHANGE: not reported

LANGUAGES: Local dialects (100% speak; V)

SCRIPTURE: none

CHRISTIAN LITERACY: not reported

RELIGION: Christianity (1% adherents/1% practicing); Animism
    (80% adherents); Islam-Animist (19% adherents)

CHURCHES AND MISSIONS	BEGAN	MEMBERSHIP	COMMUNITY
Evangelical Church Indonesia	nr	100	nr
Worldwide Evangelization Crus.	nr	nr	nr

OPENNESS TO RELIGIOUS CHANGE: very open

RECEPTIVITY TO CHRISTIANITY: not reported

EVANGELISM PROFILE: not reported

VALIDITY: 6

The term Kubu refers to remnant groups of forestdwellers who are
scattered throughout various regions of Sumatra, the Riau-Lingga
Islands, Billiton and Banka. They have undergone a process of
settlement and assimilation and may refer to themselves by the
name of the dominant group into which they have assimilated.
They have lost, for the most part, their native language and
speak the local language of the people of the particular region
in which they live.

They are known by a variety of names (the Jakun and Sakai tribes
in Malaysia; the Mamak, Akit, Talang, Tapung, Lubu, Orang Utan,
Rawas, Duwablas, Benua etc). The term Kubu is a derogatory word
(connoting "backwards" or "primitive"). Most have intermarried
so that the ancient Veddoid physical type grades into the local
physical characteristics. They are to be found most frequently
in settled agricultural villages where they build their houses
and attempt to pass as members of the dominant local group.

Most consider themselves Muslims though their practice is
intermixed with traditional shamanism. Most other customs are
approximations of the dominant local people. For example, those
associated with the Minangkabau (see article in this book) have
adopted a matrilineal structure and organized themselves as a
subtribe of the larger group.

There is very little information available on the current
activity of Churches to reach these diverse groups. The few
truly nomadic groups live in remote forested or swampy areas and
are difficult to approach by traditional missionary methods.
Because of the diversity of adjustments that Kubu have made, it
is imperative that a more detailed and specific picture be drawn,
describing the nature of each of the situations of this formerly
more uniform people.

EXPANDED DESCRIPTIONS

Kurds in Iran (Iran)

ALTERNATE NAMES: Kords

SIZE OF GROUP: 2,000,000   MARC ID: 2036

DISTINCTIVES: language; political loyalty; ethnicity; sense
    of unity; discrimination

SOCIAL CHANGE: slow

LANGUAGES: Kurdish Dialects (100% speak/1% read; V, G); Farsi
    (T, S)

SCRIPTURE: New Testament

CHRISTIAN LITERACY: not reported

RELIGION: Roman Catholic (1% adherents/1% practicing); Islam
    (95% adherents); Other (4% adherents)

CHURCHES AND MISSIONS: not reported

OPENNESS TO RELIGIOUS CHANGE: somewhat closed

RECEPTIVITY TO CHRISTIANITY: very reluctant

EVANGELISM PROFILE: not reported

VALIDITY: 6

Estimates range from 9 to 12 million Kurds in an area embracing
five countries (Turkey, Iraq, Syria, Iran, and USSR) known as
Kurdistan. Here in mountain fastness live a hardy people who
have been fighting for statehood since the 12th century. As
these words are written, the Kurds are fighting again in
Kermanshah in Iran (similar revolts occurred in 1920-25 and
1945-6).

The Kurds are a nation without a recognized country. Within the
boundaries of the countries in which they now inhabit, the
national policies are to assimilate them (e.g. see the article
on Kurds in Turkey in UNREACHED PEOPLES '79). But there is
internal diversity. Linguistically most Kurds in Iran speak the
southern Kurdish dialect of Sorani (the current literary language
since publishing is permitted, using the Arabic script in Iraq
and Iran). They also are members of various sects. In Iran both
Sunni and Shia groups are to be found. Various Sufi
brotherhoods, especially the Qadiriya and the Naqshabandiya are
prominent is rural areas. The Ali Haqq (or Ali Ilahis sect)
claim many of Iran's Kurds (see article in UNREACHED PEOPLES
'79).

The Kurds are also undergoing change brought about by
modernization in their regions. Kurds who maintain a relatively
isolated rural existence are now counterbalanced by those few who
are PhD's from western universities.

Islam is present at all levels. Christian mission to the Kurds
in the northwestern sector of Iran is present. Living Bibles
International has produced a popular New Testament in the Sorani
dialect, published in 1977. There is no current information on
how the Islamic revolution and current rebellion in Kurdistan has
affected the possibility of continued Christian activity.

Lampung (Indonesia)

ALTERNATE NAMES: Lampong; Abung

SIZE OF GROUP: 1,500,000   MARC ID: 1134

DISTINCTIVES: not reported

SOCIAL CHANGE: not reported

LANGUAGES: Lampung Abung (V); Lampung Pesisir (V); Komering
    (V)

SCRIPTURE: none

CHRISTIAN LITERACY: not reported

RELIGION: Islam-Animist (100% adherents)

CHURCHES AND MISSIONS: not reported

OPENNESS TO RELIGIOUS CHANGE: not reported

RECEPTIVITY TO CHRISTIANITY: not reported

EVANGELISM PROFILE: not reported

VALIDITY: 5

This name designates an area of southern Sumatra, bounded on its
north by the river Tulang Bawang and Lake Ranau and on the south
by the Sunda Straits. The population is actually made up of
three major ethnic elements. About 33% are Abung, various tribes
speaking a dialect similar to Riau-Malay; 39% are Paminggir and
Pubian and speak Malay; and the remainder are transmigrant
Javanese and a few smaller ethnic groups. Thus the situation is
pluralistic even though a relative degree of mutual assimilation
and homogenization has been taking place for some time.

The basic characteristics of the Javanese are discussed in
UNREACHED PEOPLES '79. The Abung are considered to be "mountain
people" in origin. They have a traditional history of
headhunting and raiding of the lowlands. Organized by clans,
their traditional way of life has been changed by forced
settlement and conquest. Normally there might be as many as 10
clans in a village with upwards of 3,000 inhabitants.

The Abung are nominally Islamic, though they know very little of
Islamic law. If anything, much of pre-Islamic life has
continued, with the substitution of farm laborers for slavery and
the killing of ox for human headhunting and sacrifice. Communal
festival houses are still to be found in the center of the
villages. The traditional initiation (papadan) is practiced, by
which males climb in a three-tiered socio-religious prestige
grading system.

The Pubian and Paminggir e the traditional lowlanders whose way
of life is being imitated to some degree by the Abung. It is
thought that they are the result of the mixture of Abung and the
Sundanese. Our sources tell little of this part of the Lampung.
In both cases we are in need of significant information on what
the Javanese Churches and missions are doing to evangelize in
southeastern Sumatra.

EXPANDED DESCRIPTIONS

Lors (Iran)

ALTERNATE NAMES: Lur

SIZE OF GROUP: 600,000   MARC ID: 2028

DISTINCTIVES: language; discrimination

SOCIAL CHANGE: slow

LANGUAGES: Luri (100% speak; V, G); Farsi (T, S)

SCRIPTURE: none

CHRISTIAN LITERACY: not reported

RELIGION: Islam (100% adherents)

CHURCHES AND MISSIONS: not reported

OPENNESS TO RELIGIOUS CHANGE: not reported

RECEPTIVITY TO CHRISTIANITY: not reported

EVANGELISM PROFILE: not reported

VALIDITY: 5

The Lors or Lur are to be found south of the Kurds in the Zagros mountains of Iran. Located in Lurestan, Bakhtiari and Kuhgiluyeh, they are divided between the semi-nomadic (who farm and tend herds for a little over half the year until the dry season forces them up into the mountain meadows in search of pasture) and the settled agriculturalists. In spite of this division, most live in villages and hamlets of a permanent nature, moving into black goat-hair tents only when following their animals to a summer mountain pasture.

The tent household or hut is the basic unit. A localized group of related households are to be found in the migratory camps or villages. Descent is traced patrilineally and federations of such descent groups form subtribes, which is turn form larger tribal groups within the Lur. Governmental pressure has ended the rule of the tribal chiefs (khans) but life is still organized along descent and subtribal units.

Change in the form of education and land reform is having an impact on the outer forms of life. More are shifting towards a predominance of agriculture over transhumant herding. The national language, Farsi, is gaining in importance along with the availability of education.

Religious practices are centered about Shiah Islam, but the piety-style is much simpler and less esoteric than the Iranians who live in cities. Most of the mullahs are from families who claim descent from Muhammad. Pir worship is popular and pilgrimages to tombs are common. Use of charms and other facets of folk Islam are common.

While Assyrian Christians are present (especially in the Pusht Kuh region of Luristan), there is apparently little evangelism taking place. Christian identity is viewed as ethnic identity. No information is available to indicate any mission activity directed specifically at the Lurs.

Maguindano (Philippines)

ALTERNATE NAMES: not reported

SIZE OF GROUP: 700,000   MARC ID: 629

DISTINCTIVES: language; ethnicity

SOCIAL CHANGE: not reported

LANGUAGES: Maguindano (100% speak/20% read; V); Tagalog (15% speak; T); English (5% speak)

SCRIPTURE: portions

CHRISTIAN LITERACY: not reported

RELIGION: Islam (99% adherents); Christianity (1% adherents/1% practicing)

CHURCHES AND MISSIONS	BEGAN	MEMBERSHIP	COMMUNITY
Roman Catholic Church	1850	nr	nr
Christian & Msny. Alliance	1930	nr	nr
Foursquare Church	1970	nr	nr
Summer Institute Linguistics	1971	nr	nr

OPENNESS TO RELIGIOUS CHANGE: not reported

RECEPTIVITY TO CHRISTIANITY: very reluctant

EVANGELISM PROFILE: not reported

VALIDITY: 6

The Maguindano are the largest of the various Islamic ethnic groups of the Philippines. They have been called the people of the flood plain since most are to be found in the vast river basin of Pulangi or Rio Grande de Mindanao. Located in the province of Cotabato of the southern island of Mindanao, the recent warfare (only the modern version of a 300 year old struggle) has stimulated a broader consciousness of solidarity with the worldwide community of Islam.

Maguindano society is structured by status distinctions (maratabat). Those with highest rank trace descent back to the legendary Muslim missionary who converted the Maguindano. Below them are the lesser nobles, the freemen and the indentured laborers. Marriage takes place between these groups so that a graded system, rather than caste, obtains. But people are aware of the clear claim to power and privilege that differential status provides.

Converted to Islam in the early 16th century, the Sunni Islam of the peole is combined with indigenous beliefs in environmental spirits, magical rituals and healing ceremonies. Rural areas are particularly lax in the observance of prototypical Islamic rites. But there has been a resurgence of Islam and a movement toward giving more formal religious training to young people. As a result the practice of orthodox Islam is on the increase.

Bitter enmity exist between the Maguindano and the Christian Filipinos. At present there is little hope for the success of direct evangelization. Until significant changes in the political atmosphere occurs, Christians will be resisted.

EXPANDED DESCRIPTIONS

Melanau of Sarawak (Malaysia)

ALTERNATE NAMES: A Liko

SIZE OF GROUP: 61,000   MARC ID: 2122

DISTINCTIVES: language; ethnicity; social class; economic
    status

SOCIAL CHANGE: moderate

LANGUAGES: Melanau (100% speak/15% read; V, G, W); Malay (20%
    speak/15% read; T); English (15% speak/15% read; S, W)

SCRIPTURE: none

CHRISTIAN LITERACY: 100%

RELIGION: Christo-Paganism (20% adherents); Islam-Animist (25%
    adherents); Animism (53% adherents); Secularism (1%
    adherents); Christianity (1% adherents/1% practicing)

CHURCHES AND MISSIONS	BEGAN	MEMBERSHIP	COMMUNITY
Roman Catholic Church	1930	nr	nr
Protestant	nr	nr	nr

OPENNESS TO RELIGIOUS CHANGE: somewhat open

RECEPTIVITY TO CHRISTIANITY: receptive

EVANGELISM PROFILE:
        0% No awareness of Christianity
       78% Aware that Christianity exists
       20% Some knowledge of the gospel
        1% Understand the message of the gospel
        0% Personally challenged to receive Christ
        1% Decision to accept Christ
        0% Incorporated into a fellowship of Christians
        0% Active propagators of the gospel

VALIDITY: 6

Located on the central west coast of Sarawak (Kalimantan), the
Melanau are an indigenous riverine people who live in a series of
villages located in the delta of the Rejang up to the Balingian
river. Each localized group designates itself as "the people of"
Oya river, or wherever it is they are located.

Traditional religion is animistic, with a special concern for
communication from the gods by means of birds. Curing and
rituals at death are the most important ceremonies in the
animistic sector. Many who converted to Islam continue to
practice traditional rituals. Islamization apparently is
continuing at the present.

Those who have become Roman Catholics also do not see such a
profession as incompatible with traditional ideas and practices.
Thus most Christians are involved in a form of Christo-paganism.
The New Testament is not available and the ETHNOLOGUE indicates
Melanau as probably the most important contemporary translation
need in Sarawak. More specifics are necessary for evaluating the
contemporary status of evangelization among this people.

Meos of Rajasthan (India)

ALTERNATE NAMES: not reported

SIZE OF GROUP: 500,000   MARC ID: 4017

DISTINCTIVES: language; religion; sense of unity

SOCIAL CHANGE: not reported

LANGUAGES: Rajasthani (100% speak; V)

SCRIPTURE: not reported

CHRISTIAN LITERACY: not reported

RELIGION: Islam (100% adherents)

CHURCHES AND MISSIONS: not reported

OPENNESS TO RELIGIOUS CHANGE: not reported

RECEPTIVITY TO CHRISTIANITY: not reported

EVANGELISM PROFILE: not reported

VALIDITY: 5

Some two million Muslims are to be found among the Rajasthani
peoples. Three subgroups are heavily urban (the merchants and
traders, the service castes, and converts from the Hindu military
caste of the Rajputs). One is principally rural -- the Meos.

The Meos are the only native Muslim population, the others
originating elsewhere. The Meos claim to be descendents of the
Rajputs but an examination of their history and the current 800
"gotras" (exogamous clans) indicates a rather mixed origin from a
number of Hindu castes. They are concentrated in an area known
as Mewat (Alwar and Bharatpur districts in the northeast of
Rajasthan and in the Gurgaon district of Harayana state).

The Meos engage in a variety of village occupational endeavors
beyond agriculture. As seems to be true in much of India, the
more rural existence has meant a stronger acceptance of a mixed
Hindu-Islamic set of religious patterns. Traditionally marriage
ceremonies incorporated Hindu rituals, including the worship of
gods. Meo women are not secluded and cousin marriage is stiffly
resisted.

But beginning in 1947 an Islamic revival took hold in reaction to
the attempt of Hindus to reconvert the Meos. Independence and
partition meant the Meos were threatened politically and
communally and they have sought stronger ties with the urban
Muslims of Rajasthan and other parts of India. The new contact
and concern with Muslim identity has lead to a strong movement
toward Islamization and the elimination of Hindu traditions that
have existed for centuries in harmony with Muslim practices.

Christians are extremely few in number in Rajasthan. There is no
indication in our sources as to whether there are any concerted
efforts toward the evangelization of the Meos. More information
is needed in order to evaluate the current status of
evangelization among this people.

EXPANDED DESCRIPTIONS

Minangkabau (Indonesia)

ALTERNATE NAMES: Orang Padang

SIZE OF GROUP: 5,000,000   MARC ID: 212

DISTINCTIVES: language; ethnicity

SOCIAL CHANGE: not reported

LANGUAGES: Minangkabau (80% speak/80% read; V); Arabic (P); Indonesian (95% speak/95% read)

SCRIPTURE: none

CHRISTIAN LITERACY: not reported

RELIGION: Islam (99% adherents/90% practicing); Christianity (1% adherents/1% practicing)

CHURCHES AND MISSIONS   BEGAN MEMBERSHIP COMMUNITY
    Overseas Missionary Fellowship nr   nr   nr

OPENNESS TO RELIGIOUS CHANGE: somewhat closed

RECEPTIVITY TO CHRISTIANITY: very reluctant

EVANGELISM PROFILE: not reported

VALIDITY: 6

Minangkabau are prominent in government and commerce, far beyond their homeland in west-central Sumatra. In fact of over five million total Minangkabau less than half are to be found in the province of West Sumatra. Some reports say more are to be found in Jakarta than in West Sumatra! Many were very active in the Indonesian revolution (1945-9) and hold high civil offices.

Virtually all are Sunni Muslims, adhering to the Shafi school. The modernist Islamic movement, Muhammadijah, held widespread popularity in West Sumatra and was influential in introducing secular schools. Islam is combined with an ancient set of Hindu-Buddhist customs (especially in the rites of passage such as birth and marriage).

The spectrum of Minangkabau life runs from traditional wet rice subsistance agriculture focused about tiny, single matrilineage hamlets to modern, salaried professionals employed in the central government. In wealthy agricultural areas men are scarce except during the rice harvest. Since they do not own or control the best land, many of them leave their wife and family for a job or land elsewhere (in rantau or emigre regions). There they may set up another household, returning only to help their sisters and mother and to visit their "homeland" wives. Women do most of the work and make the daily decisions. Only in poorer regions do men remain to farm.

Only a few churches are located near the concentrations of the Minangkabau, but little is being done to evangelize them. A few New Testament portions are available, and there is a definite translation need. A fellowship of Minangkabau Christians has been formed, but not publicized.

Mossi (Upper Volta)

ALTERNATE NAMES: not reported

SIZE OF GROUP: 3,300,000   MARC ID: 4009

DISTINCTIVES: language; ethnicity; sense of unity

SOCIAL CHANGE: slow

LANGUAGES: Mole (100% speak; V, G, W); French (T, S)

SCRIPTURE: New Testament

CHRISTIAN LITERACY: not reported

RELIGION: Roman Catholic (10% aonerents/6% practicing);
    Protestant (2% adherents/1% practicing); Islam (22%
    adherents); Animism (66% adherents)

CHURCHES AND MISSIONS	BEGAN	MEMBERSHIP	COMMUNITY
Assemblies of God	nr	16,000	30,000
Christian & Msny. Alliance	nr	nr	nr
Roman Catholic	nr	nr	300,000

OPENNESS TO RELIGIOUS CHANGE: not reported

RECEPTIVITY TO CHRISTIANITY: not reported

EVANGELISM PROFILE: not reported

VALIDITY: 6

David Barrett describes this people as "the largest pagan tribe
in Africa." For over 8 centuries they resisted the pressures and
jihads aimed at converting them to Islam. But they are now
slowly being converted.

The Mossi are the largest ethnic group in Upper Volta. The vast
majority live in villages in the Volta River Basin, practicing a
hoe-based subsistence agriculture in an arid land. Cattle are
cared for by Fulani who receive a share of the farm crops in
exchange. Most of the Mossi continue to have a heavy investment
in the traditional ancestral cult (which reinforces lineage ties)
and fertility rituals associated with customary geographical
sites.

Islam has been gaining major ground in city areas (where about
62% of the Mossi list Islam as their religious identity) as
opposed to rural areas (where only 20% are Muslim). Part of the
growth has been due to the intermingling with the Muslim Yarse
who have lived among the Mossi for 200 years. This is especially
true where Mossi have moved to Ghana, Ivory Coast and Togo.

Christianity is present, especially in the form of Roman
Catholicism. While they claim an adherence of nearly 10%, it is
infected with nominalism and syncretism that is partly due to the
fact that much of the growth happened during colonial times.
Protestants are present, mainly through the Assemblies of God
churches. Major parts of the Mossi are still without a
significant enduring witness that can make the reality of Christ
a real option. It is clear that Islam is making far more headway
in converting this tribe than is Christianity.

EXPANDED DESCRIPTIONS

Muslim Malays (Malaysia)

ALTERNATE NAMES: not reported

SIZE OF GROUP: 5,500,000   MARC ID: 59

DISTINCTIVES: ethnicity; religion

SOCIAL CHANGE: not reported

LANGUAGES: Bahasa Malaysia (100% speak; V); English (20% speak)

SCRIPTURE: New Testament

CHRISTIAN LITERACY: not reported

RELIGION: Islam (99% adherents); Christianity (-1% practicing)

CHURCHES AND MISSIONS	BEGAN	MEMBERSHIP	COMMUNITY
Southern Baptist Convention	1951	nr	nr
Brethren Assemblies	1860	nr	nr
Anglican Church	1848	nr	nr
Methodist Church	1885	nr	nr
Presbyterian Church	1820	nr	nr

OPENNESS TO RELIGIOUS CHANGE: somewhat closed

RECEPTIVITY TO CHRISTIANITY: very reluctant

EVANGELISM PROFILE: not reported

VALIDITY: 6

The Malays comprise 46.7% of the 13 million people of Malaysia. The country is composed of two major geographical segments. The southern half of the Malay Peninsula is referred to officially as Peninsula Malaysia (or popularly as West Malaysia); the states of Sabah and Sarawak, which form a strip along the northern and western rim of Borneo are known as East Malaysia.

The official religion of the country is Islam. In popular thinking, to be converted to the Islamic faith is to become a Malay. According to official reckoning, anyone who habitually speaks the Malay language, follows Malay custom and professes Islam is a Malay. In Malaysia all Malays are regarded as Muslims. It is acceptable for non-Malays to be converted to Islam and many are openly encourged to do so, but it is against the Constitution to convert a Muslim to another religion. In this respect freedom of religion is restricted.

Many Malays in the cities are spiritually receptive to the Gospel but in the present context it is not convenient - socially, culturally and economically for them to change their religion. So far there is no Malay church in the country, and there are very few Malay Christians. Some towns and cities are known to be receptive to the gospel in that many of them respond to Bible correspondence courses and the radio gospel messages. At present the Churches in Malaysia have not devised a way to follow up these responsive Malays nor have they seriously considered any evangelistic outreach towards them.

North Africans in Belgium (Belgium)

ALTERNATE NAMES: Moroccans

SIZE OF GROUP: 90,000   MARC ID: 4019

DISTINCTIVES: language; ethnicity; kinship; sense of unity;
    economic status; discrimination

SOCIAL CHANGE: moderate

LANGUAGES: Arabic (100% speak/50% read; V, T, G, W); Arabic
    Berber (100% speak; T); French (70% speak/50% read; S)

SCRIPTURE: Bible

CHRISTIAN LITERACY: not reported

RELIGION: Christianity (-1% practicing); Islam (99%
    adherents/20% practicing)

CHURCHES AND MISSIONS   BEGAN MEMBERSHIP   COMMUNITY
    Gospel Missionary Union   1970   4   20

OPENNESS TO RELIGIOUS CHANGE: very closed

RECEPTIVITY TO CHRISTIANITY: very reluctant

EVANGELISM PROFILE:
    0% No awareness of Christianity
    74% Aware that Christianity exists
    20% Some knowledge of the gospel
    5% Understand the message of the gospel
    1% Personally challenged to receive Christ
    0% Decision to accept Christ
    0% Incorporated into a fellowship of Christians
    0% Active propagators of the gospel

VALIDITY: 6

Belgium has nearly a million foreign workers, in a total
population of only 10 million. 90,000 of them come from North
Africa, the overwhelming preponderance of them from Morocco
(including Arabs and Berbers).

Islam came with them in a very vital form. Brussels now boasts
an Islamic Center and nearly thirty storefront mosques. Since
1975 Islam has been a recognized religion, and Muslim teachers
give instruction in Islam in religious classes in the public
schools. Moroccans bring with them a Sunni form of Islam,
strongly influenced by maraboutism and orientation to "baraka"
(divine favor that leads to material prosperity, well being,
completion, luck etc.).

Their sense of being Muslim has slackened very little and, while
there is greater freedom to reach them with the gospel, few have
become Christians. Since 1970 the Gospel Missionary Union has
had an evangelistic program aimed at Moroccan Arabs (by
missionaries expelled from Morocco in 1969 who speak the Magrebi
dialect of Arabic peculiar to Morocco). In 1974 an Arab center,
"The House of Life", was opened in a heavily North African area.
It is currently led by an Arab couple and participated in by an
international group, including Belgians. As yet a formula that
will win significant numbers of North Africans has not been
developed.

EXPANDED DESCRIPTIONS

Nuristani (Afghanistan)

ALTERNATE NAMES: Kafir; Sheikhan

SIZE OF GROUP: 67,000   MAPC ID: 4015

DISTINCTIVES: ethnicity; religion

SOCIAL CHANGE: not reported

LANGUAGES: Local dialects (V)

SCRIPTURE: Bible stories; portions

CHRISTIAN LITERACY: not reported

RELIGION: Islam (94% adherents); Animism (6% adherents)

CHURCHES AND MISSIONS: not reported

OPENNESS TO RELIGIOUS CHANGE: not reported

RECEPTIVITY TO CHRISTIANITY: not reported

EVANGELISM PROFILE: not reported

VALIDITY: 5

Perched high on steep mountainsides, Nuristani villages maintain an ancient adjustment to difficult circumstances. Mountain trails are not suitable even for mules, and one must walk almost everywhere. Villages range from 30 to 300 households surrounded by terraced fields fed by miles of tortuous irrigation channels.

Located in 5 main valley systems with a number of tributaries, each drainage area speaks its own dialect (Kati, Waigali, Ashkuni, Paruni). Suspicious of outsiders, even Nuristani from a few miles away, everything is regulated by village level consensus based on centuries of experience that have ensured survival. Strict rules enforced by public opinion and an elected village group specify the order in which fields are irrigated and when the men must move goats and sheep to different pastures.

For over 800 years they held out against the Muslim tide that threatened to sweep into their valleys. Traditional prestige was marked by how many Muslims a young man killed in raids. But in 1895-6 these valleys were conquered and were forcibly converted to Islam. The numerically dominant Muslims changed their name from infidels ("Kafirs"-- see description of unconverted Nuristanis who live in Pakistan, UNREACHED PEOPLES '79) to "Nuristani," that is "Land of the Light." The light of Islam had finally triumphed in these mountain villages. Each village is made up of several named wards, each with its own mosque and its own leader who acts to mediate disputes and to deal with the government. Women are not veiled or secluded and a customary wine of the area is still drunk.

There is no known evangelism taking place in the area and none would be openly permitted. It may be possible to evangelize among the pagan "Nuristani", the Kafirs of Pakistan, and through them eventually have a basis for evangelization in Afghanistan.

Nyamwezi (Tanzania)

ALTERNATE NAMES: Nyamwesi; Banyamwezi

SIZE OF GROUP: 590,000   MARC ID: 487

DISTINCTIVES: language; ethnicity

SOCIAL CHANGE: not reported

LANGUAGES: Nyamwezi (100% speak; V); Swahili (90% speak; T)

SCRIPTURE: New Testament

CHRISTIAN LITERACY: not reported

RELIGION: Animism (45% adherents); Islam-Animist (40%
     adherents); Protestant (5% adherents/3% practicing); Roman
     Catholic (10% adherents/6% practicing)

CHURCHES AND MISSIONS	BEGAN	MEMBERSHIP	COMMUNITY
Roman Catholic Church	nr	nr	nr
Moravian Church	nr	nr	nr
Salvation Army	nr	nr	nr
African Independent Church	nr	nr	nr

OPENNESS TO RELIGIOUS CHANGE: not reported

RECEPTIVITY TO CHRISTIANITY: not reported

EVANGELISM PROFILE: not reported

VALIDITY: 6

Nyamwezi can refer to two different social groupings: the larger
3 million person group that includes both Sukuma and Sumbwa.
Under such a use, the groups referred to are geographical
subunits of the Nyamwezi (e.g. the Sukuma occupy the area of
steppe country bordering Lake Victoria). Or it can refer to the
Nyamwezi "proper" who have a far more significant percentage of
Muslims (365,000 out of 460,000 Muslims of the larger group).

Islam entered the area in the 1840s. Its major point of current
growth is in the cities where it is socially advantageous. But
the actual practice of Islam is syncretistic with the traditional
ancestral rites being continued. Some argue that Islam is being
adopted (rather than Christianity) because it permits polygamy
and because it cannot control or monitor the beer drinking which
is common among the Nyamwezi. Most follow the Shafi school of
Sunni Islam, but observance of the major rituals are lax and only
a small minority carry out daily prayers or Ramadan.

Swahili is the national language and the great majority of
Nyamwezi use it as well as their mother tongue. The Church is
present in significant strength. Among the Sukumu, for example,
it is estimated that more than 30% profess Christian faith.
Among the Nyamwezi "proper" where Islam is much more influential,
15% are adherents though animism is said to be intermixed.
Evangelization has thus begun and while there are areas that are
relatively neglected, the potential is present, given the proper
motivation and personnel, to reach out to Islamic Nyamwezi.

EXPANDED DESCRIPTIONS

Pashtuns (Iran)

ALTERNATE NAMES: not reported

SIZE OF GROUP: 3,000   MARC ID: 2054

DISTINCTIVES: language; ethnicity

SOCIAL CHANGE: slow

LANGUAGES: Pashtu (100% speak; V); Farsi (T, S)

SCRIPTURE: Bible

CHRISTIAN LITERACY: not reported

RELIGION: Islam (100% adherents)

CHURCHES AND MISSIONS: not reported

OPENNESS TO RELIGIOUS CHANGE: not reported

RECEPTIVITY TO CHRISTIANITY: not reported

EVANGELISM PROFILE: not reported

VALIDITY: 6

Estimates of the total number of Pashtuns (Pushtuns or Pakhutn)
range from 13 to 19 million, most in Afghanistan and Pakistan.
Those in the Khorisan region of Iran, just over the border from
Afghanistan, are only a tiny outpost on the margins of a very
large Islamic people. We normally refer to Pashtuns in
Afghanistan as Afghans.

Most Pashtuns are farmers or herdsmen. Wheat, barley, sheep,
goats and camels are common denominators of their struggle for
existence. Nomadism is declining significantly so that more and
more are only semi-nomadic. Society is strongly patriarchal with
a reinforcing heirarchy of patrilineally-constituted, extended
families, lineages and tribes. In all there are more than 20
major tribal units within the Pashtun people as a whole. In most
periods of time the average person feels a stronger sense of
identity with the tribal designation than with a larger ethnic
group which includes all Pashtun.

Hanifi Sunni Islam is the majority religion. Village and nomadic
women wear head shawls but not the head to toe "chader" that
"orthodox" Islam advocates in Iran. Many pre-Islamic customs are
present. "Pir" worship is practiced. It is difficult to assess
the degree to which Islam is practiced among the nomadic. Some
nomadic camps have their own "mullahs" and try hard to follow
daily prayers. In many contexts they seem indifferent to
religion unless challenged by an outsider.

Evangelization has taken place among the Pakistani Pashtuns
(Pathans) in the past. Very little has occurred either among the
Pashtuns of Iran or Afghanistan. The small part of this group
living in Iran would have to be rated as almost completely
unreached with the gospel.

Persians of Iran (Iran)

ALTERNATE NAMES: not reported

SIZE OF GROUP: 2,000,000   MARC ID: 4010

DISTINCTIVES: language; religion; sense of unity

SOCIAL CHANGE: moderate

LANGUAGES: Persian (100% speak/60% read; V, T, S, W)

SCRIPTURE: Bible

CHRISTIAN LITERACY: not reported

RELIGION: Christianity (-1% practicing); Islam (98% adherents);
    Bahaism (1% adherents); Other (1% adherents)

CHURCHES AND MISSIONS	BEGAN	MEMBERSHIP	COMMUNITY
Assemblies of God	nr	nr	nr
International Missions	nr	nr	nr
Evangelical Church of Iran	nr	nr	nr
Episcopal Church	nr	nr	nr
Roman Catholic	nr	nr	nr

OPENNESS TO RELIGIOUS CHANGE: not reported

RECEPTIVITY TO CHRISTIANITY: not reported

EVANGELISM PROFILE: not reported

VALIDITY: 6

The Persians justly boast of an ancient and illustrious history.
Their identity as a people hinges not only on modern Farsi, which
serves as the medium for education, literature and government,
but also on the localization of Islam in the Ithna Ashari Shia
"denomination" which the vast majority of them follow.

In the towns and villages of the Persian population (about 50%),
life retains a great deal of its traditional homogeneity.
Religious practices are deeply ingrained and regularly observed.
In the cities modernization and urbanization has and is producing
many of the changes we are familiar with in the West, though the
current Islamic revolution is attempting to channel it in a
distinctly Shiite direction. Distinct occupational classes have
emerged including: (1) former landowners who are now the chief
entrepreneurial class. (2) The governmental administrators and
top officials. (3) The Bazaaris who control the wholesale and
retail markets. (4) Religious leaders. (5) The middle class,
made up largely of educated professionals and white collar
workers. (6) The urban proletariat, making up about a third to a
half of the city population. (7) The underclass of rural
migrants who are unemployed and occupy the shanty towns that are
increasing about the cities.

Evangelization is relatively minimal, in spite of the presence of
Christian Churches. The overwhelming majority of Christians are
from groups such as the Armenians who are "ethnically" Christian.
Very few Iranian Persians have ever converted. Part of the
problem is due to Christian churches whose forms and outlook are
not congenial to Muslim converts. Part of it is due to an
identifica ion of Christianity with the decadent West.

EXPANDED DESCRIPTIONS

Punjabis (Pakistan)

ALTERNATE NAMES: not reported

SIZE OF GROUP: 49,000,000   MARC ID: 4021

DISTINCTIVES: language; residence

SOCIAL CHANGE: moderate

LANGUAGES: Punjabi (100% speak/15% read; V); Urdu (30% speak/15% read; T, S); English (5% speak; V)

SCRIPTURE: Bible

CHRISTIAN LITERACY: not reported

RELIGION: Roman Catholic (1% adherents/1% practicing); Protestant (1% adherents/1% practicing); Islam (99% adherents/49% practicing)

CHURCHES AND MISSIONS	BEGAN	MEMBERSHIP	COMMUNITY
Church of Pakistan	nr	nr	250,000
United Presbyterian	nr	nr	200,000
Lahore Church Council	nr	nr	45,000
Assoc. Reformed Presbyterian	nr	nr	23,000
Roman Catholic	nr	nr	360,000

OPENNESS TO RELIGIOUS CHANGE: not reported

RECEPTIVITY TO CHRISTIANITY: not reported

EVANGELISM PROFILE: not reported

VALIDITY: 6

The Punjabis take their name from the five rivers (panj-ab) which join to form the Punjab river flowing southwest into the Indus. Two-thirds of Pakistan's population is located in this region.

Partition created a mass migration, with 12 million people finding new homes: Hindus moving eastward to India and Muslims west to Pakistan. As a result the Pakistan Punjab is 99% Islamic while India's Punjab is less than 1% Muslim. Diversity of several types is to be found among the Muslim Punjabis: four dialects are spoken, interpretation and pracitice of Islam is divided into Hanafi Sunni (87%), Shia (9%) and Ahmadi (2% - now officially declared not a legitimate Islamic sect by the government), three Sufi brotherhoods are present in strength, and occupational diversity is rooted in the rural-urban split.

Punjabi society is strongly male-oriented. Male dominance and agressiveness is strongly emphasized and kinship is traced patrilineally. Landholding is usually small plots, farmed in an unmechanized fashion. Most marriages are contracted within one's own lineage, within one's own village.

The Church is present in what appears to be large numerical strength, even though Christians are only a small percentage of the population. It must be noted that over 99% of the present Christians are converts from Hinduism or descendents of Hindu converts. Only a small proportion have converted from Islam. At present there is little attraction for the Muslims to become part of such a church.

Qashqa'i (Iran)

ALTERNATE NAMES: not reported

SIZE OF GROUP: 350,000   MARC ID: 2038

DISTINCTIVES: language; political loyalty; occupation;
     ethnicity; sense of unity; discrimination

SOCIAL CHANGE: not reported

LANGUAGES: Qashqa'i (100% speak; V); Farsi (T)

SCRIPTURE: none

CHRISTIAN LITERACY: not reported

RELIGION: Islam (100% adherents)

CHURCHES AND MISSIONS: not reported

OPENNESS TO RELIGIOUS CHANGE: not reported

RECEPTIVITY TO CHRISTIANITY: not reported

EVANGELISM PROFILE: not reported

VALIDITY: 5

The Qashqa'i identity is the result of generations of various
groups allying themselves in a tribal confederacy to compete for
scarce resources in the southwest of Iran in the Zagros
mountains. Several criteria mark a person as a member of this
group: use of Turkic speech, common customs (especially wedding
celebrations), clothing and integration into one of the tribal
subunits, as signalled by descent and acceptance of the
leadership of a headman of one of the subtribes. There are six
major tribes (Amaleh, Dareshuri, Farsimadan, Shesh Boluki,
Kashkuli, Bozorg) and a number of smaller ones.

The vast majority are nomadic pastoralists, engaging in
transhumance of up to 585 Kilometers (350 miles), to find
pasturage with the change of the seasons. Their encampments are
marked by black, goat-hair tents. There is some sedentarization
with families settling down to grow grain but no estimates of its
size are available.

The Qashqa'i view the town and city Muslims with great suspicion,
feeling that more often than not they are oppressed and cheated
by them in commercial dealings. For the same reason they reject
a strict observance of Islam (though they all identify themselves
as Ithna Ashari sect of Shia). They feel that fasting and daily
prayers do not a good Muslim make and point to dishonest Muslim
merchants in the towns who devoutly follow the law. There are a
few who are knowledgeable of Persian and can perform various
ceremonies on demand. Some traveling dervishes also serve to
supply charms and cures.

No scripture has been translated and our sources do not indicate
any evangelization of this group. With the tension of the
Qashqa'i with city Islam, there is a potential for developing
relationships of trust on the basis of honest dealings that could
lead to opportunities for evangelization.

179

EXPANDED DESCRIPTIONS

Redjang (Indonesia)

ALTERNATE NAMES: Rejang; Rejong-Lebong

SIZE OF GROUP: 300,000   MARC ID: 694

DISTINCTIVES: sense of unity; language; ethnicity; occupation

SOCIAL CHANGE: not reported

LANGUAGES: Rejang (100% speak/45% read; V); Bahasa Indonesian (40% speak; T)

SCRIPTURE: none

CHRISTIAN LITERACY: not reported

RELIGION: Islam (99% adherents); Christianity (-1% practicing)

CHURCHES AND MISSIONS	BEGAN	MEMBERSHIP	COMMUNITY
Gereja Kristen Injili Sumatera	nr	nr	nr
Selatan (Gekisus)	1974	nr	nr
Gereja Kristen Injili	nr	nr	nr
Indonesia (GKII)	1968	nr	nr

OPENNESS TO RELIGIOUS CHANGE: somewhat closed

RECEPTIVITY TO CHRISTIANITY: very reluctant

EVANGELISM PROFILE: not reported

VALIDITY: 6

Among the Redjang, one cannot yet count a single Christian. Muslim since the 1860s, their sense of history and their isolation from Christian contact has reinforced a dynamic cultural complex that shows little dissatisfaction.

Located on the Western coast of South Sumatra in the province of Bengkulu, 85% live in remote rural areas. No missionary activity was permitted from 1824 until WEC missionaries moved into the area in 1952.

The Redjang are divided into five main groups by areas of residence: the Djang Lebong in the fertile upland Lebong region, the Djang Musai (in the Musai valley), the Djang Lai, the Djang Bekulau and the Djang Abeus. They are stratified by a traditional heirarchy. The social structure is also reinforced by the government's recognition of village headmen who rule with the aid of a tribunal of village elders from the various households.

Life promises to change in significant ways. The Indonesian government is planning on transmigrating 100,000 Javanese and Balinese to live in the Bengkulu province. Among those new families will be numbers of Christians.

Except for private contacts with a few members of the Redjang tribe, no special effort has ever been made to reach this tribe. To the north the Serawai have a small indigenous church won out of a similar animist-Islamic cultural complex. Until significant effort is made, it is difficult to know what God might do in evangelizing the Redjang.

Sama Bangingi (Philippines)

ALTERNATE NAMES: Samal Balangingi

SIZE OF GROUP: 70,000   MARC ID: 1148

DISTINCTIVES: language; occupation; ethnicity; religion

SOCIAL CHANGE: moderate

LANGUAGES: Sinama Bangini (100% speak; V); Tausug (90% speak;
    T); Chavacano

SCRIPTURE: none

CHRISTIAN LITERACY: not reported

RELIGION: Islam-Animist (90% adherents); Christianity (-1%
    practicing); Islam (9% adherents)

CHURCHES AND MISSIONS	BEGAN	MEMBERSHIP	COMMUNITY
Christian & Msny. Alliance	nr	nr	nr
Summer Institute Linguistics	nr	nr	nr

OPENNESS TO RELIGIOUS CHANGE: very closed

RECEPTIVITY TO CHRISTIANITY: reluctant

EVANGELISM PROFILE: not reported

VALIDITY: 6

The Bangingi or Balangingi are the most widely dispersed of the
eastern Sama with communities to be found from the eastern coast
of Basilan and the southern and eastern coasts of Zamboanga
Penisula, to the Samales islands. Their name is taken from the
island of Balanguinigui where they trace their origin and
dialect. They recognize themselves as a distinctive people
(bangsa) within the larger Muslim people of the Sulu archipelago.

The Bangingi are the most completely Islamized of the Sama
peoples. But, in common with neighboring groups, the Sunni Islam
of the Shafi school is combined with a variety of traditional
beliefs and practices without a clear awareness that they are
non-Muslim in nature. Religious involvement varies widely, with
the local imam and wealthy families being the most devout in the
observance of Muslim custom. Traditional religious pratitioners
such as the healers and midwives are to be found in all
communities.

The recent fighting between the Philippine government and the
Muslim rebellion has had major disruptive effects on all of the
Sama peoples. It is only part of a continuing history of
warfare, piracy and struggle through which the Sama peoples have
maintained continuity partly because so much of their life has
been sea-focused rather than agriculture based. When trouble
grows too intense, they are able to slip away to other bays and
coasts.

Missions has also been disrupted. With missionaries kidnapped on
three occasions since 1976, many agencies have withdrawn
personnel from outlying areas. At present resistance to
Christians in any form is high while the opportunity for
evangelism is very low.

EXPANDED DESCRIPTIONS

Sama Pangutaran (Philippines)

ALTERNATE NAMES: Samal of Pangutaran

SIZE OF GROUP: 15,000   MARC ID: 1159

DISTINCTIVES: language; occupation; social class; religion

SOCIAL CHANGE: not reported

LANGUAGES: Sama Pangutaran (100% speak; V); Tausug (80% speak; T); English (15% speak); Tagalog (20% speak)

SCRIPTURE: none

CHRISTIAN LITERACY: 35%

RELIGION: Christianity (-1% practicing); Islam (99% adherents)

CHURCHES AND MISSIONS	BEGAN	MEMBERSHIP	COMMUNITY
Evangelical Church	nr	1	10
Christian & Msny. Alliance	nr	nr	nr

OPENNESS TO RELIGIOUS CHANGE: very closed

RECEPTIVITY TO CHRISTIANITY: reluctant

EVANGELISM PROFILE: not reported

VALIDITY: 6

When Spain arrived in the mid-16th century to seize the Philippines, most Filipinos accepted its rule. But not the Muslims, entrenched in the south and west. Thus began a basic division in Filipino society that festers even to the present.

The Samal peoples (one of four major Muslim groups) are located on the islands of the Sulu Archipelago which stretch from Mindanao to the north eastern tip of Kalimantan (what formerly was called the island of Borneo). Pangutaran is in west central Sulu, to the west of the large island of Jolo.

The Sama Pangutaran speak their own dialect and are relatively isolated from the rest of Philippine life because of the remoteness of their island home. While they are in a Tausug area, they have their own indigenous roots. Attempts to evangelize them in the Tausug or English language using interpreters have failed.

Islam is well established, but coexists with many unorthodox interpretations and practices that continue from the 18th century when they were "converted." They are largely satisfied with their way of life and the current warfare and hostility has simply stiffened their determination not to change.

Since the 1940s itinerant missionary work by Christian Missionary Alliance has been present. A small church has been established in Pangutaran but very few indigenous people have responded. At present there is no resident pastor. SIL is engaged in Bible translation work with Pangutaran people who settled on another island some 50 years ago. Portions of the Torah, three of the Gospels and Acts are to be published in 1980. Until the political climate improves Filipinos will be the only evangelists possible. Literacy evangelism and vernacular home Bible studies have the most promise for future evangelism.

Sarakole (Senegal)

ALTERNATE NAMES: Soninke

SIZE OF GROUP: 67,600   MARC ID: 1139

DISTINCTIVES: not reported

SOCIAL CHANGE: not reported

LANGUAGES: Soninke (100% speak; V)

SCRIPTURE: none

CHRISTIAN LITERACY: not reported

RELIGION: Islam (100% adherents)

CHURCHES AND MISSIONS: not reported

OPENNESS TO RELIGIOUS CHANGE: not reported

RECEPTIVITY TO CHRISTIANITY: not reported

EVANGELISM PROFILE: not reported

VALIDITY: 6

Over one million people derive their identity from the Sarakole. Most are to be found in Mali (about 300,000), Upper Volta and Ivory Coast. Only in more isolated pockets do they speak the Azer dialect of Soninke, their native tongue (and Bakel in Senegal is one of them). In many other places of settlement, they have adopted the tongues of the dominant tribes that surround them (e.g. Diola in Upper Volta).

The Sarakole are agriculturalists, living in villages and towns in six West African countries. Many also have taken up trading as a profession. They were forcibly converted to Islam in the 11th century and were for a period of time very active propagators. Even today the most learned Islamic scholars of West Africa tend to be Sarakole.

This is not to say that the traditional elements of animism have disappeared with the passing of the centuries. The average Sarakole still views much of the world in terms of spiritual forces and the "witchcraft" complex is vitally present in everyday life. Charms and amulets are given to each child at birth to protect it in this difficult world. The "shadow soul" of an individual is subject to being attacked and being eaten by a witch.

There is a stratification of clans in the society which includes a "clerical" clan which supplies the candidates for imam status. Many of the men belong to Tijaniya, though there are other tariqa to be found among the Soninke, including the Hammal sect centered in Mauritania.

Our sources do not indicate any Christians or current evangelism among the Sarakole in Senegal. There is a translation need. No scripture is known to exist in the Azer dialect of Soninke. More information is needed to assess the current status of evangelization among the Sarakole.

EXPANDED DESCRIPTIONS

Sasak (Indonesia)

ALTERNATE NAMES: Waktu Lima; Waktu Telu

SIZE OF GROUP: 1,600,000   MARC ID: 1095

DISTINCTIVES: language; ethnicity

SOCIAL CHANGE: not reported

LANGUAGES: Sasak (100% speak; V)

SCRIPTURE: portions

CHRISTIAN LITERACY: not reported

RELIGION: Islam-Animist (99% adherents); Protestant (1%
    adherents/1% practicing)

CHURCHES AND MISSIONS: not reported

OPENNESS TO RELIGIOUS CHANGE: very closed

RECEPTIVITY TO CHRISTIANITY: not reported

EVANGELISM PROFILE: not reported

VALIDITY: 6

The Sasak are indigenous inhabitants of Lombok, an island just
east of Bali in Indonesia. Since the Dutch Colonial period
(1895) this people has exhibited a marked division between the
more isolated, traditional Waktu Telu and the more Islamized,
outward going Waktu Lima.

The Waktu Telu are found in the more marginal, rural areas.
Their village life continues to be strongly communal, with
religion revolving about indigenous ritual feasts oriented to
life crises. While nominally Muslim, their concern is largely
with customary law (adat). Islamic rituals such as prayer and an
abbreviated observance of Ramadan is performed on behalf of the
village by the local religious practitioner. They view the far
more numerous Waktu Lima as those who have left their true
birthright.

The Waktu Lima are found in the plains and near the major roads
and towns. Whereas most Waktu Telu own farms, nearly two-thirds
of the Waktu Lima are landless. They are oriented to the cash
economy. Their diversity and specialization in occupations is
marked. They travel and have a great deal more contact with the
outside. Islamic religion is more central to their lifestyle and
they see hajj as an important goal for family effort and savings.
They proselyte the Waktu Telu and view them as backward pagans.

Each village is classed as one or the other, containing its own
mosque and school. Village headmen are assisted by a number of
other elders and "adat" specialists. Social relationships are
stratified by a "caste" system dividing families into aristocracy
and commoners. The aristocracy has subcastes and caste titles
preface a person's name.

Evangelization has had little impact on Lombok. The number of
"foreigners" (Indonesians or expatriates) is small and most
Christians are temporary government workers or immigrants from
other parts of Indonesia.

Senufo (Ivory Coast)

ALTERNATE NAMES: Sienamana

SIZE OF GROUP: 300,000   MARC ID: 181

DISTINCTIVES: language; ethnicity

SOCIAL CHANGE: not reported

LANGUAGES: Senari (100% speak; V); Dyoula (25% speak); French
    (9% speak)

SCRIPTURE: portions

CHRISTIAN LITERACY: 25%

RELIGION: Animism (70% adherents); Islam-Animist (20%
    adherents); Christianity (2% adherents/2% practicing)

CHURCHES AND MISSIONS	BEGAN	MEMBERSHIP	COMMUNITY
Eglise Baptiste	1964	nr	255
Roman Catholic Church	nr	nr	nr

OPENNESS TO RELIGIOUS CHANGE: somewhat open

RECEPTIVITY TO CHRISTIANITY: reluctant

EVANGELISM PROFILE: not reported

VALIDITY: 6

The Senufo of Ivory Coast (located around Korhogo and Odienne)
are part of the southern subdivision of a larger ethnic unit that
totals perhaps two million. Sienamana is the indigenous name,
but one that is not widely used in the literature on this group.

Until World War II the Senufo were rather resistant to
Islamization. They engaged in agricultural life in a highly
communal society. The communal nature of their life with its
associated strong ancestral cult made them rather resistant to
outsider innovations such as Islam or Christian faith. Everyone
is seen as a member of an extended family and a hamlet. Fields
are worked collectively and goods are shared communally with
those in need. No individual becomes a Christian or Muslim
unless the group within which he or she is located makes the same
commitment.

Islam penetrated the southern Senufo principally through the
chiefs who embraced Islam in the 19th century. At present those
who are becoming Muslims are younger people who have left their
traditional villages and migrated to the city. Islam has been
generally preferred to Christianity because it permits more of
the ancestral beliefs than Christian churches do. To become
either Muslim or Christian is seen as politically and
economically advantageous in the city.

The Baptist and Roman Catholics are present and there is a small
church. The Conservative Baptist are at work on a translation of
the New Testament which should be completed in the next few
years. The history and structure of Senufo life suggests that
significant advances are possible only through evangelization
that aims at converting whole villages or extended families.

EXPANDED DESCRIPTIONS

Shahsavans (Iran)

ALTERNATE NAMES: not reported

SIZE OF GROUP: 180,000   MARC ID: 2043

DISTINCTIVES: language; occupation; ethnicity

SOCIAL CHANGE: very slow

LANGUAGES: Azerbaijani (Shahsavani) (100% speak; V); Farsi (T)

SCRIPTURE: none

CHRISTIAN LITERACY: not reported

RELIGION: Islam (100% adherents)

CHURCHES AND MISSIONS: not reported

OPENNESS TO RELIGIOUS CHANGE: not reported

RECEPTIVITY TO CHRISTIANITY: not reported

EVANGELISM PROFILE: not reported

VALIDITY: 6

It would be difficult to live with a name that means "lovers of
the Shah" after the Iranian revolution of 1979. The some 180,000
(estimates range from 65-300,000 total) Shahsavans are so named
because 380 years ago they were placed in the region southwest of
the Caspian Sea to help control the region as loyalists of the
Shah. Originally they had been fierce warriors, followers of
fanatic religious chieftans (of the Qizilbash tribes) but
abandoned them when Shah Abbas appealed to the Shah lovers to
follow him.

Most are now settled villagers. Some 5,000 families still retain
the pastoral nomadism from which they were derived. They are
organized into "tribes" (tayfeh), each led by a chief and
constituted by a number of lineages made up of all who trace
descent four generations back to a common ancestor. A lineage
(tireh) forms the important unit of participation in marriage,
Ramadan and Muharran. Each lineage is itself divided into about
25 families. The "grey beard" is the most important man among
these families and he is looked to to direct communal activities.

Families normally live together so that a single "tent" will have
four or five households (usually brothers or patrilineally
related cousins) who share herds and work. Women are not
secluded and they normally do not wear the veil, though they will
cover the bottom part of their face in the presence of unrelated
men. The most visible distinctive mark of the Shahsavans is
their use of a round tent similar to the yurts of Central Asia.

Shahsavans are Shia Muslims and have a clear sense of self
identity that revolves around Islam. Our sources do not indicate
any known Christians in this group. Nor is there information as
to literacy or whether the Shahsavans could read the Azerbaijani
Bible now being revised.

Subanen, Sindangan (Philippines)

ALTERNATE NAMES: Subanen, Eastern

SIZE OF GROUP: 80,000   MARC ID: 1062

DISTINCTIVES: language; ethnicity

SOCIAL CHANGE: not reported

LANGUAGES: Subanun (100% speak/6% read; V); Cebuano bisaya
     (70% speak; T); English (7% speak); Filipino (1% speak)

SCRIPTURE: portions

CHRISTIAN LITERACY: not reported

RELIGION: Animism (94% adherents); Christianity (-1%
     practicing); Christo-Paganism (3% adherents);
     Islam-Animist (2% adherents)

CHURCHES AND MISSIONS   BEGAN MEMBERSHIP COMMUNITY
     Christian & Msny. Alliance   nr   nr   nr

OPENNESS TO RELIGIOUS CHANGE: somewhat closed

RECEPTIVITY TO CHRISTIANITY: receptive

EVANGELISM PROFILE: not reported

VALIDITY: 6

Subanen literally means "up-stream people." It is a term used by
the low land dwellers to designate any interior pagans living in
Zamboanga and the mountains of western Mindanao. The vast
majority of them have in the past practiced slash and burn
agriculture, growing rice and maize. Some fishing is done in the
nearby streams.

Traditionally the Subanen have been exploited by the Muslims.
Now with the large influx of Christians they face another form of
economic discrimination and have been threatened with the loss of
the lands they have farmed. Some have been forced into adopting
a more settled form of agriculture as a strategy for holding onto
land.

Few have become either Muslim or Christian. Those who have
married into Muslim families or converted are locally known as
Kalibugan. In the past religious practices have not played a
major role in life except in the concern with health. There are
a significant number of rites and formula for dealing with
various types of illnesses. The religious specialists act as
priest, shaman and medium. Traditional festivals include beer
drinking and the pig is also eaten on ceremonial occasions.

The traditional tensions between the Subanen and the Muslim
population would indicate that there is the potential for
Christian intervention that would be favorably received. But the
influx of nominal Christian Filipinos and their desire for land
is creating a negative image. The Christian and Missionary
Alliance is present and engaged in translation work, but very few
of the Subanen have had a clear opportunity to understand the
gospel.

EXPANDED DESCRIPTIONS

Sundanese (Indonesia)

ALTERNATE NAMES: Orang Sunda

SIZE OF GROUP: 20,000,000   MARC ID: 273

DISTINCTIVES: language; ethnicity; religion; residence

SOCIAL CHANGE: not reported

LANGUAGES: Sundanese (100% speak/30% read; V); Indonesian (60%
    speak; T); Dutch (5% speak)

SCRIPTURE: Bible

CHRISTIAN LITERACY: 50%

RELIGION: Islam-Animist (99% adherents); Christianity (1%
    adherents/-1% practicing)

CHURCHES AND MISSIONS	BECAN	MEMBERSHIP	COMMUNITY
Christian & Msny. Alliance	1970	nr	100
Indigenous Churches	nr	nr	300
Methodist Church	1971	nr	100
Pentecostal Churches	1919	nr	nr
Sundanese Reformed Church	1940	nr	nr

OPENNESS TO RELIGIOUS CHANGE: somewhat open

RECEPTIVITY TO CHRISTIANITY: receptive

EVANGELISM PROFILE: not reported

VALIDITY: 6

Most Sundanese are wet rice farmers. Average land holdings are
small and most families engage in small craft, trade and seasonal
labor to provide essential cash for other goods.

Islam came to the Sundanese in the 1500s and virtually all
consider themselves to be Muslims. Islamic law is adapted to
local customary law (adat). The distinction between the abangan
(lax) and santri (rigorous observance of Islamic principles) is
not made among the Sundanese as it is among the Javanese.

A variety of pre-Islamic practices are integrated into the
religious life. Magic is important for healing, divination and
numerology. Mystical movements seeking unity through ecstasy are
centered in rural Islamic schools. The rice goddess, Dewi Sri,
figures importantly in such things as the wedding ceremony.
Since World War II significant progress has been made in teaching
Islam. Public schools offer instruction as well as private
teachers so that the level of awareness of Islam is rising.
About 60% of the men and 5% of the women are estimated as
regularly attending the mosque.

The Church is present in a variety of denominations. It is
estimated that the eighteen Pentecostal denominations and the
Sundanese Reformed Church have a total membership of about 50,000
(or no more than 1/4th of 1% of the population). Less than 10%
are possibly hearing the gospel. The Bible, originally
translated in 1891, is undergoing translation.

Tajik (Iran)

ALTERNATE NAMES: not reported

SIZE OF GROUP: 15,000   MARC ID: 2053

DISTINCTIVES: language; ethnicity

SOCIAL CHANGE: slow

LANGUAGES: Dari (100% speak/10% read; V); Farsi (T, S)

SCRIPTURE: portions

CHRISTIAN LITERACY: not reported

RELIGION: Islam (100% adherents)

CHURCHES AND MISSIONS: not reported

OPENNESS TO RELIGIOUS CHANGE: not reported

RECEPTIVITY TO CHRISTIANITY: not reported

EVANGELISM PROFILE: not reported

VALIDITY: 5

Tajik total about 6 million in at least four countries. By far
the largest concentration are to be found in northern Afghanistan
(3.6 million) and the USSR (2.5 million). The small group in
Iran is thus only a marginal settlement, separated from the main
body of their people.

Most Tajik are mountain farmers and herdsmen, living in the
valleys of high mountains. Iranian Tajik are located in the area
of Zabol, Sistan and the Baluchistan province. They occupy domed
beehive huts that are common to the Iranian plateau. Farms are
individually owned though often more than one family will have a
hand in the work or provision of water.

Islam is the universal profession. Our source does not indicate
what school is followed. The vast majority of the larger group
is Hanafi Sunni, though there are Ismailis in the Pamir mountains
of Afghanistan. Most typically the rural woman is not veiled but
wears a head shawl which can be used to partially hide the face
at the approach of strangers. Tajik who have settled in the city
begin to take on the more "orthodox" ways and women often adopt
the head to toe "chador" as a symbol of their advance in status.

Family structure is patrilineal and patriarchal. Affairs in a
village are governed by a council of elders, though the opinion
of women is consulted. Some short-range seasonal migration to
find pasture for the livestock may break a family group up
temporarily.

There is no indication of evangelization efforts. Portions of
the Bible have been translated and work is in progress to produce
more of the New Testament. The 1979 revolution in Iran will
undoubtedly have a major effect on the potential for further
evangelization, but no current information is available as to
what effect it has had up to the present.

EXPANDED DESCRIPTIONS

Tatars (Soviet Russia)

ALTERNATE NAMES: not reported

SIZE OF GROUP: 6,000,000   MARC ID: 4008

DISTINCTIVES: ethnicity; sense of unity

SOCIAL CHANGE: moderate

LANGUAGES: Tatar dialects (V); Tatar (S)

SCRIPTURE: Bible

CHRISTIAN LITERACY: not reported.

RELIGION: Christianity (1% adherents/1% practicing); Islam (60%
    adherents); Secularism (39% adherents)

CHURCHES AND MISSIONS	BEGAN	MEMBERSHIP	COMMUNITY
Russian Orthodox	nr	nr	nr
Protestant	nr	nr	nr

OPENNESS TO RELIGIOUS CHANGE: not reported

RECEPTIVITY TO CHRISTIANITY: not reported

EVANGELISM PROFILE: not reported

VALIDITY: 6

The Tatars are the fifth largest ethnic group within the USSR.
Though almost 2 million are to be found concentrated in the Tatar
Autonomous USSR, the remaining Tatars are scattered in 30
different provinces, the majority of them in cities where
industry is growing. Those engaged in agriculture are to be
found especially on collectives in the Volga region.

Islam remains a point of self-identification though its hold is
weakening much more substantially than among Russia's other
Muslims. This is due in part to the urban character of the
Tatars. They have been more thoroughly Russified than other
Islamic populations and a significant number live in a way
indistinguishable from Russians. The true estimate of
secularists as opposed to those still strongly adhering to Islam
is not known. The figures given are a guess based on a higher
percentage Muslim than Soviet scientists have "found" in their
survey of rural Tatars.

The Tatars are a diverse group, disperate both in the dialects
they speak, and in their geographical spread. There are some
7,000 Tatars in New York City! Pockets of population are known
to exist in at least five countries outside the USSR.

Christians are present among this group but their numbers are
small and can only be guessed at. Some translation work is in
progress. Much more information is needed if we are to give an
estimate of the contemporary status of evangelization. We have
no indications of the status of evangelization among the Tatars
of New York who might act as a possible link to the larger Tatar
populations. The Tatars of Finland also have close contact with
Tatar ASSR and might serve as a base for evangelistic work.

Tancouleur (Senegal)

ALTERNATE NAMES: Futankobe; Haopholaren; Tukulor

SIZE OF GROUP: 464,700   MARC ID: 1137

DISTINCTIVES: religion; residence

SOCIAL CHANGE: not reported

LANGUAGES: Tancouleur (V)

SCRIPTURE: portions

CHRISTIAN LITERACY: not reported

RELIGION: Islam (100% adherents)

CHURCHES AND MISSIONS: not reported

OPENNESS TO RELIGIOUS CHANGE: not reported

RECEPTIVITY TO CHRISTIANITY: not reported

EVANGELISM PROFILE: not reported

VALIDITY: 5

While the Taucouleur (Tukulor) speak a dialect closely related to
Fulani, they are distinguished from them by virtue of the
important role they played in the history of Islam in West Africa
and by the fact that they are sedentary. While they show
evidence of intermarriage with the Fulani (and the Soninke), they
have a clearly distinct identity.

Their society is divided up into four social strata. The
aristocratic, clerical class reflects the fact that the first to
embrace Islam in the 11th century was the ruling class. Now most
Islamic learning and scholarship comes from this strata. The
middle class is composed of fishers, farmers, administrators and
tradesmen. The lower middle strata includes skilled craftsmen
and such occupational slots as storytellers and musicians. The
lower class is made up of day laborers, servants and slaves, both
free and bound. Mobility between these classes is virtually nil.

In spite of the great length of time in which Islam has been
present and the popularity of the strict Tijaniya brotherhood,
Islam is inextricably penetrated by traditional animistic ideas
and practices. Divination, witchcraft (often practiced by the
Islamic cleric -- the midibbo), and magic are widespread.
Amulets and charms are made and sold by Islamic religious
leaders. A belief in "baraga" (supernatural power) is common and
religious leaders thought to possess it are sought after for the
miracles they can work.

The Taucouleur are concentrated in Senegal along the banks of the
Dagana river to about halfway between Matam and Bakel. They are
also found in Gambia and western Mali. Settlement pattern tends
to be in villages governed by elders.

There are no known Christians among the Taucouleur. There
apparently is a very minimal amount of evangelization taking
place and some translation work is in progress.

EXPANDED DESCRIPTIONS

Tansug (Philippines)

ALTERNATE NAMES: Tawsug; Sulu; Joloano

SIZE OF GROUP: 500,000   MARC ID: 635

DISTINCTIVES: language; ethnicity; religion

SOCIAL CHANGE: not reported

LANGUAGES: Tausug (100% speak/15% read; V); Tagalog (30% speak); English (30% speak)

SCRIPTURE: portions

CHRISTIAN LITERACY: not reported

RELIGION: Islam (99% adherents); Christianity (1% adherents/1% practicing)

CHURCHES AND MISSIONS   BEGAN   MEMBERSHIP   COMMUNITY
    Christian & Msny. Alliance   1930   nr   nr
    Roman Catholic Church   1900   nr   nr

OPENNESS TO RELIGIOUS CHANGE: not reported

RECEPTIVITY TO CHRISTIANITY: very reluctant

EVANGELISM PROFILE: not reported

VALIDITY: 6

The Tausug are numerically and culturally dominant in the Sulu Archipelago between Mindanao of the Philippines and the northeastern coast of Kalimantan. Never at rest under any central Filipino control, the Tausug are known for their fierce piracy and slave trade. Under various Sultanates beginning in the middle of the fifteenth century, the Tausug have become firm Sunni Muslims of the Shafi school.

Their main concentration is on the island of Jolo, but they are also on Pata, Marunggas, Tapul, Lusus, Siasi, coastal Basilan, and Zamboanga del Sur and Cotabato. In Sabah they are known as Suluk. The present Moro National Liberation Front had its origins in large measure among Muslim students from Sulu. Even at present the Philippine government has not established control over the interior of Jolo. As a result of the warfare and the traditional independence of the area, the Tausug have a strong solidarity against "Christians" who dominate them and repress their aspirations for a separate state.

Islam is combined with traditional customary elements. Folk medicine is important as well as the advice and leadership of the local imam. Charms and beliefs in spirits are crucial in understanding the daily adjustments people make in order to guarantee success and good fortune.

Because of the tensions of the political situation as well as long standing feelings of superiority, the Tausug are not open to Christian faith. They see the Christian Filipino as an oppressor and frustrator of national and Muslim aspirations. Only an outsider with Muslim sympathies could serve effectively among this people.

Teda (Chad)

ALTERNATE NAMES: not reported

SIZE OF GROUP: 10,000   MARC ID: 4012

DISTINCTIVES: language; occupation; religion; kinship

SOCIAL CHANGE: slow

LANGUAGES: Teda (V); Arabic (T); Dazaga (T)

SCRIPTURE: not reported

CHRISTIAN LITERACY: not reported

RELIGION: Islam (100% adherents)

CHURCHES AND MISSIONS: not reported

OPENNESS TO RELIGIOUS CHANGE: not reported

RECEPTIVITY TO CHRISTIANITY: not reported

EVANGELISM PROFILE: not reported

VALIDITY: 6

Most of the Teda are isolated in the mountains of the Tibesti
massif on the Libyan-Chad border. They are categorized with a
number of groups which are very similar in cultural patterns,
live in the same general area, and are thought to have originated
in the Tibesti massif. But their particular dialect is mutually
intelligible only with Dazaga speaking groups such as the Daza
and their vassals the Azza.

Life for the Teda revolves about pastoralism. The women do most
of the herding. The men sell animals and travel for trade
purposes. Both share the labor connected with growing various
grains and vegetables.

Family life is organized by patrilineal clans, though bilateral
kindreds are present and considered important for indicating all
those a person cannot marry. Each person can trace descent back
to one of a dozen common male ancestors. The recent drought has
had major impact in that many men have had to leave their homes
altogether in search of food and income from well-drilling and
work in the oil industry in Libya.

Islam dates from the Arab conquest of the area, but schools have
been present only for the past 100 years. Pre-Islamic ideas are
unconsciously integrated into their life-style with no awareness
of discrepancy. The prayers and Jamadan as well as the other
pillars are carefully observed. "Mallams" are not normally
present in the mountain areas. Those who receive education to
become religious leaders generally do not return to such Spartan
areas.

Our sources do not indicate any current evangelization efforts.
There is a definite translation need. This part of Chad has been
politically sensitive, since it has harbored Muslim guerrilla
forces fighting the Chad government for the rights of the Muslim
population.

EXPANDED DESCRIPTIONS

Temne (Sierra Leone)

ALTERNATE NAMES: Aythemne

SIZE OF GROUP: 1,000,000   MARC ID: 123

DISTINCTIVES: language; ethnicity; kinship

SOCIAL CHANGE: not reported

LANGUAGES: Temne (100% speak/6% read; V); Krio (25% speak);
      English (5% speak)

SCRIPTURE: New Testament

CHRISTIAN LITERACY: 3%

RELIGION: Animism (60% adherents); Islam (34% adherents);
      Protestant (4% adherents/4% practicing); Roman Catholic (2%
      adherents/2% practicing)

CHURCHES AND MISSIONS	BEGAN	MEMBERSHIP	COMMUNITY
Assemblies of God	nr	nr	350
Missionary Church Association	nr	nr	400
Roman Catholic Church	nr	nr	nr
Sierra Leone Wesleyan Church	1893	nr	750
United Pentecostal Church	nr	nr	250

OPENNESS TO RELIGIOUS CHANGE: somewhat open

RECEPTIVITY TO CHRISTIANITY: receptive

EVANGELISM PROFILE: not reported

VALIDITY: 6

Fully one-third of Sierra Leone is inhabited by the Temne
Chiefdoms. Divided into nearly 40 chiefdoms, the Temne are found
in the northern part of the coastal bush region and the
neighboring sections of rain forest. The vast majority (95%) are
farmers growing rice as the basic staple. Fishing is found in
areas along rivers and the coast.

The chiefdoms are divided into those in which the Muslim clerics
conduct the installation ceremony and those where the new chiefs
are installed by the male societies (Poro, Ragbenle or Ramena).
Islam is growing in influence and strength among the Temne but in
the southern areas where Poro is strong, Islam is resisted.

Christian witness has been present for a great length of time and
there is a sizeable minority (nearly 6%) who profess some form of
Christian commitment. The new Testament was completed in 1955
and some revisions of it and Old Testament portions are underway.
Lutheran Bible Translators are present and active. The Temne are
easily accessible and there is a leadership training program for
Temne pastors and evangelists. At present, however, Islam is
growing more rapidly and is also in the process of purifying the
practice of its adherents. The next 25 years will be crucial to
the evangelization of the still predominant animist sector and
for the creation of new approaches to evangelizing those who have
become Muslims.

Thai Islam (Malay) (Thailand)

ALTERNATE NAMES: Pattani Malay

SIZE OF GROUP: 1,700,000   MARC ID: 39

DISTINCTIVES: language; ethnicity; religion; sense of unity; residence

SOCIAL CHANGE: slow

LANGUAGES: Mala, Pattani (100% speak/15% read; V); Thai, Central (35% speak/18% read; S, T)

SCRIPTURE: portions

CHRISTIAN LITERACY: 20%

RELIGION: Christianity (1% adherents/1% practicing); Islam (2% adherents); Islam-Animist (97% adherents)

CHURCHES AND MISSIONS	BEGAN	MEMBERSHIP	COMMUNITY
Independent Church (OMF)	1953	20	40

OPENNESS TO RELIGIOUS CHANGE: somewhat closed

RECEPTIVITY TO CHRISTIANITY: very reluctant

EVANGELISM PROFILE: not reported

VALIDITY: 6

The largest concentration of Thai Islam is among the ethnic Malays who are predominant in the southernmost province of the peninsula. It is difficult to distinguish them from the southern Thais who are also Muslims because of similarity and bilingualism. Both groups account for approximately 80-90% of the population in the provinces of Yala, Pattani, Narathiwat and Satun, with Malays by far the most common.

Some 300 years ago the southern peoples converted en masse to Islam from Hinduism. This significant minority within the Thai nation fears exploitation and hence is suspicious of other ethnic groups. Malay Muslims tend to look down on Thai speaking Muslims, as those in the process of acculturation and compromisers by their acceptance of Thai ways and customs. Malay Muslims belong to the Shafi school of the Sunni tradition. Yet this orthodoxy is complemented by beliefs and rituals that are clearly Hindu-Buddhist or animist in origin.

The Overseas Missionary Fellowship is the only mission working with Thai Islamic populations. Since 1953 OMF has focused in the south, with 19 missionaries at present. Linguistic studies have led to the projected 1980 publication of a Pattani Malay dialect New Testament. The Saiburi Christian hospital and various leprosy treatment clinics have been the most welcome presence among the Muslims. As of 1979 there were only a couple of small groups of Malay believers and adherents. The most receptive have been Islamic people who have been treated for leprosy.

Thailand's religious tolerance provides a context within which evangelization can take place. Social control is still strong and the pressure against conversion among the Malay Muslims is still present. Yet the nominalism and accomodation of animistic elements suggests there are opportunities not being seized.

195

EXPANDED DESCRIPTIONS

Turkish Workers (Belgium)

ALTERNATE NAMES: not reported

SIZE OF GROUP: 60,000   MARC ID: 4020

DISTINCTIVES: occupation; ethnicity; religion; kinship;
    social class

SOCIAL CHANGE: moderate

LANGUAGES: Turkish (V); Kurdish (V)

SCRIPTURE: Bible

CHRISTIAN LITERACY: not reported

RELIGION: Christianity (3% adherents/1% practicing); Islam (97%
    adherents)

CHURCHES AND MISSIONS	BEGAN	MEMBERSHIP	COMMUNITY
Gospel Missionary Union	nr	nr	nr
Operation Mobilization	nr	nr	nr
Orthodox Church	nr	nr	nr

OPENNESS TO RELIGIOUS CHANGE: not reported

RECEPTIVITY TO CHRISTIANITY: not reported

EVANGELISM PROFILE: not reported

VALIDITY: 6

Belgium factories and construction industries are increasingly
powered by the labor of foreign workers. Nearly 60,000 workers
originate in Turkey. While this is less than a 20th the number
found in neighboring Germany, it represents a major opportunity
for evangelization (see description on Turkish Workers, UNREACHED
PEOPLES, '79, p. 243). The majority are concentrated in one
section of Brussels, with a few thousand to be found in the other
industrial cities of Belgium.

Ethnically, Turkish workers include the Turks proper, the Kurds,
and a small Syrian Community from the Eastern part of Turkey.
The Syrians are the only Christian portion. Most others are
Muslims, overwhelmingly Sunni with some Alevi Muslims.
Secularization is advanced and piety is often more strongly a
nationalistic and cultural affair than a matter of religiosity.
Consequently community life manifests fewer mosques and
religiously organized events than is true for the North African
Arabs who also are present in Brussels in large numbers.

Little is being done to evangelize the Turkish workers in
Belgium. Unlike Germany, where several missionaries are
deployed, most evangelism is sporadic and sponsored by Operation
Mobilization in the summertime. Colportage and films are
utilized. The Gospel Missionary Union has a small outreach to
the Orthodox Christian community of Syrians. But at present
almost nothing is directed at the Turks and Kurds in a manner
that would either win their confidence or provide a context where
they might feel comfortable. At present the only center for
Muslim evangelization and worship is Arab in orientation.

Turkomans (Iran)

ALTERNATE NAMES: Turkmen

SIZE OF GROUP: 550,000   MARC ID: 2032

DISTINCTIVES: language; occupation; ethnicity; religion;
    sense of unity

SOCIAL CHANGE: very slow

LANGUAGES: Turkomani (100% speak; V); Farsi (T)

SCRIPTURE: portions

CHRISTIAN LITERACY: not reported

RELIGION: Islam (100% adherents)

CHURCHES AND MISSIONS: not reported

OPENNESS TO RELIGIOUS CHANGE: very closed

RECEPTIVITY TO CHRISTIANITY: very reluctant

EVANGELISM PROFILE: not reported

VALIDITY: 6

Even the name of their home sounds ominous: the Black Sand
Desert (Kara Kum). For surrounding peoples it has been the
source of raids and frustration. For centuries the Turkoman have
used its arid difficulties as a refuge from the power of
surrounding states. The desert itself spans the countries of
USSR (where 1.8 million Turkoman live), Afghanistan (390,000) and
Iran. Other Turkmen are to be found in Iraq (170,000) and Syria
(80,000).

The separation by political boundaries has not as yet produced
major differences in language and lifestyle. Turkoman is written
in a Cyrillic script in the USSR and an extensive literature has
grown up in that script. It can be expected over time to produce
major changes especially when combined with the change from
semi-nomadic herding to cash crop cotton production.

Most Turkoman in the past have lived partly in permanent homes
where wheat and dryland crops could be grown in the semi-arid
border regions surrounding the Black Sand Desert. Part of the
year was spent in the round yurts (tents) following the migration
of animals to better pasture. Only in the last 50 years have
they finally been subdued and made a part of the political states
they have fended off for so many centuries.

Observance of the prayers and Ramadan is relatively high. The
ideal of hajj is alive and those who have done so are shown an
enhanced degree of respect. Religious teachers also have high
prestige. The Turkomen are Hanafi Sunni Muslims.

Some evangelization has taken place in the past. The ETHNOLOGUE
indicates a definite translation need and some portions were to
have been published in 1979. But the vast majority of this group
is currently unreached.

EXPANDED DESCRIPTIONS

Uugur (China)

ALTERNATE NAMES: not reported

SIZE OF GROUP: 4,899,000   MARC ID: 4913

DISTINCTIVES: language; ethnicity; religion

SOCIAL CHANGE: moderate

LANGUAGES: Uigur (100% speak; V); Mandarin (T)

SCRIPTURE: Bible

CHRISTIAN LITERACY: not reported

RELIGION: Islam (100% adherents)

CHURCHES AND MISSIONS: not reported

OPENNESS TO RELIGIOUS CHANGE: not reported

RECEPTIVITY TO CHRISTIANITY: not reported

EVANGELISM PROFILE: not reported

VALIDITY: 5

Uigur is a twentieth century revival of a 16th century name.
Until it began to be applied to the peoples of Sinkiang-Uigur
Autonomous Region, most called themselves by the place where they
lived. Though they speak a common Turkic language, they had no
broader identity than the locale in which they lived.

Most were oasis ariculturalists, living near the oases of the old
silk trade routes. The emphasis on settled life and caravan
trade had been predominant for nearly a thousand years. The
urban Uigur lived a more sophisticated life, with merchants,
educators, inn-keepers, and artisans. Much of this has changed,
though it is difficult to say precisely how since information is
very limited. The Han Chinese have been resettled into this area
in massive numbers, probably making the Uigur a minority in their
own region. Industrialization is taking place, causing
population shifts. Reforestation and irrigation projects have
opened up great tracts of land. How collectivization of
agriculture has affected the traditional independent Uigur
farmers is also not clear though they have been organized into
communes.

Prior to Communist control the Uigur were considered devout Sunni
Muslims. Islam penetrated these peoples as early as the tenth
century. Sufi orders were particularly influential in their
history. How Communism has affected Islamic practices is not
clear. One might guess from the preferential treatment of the
Muslim Hui that other Muslim groups may also be seen as crucial
for foreign relation purposes. It is clear that many mosques
remain open and that Islamic practices are continued, even if
somewhat curbed.

More information is needed for evaluating the status of
evangelization among this people. No known foreign witness is
present in the region and so far as we know, there is not a
single Christian Church to be found in the region.

Vai (Liberia)

ALTERNATE NAMES: not reported

SIZE OF GROUP: 31,000   MARC ID: 688

DISTINCTIVES: language; ethnicity

SOCIAL CHANGE: not reported

LANGUAGES: Vai (100% speak/10% read; V); English (20% sp k;
    T); Gola

SCRIPTURE: portions

CHRISTIAN LITERACY: not reported

RELIGION: Islam (90% adherents); Animism (9% adherents);
    Protestant (1% adherents/1% practicing)

CHURCHES AND MISSIONS	BEGAN	MEMBERSHIP	COMMUNITY
Baptist Church	nr	nr	nr
Episcopal Church	nr	nr	nr

OPENNESS TO RELIGIOUS CHANGE: somewhat closed

RECEPTIVITY TO CHRISTIANITY: indifferent

EVANGELISM PROFILE: not reported

VALIDITY: 6

According to old history, the Vai nation originated when a group
of some 500 warriors migrated from Timbuktu to the Atlantic coast
to establish a trade in salt with the peoples of the interior.
Today they number about 30,000 in Liberia and 45,000 in Sierra
Leone. In Sierra Leone assimilation to Mende life is taking
place. The Liberian Vai however, are maintaining their separate
way of life. Religiously, the Vai became Muslim in mass
conversions beginning in the 1930s. This came about after the
governments established control over a heretofore independent Vai
and undermined the traditional power system that was rooted in an
elder-ancestor cult mediated through a male secret society, the
Poro.

Externally the Vai are Sunni Muslims, with some Ahmadi in the
cities. Both the Tijaniya and Qadiriya brotherhoods are present
and there are strong movements afoot to purify Vai religious
practice of its animistic world view and rituals. Many of those
who move to the city find themselves moving into a more secular
life style and outlook.

Christian missions have been established in the Vai territory for
more than a century. The basic approach has been evangelism
through education. As a result, virtually all educated Vai are
at least nominally Christian and have become a disproportionate
part of the political, economic and educational leadership of
Liberia. Because of their prestige, there is no stigma attached
to conversion to Christian faith as in many other Muslim
societies.

Most education is being taken over by the government and
secularized so that this one evangelical contact is being lost.
Since most Vai who become Christian leave the area, there is
virtually no Christian witness among the Vai today.

EXPANDED DESCRIPTIONS

Wolof (Senegal)

ALTERNATE NAMES: not reported

SIZE OF GROUP: 1,560,000   MARC ID: 96

DISTINCTIVES: language; ethnicity; religion

SOCIAL CHANGE: not reported

LANGUAGES: Wolof (100% speak/30% read; V, T); French (10% speak/5% read); Arabic (2% speak)

SCRIPTURE: portions

CHRISTIAN LITERACY: 99%

RELIGION: Islam-Animist (99% adherents); Christianity (1% adherents/1% practicing)

CHURCHES AND MISSIONS	BEGAN	MEMBERSHIP	COMMUNITY
Assemblies of God	1960	nr	3
United World Mission	1960	nr	nr
Southern Baptist Convention	1970	nr	nr
Conservative Baptist Church	1965	nr	3
Roman Catholic Church	nr	nr	nr

OPENNESS TO RELIGIOUS CHANGE: somewhat closed

RECEPTIVITY TO CHRISTIANITY: very reluctant

EVANGELISM PROFILE: not reported

VALIDITY: 6

The Wolof are Senegal's largest tribal group, making up about 36% of the population. Its dominance is reflected in the fact that an additional 30% of the tribals speak Wolof and it is used even more widely as a trade language in West Africa.

Such a large group can hardly help but be diverse. Wolof society, like that of all tribes of Senegal, is highly stratified by a caste system of five ranks: nobles, freeborn, artisans, musicians and descendants of former slaves. Intermarriage across tribal lines within caste is far more frequent than the rare cross-caste marriage. Polygamy is found in about 25% of the households.

Islam entered Wolof life as early as the 11th century. But large-scale conversions only came with the jihads of the nineteenth century. As a result, almost all Wolof became Muslims at that time. They have lost almost all of their traditional religious customs, though they follow a form of "folk" Islam. Three main brotherhoods are widespread: Tijaniya (about 60% of brotherhood membership), Mourid (30%) and Qadiriya (10%).

Christian missions is a very thin presence and most Wolof cannot be said to have faced the question of Christian faith. They simply do not know about it. The most effective presence seems to be one that enters Wolof life to bring education, medicine and rural community development. Christianity is not actively opposed because it brings desired help. But neither is it espoused as an option which one might embrace in an act of conversion and commitment.

Yakan (Philippines)

ALTERNATE NAMES: Yacanes

SIZE OF GROUP: 97,000   MARC ID: .25

DISTINCTIVES: language; ethnicity; religion

SOCIAL CHANGE: not reported

LANGUAGES: Yakan (100% speak/15% read; V); Tausug (50% speak;
    T); Chavacano (20% speak)

SCRIPTURE: portions

CHRISTIAN LITERACY: 1%

RELIGION: Christianity (1% adherents/1% practicing); Islam (15%
    adherents); Islam-Animist (74% adherents)

CHURCHES AND MISSIONS	BEGAN	MEMBERSHIP	COMMUNITY
Anglican Church	1946	nr	10
Christian & Msny. Alliance	1946	nr	100
Foursquare Church	1950	nr	nr
Pentecostal Church	1971	nr	nr
Roman Catholic Church	1700	nr	90

OPENNESS TO RELIGIOUS CHANGE: somewhat closed

RECEPTIVITY TO CHRISTIANITY: reluctant

EVANGELISM PROFILE: not reported

VALIDITY: 6

Basilan is a volcanic island just off the southern tip of
Zamboanga Peninsula of western Mindanao. The Yakan are the
indigenous people, concentrated in the interior. At present they
make up but half the island population, sharing it with the
"Christian" Filipino and the Muslim Tausug and Sama.

Yakan consider themselves good Sunni Muslims of the Shafi school,
even if other Muslims do not. They follow the Muslim calendar,
are lead by imams religiously and judicially. The pagan rituals
and traditions which are incorporated into the rites lead by the
imam are seen by the people as good Muslim ritual.

Few make the pilgrimage, most fast only several days of Ramadan,
and ritual praying is done only on Friday. The Muslim law is
followed in protecting the property a woman brings into marriage
but ignored by giving equal inheritance shares to sons and
daughters. The profession of imam is inherited, though it
requires study on the part of the aspirant since he must live
more strictly and judge civil and criminal cases. Muslim
missionaries have attempted to purify Yakan Islam but with only
marginal success.

Christian missionaries have been present for a number of years
but with little success among the Yakan. Churches on Basilan are
almost entirely found among the Christian Filipinos of the two
municipalities of Isabela and Lamitan.

EXPANDED DESCRIPTIONS

Yalunka (Sierra Leone)

ALTERNATE NAMES: not reported

SIZE OF GROUP: 25,000   MARC ID: 455

DISTINCTIVES: language; ethnicity; religion

SOCIAL CHANGE: not reported

LANGUAGES: Yalunka (100% speak/2% read; V); Menika (T);
    Creole

SCRIPTURE: New Testament

CHRISTIAN LITERACY: 2%

RELIGION: Islam-Animist (90% adherents); Christianity (1%
    adherents/1% practicing); Unknown (9% adherents)

CHURCHES AND MISSIONS	BEGAN	MEMBERSHIP	COMMUNITY
MCA Mission	1952	103	150

OPENNESS TO RELIGIOUS CHANGE: somewhat closed

RECEPTIVITY TO CHRISTIANITY: indifferent

EVANGELISM PROFILE: not reported

VALIDITY: 6

The Yalunkas moved into southern Guinea and northern Sierra Leone
in the 16th century because of the military pressures of the
Muslim Fula tribe. Tradition indicates that the Yalunkas were
enslaved by the Fulas but sucessfully revolted. In the process
of these events they adopted a thin veneer of Islam which now
serves as the outer face of a strong traditional animism.

The Yalunkas are agriculturalists, settled in scattered villages.
Semi-nomadic Fula with their cattle still live and move
throughout Yalunka territory. Creole is used as the lingua
franca in Sierra Leone.

The earliest attempts to evangelize took place at the turn of the
century by the Church Missionary Society. Poor response stalled
the initial evangelization so that not a single church or school
was established. In 1952 the Missionary Church Association
(Mennonite Brethren) entered an area where no prior
evangelization had taken place. Language work has progressed
with the New Testament now published. Response has still been
slow with churches in only three towns.

In recent years the government has established schools in six
towns and placed the Missionary Church Association in charge of
managing them. While the Roman Catholics are present (and also
managing two other government schools) they have no churches
established and no resident missionary in the tribe.

With the slow response and the minimal growth, much of the effort
of the MCA has been to establish a foundation for a later period
of harvest. A leadership base is being developed with three
ordained national pastors, three licensed pastors and seven
attending Bible school.

MUSLIM AND LARGELY MUSLIM PEOPLE GROUPS

With Descriptions in *Unreached Peoples '79*

Page number
in *Unreached Peoples '79*

Afar (Ethiopia) 145
Ahl-i-Haqq (Iran) 146
Ajuran (Kenya) 147
Alawites (Syria) 150
Chitralis (Pakistan) 169
Comorians (Comoros) 172
Dagon (Mali) 176
Fulani (Cameroon) 181
Hunzakut (Pakistan) 188
Javanese (rural) (Indonesia) 194
Kabyle (Algeria) 195
Kashmiri Muslims (India) 199
Koalib (Sudan) 200
Kurds (Turkey) 202
Madurese (Indonesia) 206
Malays of Singapore (Singapore) 209
Mandingo (Liberia) 210
Maranao (Philippines) 211
Moor and Malays (Sri Lanka) 218
Muslims in United Arab Emirates (U.A.E.) 220
Sama-Badjaw (Philippines) 231
Serere (Senegal) 232
Somali (Somalia) 233
Swatis (Pakistan) 236
Tuareg (Niger) 240
Turkish Immigrant Workers (West Germany) 243

EXPANDED DESCRIPTIONS

Uzbeks (Afghanistan)   247
Yemenis (Yemen, Arab Republic)   251

PART 4
Registry of the Unreached

The information on the 1,982 unreached peoples in the registry is presented in five different lists. Each list organizes the information differently. Only the first list, which indexes the peoples alphabetically by group name, includes the estimated percentage of those that practice Christianity and a code that indicates the overall accuracy of the data.

Groups are also listed by receptivity, principal professed religion, language, and country. All five lists indicate those groups reported to be very receptive (***), receptive (**), or indifferent (*). There is also another code (79 or 80) attached to the group name to indicate that a description has been written about this people group in *Unreached Peoples '79* (79) or *Unreached Peoples '80* (80). These descriptions are included in Part 3 of these books.

A more detailed explanation of the information contained in each of the following lists may be found at the beginning of the appropriate sections.

INDEX
by
Group
Name

INDEX BY GROUP NAME

This is the basic listing of people groups in this registry. Peoples are listed by their primary **name,** and effort has been made to standardize names and use the most commonly accepted English spelling. This listing includes the **country** for which the information was provided, principal vernacular **language** used by the group, population estimate of the **group size** in the country listed and principal professed religion **(primary religion),** which in some cases is less than 50 percent of the total group membership.

In addition, this index includes the estimated percentage of the group that practices Christianity in any recognized tradition **(practicing Christian).** Included in this percentage are Protestant, Roman Catholic, Orthodox, African Independent, and other Christian groups. Excluded in this percentage were Christo-pagans and Christian cultic groups. It is important to note that this figure is the estimated percentage of *practicing* Christians within the group. If the group was listed in *Unreached Peoples '79,* the figure recorded here will most likely be different, because that volume recorded the percentage of *professing* Christians (or adherents), which most often will be a higher number. Thus these figures should not be compared or used as a time series, since the changes indicate a different kind of data. Differences might also be due to a new and better data source or revised data, as we are continually updating our files.

The index also lists a validity code **(valid)** which estimates the accuracy and completeness of the data on a scale from 1 to 9. The code is:

1. The only information available at this point is the group name, country, language, population, and primary religion. The percentage listed under practicing Christians is at best a rough estimate.

2. There has been more data collected than the "baseline" information in 1, but it is scanty and/or of poor quality.

3. About one-half of the information on the unreached peoples questionnaire (Appendix B) has been collected, and information on the Christian community, if any, is missing or probably inaccurate.

4. Almost all the data on the unreached peoples questionnaire has been collected *or* the source document has supplied most of the necessary information.

5. Information has been supplied by a completed unreached peoples questionnaire and at least one other document.

6. In addition to 5, there is enough detailed information about the people group to write an accurate, up-to-date description.

7. There exists an extensive description of the people group in secular or Christian literature.

8. There has been a major research study (thesis or dissertation quality) done on the group which includes detailed information on the Christian community.

9. In addition to 8, the study includes a thorough exploration of evangelism strategy for the particular group,
based on firsthand experience.

The final column in this section indicates the year of the
volume **(Year Described)** of *Unreached Peoples* in which
a description of this group appeared.

Name	Alt. Name	Country	Population	Religion	Code
Abaknon	Abaknon	Philippines	10,000	Christo-Paganism	–18 0 1
Abanyom	Abanyom	Nigeria	3,850	Animism	–18 0 1
Abau	Abau	Indonesia	3,390	Animism	–18 0 1
Abe	Abe	Ivory Coast	28,500	Islam-Animist	–18 0 1
Abidji	Adidji	Ivory Coast	23,000	Islam-Animist	–18 0 1
Abkhaz	Abkhaz	Turkey	12,400	Islam	–18 0 1
Abong	Abong	Nigeria		Islam	–18 0 1
Abou Charib	Abou Charib	Chad	25,000	Islam-Animist	–18 0 1
Abua	Abua	Nigeria	24,000	Animism	–18 0 1
Abujmaria	Abujmaria	India	11,000	Hindu-Animist	–18 0 1
Abure	Abure	Ivory Coast	25,000	Islam-Animist	–18 0 1
Ach'ang	Ach'ang	China	10,000	Traditional Chinese	–18 0 1
Achagua	Achagua	Colombia	100	Animism	–18 0 1
Achehnese	Achehnese	Indonesia	2,200,000	Islam	–18 0 6 80
Achipa	Achipa	Nigeria	3,600	Islam	–18 0 1
Achual	Achual	Peru	5,000	Animism	–18 0 1
Adamawa	Fulani	Cameroon	380,300	Animism	–18 0 5
***Adi	Adi	India	95,000	Animism	–28 0 4
***Adivasis of Dang	Dangi	India	80,300	Animism	–18 0 4
Adiyan	Adiyan	India	2,500	Hinduism	–18 0 1
**Adja	Ge	Benin	250,000	Animism	–58 0 4
Adyukru	Adyukru	Ivory Coast	50,450	Islam-Animist	–18 0 4
Aeta	Aeta	Philippines	500	Christo-Paganism	–18 0 1
Afar	Afar	Ethiopia	300,000	Islam	–18 6 79
**Afawa	Afanci	Nigeria	10,000	Animism	–18 6 80
**Afo	Eloyi	Nigeria	25,000	Animism	–18 6 80
**African Students in Cairo	Various dialects	Egypt	700	Islam	–98 0 4
Afshars	Afshari	Iran	290,000	Islam	0% 3
Agajanis	Agajanis	India	1,000	Islam	0% 3
Agariya	Agariya	India	11,790	Hinduism	–18 0 1
Aghu	Aghu	Indonesia	3,000	Animism	–18 0 1
Agoi	Agol	Nigeria	3,650	Animism	–18 0 1
Aguaruna	Aguaruna	Peru	22,000	Animism	–18 0 1
Agutaynon	Agutaynon	Philippines	7,000	Islam-Animist	–18 0 1
Agwagwune	Agwagwune	Nigeria	20,000	Animism	–18 0 1
Ahir	Ahir	India	132,520	Islam	–18 0 1
**Ahl-i-Haqq in Iran	Kurdish dialects	Iran	500,000	Islam	0% 6 79
Aibondeni	Aibondeni	Indonesia	150	Animism	–18 0 1
Aikwakai	Aikwakai	Indonesia	400	Animism	–18 0 1
Aimol	Aimol	India	110	Hindu-Animist	–18 0 1
Airo-Sumaghaghe	Airo-Sumaghaghe	Indonesia	2,000	Animism	–18 0 1
Airoran	Airoran	Indonesia	350	Animism	–18 0 1
Ajmeri	Ajmeri	India	580	Hindu-Animist	–18 0 1

People	Country	Language	Population	Religion	%	Code	Yr
Aka	India	Aka	2,257	Animism	0%	3	
Akan, Brong	Ivory Coast	Akan, Brong	50,000	Islam-Animist	-1%	1	
Ake	Nigeria	Ake	300	Animism	-1%	1	
**Akha	Thailand	Akha	9,916	Ancestor Worship	-1%	6	79
Akpa-Yache	Nigeria	Akpa-Yache	15,000	Animism	-1%	1	
Alaba	Ethiopia	Alaban	50,000	Islam	3%	4	
Aladian	Ivory Coast	Aladian	14,770	Islam-Animist	2%	5	
Alago	Nigeria	Alago	35,000	Animism	1%	5	
Alak	Laos	Alak	8,000	Animism	-1%	1	
Alangan	Philippines	Alangan	6,000	Christo-Paganism	0%	5	
*Alars	India	Allar	400	Folk Religion	0%	6	
Alas	Indonesia	Gayo	30,000	Islam	0%	6	79
*Alawites	Syria	Arabic	600,000	Islam	0%	6	
*Albanian Muslims	Albania	Albanian Tosk	1,700,000	Islam	-1%	6	
Alege	Nigeria	Alege	1,200	Animism	-1%	6	80
Algerian (Arabs)	Algeria	Arabic	8,000,000	Islam	-1%	6	80
Algerian Arabs in France	France	Arabic	804,000	Islam	-0%	3	
Allar	India	Allar	90,350	Hinduism	-1%	1	
Alor, Kolana	Indonesia	Alor, Kolana	1,500	Animism	-1%	6	
Amahuaca	Peru	Amahuaca	2,800	Animism	-1%	1	
Amanab	Indonesia	Amanab	22,500	Animism	-1%	1	
Amar	Ethiopia	Amar	500	Animism	-1%	1	
Amarakaeri	Peru	Amarakaeri	6,000	Animism	-1%	1	
Ambai	Indonesia	Ambai	300	Animism	-1%	1	
Amber	Indonesia	Amber	5,000	Animism	-1%	1	
Amberbaken	Indonesia	Amberbaken	80,000	Animism	-1%	1	
Ambonese	Indonesia	Ambonese	30,000	Animism	2%	4	
	Netherlands	Ambonese		Animism	-1%	4	
Amo	Nigeria	Amo	3,550	Animism	-1%	1	
**Ampeeli	Papua New Guinea	Ampale	1,000	Christo-Paganism	-1%	1	
Amuesha	Peru	Amuesha	5,000	Animism	-1%	1	
Anaang	Nigeria	Anaang	246,000	Animism	-1%	1	
Anal	India	Anal	6,590	Animism	-1%	1	
Andha	India	Andha	64,650	Animism	-1%	1	
Andoque	Colombia	Andoque	100	Animism	-1%	4	
Anga	India	Anga	423,500	Hinduism	-1%	1	
Angas	Nigeria	Angas	100,000	Animism	-1%	1	
Ankwe	Nigeria	Ankwai	10,000	Animism	-1%	4	
Ansus	Indonesia	Ansus	3,000	Animism	-1%	5	
Anuak	Ethiopia	Anuak	52,000	Animism	-1%	5	
Anuak	Sudan	Anuak	30,000	Animism	4%	5	
Apalai	Brazil	Apalai	100	Animism	-1%	1	
**Apartment Residents-Seoul	Korea, Republic of	Korean	87,000	Folk Religion	11%	4	

Group	Country	People	Population	Religion	
**Apatani	India	Apatani	11,000	Animism	18 4
**Apayao	Philippines	Isneg	12,000	Christo-Paganism	158 5
Apinaye	Brazil	Apinaye	210	Animism	-18 1
Apurina	Brazil	Apurina	1,000	Animism	-18 1
Ara	Indonesia	Ara	75,000	Islam	-18 1
Arab-Jabbari (Kamesh)	Iran	Arabic	13,000	Islam	(? 3
Arab-Shaibani (Kamesh)	Iran	Arabic	16,000	Islam	(? 3
Arabela	Peru	Arabela	200	Animism	-18 4
Arabs of Khuzestan	Iran	Arabic	520,200	Islam	-18 4
Aranadan	India	Aranadan	600	Hindu-Animist	-18 1
Arandai	Indonesia	Arandan	2,000	Animism	-18 1
Arapaco	Brazil	Tucanoan	310	Animism	-18 1
Arawa	Nigeria	Hausa	200,000	Animism	-18 4
Arbore	Ethiopia	Arbore	2,000	Animism	-18 1
Argobba	Ethiopia	Argobba	2,000	Animism	-18 1
Arguni	Indonesia	Arguni	200	Animism	-18 1
*Arnatas	India	Arnatan	??	Animism	?? 6
Arusha	Tanzania	Arusha	110,?	Animism	-? 1
Arya	India	Arya	2,590	Hinduism	-18 1
Asienara	Indonesia	Asienara	700	Animism	-18 1
*Asmat	Indonesia	Asmat	30,000	Animism	78 6 79
Assamese	Bangladesh	Assamese	4,540	Islam	-18 1
Asuri	India	Manobo	10,000	Animism	48 4
*Ate of Davao	Philippines	Aten	4,000	Islam	-18 1
Ati	Philippines	Ati	1,500	Christo-Paganism	-18 1
Atruahi	Brazil	Atruahi	520	Animism	-18 1
*Atta	Philippines	Atta	1,000	Animism	18 5
Attie	Ivory Coast	Attie	160,000	Islam-Animist	-18 1
Avikam	Ivory Coast	Avikam	7,940	Islam-Animist	-18 1
Awngi	Ethiopia	Awngi	50,000	Islam	-18 1
Awyi	Indonesia	Awyi	400	Animism	-18 1
Awyu	Indonesia	Awyu	18,000	Animism	-18 1
**Aymara	Bolivia	Aymara	850,000	Animism	78 5
Ayu	Nigeria	Ayu	4,000	Islam	-18 1
*Azerbaijani	Afghanistan	Azerbaijani	5,000	Islam	-18 1
*Azerbaijani Turks	Iran	Azerbaijani Turkish	6,000,000	Islam	69 5 80
***Azteca	Mexico	Nahuatl, Hidalgo	250,000	Christo-Paganism	28 6 79
Babri	India	Babri	29,700	Hinduism	-18 1
**Babur Thali	Nigeria	Bura (Babur)	75,000	Animism	38 6 80
Baburiwa	Indonesia	Baburiwa	160	Animism	-18 1
Bachama	Nigeria	Bachama	20,000	Islam	-18 1
Bada	Nigeria	Bada	10,000	Animism	-18 1

215

People	Language	Country	Population	Religion		
Badagu	Badagu	India	104,920	Animism	-1%	1
Bade	Bade	Nigeria	100,000	Islam	-1%	1
Bagelkhandi	Bagelkhandi	India	231,230	Hindu-Animist	-1%	1
Baghati	Baghati	India	3,980	Animism	-1%	1
Bagirmi	Bagirmi	Chad	40,000	Islam-Animist	-1%	4
Bagri	Bagri	Pakistan	20,000	Hinduism	-1%	4
Baham	Baham	Indonesia	500	Animism	0%	3
Baharlu (Kamesh)	Turkish	Iran	7,500	Islam	-1%	1
Bahawalpuri	Bahawalpuri	India	7,640	Animism	-1%	1
Baiga	Baiga	India	11,110	Animism	-1%	1
Bajania	Gujrati Dialect	Pakistan	20,000	Hinduism	-1%	6 79
Bajau, Indonesian	Bajau, Indonesian	Indonesia	50,000	Islam	-1%	1
Bakairi	Bakairi	Brazil	300	Animism	-1%	1
Bakhtiaris	Bakhtiaris	Iran	590,000	Islam	0%	5 80
**Bakuba	Tshiluba	Zaire	75,000	Animism	14%	5
Bakwe	Bakwe	Ivory Coast	5,060	Islam-Animist	-1%	1
**Balangao	Balangao	Philippines	4,500	Christo-Paganism	3%	4
Balangaw	Balangaw	Philippines	5,000	Animism	-1%	1
Balanta	Balanta	Senegal	49,200	not reported	-1%	3
Balantak	Balantak	Indonesia	125,000	Islam-Animist	-1%	1
Balante	Balanta	Guinea-Bissau	100,000	Animism	7%	4
Bali	Bali	Indonesia	1,000	Islam-Animist	-1%	1
Balinese	Balinese	Indonesia	2,000,000	Hinduism	-1%	5
Balmiki	Hindustani	Pakistan	20,000	Hinduism	-1%	5
Balti	Balti	India	40,140	Animism	-1%	1
Baluchi	Baluchi	Iran	1,100,000	Islam	0%	6 80
Bambara	Bambara	Ivory Coast	1,000,000	Islam-Animist	-1%	5
Bambara	Bambara	Mali	1,000,000	Islam	-1%	1
Bambuka	Bambuka	Nigeria	10,000	Islam	-1%	1
**Banai	Bengali	Bangladesh	2,000	Buddhism	1%	4
***Banaro	Banaro	Papua New Guinea	2,500	Animism	5%	4
Bandawa-Minda	Bandawa-Minda	Nigeria	10,000	Islam	-1%	1
Bandi	Bandi	Liberia	32,000	Animism	-1%	4
Banga	Banga	Nigeria	8,000	Islam	-1%	1
Bangaru	Bangri	India	4,000,000	Hindu-Animist	-1%	1
Banggai	Banggai	Indonesia	200,000	Islam	-1%	1
Baniwa	Baniwa	Brazil	2,446	Animism	-1%	1
Bantuanon	Bantuanon	Philipines	50,000	Christo-Paganism	6%	4
Banyun	Banyun	Guinea-Bissau	15,000	Animism	9%	4
***Baoule	Baule	Ivory Coast	1,200,000	Animism	2%	5 79
Barabaig	Tatoga	Tanzania	49,000	Animism	-1%	1
Barasano	Barasano	Colombia	400	Animism	2%	1
Barasano, Northern	Barasano, Northern	Colombia	450	Animism	3%	5

216

Name	Country	Alt. Name	Population	Religion	
Barasano, Southern	Colombia	Janena	400	Animism	28 4
Barau	Indonesia	Barau	150	Animism	-18 1
Bare'e	Indonesia	Bare'e	325,000	Animism	-18 1
Bareli	India	Bareli	230,030	Hinduism	-18 1
*Bariba	Benin	Bariba	400,000	Animism	48 6 80
Bariba	Nigeria	Bariba	60,000	Islam-Animist	-18 1
Basakomo	Nigeria	not reported	55,000	Animism	12% 4
Basari	Senegal	Gasari	8,000	Animism	09 3
	Togo	Basari	100,000	Animism	10% 5
Bashar	Nigeria	Bashar	20,000	Animism	-18 1
Bashgali	Afghanistan	Bashgali	10,000	Islam	-18 1
Bashkir	Soviet Russia	Tatar	1,200,000	Islam	09 5 80
Basketo	Ethiopia	Basketo	9,000	Animism	-18 1
***Basotho, Mountain	Lesotho	Southern Sesotho	70,000	Animism	88 6 79
*Bassa	Liberia	Bassa	200,000	Animism	11% 5
*Bassa	Nigeria	Bassa	100,000	Animism	8% 5
Bata	Nigeria	Bata	26,400	Islam-Animist	-18 1
*Batak, Angkola	Indonesia	Batak, Angkola	nr	Islam	68 6
Batak, Karo	Indonesia	Batak, Karo	400,000	Islam	-18 1
Batak, Palawan	Philippines	Batak, Palawan	390	Christo-Paganism	-18 1
Batak, Simalungun	Indonesia	Batak, Simalungun	800,000	Animism	-18 1
Batak, Toba	Indonesia	Batak, Toba	1,600,000	Animism	-18 1
Bathudi	India	Bathudi	73,890	Hinduism	-18 1
Batu	Nigeria	Batu	25,000	Islam	-18 1
Baushi	Nigeria	Baushi	2,650	Islam	-18 1
Bawm	Bangladesh	Bawm	7,000	Islam	-18 1
Bayats	Iran	Bayat	nr	Islam	09 3
Bayot	Gambia	Bayot	4,000	Islam-Animist	-18 1
Bazigar	India	Bazigar	100	Animism	-18 1
Bediya	India	Bediya	32,200	Animism	-18 1
Bedoanas	Indonesia	Bedoanas	250	Animism	-18 1
Beja	Ethiopia	Beja	39,000	Islam	-18 1
Bekwarra	Nigeria	Bekwarra	34,000	Animism	-18 1
Bencho	Ethiopia	Bencho	5,000	Animism	-18 1
Bengali	Bangladesh	Bengali	80,000,000	Islam	18 6 80
Berik	Indonesia	Berik	800	Animism	-18 1
Berom	Nigeria	Berom	116,000	Animism	-18 1
Bete	India	Bete	2,960	Animism	-18 1
Bete-Bende	Ivory Coast	Bete-Bende	350,000	Islam-Animist	-18 1
Bhakta	Nigeria	Bhakta	36,800	Animism	-18 1
Bharia	India	Bharia	55,150	Hindu-Animist	-18 1
Bhatneri	India	Bhatneri	5,380	Animism	-18 1
Bhatneri	India	Bhatneri	190	Islam	-18 1

Name	Country	Language	Population	Religion		
Bhattri	India	Bhattri	103,770	Hindu-Animist	18 1	
**Bhil	Pakistan	Marwari	800,000	Hinduism	18 6	
Bhilala	India	Bhilala	246,720	Hindu-Animist	18 1	
**Bhils	India	Dangi	806,000	Animism	18 6	79
*Bhojpuri	Nepal	Bhojpuri	806,480	Hinduism	18 4	
Bhoyari	India	Bhoyari	5,390	Hindu-Animist	18 1	
Bhuiya	India	Bhuiya	4,430	Animism	18 1	
Bhumij	India	Bhumij	48,240	Hindu-Animist	18 1	
Bhunjia	India	Bhunjia	5,240	Hindu-Animist	18 1	
Bhutias	Bhutan	Sharchagpakha	780,000	Buddhism	18 6	
Biafada	Guinea-Bissau	Biafada	15,000	Animism	18 4	
Biak	Indonesia	Biak	40,000	Animism	68 4	
**Bidayuh of Sarawak	Malaysia	Biatah	110,000	Christo-Paganism	18 4	
Bihari	India	Bihari	23,220	Hindu-Animist	18 4	
**Bijogo	Guinea-Bissau	Bidyogo	25,000	Animism	88 4	
Bijori	India	Bijori	2,390	Hindu-Animist	18 1	
Biksi	Indonesia	Biksi	200	Animism	18 1	
Bilala	Chad	Bilala	42,000	Islam-Animist	18 1	
**Bilan	Philippines	Bilaan	75,000	Islam-Animist	18 5	
Bile	Nigeria	Bile	1,000	Islam-Animist	18 1	
Bilen	Ethiopia	Bilen	32,000	Islam	18 5	
Bimanese	Indonesia	Bima	300,000	Islam	18 5	
Binawa	Nigeria	Binawa	2,000	Islam	18 1	
Bingkokak	Indonesia	Bingkokak	150,000	Islam	18 1	
Binjhwari	India	Binjhwari	48,800	Hindu-Animist	18 1	
Bipim	Indonesia	Bipim	450	Christo-Paganism	58 4	
Bira	Indonesia	Bira	75,590	Islam-Animist	18 5	
Birhor	India	Birhor	590	Hindu-Animist	18 1	
Birifor	Ghana	Birifor	40,000	Animism	18 4	
Bitare	Nigeria	Bitare	3,000	Islam-Animist	38 5	
**Black Caribs, Belize	Belize	Moreno	10,000	Christo-Paganism	18 6	79
**Black Caribs, Guatemala	Guatemala	Moreno	1,500	Christo-Paganism	18 5	
**Black Caribs, Honduras	Honduras	Moreno	20,000	Christo-Paganism	18 5	
Bodo	India	Bodo	509,010	Animism	18 4	
**Bodo Kachari	India	Bodo	610,000	Hinduism	28 4	
Boghom	Nigeria	Boghom	50,000	Animism	18 1	
**Boko	Benin	Boko (Busa)	40,000	Animism	28 4	
Bokyi	Nigeria	Bokyi	87,000	Animism	18 1	
Bole	Nigeria	Bole	32,000	Islam	18 1	
Bomou	Chad	Bomou	15,000	Islam-Animist	18 1	
Bondo	India	Bondo	2,370	Hinduism	18 1	
Bonerif	Indonesia	Bonerif	100	Animism	18 1	
Bonggo	Indonesia	Bonggo	430	Animism	18 1	

Group	Language/People	Country	Population	Religion	Code
*Bontoc, Central	Bontoc, Central	Philippines	20,000	Animism	18 5
**Bontoc, Southern	Southern Bontoc	Philippines	12,000	Christo-Paganism	48 5
Bora	Bora	Colombia	400	Animism	-18 1
Borai	Borai	Indonesia	1,000	Animism	-18 1
Boran	Boran	Ethiopia	132,000	Islam-Animist	-18 1
Bororo	Bororo	Brazil	500	Animism	-18 5
*Bosnian	Serbo-Croation	Yugoslavia	1,740,000	Islam	18 6 80
Bovir-Ahmadi	Lori	Iran	110,000	Islam	0% 4
Boya	Boya	Sudan	15,000	Animism	-18 4
Braj	Braj	India	6,000,000	Animism	-18 4
Brao	Brao	Laos	18,000	Animism	18 6 79
Brat	Brat	Indonesia	20,000	Animism	-18 1
Bua	Bua	Chad	6,000	Animism	0% 3
Bual	Bual	Indonesia	150,000	Islam	-18 1
Budugum	Masa	Cameroon	10,000	Animism	-18 1
Buduma	Buduma	Nigeria	80,000	Islam	-18 1
Bugis	Bugis	Indonesia	3,500,000	Islam	18 6 80
Buhid	Buhid	Philippines	6,000	Christo-Paganism	-18 4
Buisa	Buisa	Ghana	97,000	Animism	-18 4
**Bukidnon	Manobo, Binukid	Philippines	100,000	Christo-Paganism	15% 5
Buli	Buli	Indonesia	1,000	Islam-Animist	-18 1
Bunak	Bunak	Indonesia	50,000	Animism	-18 1
Bunan	Bunan	India	2,000	Animism	-18 1
Bungku	Bungku	Indonesia	180,000	Animism	-18 4
Bunu	Bunu	Nigeria	150,000	Animism	-18 1
Burak	Burak	Nigeria	2,000	Islam	-18 1
Buriat	Buriat	China	26,500	Traditional Chinese	-18 1
Burig	Burig	China	148,000	Traditional Chinese	-18 1
Burji	Burji	India	132,200	Animism	-18 1
Buru	Buru	Ethiopia	6,000	Animism	-18 1
Burungi	Burungi	Tanzania	20,000	Animism	78 4
**Bus Drivers, South Korea	Korean	Korea, Republic of	26,000	Unknown	88 4
Busa	Busa (Bokobarn Akiba)	Nigeria	50,000	Islam	18 6 80
**Busami	Busami	Indonesia	350	Animism	-18 1
Busanse	Bisa (Busanga)	Ghana	50,000	Animism	28 5
Bushmen (Heikum)	Heikum	Namibia	16,000	Animism	68 5
*Bushmen (Hiechware)	Kwe-Etshari	Rhodesia	1,600	Animism	68 5
*Bushmen (Kung)	Xu	Namibia	10,000	Animism	68 6 79
Bushmen in Botswana	Buka-khwe	Botswana	30,000	Animism	78 4
Bussa	Bussa	Ethiopia	1,000	Animism	-18 1
Butawa	Buta	Nigeria	20,000	Islam	08 5
Butung	Butung	Indonesia	200,000	Islam-Animist	-18 1

People	Country	Group	Population	Religion	9 6 80
Bwa	Upper Volta	Buamu (Bobo Wule)	140,000	Animism	9% 6 80
Cacua	Colombia	Cacua	150	Animism	-1% 1
Caiwa	Brazil	Caiwa	7,000	Animism	-1% 1
Caluyanhon	Philippines	Caluyanhon	30,000	Christo-Paganism	-1% 1
*Cambodians	Thailand	Northern Kamer	1,000,000	Buddhism	1% 5
Campa	Peru	Campa	5,000	Animism	-1% 1
Camsa	Colombia	Camsa	2,000	Animism	-1% 1
Candoshi	Peru	Candoshi	3,000	Animism	-1% 1
Canela	Brazil	Canela	1,400	Animism	-1% 1
Capanahua	Peru	Capanahua	500	Animism	-1% 1
Carapana	Colombia	Carapana	200	Animism	-1% 1
Cashibo	Peru	Cashibo	1,500	Animism	-1% 1
Caste Hindus (Andra Prd)	India	Telugu	44,000,000	Hinduism	3% 4
Cayapa	Ecuador	Cayapa	3,000	Animism	-1% 1
***Cebu, Middle-Class	Philippines	Cebuano	500,000	Animism	12% 4
Chiang	China	Ch'iang	128,000	Christo-Paganism	5% 4
***Ch'ol Sabanilla	Mexico	Tila Chol	77,000	Traditional Chinese	5% 4
Ch'ol Tila	Mexico	Ch'ol	20,000	Christo-Paganism	5% 4
Chacobo	Bolivia	Chacobo	38,000	Animism	-1% 5
Chaghatai	Afghanistan	Chaghatai	250	Animism	-1% 1
Chakfem-Mushere	Nigeria	Chakfem-Mushere	300,000	Islam	-1% 1
Chakma	India	Chakma	5,000	Animism	-1% 1
***Chakossi	Ghana	Chakossi	68,710	Hindu-Animist	6% 5
Chakossi	Togo	Chakossi	22,000	Animism	3% 4
Cham	Viet Nam	Cham	29,000	Animism	-1% 1
*Cham (Western)	Kampuchea, Democratic	Cham	45,000	Hinduism	1% 5
***Chamars of Bundelkhand	India	Chamari	90,000	Islam	0% 6 80
Chamba Daka	Nigeria	Bundelkhandi	5,320	Hindu-Animist	-1% 4
Chamba Leko	Nigeria	Chamba Daka	nr	Hinduism	-1% 1
Chameali	India	Chamba Leko	66,000	Islam-Animist	-1% 1
Chami	Colombia	Chameali	30,000	Islam-Animist	-1% 1
Chamicuro	Peru	Chami	52,970	Hindu-Animist	-1% 1
Chamorro	Turks and Caicos Islands	Chamicuro	3,000	Animism	-1% 1
Chamula	Mexico	Chamorro	150	Animism	-1% 1
Chara	Ethiopia	Tzotzil (Chamula)	15,000	Christo-Paganism	10% 4
Chaungtha	Burma	Chara	50,000	Christo-Paganism	18% 6 79
Chawal	Nigeria	Chaungtha	1,000	Animism	-1% 1
**Chayahuita	Peru	Chawai	34,600	Buddhist-Animist	-1% 1
Chenchu	India	Chayawita	30,000	Animism	11% 4
Chero	India	Chenchu	6,000	Christo-Paganism	-1% 1
Chik-Barik	India	Chero	17,610	Hindu-Animist	-1% 1
Chin	China	Chik-Barik	28,370	Animism	-1% 1
		Chin	30,240	Animism	-1% 1
			95,500	Traditional Chinese	-1% 1

Group	Country	Language	Population	Religion	%
Chin, Asho	Burma	Chin, Asho	11,000	Buddhist-Animist	-1% 1
Chin, Falam	Burma	Chin, Falam	92,000	Buddhist-Animist	-1% 1
Chin, Haka	Burma	Chin, Haka	85,000	Buddhist-Animist	-1% 1
Chin, Khumi	Burma	Chin, Khumi	30,000	Buddhist-Animist	-1% 1
Chin, Ngawn	Burma	Chin, Ngawn	5,000	Buddhist-Animist	-1% 1
Chin, Tiddim	Burma	Chin, Tiddim	38,000	Buddhist-Animist	-1% 1
*Chinbok	Burma	Chinbok	21,000	Buddhist-Animist	-1% 1
*Chinese (Hoklo) in Taiwan	Taiwan	Taiwanese (Minnan)	11,470,000	Traditional Chinese	2% 4
Chinese Businessmen	Hong Kong	Cantonese	10,000	Traditional Chinese	8% 4
Chinese Factory Workers	Hong Kong	Cantonese	500,000	Traditional Chinese	2% 3
**Chinese Hakka of Taiwan	Taiwan	Hakka	1,750,000	Traditional Chinese	2% 4
*Chinese in Amsterdam	Netherlands	Cantonese	15,000	Unknown	1% 6 79
**Chinese in Australia	Australia	Cantonese	30,000	Traditional Chinese	8% 4
*Chinese in Austria	Austria	Mandarin	1,000	Traditional Chinese	5% 4
*Chinese in Brazil	Brazil	Hakka	45,000	Traditional Chinese	8% 4
Chinese in Burma	Burma	Mandarin	600,000	Traditional Chinese	2% 4
Chinese in Costa Rica	Costa Rica	Cantonese	5,000	Unknown	1% 3
*Chinese in Holland	Netherlands	Mandarin	35,000	Unknown	1% 4
**Chinese in Hong Kong	Hong Kong	Cantonese	4,135,000	Traditional Chinese	8% 4
**Chinese in Indonesia	Indonesia	Indonesian	3,600,000	Traditional Chinese	6% 4
*Chinese in Japan	Japan	Mandarin	50,000	Traditional Chinese	1% 4
*Chinese in Korea	Korea, Republic of	Chinese	35,000	Secularism	5% 4
*Chinese in Laos	Laos	Mandarin	25,000	Traditional Chinese	1% 4
*Chinese in Malaysia	Malaysia	Chinese dialects	3,555,879	Traditional Chinese	8% 5
*Chinese in New Zealand	New Zealand	Cantonese	9,500	Traditional Chinese	4% 4
*Chinese in Osaka, Japan	Japan	Japanese	9,000	Unknown	1% 3
*Chinese in Puerto Rico	Puerto Rico	Hakka	1,200	Traditional Chinese	0% 2
**Chinese in Sabah	Malaysia	Hakka	180,000	Traditional Chinese	10% 2
*Chinese in Sarawak	Malaysia	Mandarin	330,000	Traditional Chinese	7% 4
**Chinese in South Africa	South Africa	Cantonese	10,000	Traditional Chinese	9% 4
*Chinese in Thailand	Thailand	Hakka	3,100,000	Buddhism	2% 4
**Chinese in United Kingdom	United Kingdom	Mandarin	105,000	Traditional Chinese	3% 4
**Chinese in United States	United States of America	Mandarin	550,000	Traditional Chinese	9% 4
*Chinese in Vancouver B.C.	Canada	Cantonese	80,000	Traditional Chinese	6% 4
*Chinese in West Germany	German Federal Rep.	Mandarin	5,200	Secularism	2% 4
*Chinese Mainlanders	Taiwan	Mandarin	2,010,000	Secularism	8% 4
Chinese Merchants	Ghana	Chinese dialects	40	Unknown	0% 3
*Chinese of W. Malaysia	Malaysia	Cantonese	3,500,000	Traditional Chinese	4% 4
**Chinese Refugees in Macau	Macau	Burmese	18,000	Traditional Chinese	1% 4
**Chinese Refugees, France	France	Tien-Chiu	100,000	Traditional Chinese	2% 4 79
**Chinese Restaurant Wrkrs.	France	Won Chow	50,000	Traditional Chinese	2% 4
**Chinese Stud., Australia	Australia	Chinese Dialects	5,500	Secularism	5% 4
**Chinese Students Glasgow	United Kingdom	Mandarin	1,000	Traditional Chinese	15% 4

	Country	Name	Population	Religion			
Chinese Villagers	Hong Kong	Cantonese	500,000	Traditional Chinese	18	3	
Chip'o	China	Chingp'o	101,850	Traditional Chinese	-18	1	
Chip	Nigeria	Chip	6,000	Animism	-18	1	
Chipaya	Bolivia	Chipaya	850	Animism	-18	1	
Chiquitano	Bolivia	Chiquitano	20,000	Animism	-18	5	
**Chiriguano	Argentina	Guarani (Bolivian)	15,000	Animism	8%	5	
Chiru	India	Chiru	3,060	Animism	-18	1	
Chitralis	Pakistan	Khuwar	126,000	Islam	0%	6	79
Chodhari	India	Chodhari	138,980	Hindu-Animist	-18	1	
Chokobo	Nigeria	Chokobo	425	Animism	-18	1	
Chokwe (Lunda)	Angola	Chokwe	400,000	Animism	9%	5	
Chola Naickans	India	Canarese	100	Animism	0%	3	
Chorote	Argentina	Chorote	500	Animism	-18	1	
**Chrau	Viet Nam	Jro	15,000	Animism	14%	4	
Chuabo	Mozambique	Chwabo	250,000	Animism	9%	4	
Chuj of San Mateo Ixtatan	Guatemala	Chuj	17,000	Animism	12%	5	
Chungchia	China	Chungchia	1,500,000	Traditional Chinese	-18	1	
Churahi	India	Churahi	34,670	Hindu-Animist	-18	1	
Chwang	China	Chwang	7,785,410	Traditional Chinese	-18	1	
Cinta Larga	Brazil	Cinta Larga	500	Animism	-18	1	
Circassian	Turkey	Circassian	113,370	Islam	-18	5	
Cirebon	Indonesia	Javanese, Tjirebon	2,500,000	Islam	-18	5	
***Citak	Indonesia	Citak (Asmat)	6,500	Animism	-18	1	
Citak	Indonesia	Citak	6,000	Animism	-18	1	
Cocama	Peru	Cocama	18,000	Animism	-18	1	
Cofan	Colombia	Cofan	250	Animism	-18	1	
Cogui	Colombia	Cogui	4,000	Animism	-18	1	
*College Students in Japan	Japan	Japanese	350,000	Secularism	2%	4	
*Comorians	Comoros	Comorian (Shingazidja)	300,000	Islam	-18	6	79
**Coreguaje	Colombia	Coreguaje	500	Animism	-18	4	
Coreguaje	Colombia	Coreguaje	500	Animism	-18	1	
Cubeo	Colombia	Cubeo	2,000	Animism	-18	1	
Cuiba	Colombia	Cuiba	2,000	Animism	-18	1	
Cujareno	Peru	Cujareno	100	Animism	-18	1	
Culina	Brazil	Culina	800	Animism	-18	1	
*Cuna	Colombia	Cuna	600	Animism	-18	1	
Cuna	Colombia	Cuna	600	Animism	7%	5	79
Curipaco	Colombia	Curipaco	2,500	Animism	7%	1	
Cuyonon	Philippines	Cuyonon	49,000	Christo-Paganism	-18	1	
Dabra	Indonesia	Dabra	100	Animism	-18	1	
Dadiya	Nigeria	Dadiya	2,300	Islam	-18	1	
Dagada	Indonesia	Dagada	30,000	Animism	-18	1	
Dagari	Ghana	Dagari	200,000	Animism	-18	4	

People	Country	Language	Population	Religion	
**Dagomba	Ghana	Dagbanli	350,000	Islam	18 4
Dagur	China	Dagur	22,600	Traditional Chinese	18 1
Dai	Burma	Dai	10,000	Buddhist-Animist	18 1
Daju of Dar Dadju	Chad	Daju of Dar Dadju	27,000	Islam-Animist	18 1
Daju of Dar Sila	Chad	Daju of Dar Sila	33,000	Islam-Animist	18 4
*Daka	Nigeria	Dakanci	10,000	Animism	38 4
Dan	Ivory Coast	Dan	245,000	Islam-Animist	18 1
Dangaleat	Chad	Dangaleat	20,000	Islam-Animist	18 1
*Dani, Baliem	Indonesia	Dani, Grand Valley	50,000	Animism	38 6 79
Dass	Nigeria	Dass	8,830	Islam-Animist	18 1
Dathanik	Ethiopia	Dathanik	18,000	Animism	18 1
Davaweno	Philippines	Davaweno	13,000	Christo-Paganism	18 1
Dawoodi Muslims	India	Gujarati	225,000	Islam	08 4
Degema	Nigeria	Degeme	10,000	Animism	18 1
Dem	Indonesia	Dem	2,000	Animism	08 1
Demta	Indonesia	Demta	840	Animism	18 1
Dendi	Benin	Dendi	40,000	Islam	08 3
Deno	Nigeria	Deno	10,000	Islam	18 1
Deori	India	Deori	14,940	Animism	18 1
Dera	Nigeria	Dera	20,000	Islam	18 1
Desano	Brazil	Desano	1,040	Animism	18 1
*Dewein	Liberia	De	5,000	Islam	18 4
*Dghwede	Nigeria	Zighvana (Dghwede)	13,000	Animism	18 5
Dhanka	India	Dhanka	10,230	Animism	18 1
Dhanwar	India	Dhanwar	21,140	Animism	18 4
*Dhodias	India	Dhodia Dialects	300,000	Hinduism	18 4
Dida	Ivory Coast	Dida	115,000	Islam-Animist	18 1
Didinga	Sudan	Didinga	30,000	Animism	18 4
Dimasa	India	Dimasa	37,900	Animism	18 1
Dime	Ethiopia	Dime	2,000	Animism	18 1
Dinka	Sudan	Dinka	1,940,000	Animism	48 5
Diola	Guinea-Bissau	Diola	15,000	Islam	38 5 80
Diola	Senegal	Diola	266,000	Islam	18 5
Dirim	Nigeria	Dirim	11,000	Islam-Animist	18 1
Dirya	Nigeria	Dirya	3,750	Islam	18 1
Divehi	Maldives	Divehi	120,000	Islam	08 6 80
*Dogon	Mali	Dogon	312,000	Animism	108 6 79
Dompago	Benin	Dompago	19,000	Animism	78 4
**Doohwaayo	Cameroon	Doohyaayo	15,000	Animism	128 5
Dorli	India	Dorli	24,320	Hindu-Animist	18 1
Dorobo	Kenya	Nandi	22,000	Animism	18 4
	Tanzania	Hadza	3,000	Animism	18 4
Dorze	Ethiopia	Dorze	3,000	Animism	18 1

223

Name	Country	Language	Population / Religion	Code
Druzes	Israel	Arabic	33,000 Folk Religion	08 6 79
**Dubla	India	Gujarati	202,218 Hinduism	48 4
Dubu	Indonesia	Dubu	Animism	-18 1
Duguir	Nigeria	Duguri	12,000 Islam	-18 1
Duguza	Nigeria	Duguza	2,000 Islam	-18 1
**Duka	Nigeria	Dukanci	10,000 Animism	18 5
*Dumagat , Casiguran	Philippines	Dumagat	1,000 Animism	38 6
Duru	Cameroon	Duru	20,000 Animism	-38 4
Duvele	Indonesia	Duvele	500 Animism	-18 1
Dyerma	Niger	Dyerma	1,000,000 Islam	18 6 80
Dyimini	Nigeria	Dyimini	42,000 Islam	-18 1
Dyola	Ivory Coast	Dyola	50,000 Islam-Animist	-18 1
Ebira	Gambia	Ebira	216,000 Islam-Animist	-18 1
Ebrie	Ivory Coast	Ebrie	325,000 Islam-Animist	-18 1
Edo	Nigeria	Edo	50,000 Islam-Animist	-18 1
Efik	Nigeria	Efik	430,000 Animism	-18 1
Efutop	Nigeria	Efutop	26,300 Animism	-18 1
Eggon	Nigeria	Eggon	10,000 Animism	-18 1
Ejagham	Nigeria	Ejagham	80,000 Animism	128 5
Ekagi	Indonesia	Ekagi	100,000 Animism	-18 1
Ekajuk	Nigeria	Ekajuk	15,000 Animism	-18 1
Eket	Nigeria	Eket	22,000 Animism	-18 1
Ekpeye	Nigeria	Ekpeye	30,000 Animism	-18 1
El Molo	Kenya	Samburu	1,000 Animism	-18 1
Eleme	Nigeria	Eleme	16,000 Animism	38 4
Emai-Iuleha-Ora	Nigeria	Emai-Iuleha-Ora	48,000 Animism	-18 1
Embera, Northern	Colombia	Embera	2,000 Animism	-18 1
Emumu	Indonesia	Emumu	1,100 Animism	-18 1
Endeh	Indonesia	Endeh	34,000 Christo-Paganism	-18 1
Engenni	Nigeria	Engenni	10,000 Animism	-18 1
Enggano	Indonesia	Enggano	400 Animism	-18 1
Eotile	Ivory Coast	Eotile	4,000 Islam-Animist	-18 1
Epie	Nigeria	Epie	12,000 Animism	-18 1
Erokwanas	Indonesia	Erokwanas	250 Animism	-18 1
Esan	Nigeria	Esan	200,000 Animism	-18 1
Etulo	Nigeria	Etulo	2,900 Animism	-18 1
Evant	Nigeria	Evant	5,000 Animism	-18 1
Evenki	China	Evenki	7,200 Traditional Chinese	-18 1
**Factory Workers, Young	Hong Kong	Cantonese	40,000 Unknown	58 4
***Fakai	Nigeria	Faka	15,000 Animism	18 5
***Falasha	Ethiopia	Agau	30,000 Judaism	78 7 79
**Fali	Nigeria	Fali	25,000 Animism	28 5

Farmers of Japan	Japan	Japanese	24,988,740	Traditional Japanese	18	4	
Fishing Village People	Taiwan	Amoy	150,000	Traditional Chinese	28	4	
Foau	Indonesia	Foau	230	Animism	-18	1	
Fordat	Indonesia	Fordat	9,770	Animism	-18	1	
Fra-Fra	Ghana	Fra-Fra	230,000	Animism	-18	5	
Fula	Guinea	Fula	1,500,020	Islam	-18	5	
Fula, Cunda	Gambia	Fula	70,200	Islam-Animist	18	5	
Fulah	Upper Volta	Fulani	300,000	Islam	18	5	
*Fulani	Benin	Fulani	70,000	Islam	18	5	
Fulani	Cameroon	Fulani	250,000	Islam	18	5	79
*Fulbe	Ghana	Fulani	5,500	Islam	08	5	
Fulnio	Brazil	Fulnio	1,500	Animism	-18	1	
Fyam	Nigeria	Pyam	14,000	Animism	-18	1	
Fyer	Nigeria	Fyer	3,000	Animism	-18	5	
Ga-Dang	Philippines	Ga-Dang	5,500	Animism	-18	1	
Gaanda	Nigeria	Gaanda	10,000	Islam-Animist	-18	4	
*Gabbra	Ethiopia	Gabrinja	nr	Folk Religion	-18	1	
Gabbra	Kenya	Galla	12,000	Folk Religion	-18	4	
Gabri	Chad	Gabri	20,000	Islam-Animist	-18	5	
Gadaba	India	Gadaba	20,410	Hindu-Animist	-18	4	
Gaddi	India	Gaddi	70,220	Hindu-Animist	-18	4	
Gade	Nigeria	Gade	25,000	Animism	18	4	
*Gagre	Ivory Coast	Punjabi	40,000	Animism	18	4	
Gagu	Nigeria	Gagou	25,000	Animism	18	4	
Galambi	Nigeria	Galambi	1,000	Islam	-18	1	
Galeshis	Iran	Galeshi	2,000	Islam	78	5	
*Galla (Bale)	Ethiopia	Galla	750,000	Islam	-18	3	
Galla of Bucho	Ethiopia	Galla (Oromo)	1,500	Christo-Paganism	-18	5	
Galla, Harar	Ethiopia	Gallinya	1,305,400	Islam	-18	4	
Galler	Laos	Gallinya	50,000	Animism	-18	1	
Galong	India	Galler	36,860	Hindu-Animist	-18	1	
Gambai	Chad	Gambai	200,000	Islam-Animist	-18	1	
Gamti	India	Gamti	136,210	Hindu-Animist	-18	1	
Gane	Indonesia	Gane	1,500	Animism	-18	1	
Gange	India	Gangte	6,030	Hindu-Animist	-18	1	
Gawar-Bati	Afghanistan	Gawar-Bati	8,000	Islam	-18	1	
Gawari	India	Gawari	21,100	Hindu-Animist	-18	1	
Gawwada	Ethiopia	Gawwada	4,000	Animism	-18	1	
Gayo	Indonesia	Gayo	200,000	Islam	08	4	80
Gbande	Guinea	Bandi	66,000	Animism	08	3	
Gbari	Nigeria	Gbari	500,000	Animism	28	6	80
Gbaya	Nigeria	Gbaya	350,000	Islam	-18	1	
Gbazantche	Benin	Gbazantche	9,000	Islam	08	3	

225

Gedeo	Gedeo	Ethiopia	250,000	Animism	-1 8 1
Geji	Geji	Nigeria	2,650	Islam	-1 8 1
Gera	Gera	Nigeria	13,300	Islam	-1 8 1
Geruma	Geruma	Nigeria	4,700	Islam	-1 8 1
Gesa	Gesa	Indonesia	200	Animism	-1 8 1
Gheko	Gheko	Burma	4,000	Buddhist-Animist	4 8 5
**Chimeera	Gimira	Ethiopia	50,000	Animism	-1 8 1
Ghotuo	Ghotuo	Nigeria	9,000	Animism	-1 8 1
Gidar	Gidar	Chad	50,000	Islam-Animist	-1 8 1
Gidicho	Gidicho	Ethiopia	500	Animism	-1 8 1
Gilaki	Gilaki	Iran	1,950,000	Islam	-1 8 4
Gio	Dan (Yacouba)	Liberia	92,000	Animism	5 8 5
Giryama	Giryama	Kenya	335,900	Animism	9 8 4
Gisel	Masa	Cameroon	10,000	Animism	-1 8 4
Gisiga	Gisiga	Cameroon	30,000	Animism	-1 8 4
*Glavda	Glavda	Nigeria	19,000	Animism	4 8 5
Gobato	Gobato	Ethiopia	1,000	Animism	-1 8 1
Gobeze	Gobeze	Ethiopia	22,000	Animism	-1 8 1
***Godie	Godie	Ivory Coast	20,000	Animism	12 8 4
Goemai	Goemai	Nigeria	80,000	Animism	-1 8 1
Gokana	Gokana	Nigeria	54,000	Animism	-1 8 1
Golo	Golo	Chad	3,400	Islam-Animist	-1 8 1
*Gonds	Gondi	India	4,000,000	Animism	1 8 5
Gonja	Gonja	Ghana	108,000	Islam	2 8 5
*Gorkha	Napali	India	180,000	Hinduism	0 8 4
Gorontalo	Gorontalo	Indonesia	500,000	Islam	-1 8 1
Goudari	Goudari	Iran	2,000	Islam	0 8 3
Goulai	Goulai	Chad	30,000	Islam-Animist	-1 8 1
**Gourcy	Gourendi	Upper Volta	200,000	Animism	5 8 4
Gouro	Gouro	Ivory Coast	100,000	Animism	4 8 6
Government officials	Thai	Thailand	27,160	Buddhism	0 8 3
Grasia	Grasia Dialects	India	65,000	Hindu-Animist	-1 8 1
*Grebo	Grebo Dialects	Liberia	200,000	Animism	8 8 4
Grunshi	not reported	Ghana	5,000	Animism	-1 8 4
Guajajara	Guajajara	Brazil	15,000	Animism	-1 8 1
Guajibo	Guajibo	Colombia	60,000	Animism	-1 8 1
*Guajiro	Guajiro	Colombia	9,000	Animism	12 8 5
Guambiano	Guambiano	Colombia	800	Animism	-1 8 1
*Guanano	Guanano	Colombia	15,000	Animism	1 8 4 79
***Guarani	Guarani	Bolivia	15,000	Christo-Paganism	10 8 6 79
Guarayu	Guarayu	Bolivia	5,000	Christo-Paganism	1 8 5
Guayabero	Guayabero	Colombia	700	Animism	-1 8 1
Guayabevo	Guayabero	Colombia	600	Animism	8 8 5

	Language	Country	Population	Religion	
Gude	Gude	Cameroon	100,000	Animism	18 4
Gudu	Gudu	Nigeria	40,000	Animism	18 1
Guduf	Guduf	Nigeria	1,200	Animism	18 1
Guere	Guere	Ivory Coast	21,300	Animism	18 1
Gugu-Yalanji	Gugu-Yalanji	Australia	117,870	Islam-Animist	18 4
Gujarati	Gujarati	United Kingdom	5,400	Animism	18 6
Gujuri	Gujuri	Afghanistan	300,000	Hinduism	18 1
Gula	Gula	Chad	10,000	Islam	18 1
Gumuz	Gumuz	Ethiopia	2,500	Islam-Animist	18 1
Gurage	Gurage Dialects	Ethiopia	53,000	Animism	18 1
Gure-Kahugu	Gure-Kahugu	Nigeria	750,000	Islam	30 6 80
Gurensi	Gurene	Ghana	5,000	Islam	18 4
Gurung	Gurung	Nepal	250,000	Animism	18 1
Guruntum-Mbaaru	Guruntum-Mbaaru	Nigeria	172,000	Hinduism	08 5
Gwa	Gwa	Ivory Coast	10,000	Islam	18 1
Gwandara	Gwandara	Nigeria	8,300	Islam-Animist	18 5
Gwari Matai	Gwari Matai	Nigeria	25,000	Animism	18 1
*Gypsies in Spain	Rom	Spain	200,000	Islam	18 1
Hadiyya	Hadiyya	Ethiopia	700,000	Folk Religion	30 6 79
**Hajong	Bengali	Bangladesh	17,000	Animism	18 1
Halbi	Halbi	India	349,260	Hinduism	18 5
Hallam	Hallam	Burma	11,000	Hindu-Animist	18 1
Hani	Hani	China	138,000	Buddhist-Animist	18 1
Hanonoo	Hanonoo	Philippines	6,000	Traditional Chinese	18 1
Harari	Harari	Ethiopia	13,000	Christo-Paganism	18 1
Harauti	Harauti	India	334,380	Islam	18 1
Havunese	Havunese	Indonesia	40,000	Hindu-Animist	18 1
Helong	Helong	Indonesia	5,000	Animism	18 1
**Hewa	Hewa	Papua New Guinea	1,500	Animism	58 6 79
Hezareh	Hezara'i	Iran	nr	Islam	78 4
**High School Students	Cantonese	Hong Kong	453,000	Traditional Chinese	78 5
Higi	Higi	Nigeria	150,000	Animism	18 1
Hixkaryana	Hixkaryana	Brazil	150	Animism	18 1
Ho	Ho	India	749,800	Hindu-Animist	18 1
Hohodene	Hohodene	Brazil	1,000	Animism	18 1
Holiya	Holiya	India	3,090	Hindu-Animist	18 1
Hopi	Hopi	United States of America	6,000	Animism	48 5
Hrangkhol	Hrangkhol	Burma	8,500	Buddhist-Animist	18 1
Huachipaire	Huachipaire	Peru	215	Animism	18 1
Huambisa	Huambisa	Peru	5,000	Animism	18 1
**Huave	Huave	Mexico	18,000	Christo-Paganism	58 5
Hui	Hui-hui-yu	China	5,200,000	Islam	08 6 80

Name	Language/Dialect	Country	Population	Religion	
**Huila	Huila	Angola	200,000	Animism	-1% 4
Huitoto, Meneca	Huitoto, Meneca	Colombia	600	Animism	-1% 1
Huitoto, Murui	Huitoto, Murui	Peru	800	Animism	-1% 1
Hukwe	Hukwe	Angola	9,000	Animism	3% 4
**Hunzakut	Burushaski	Pakistan	10,600	Islam	0% 6 79
Hupda Maku	Hupda Maku	Colombia	150	Animism	-1% 1
Hwana	Hwana	Nigeria	20,000	Islam-Animist	-1% 1
Hwela-Numu	Hwela-Numu	Ivory Coast	50,000	Islam-Animist	-1% 1
Hyam	Hyam	Nigeria	60,000	Islam	-1% 1
Ibaji	Ibaji	Nigeria	20,000	Animism	-1% 4
Ibanag	Ibanag	Philippines	319	Animism	-1% 1
Ibibio	Ibibio	Nigeria	2,000,000	Animism	-1% 1
Ica	Ica	Colombia	3,000	Animism	2% 5
Icen	Icen	Nigeria	7,000	Islam-Animist	-1% 1
Idoma	Idoma	Nigeria	300,000	Animism	-1% 1
Idoma, North	Idoma, North	Nigeria	56,000	Animism	-1% 1
Ifuago, Antipolo	Keley-i	Philippines	5,000	Animism	6% 5
*Ifugao	Ifugao	Philippines	95,000	Animism	6% 5
**Ifugao (Kalangoya)	Kalangoya	Philippines	35,000	Animism	5% 4
Ifugao in Cababuyan	Ifugao, Ambanad	Philippines	4,000	Animism	14% 4
Ifugao, Ambanad	Ifugao, Ambanad	Philippines	15,000	Animism	-1% 1
Ifugao, Kiangan	Ifugao, Kiangan	Philippines	25,000	Animism	-1% 1
Igala	Igala	Nigeria	350,000	Animism	-1% 1
Igbira	Igbirra	Nigeria	400,000	Islam	14% 6 80
Igede	Igede	Nigeria	70,000	Animism	-1% 1
Ignaciano	Ignaciano	Bolivia	5,000	Animism	-1% 1
Igorot	Igorot	Philippines	20,000	Animism	-1% 1
Iha	Iha	Indonesia	5,500	Animism	-1% 1
Ihceve	Icheve	Nigeria	5,000	Animism	-1% 1
Ijo, Central-Western	Ijo	Nigeria	338,700	Animism	-1% 1
Ijo, Northeast	Ijo	Nigeria	395,300	Animism	-1% 1
Ijo, Northeast Central	Ijo	Nigeria	8,400	Animism	-1% 1
Ikulu	Ikulu	Nigeria	6,000	Islam	-1% 1
Ikwere	Ikwere	Nigeria	200,000	Animism	-1% 1
Ilongot	Ilongot	Philippines	7,640	Animism	-1% 1
Inallu	Afshari	Iran	5,000	Islam	-1% 1
Inanwatan	Inanwatan	Indonesia	1,100	Animism	0% 3
Indians in Fiji	Hindustani	Fiji	265,000	Hinduism	2% 6 79
*Indians In Rhodesia	Gujarati	Rhodesia	9,600	Hinduism	9% 4
**Indians, East	English with Hindi	Trinidad and Tobago	400,000	Hinduism	5% 6 79
*Indust-Workers Yongdungpo	Korean	Korea, Republic of	140,000	Folk Religion	6% 4
*Industry Laborers-Japan	Japanese	Japan	21,000,000	Traditional Japanese	1% 4
Inga	Inga	Colombia	6,000	Christo-Paganism	-1% 1

Group	Country	People/Language	Population & Religion			
Ingassana	Sudan	Tabi	35,000 Animism	08	5	
*Inland Sea Island Peoples	Japan	Japanese	1,000,000 Traditional Japanese	-18	4	
Insinai	Philippines	Insinai	10,000 Animism	-18	4	
*Int'l Stud., Los Banos	Philippines	Vietnamesc	nr Islam	-28	4	
Intha	Burma	Intha	80,000 Buddhist-Animist	-18	1	
Iquito	Peru	Spanish	150 Animism	-18	1	
Itahutu	Indonesia	Irahutu	4,000 Animism	-18	4	
Iraqw	Tanzania	Iraqw	218,000 Animism	118	4	
Iraya	Philippines	Iraya	6,000 Christo-Paganism	-18	1	
Iresim	Indonesia	Iresim	100 Animism	-18	1	
Iria	Indonesia	Iria	850 Animism	-18	1	
Irigwe	Nigeria	Irigwe	15,000 Animism	-18	1	
***Irulas	India	Irula	10,000 Hinduism	08	4	
Isekiri	Nigeria	Isekiri	33,000 Animism	-18	1	
Isneg, Dibagat-Kabugao	Philippines	Isneg, Dibagat-Kabugao	10,000 Animism	-18	1	
Isneg, Karagawan	Philippines	Isneg, Karagawan	8,000 Animism	-18	1	
Isoko	Nigeria	Isoko	20,000 Animism	-18	1	
Itawit	Philippines	Itawit	15,000 Christo-Paganism	-18	1	
Itik	Indonesia	Itik	100 Animism	-18	1	
Itneg, Adasen	Philippines	Itneg, Adasen	4,000 Christo-Paganism	-18	1	
Itneg, Binongan	Philippines	Itneg, Binongan	7,000 Christo-Paganism	-18	1	
Itneg, Masadiit	Philippines	Itneg, Masadiit	7,500 Christo-Paganism	-18	1	
Itonama	Bolivia	Itonama	110 Animism	-18	1	
Ivbie North-Okpela-Atte	Nigeria	Ivbie North-Okpela-Atte	20,000 Animism	-18	4	
*Iwaidjo	Austria	Iwaidjo	150 Animism	18	4	
Iwur	Indonesia	Iwur	1,000 Animism	08	4	
Ixil	Guatemala	Cuyolbal	45,000 Christo-Paganism	18	4	
Iyon	Nigeria	Iyon	2,000 Animism	-18	4	
Izarek	Nigeria	Izarek	30,000 Animism	-18	1	
**Izi	Nigeria	Izi	200,000 Animism	118	4	
Jaba	Nigeria	Jaba	60,000 Animism	-18	4	
Jagannathi	India	Jagannathi	1,310 Hindu-Animist	-18	4	
Jains	India	Hindi	2,000,000 Jain	-18	5	80
Jama Mapun	Philippines	Cagayan	15,000 Islam	-18	1	
Jamamadi	Brazil	Jamamadi	1,200 Animism	-18	3	
Jamden	Indonesia	Jamden	14,330 Animism	08	3	
Jamshidis	Iran	Jamshidi	1,000 Islam	-18	1	
Janjero	Ethiopia	Janjero	1,000 Animism	-18	1	
Janjo	Nigeria	Janjo	6,100 Animism	-18	1	
Japanese in Brazil	Brazil	Japanese	750,000 Buddhism	88	8	79
*Japanese in Korea	Korea, Republic of	Japanese	5,000 Traditional Japanese	18	3	
*Japanese Students In USA	United States of America	Japanese	nr Secularism	18	4	
Jagaru	Peru	Jaqaru	2,000 Animism	-18	1	

People	Language	Country	Population	Religion	
Jara	Jara	Nigeria	40,000	Islam	-18 1
**Jarawa	Jaranchi	Nigeria	150,000	Animism	68 5
Jatapu	Jatapu	India	36,450	Hindu-Animist	-18 1
Jati	Jati	Afghanistan	1,000	Islam	-18 1
Jaunsari (rural)	Jaunsari	India	56,560	Hindu-Animist	28 6 79
**Javanese of Central Java	Javanese	Indonesia	60,000,000	Islam	28 6
**Javanese of Pejompongan	Bahasa Jawa	Indonesia	20,000,000	Islam	58 5
Jebero	Spanish	Peru	5,000	Islam	78 4
Jemez Pueblo	Tewa (Jemez)	United States of America	3,000	Animism	-18 1
Jeng	Jeng	Laos	1,800	Christo-Paganism	58 4
Jera	Jera	Nigeria	50%	Animism	08 1
Jerawa	not reported	Nigeria	23,000	Islam	-18 1
*Jewish Imgrnts.-American	Hebrew	Israel	70,000	Judaism	-18 4
*Jewish Imgrnts.-Argentine	Hebrew	Israel	25,797	Judaism	08 3
*Jewish Imgrnts.-Australia	Hebrew	Israel	17,686	Judaism	08 3
*Jewish Imgrnts.-Brazilian	Hebrew	Israel	1,257	Judaism	08 3
*Jewish Imgrnts.-Mexican	Hebrew	Israel	4,005	Judaism	08 3
*Jewish Imgrnts.-Uruguayan	Hebrew	Israel	1,065	Judaism	09 3
*Jewish Immigrants, Other	Hebrew	Israel	2,720	Judaism	09 3
	Hebrew	Israel	5,520	Judaism	09 3
Jews of Iran	Farsi	Iran	93,000	Judaism	19 4
Jews of Montreal	English	Canada	120,000	Judaism	18 5
Jews, Sephardic	French	Canada	26,000	Judaism	18 3
Jharia	Jharia	India	2,050	Hinduism	-18 1
Jibu	Jibu, Jibanci	Nigeria	20,000	Animism	-18 5
Jimbin	Jimbin	Nigeria	1,500	Islam	-18 1
**Jivaro (Achuara)	Jivaro	Venezuela	20,000	Christo-Paganism	68 4
Jiye	Jiye (Karamojong)	Sudan	7,000	Animism	C9 5
Jiye	Jiye	Uganda	34,000	Animism	-18 1
Jongor	Jongor	Chad	16,000	Islam-Animist	-18 1
Juang	Juang	India	12,170	Hinduism	-18 4
Jukun	not reported	Nigeria	20,000	Animism	-18 1
Jyarung	Jyarung	China	70,000	Traditional Chinese	-18 1
**Ka'nis	K'anjobal	Guatemala	18,000	Ancestor Worship	18 1
**K'anjobal of San Miguel	Waffa Dialect	Papua New Guinea	50	Christo-Paganism	28 3
Kaagan	Kaagan	Philippines	20,000	Christo-Paganism	-18 1
Kabixi	Kabixi	Brazil	100	Animism	-18 1
Kabre	Kabre	Togo	273,000	Animism	98 5
Kabyle	Kabyle	Algeria	1,000,000	Islam	18 6 79
Kachama	Kachama	Ethiopia	500	Animism	-18 1
Kachchi	Kachchi	India	470,990	Hinduism	-18 1
Kadaklan-Barlig Bontoc	Kadaklan-Barlig Bontoc	Philippines	4,000	Animism	-18 1
Kadar	Kadar	India	800	Hindu-Animist	-18 1

Name	Country	Name	Population	Religion			
Kadara	Nigeria	Kadara	40,000	Animism	98	5	
Kadiweu	Brazil	Kadiweu	550	Animism	-18	1	
Kaeti	Indonesia	Kaeti	4,000	Animism	-18	1	
*Kaffa	Ethiopia	Kaffenya (Kefa)	320,000	Christo-Paganism	28	6	80
**Kafirs	Pakistan	Kafiristani (Bashgali)	3,000	Animism	-18	6	79
Kagoma	Nigeria	Kagoma	6,250	Islam	-18	1	
Kagoro	Mali	Logoro (Bambara)	30,000	Animism	-18	4	
Kahluri	India	Kahluri	66,190	Hindu-Animist	-18	1	
Kaibu	Nigeria	Kaibu	650	Islam	-18	1	
Kaikadi	India	Kaikadi	11,850	Hindu-Animist	-18	1	
Kaili	Indonesia	Kaili	300,000	Animism	-18	1	
Kaingang	Brazil	Kaingang	7,000	Christo-Paganism	-18	1	
**Kaipeng-Koloi	India	Kaipeng	30,000	Animism	-18	5	
Kaiwai	Indonesia	Kaiwai	600	Animism	-18	1	
Kajang	Indonesia	Kajang	50,000	Animism	-18	1	
Keka	Nigeria	Keka	2,000	Islam	-18	1	
**Kalagan	Philippines	Kalagan	19,000	Animism	-18	5	
*Kalanga	Botswana	ChiKalanga	150,000	Animism	28	5	
Kalinga, Kalagua	Philippines	Kalinga, Kalagua	3,600	Animism	-18	1	
Kalinga, Limus-Linan	Philippines	Kalinga, Limus-Linan	20,000	Animism	-18	1	
Kalinga, Quinaang	Philippines	Kalinga, Quinaang	41,000	Animism	-18	1	
*Kalinga, Southern	Philippines	Kalinga,Sumadel-Tinglayan	11,000	Animism	4	5	
*Kalinga,Northern	Philippines	Kalinga	20,000	Christo-Paganism	38	5	
Kam	China	Kalmytz	70,000	Traditional Chinese	-18	1	
Kamantan	Nigeria	Kam	825,320	Traditional Chinese	-18	4	
Kamar	India	Kamar	10,110	Hindu-Animist	-18	1	
Kamayura	Brazil	Kamayura	110	Animism	-18	1	
*Kambari	Nigeria	Kambari	100,000	Animism	-18	1	
Kambera	Indonesia	Kambera	200,000	Animism	68	6	80
Kamberataro	Indonesia	Kamberataro	970	Animism	-18	1	
Kamo	Nigeria	Kamo	3,000	Islam	-18	1	
Kamoro	Indonesia	Kamoro	8,000	Animism	-18	1	
Kampung Baru	Indonesia	Kampung Baru	400	Animism	-18	1	
Kamtuk-Gresi	Indonesia	Kamtuk-Gresi	5,000	Animism	-18	1	
*Kamuku	Nigeria	Kamuku	20,000	Animism	38	6	80
Kana	Nigeria	Kana	90,000	Animism	-18	1	
*Kanarese	India	Kannada	21,707,000	Hinduism	98	5	
Kanauri	India	Kanauri	28,500	Hindu-Buddhist	-18	1	
Kanembu	Chad	Kanembu	2,250	Islam-Animist	-18	1	
Kanikkaran	India	Kanikkaran	10,000	Hindu-Animist	-18	1	
Kanjari	India	Kanjari	55,390	Hindu-Animist	-18	1	
**Kankanay, Central	Philippines	Kankanay	40,000	Animism	28	5	

			Population	Religion			
Kanum	Indonesia	Kanum	320	Animism	-18	6	80
Kanuri	Nigeria	Kanuri Dialects	3,000,000	Islam	-18	6	1
Kao	Ethiopia	Karo	600	Animism	-18		1
Kapori	Indonesia	Kapori	60	Animism	-18		1
Karakalpak	Soviet Russia	Karakalpak	277,000	Islam	08	6	80
Karanga	Chad	Karanga	57,000	Islam-Animist	-18		1
Karas	Indonesia	Karas	200	Animism	-18		1
**Karbis	India	Mikir	300,000	Hinduism	58		5
Karekare	Nigeria	Karekare	39,000	Islam	-18		1
Karen	Thailand	Sgaw Karen	80,000	Animism	18	6	79
Karen, Pwo	Thailand	Pwo Karen	40,000	Animism	18		5
Kari	Chad	Kari	40,000	Islam-Animist	-18		1
Karipuna Creole	Brazil	Karipuna Creole	500	Animism	-18		1
Karipuna Do Guapore	Brazil	Karipuna Do Guapore	150	Animism	-18		1
Kariya	Nigeria	Kariya	2,200	Islam	-18		1
Karmali	India	Karmali	69,620	Hindu-Animist	-18		1
Karon Dori	Indonesia	Karon Dori	5,000	Animism	-18		1
Karon Pantai	Indonesia	Karon Pantai	2,500	Animism	-18		1
**Kasena	Ghana	Kasem	70,000	Animism	11	6	4
**Kashmiri Muslims	India	Kashmiri	3,060,000	Islam	18	6	79
Kasseng	Laos	Kasseng	15,000	Animism	08		5
Kasuweri	Indonesia	Kasuweri	1,200	Animism	-18		1
Katab	Nigeria	Katab	32,370	Islam	-18		1
Katakari	India	Katakari	4,956	Hindu-Animism	-18		1
Kati, Northern	Indonesia	Kati, Northern	8,000	Animism	-18		1
Kati, Southern	Indonesia	Kati, Southern	4,000	Animism	-18		1
Katukina, Panoan	Brazil	Katukina, Panoan	180	Animism	-18		1
Kaugat	Indonesia	Kaugat	1,000	Animism	-18		1
Kaure	Indonesia	Kaure	800	Animism	-18		1
Kavwol	Indonesia	Kavwol	500	Animism	-18		1
Kawar	India	Kawar	33,770	Hindu-Animist	-18		1
Kawe	Indonesia	Kawe	300	Animism	-18		1
Kayabi	Brazil	Kayabi	300	Animism	-18		1
Kayagar	Indonesia	Kayagar	9,000	Animism	88		4
Kayapo	Brazil	Kayapo	600	Animism	-18		1
Kaygir	Indonesia	Kaygir	4,000	Animism	08		4
Kayupulau	Indonesia	Kayupulau	570	Animism	-18		1
Kazakhs	Iran	Kazakhi	3,000	Islam	08	5	80
Kebumtamp	Bhutan	Kebumtamp	400,000	Buddhist-Animist	-18		1
Keer	India	Keer	2,890	Hindu-Animist	-18		1
Kei	Indonesia	Kei	30,000	Animism	-18		1
Kelao	China	Kelao	23,000	Traditional Chinese	-18		1
Kemak	Indonesia	Kemak	50,000	Animism	-18		1

Name	Name	Country	Population	Religion			
Kembata	Kembata	Ethiopia	250,000	Animism	-1	8	1
Kendari	Kendari	Indonesia	500,000	Islam-Animist	-1	8	1
Kenga	Kenga	Chad	25,000	Islam-Animist	-1	8	1
Kenyah	Kenyah	Indonesia	37,500	Animism	-1	8	1
*Kepas	Kewa	Papua New Guinea	5,000	Animism	-1	8	3
Kera	Kera	Chad	5,000	Islam-Animist	-1	8	1
Kerewe	Kikerewe	Tanzania	35,000	Animism	-1	8	4
Kerinchi	Kerinchi	Indonesia	170,000	Islam-Animist	-1	8	1
Khalaj	Khalaj	Iran	20,000	Islam	-1	8	1
Khalka	Khalka	China	68,000	Traditional Chinese	-1	8	1
Kham	Kham	China	11,400	Traditional Chinese	-1	8	1
Khamti	Khamti	India	300	Hindu-Buddhist	-1	8	1
*Khamu	Khamu	Thailand	6,300	Animism	0	8	4
Khana	Khana	Nigeria	90,000	Unknown	-1	8	5
Khandesi	Khandesl	India	14,700	Hindu-Animist	-1	8	1
Kharia	Kharia	India	88,400	Hindu-Animist	-1	8	1
Khasi	Khasi	India	384,010	Hinduism	-1	8	1
Khirwar	Khirwar	India	34,250	Hindu-Animist	-1	8	1
**Khmer Refugees	Cambodia	Thailand	15,000	Buddhism	0	8	4
Khojas, Agha Khani	Gujarati	India	175,000	Islam	-1	8	1
Khowar	Khowar	India	6,960	Hindu-Animist	-1	8	1
Kibet	Kibet	Chad	22,000	Islam-Animist	0	8	3
Kichepo	Kichepo	Sudan	16,000	Animism	-1	8	1
Kilba	Kilba	Nigeria	80,000	Islam	-1	8	1
Kim	Kim	Chad	5,000	Islam-Animist	-1	8	1
Kimaghama	Kimaghama	Indonesia	3,000	Animism	-1	8	1
*Kimyal	Kimyal	Indonesia	7,000	Animism	2	8	4
Kinaray-A	Kinaray-A	Philippines	288,000	Christo-Paganism	-1	8	1
Kirchiz	Kirghiz	China	68,000	Traditional Chinese	-1	8	1
Kirghiz	Kirgiz	Afghanistan	45,000	Islam	-1	8	1
Kirgiz	Kirgiz	Soviet Russia	1,700,000	Islam	0	8	6	80
Kirifi	Kirfi	Nigeria	14,000	Islam	-1	8	1
Kisan	Kisan	India	73,850	Hindu-Animist	-1	8	1
Kishanganjia	Kishanganjia	India	56,920	Hindu-Animist	-1	8	1
Kishtwari	Kishtwari	India	12,170	Hindu-Animist	-1	8	1
*Kissi	Kissi	Guinea	266,000	Animism	2	8	4
Kissi	Kissi	Liberia	35,000	Animism	3	8	4
*Kissi	Kissi, Southern	Sierra Leone	48,000	Animism	12	8	3
Kita	not reported	Mali	150,000	Islam	6	8	6	79
Koalib	Koalib (Nuba)	Sudan	320,000	Animism	-1	8	5
**Koch	Bengali	Bangladesh	35,000	Hinduism	-1	8	1
Koda	Koda	India	14,140	Hindu-Animist	-1	8	1
Kodi	Kodi	Indonesia	25,000	Animism	-1	8	1

Name	Country	Group	Population	Religion	Code
Koenoem	Nigeria	Koenoem	3,000	Animism	-18 1
Kofyar, Kutchi	Nigeria	Kofyar	40,000	Animism	-18 1
**Kohli, Tharadari	Pakistan	Gujarati, Koli	50,000	Hinduism	48 4
**Kohli, Wadiara	Pakistan	Gujarati, Koli	40,000	Hinduism	18 5
**Kohlis, Parkari	Pakistan	Gujarati, Koli	100,000	Hinduism	58 4
Kohoroxitari	Brazil	Kohoroxitari	620	Animism	-18 1
Kohumono	Nigeria	Kohumono	11,870	Animism	-18 1
Koke	Chad	Koke	1,000	Islam-Animist	-18 1
Kol	India	Kol	82,900	Hindu-Animist	18 5
**Kolam	India	Kolami	60,000	Hinduism	-18 5
Kolbila	Cameroon	Kolbila	1,000	Islam	18 5
Kom	India	Kom	6,970	Hindu-Animist	08 5
Koma	Ghana	Koma	1,000	Animism	-18 1
*Komo	Nigeria	Koma	15,000	Animism	-18 4
***Kond	Ethiopia	Komo	20,000	Animism	-38 5
Konda-Dora	India	Kui	900,000	Animism	-18 1
Koneraw	India	Konda-Dora	15,650	Hindu-Animist	-18 1
Konkani	Indonesia	Koneraw	300	Animism	18 1
Konkomba	India	Konkani	1,522,680	Hindu-Animist	98 5
*Konkomba	Ghana	Konkomba	175,000	Animism	-18 4
Kono	Togo	Kom Komba	25,000	Animism	-18 1
**Kono	Nigeria	Kono	1,550	Islam	58 5
Konso	Sierra Leone	Kono	133,000	Animism	-18 5
Koraga	Ethiopia	Konso	30,000	Animism	-18 1
**Koranko	India	Koraga	1,500	Hindu-Animist	18 5
Korapun	Sierra Leone	Kuranko (Maninka)	103,000	Islam	18 5
**Korean Prisoners	Indonesia	Korapun	4,000	Animism	-18 1
***Koreans in Germany	Korea, Republic of	Korean	45,000	Secularism	48 4
Koreans of Japan	German Federal Rep.	Korean	10,000	Unknown	48 4
*Korku	Japan	Korean	600,000	Folk Religion	68 5
Koro	India	Korku	250,000	Animism	18 5
Koroma	Nigeria	Koro	35,000	Animism	18 5
Korop	Sudan	Koroma	30,030	Animism	08 3
Korwa	Nigeria	Korop	10,000	Animism	-18 1
Kota	India	Korwa	14,250	Hindu-Animist	-18 1
Kotia	India	Kota	860	Hindu-Animist	-18 1
Kotogut	India	Kotia	15,000	Hindu-Animist	-18 1
Kotoko	Indonesia	Kotogut	1,000	Animism	-18 1
Kotokoli	Chad	Kotoko	31,000	Islam-Animist	08 3
Kotopo	Benin	Kotokoli	75,000	Islam	08 4
Kotta	Cameroon	Kotopo	10,000	Animism	08 5
	India	Kota	1,200	Animism	

Name	Language / People	Country	Population	Religion	
Kouya	Kouya	Ivory Coast	5,690	Islam-Animist	-18 1
**Kowaao	Kowaao	Liberia	7,000	Animism	3 8 4
Koya	Koya	India	211,880	Hindu-Animism	-18 1
Koyra	Koyra	Ethiopia	5,000	Animism	6 8 5
Kpelle	Kpelle	Liberia	200,000	Animism	3 8 4
*Krahn	Guere	Ivory Coast	250,000	Animism	7 8 4
***Krahn	Krahn	Liberia	55,000	Animism	-18 1
Kreen-Akakore	Kreen-Akakore	Brazil	90	Animism	-18 1
Krio	Krio	Gambia	3,400	Islam-Animist	-18 1
Krobou	Krobou	Ivory Coast	3,400	Islam-Animist	1 8 4
Krongo	Krongo	Sudan	121,000	Animism	0 8 6
Kuatinema	Asurini	Brazil	70	Animism	-18 1
Kubu	Local dialects	Indonesia	6,000	Islam	-2 8 3
Kuda-Chamo	Kuda-Chano	Nigeria	4,000	Animism	-18 1
*Kudisai Vagh Makkal	Tamil	India	1,000,000	Hinduism	1 8 6 80
	Kudiya	India	100	Hindu-Animist	-18 1
Kugbo	Kugbo	Nigeria	2,000	Animism	-18 1
*Kui	Kui	Thailand	160,000	Buddhism	-18 1
Kuikuro	Kuikuro	Brazil	120	Animism	-18 1
Kuka	Kuka	Chad	38,000	Islam-Animist	3 8 4
*Kukele	Kukele	Nigeria	31,700	Animism	-18 1
*Kuknas	Kukni	India	125,000	Hinduism	3 8 4
Kulango	Kulango	Ivory Coast	60,000	Animism	-18 1
Kulele	Kulere	Ivory Coast	15,000	Islam-Animist	-18 1
	Kulere	Nigeria	8,000	Animism	-18 1
Kullo	Kullo	Ethiopia	82,000	Islam-Animist	1 8 4
**Kuluis	Kului	India	200,000	Hinduism	-18 1
Kulung	Kulung	Nigeria	15,000	Islam-Animist	-18 1
Kumauni	Kumauni	India	1,234,940	Hindu-Animism	-18 1
	Kunama	Ethiopia	70,000	Islam	6 8 5
**Kunimaipa	Kunimaipa	Papua New Guinea	9,000	Christo-Paganism	-18 1
Kupia	Kupia	India	4,000	Hindu-Animist	1 8 6 80
Kurds in Iran	Kurdish Dialects	Iran	2,000,000	Islam	1 8 6 79
*Kurds of Turkey	Kurdish (Kirmancho)	Turkey	1,900,000	Islam	-18 1
Kurfei	Hausa	Niger	50,000	Animism	-18 1
Kurichiya	Kurichiya	India	12,130	Hindu-Animist	-18 1
Kuruba	Kuruba	India	7,900	Hindu-Animist	-18 1
Kurudu	Kurudu	Indonesia	1,100	Animism	-18 1
Kurux	Kurux	Ghana	1,240,400	Hindu-Animist	3 8 5
**Kusaasi	Kusaal	Nigeria	150,000	Animism	-18 1
Kusbi	Kushi	Nigeria	4,000	Islam	-18 1
Kuteb	Kuteb	Nigeria	26,000	Islam	-18 1
Kuturmi	Kuturmi	Nigeria	2,950	Islam	-18 1

People	Country	Population	Religion	Code
Kuvi	India	190,000	Hindu-Animist	-1% 1
Kuzamani	Nigeria	1,000	Islam	-1% 1
Kwa	Nigeria		Islam	-1% 1
Kwansu	Indonesia	350	Animism	-1% 1
Kwerba	Indonesia	2,000	Animism	-1% 5
Kwere	Tanzania	63,000	Animism	10% 5
Kwesten	Indonesia	2,480	Animism	-1% 1
Kyibaku	Nigeria	20,000	Islam	-1% 1
Laamang	Nigeria	40,000	Islam	-1% 1
Labans	India	nr	Hinduism	0% 3
Labaani	India	1,203,340	Hindu-Buddhist	-1% 1
Labhani	India	1,500	Hinduism	10% 4
*Labourers of Jhoparpatti	India	56,740	Hindu-Buddhist	10% 4
Ladakhi	India	18,000	Buddhism	-1% 1
Ladinos	Lebanon	7,300	Judaism	-1% 1
**Lahoulis	Thailand	22,500	Animism	7% 4
*Lahu	China	1,600	Traditional Chinese	-1% 4
Lahul	Cameroon	10,000	Animism	0% 4
Laka	Chad	6,000	Islam-Animist	-1% 1
Laka	China	500	Traditional Chinese	-1% 1
Lakka	Nigeria		Islam	-1% 1
Lalung	India	10,650	Hindu-Buddhist	-1% 1
Lama	Burma	3,000	Buddhist-Animist	-3% 4
Lamba	Togo	29,000	Animism	0% 5 80
Lame	Nigeria	2,000	Islam	-1% 1
Lampung (Komering)	Indonesia	1,500,000	Islam	0% 3
Langa	Ethiopia	2,000	Animism	-1% 7 79
Lango	Ethiopia	8,000	Animism	-1% 1
*Lao	Laos	1,908,600	Buddhism	-1% 1
*Lao Refugees	Thailand	20,000	Buddhism	-1% 1
Lara	Indonesia	1,000	Animism	-1% 1
Laru	Nigeria	860	Islam	-1% 1
Latdwalam	Indonesia	450	Animism	-1% 1
Lati	China	125,000	Traditional Chinese	4% 5
Laudje	Indonesia	10,000	Animism	-1% 5
Lawa	Thailand	30,000	Buddhism	0% 5
Lebgo	Nigeria	nr	Islam	-1% 1
Lebong (Redjang-Lebong)	Indonesia	200	Animism	10% 4
Leco	Bolivia	30,000	Islam-Animist	-1% 4
Lele	Chad	18,000	Hinduism	10% 4
**Lepcha	Sikkim	390,000	Buddhism	-1% 4
**Lepers of N.E. Thailand (Northeast Thai)	Thailand	6,000	Buddhism	10% 4
Letti	Indonesia		Animism	-1% 1

Group	Country	Language	Population	Religion	Index
Li	China	Li	1,000,000	Traditional Chinese	-18 1
Libyans	Libya	Arabic	2,300,000	Islam	08 3
Ligbi	Ghana	Ligbi	6,000	Islam	08 5
	Ivory Coast	Ligbi	26,000	Animism	-18 4
Limba	Sierra Leone	Limba	233,000	Animism	48 4
Lio	Indonesia	Lio	100,000	Christo-Paganism	-18 1
*Lisu	Thailand	Lisu	12,500	Animism	68 4
Lo	Nigeria	Lo	2,000	Animism	-18 1
Lobi	Ivory Coast	Lobi	40,000	Animism	-18 4
Lodhi	India	Lodhi	44,070	Hindu-Animism	-18 1
Lohar	Pakistan	Gujarati Dialect	nr	Hinduism	08 3
**Loho Loho	Indonesia	Kolaka	10,000	Animism	08 1
Loinang	Indonesia	Loinang	80,000	Animism	-18 1
Loko	Sierra Leone	Loko	22,000	Animism	58 4
*Lokoro	Sudan	Lokoro	180,000	Christo-Paganism	38 4
Loma	Guinea	Loma	60,000	Animism	128 4
	Liberia	not reported	1,000,000	Animism	98 4
Lomwe	Mozambique	Lomwe	32,000	Animism	-18 1
Longuda	Nigeria	Lonquda	140,000	Islam	-18 1
Lors	Indonesia	Lore	600,000	Islam	08 5
Lotsu-Piri	Iran	Lurl	12,000	Islam	-18 1
**Lotuka	Nigeria	Lotsu-Piri	150,000	Other	68 5
Loven	Sudan	Latuka	25,000	Buddhism	58 5
Lu	Laos	Loven	400,000	Buddhist-Animist	-18 1
Lubu	China	Lu	1,000,000	Islam	-18 1
Lugbara	Indonesia	Lubu	260,000	Unknown	128 5
Lungu	Uganda	Lugbara	10,000	Animism	-18 4
Lushai	Nigeria	Lungu	270,310	Hindu-Animist	-18 1
Luwu	India	Lushai	500,000	Islam	-18 1
Maanyan	Indonesia	Luwu	15,000	Animism	-18 1
**Maasai	Indonesia	Maanyan	56,000	Islam-Animist	58 6 79
Maba	Kenya	Masai	10,000	Animism	-18 1
Machiguenga	Chad	Maba	1,000	Animism	-18 3
Macu	Peru	Machiguenga	300	Animism	-18 1
Macuna	Colombia	Macu	6,000	Animism	58 3
*Macuxi	Colombia	Macuna	30,000	Animism	-18 1
Madda	Brazil	Macuxi	1,000	Animism	-18 6
Madik	Nigeria	Madda	7,000,000	Animism	-18 1
Madurese	Indonesia	Madik	300,000	Islam	-18 6 79
*Magar	Indonesia	Madurese	309,000	Hinduism	-18 6 80
Maghi	Nepal	Magar		Buddhist-Animist	
Maguindano	Burma	Maghi		Islam	
	Philippines	Maguindano	700,000		

Name	Country	People/Language	Population	Religion	Code
***Maguzawa	Nigeria	Hausa	100,000	Animism	18 6 79
Mahali	India	Mahali	14,300	Hindu-Animist	18 1
Mahri	Oman	Mahri	50,000	Animism	18 1
Maiongong	Brazil	Maiongong	86	Animism	18 3
Maithili	Indonesia	Mairasi	1,000	Animism	18 4
Majhwar	Nepal	Maithili	1,000,000	Hinduism	08 4
Maji	India	Majhwar	27,960	Hindu-Animist	18 4
Majingai-Ngama	Ethiopia	Maji	15,000	Animism	18 1
Makasai	Chad	Majingai-Ngama	47,000	Islam-Animism	18 1
Makian, West	Indonesia	Makasai	70,000	Animism	18 1
Maklew	Indonesia	Makian, West	12,000	Animism	18 1
Makonde	Indonesia	Maklew	120	Animism	18 1
Makua	Tanzania	not reported	550,000	Islam	68 5
Mala Muthas	Mozambique	Makua	1,200,000	Animism	08 4
Malankuravan	India	Malamutha	1,000	Hinduism	09 4
Malapandaram	India	Malankuravan	5,000	Hindu-Animist	18 1
Malappanackers	India	Malapandaram	500	Hindu-Animist	08 4
Malaryan	India	Malappanackan	1,000	Animism	18 1
Malavedan	India	Malaryan	5,000	Hindu-Animist	18 1
*Malayalars	India	Malavedan	2,000	Hinduism	08 4
Malayo	India	Malayalam	nr	Animism	68 4
Malays of Singapore	Colombia	Malayo	1,000	Animism	18 6 79
Male	Singapore	Malay	300,000	Islam	18 1
Mali	Ethiopia	Male	12,000	Animism	18 1
Malki	India	Mali	970	Hindu-Animist	18 1
Malpaharia	India	Malki	88,650	Hindu-Animist	18 1
**Mam Indian	India	Malpaharia	9,080	Hindu-Animist	18 1
*Mamanwa (Mamanua)	India	Malvi	644,030	Hindu-Animist	78 5
Mamasani	Guatemala	Mam	470,000	Christo-Paganism	18 1
Mambai	Nigeria	Mama	20,000	Animism	09 4
Mambila	Philippines	Minamanwa	1,000	Christo-Paganism	18 1
Mamprusi	Iran	Luri	110,000	Islam	18 4
Mancang	Indonesia	Mambai	80,000	Animism	18 1
Manchu	Cameroon	Mambila	40,000	Animism	08 3
Mandar	Ghana	not reported	80,000	Animism	18 1
Mandara	Senegal	Mankanya	35,200	not reported	18 1
Mandaya	China	Manchu	200,000	Traditional Chinese	18 1
Mandaya, Mansaka	Indonesia	Mandar	302,000	Islam	18 1
Mander	Nigeria	Mandara	19,300	Islam	18 1
Manding	Philippines	Mandaya	3,400	Animism	18 1
	Philippines	Mandaya, Mansaka	35,400	Animism	18 1
	Indonesia	Mander	100	Animism	18 1
	Senegal	Malinke, Senegalese	208,400	not reported	08 3

Group	Country	Population	Religion			
Mandingo	Liberia	30,000	Islam	18	6	1
Mandyak	Gambia	85,000	Islam-Animist	18		1
Manem	Indonesia	400	Animism	18		1
Mangbai	Chad	2,000	Islam-Animist	18		1
Manggarai	Indonesia	251,000	Islam-Animist	18		1
Mangs	India	nr	Hinduism	08		3
**Mangyan	Philippines	60,000	Various Dialects	68		5
**Manikion	Indonesia	8,000	Animism	18		5
Manjack	Senegal	44,200	not reported	08		3
**Manjaco	Guinea-Bissau	80,000	Animism	78		4
Manna-Dora	India	8,480	Hindu-Animist	18		1
Mannan	India	4,980	Hindu-Animist	18		1
Mano	Liberia	65,000	Animism	48		4
Manobo, Agusan	Philippines	15,000	Animism	18		1
Manobo, Ata	Philippines	7,000	Animism	18		1
Manobo, Binokid	Philippines	40,550	Animism	18		4
**Manobo, Cotabato	Philippines	10,000	Animism	18		4
Manobo, Dibabawon	Philippines	1,792	Animism	38		5
*Manobo, Ilianen	Philippines	5,000	Animism	18		1
*Manobo, Obo	Philippines	4,000	Animism	18		1
**Manobo, Salug	Philippines	4,000	Animism	48		5
Manobo, Sarangani	Philippines	15,000	Animism	18		1
Manobo, Tagabawa	Philippines	9,900	Animism	18		1
**Manobo, Tigwa	Philippines	4,000	Animism	38		5
**Manobo, Western Bukidnon	Philippines	12,000	Animism	68		5
Manobos, Pulangi	Philippines	5,000	Animism	18		5
**Mansaka	Philippines	25,000	Christo-Paganism	108		5
Mantion	Indonesia	12,000	Animism	18		1
*Manu Park Panoan	Peru	200	Animism	18		1
*Mao Refugees from Laos	Thailand	7,000	Animism	48		4
Mao, Northern	Ethiopia	13,000	Islam-Animist	18		1
Maou	Ivory Coast	80,000	Islam-Animist	18		5
Mapuche	Chile	300,000	Christo-Paganism	18		5
Mara	India	11,870	Hindu-Animist	18		1
Maranao	Philippines	500,000	Islam	28	6	79
Maranao, Lanad	Philippines	500,000	Islam-Animist	18		1
Mararit	Chad	42,000	Islam-Animist	18		1
Marau	Indonesia	1,200	Animism	18		1
Marba	Chad	30,000	Islam-Animist	18		1
Marghi Central	Nigeria	135,000	Islam	18		1
Maria	India	78,500	Hindu-Animist	18		1
Marind	Indonesia	7,000	Animism	18		1
Marind, Bian	Indonesia	900	Animism	18		1

Name	People / Language	Country	Population	Religion	Code
Marubo	Marubo	Brazil	400	Animism	-18 1
Marwari	Marwari	India	6,807,650	Hindu-Animism	-18 1
Masa	Masa	Chad	80,000	Animism	-68 4
Masalit	Masalit	Chad	73,500	Islam-Animism	-18 1
*Masengo	Majangiir	Ethiopia	7,000	Animism	-18 5
Masenrempulu	Masenrempulu	Indonesia	250,000	Islam	-18 1
Massalat	Massalat	Chad	23,000	Islam-Animism	-18 1
Mataco	Mataco	Argentina	10,000	Animism	-18 1
Matakam	Matakam	Cameroon	140,000	Animism	28 4
Matakam	Matakam	Nigeria	2,000	Animism	-18 1
Matbat	Matbat	Indonesia	550	Islam	-18 1
Matipuhy-Nahukua	Matipuhy-Nahukua	Brazil	100	Animism	-18 1
Matumbi	Matumbi	Tanzania	72,000	Islam	88 4
Maures	Arabic	Senegal	57,000	Islam	88 3
Mauri	Hausa	Niger	100,000	Animism	-18 4
Mavchi	Mauri	India	44,240	Hindu-Animism	-18 1
Mawes	Mawes	Indonesia	690	Animism	-18 1
Maxakali	Maxakali	Brazil	400	Animism	-18 4
Mayoruna	Mayoruna	Peru	1,000	Animism	-18 1
**Mazahua	Mazahua	Mexico	150,000	Christo-Paganism	68 4
Mazandaranis	Mazandarani	Iran	1,620,000	Islam	88 4
Mbai	Mbai	Chad	73,000	Islam-Animism	-18 1
Mbe	Mbe	Nigeria	14,300	Animism	-18 1
Mbembe (Tigong)	Mbembe	Nigeria	2,900	Animism	-18 1
Mboi	Mboi	Nigeria	3,200	Islam	-18 1
Mbukushu	Kusso	Angola	6,000	Animism	68 4
Mbula-Bwazza	Mbula-Bwazza	Nigeria	7,900	Islam-Animism	-18 1
Mbum	Mbum	Chad	20,000	Islam-Animism	-18 1
Me'en	Me'en	Ethiopia	38,000	Animism	-18 1
Meax	Meax	Indonesia	10,000	Animism	-18 1
Meban	Maban-Jumjum	Sudan	130,000	Animism	18 6 79
**Meghwar	Marwari	Pakistan	130,000	Hinduism	18 6 79
**Meitei	Manipuri	India	700,000	Hinduism	18 6 79
**Mejah	Mejah	India	5,500	Animism	14 4
Mekwei	Mekwei	Indonesia	1,200	Animism	-18 1
**Melanau of Sarawak	Melanau	Malaysia	61,000	Animism	18 6 80
Mende	Mende	Sierra Leone	600,000	Animism	138 5
Mentawi	Mentawi	Indonesia	50,000	Islam-Animism	-18 1
**Meo	Meo	Thailand	29,173	Animism	98 5
Meos of Rajasthan	Rajasthani	India	500,200	Islam	08 5 80
Mesengo	Mesongo	Ethiopia	28,000	Islam-Animism	-18 1
Mesme	Mesme	Chad	28,000	Islam-Animism	-18 1
Mesmedje	Mesmedje	Chad	11,000	Islam-Animism	-18 1

Name	Country	Language	Population	Religion		
**Miching	India	Miching	259,551	Hinduism	-18	4
Migili	Nigeria	Migili	10,000	Animism	-18	1
*Mimi	Chad	Mimi	15,000	Islam-Animist	-38	5
Mimika	Indonesia	Mimika	10,000	Christo-Paganism	-18	1
Mina	India	Mina	764,850	Hindu-Animist	-18	6 80
Minangkabau	Indonesia	Minangkabau	5,000,000	Islam	-18	4
Minianka	Mali	Suppire	300,000	Animism	-18	4
**Minnan Hoklo	Taiwan	Amoy Dialect	11,625,000	Buddhism	48	4
Mirdha	India	Mirdha	5,820	Hindu-Animist	-18	1
Mirung	Bangladesh	Mirung	12,000	Animism	-18	1
Mishmi	India	Mishmi	5,230	Hindu-Animist	-18	1
**Mixes	Mexico	Mixe	60,000	Christo-Paganism	28	5
*Mixteco,San Juan Mixtepic	Mexico	Mixteco	15,000	Christo-Paganism	-18	4
Miya	Nigeria	Miya	5,200	Animism	-18	5
Mo	Ghana	Mo (Degha)	13,000	Animism	-18	5
	Ivory Coast	Mo	800	Islam-Animist	-18	4
Moba	Ghana	Bimoba	80,000	Animism	-18	4
	Togo	Bimoba	70,000	Animism	88	4
Mober	Nigeria	Mober	44,800	Islam	-18	4
***Mocha	Ethiopia	Mocha	170,000	Animism	48	4
Mogholi	Afghanistan	Mogholi	2,000	Islam	-18	1
Mogum	Chad	Mogum	6,000	Islam-Animist	-18	1
Moi	Indonesia	Moi	4,000	Animism	-18	1
Moken	Burma	Moken	5,000	Animism	-18	6 79
Moken of Thailand	Thailand	Local dialects	3,000	Animism	-18	6
*Mokole	Benin	Mokole	7,000	Animism	68	3
*Molbog	Philippines	Molbog	5,000	Islam	-?	7
Molof	Indonesia	Molof	200	Animism	-18	1
Mombum	Indonesia	Mombum	250	Animism	-18	1
Mon	Burma	Mon	350,000	Buddhist-Animist	-18	1
Mona	Ivory Coast	Mona	5,570	Islam-Animist	-18	1
Mongondow	Indonesia	Mongondow	400,000	Islam	-18	1
Mongour	China	Mongour	50,000	Traditional Chinese	-18	1
Moni	Indonesia	Moni	20,000	Animism	-18	3
Monpa	India	Monpa	22,000	Buddhism	0?	3
Montol	Nigeria	Montol	20,000	Islam	-18	1
Moor & Malays	Sri Lanka	Tamil	895,322	Islam	-18	6 79
**Mopan Maya	Belize	Mopan Maya	4,000	Christo-Paganism	158	5
**Mopan Maya	Guatemala	Mopan Maya	2,000	Christo-Paganism	158	5
Moqaddam	Iran	Moqaddam	1,000	Islam	0?	3
Mor	Indonesia	Mor	1,000	Animism	-18	1
Mori	Indonesia	Mori	200,000	Animism	-18	1
Moru	Ivory Coast	Moru	10,000	Islam-Animist	-18	1

Name	Country	Language	Population	Religion	
Morunahua	Peru	Morunahua	150	Animism	-1 8 1
Morwap	Indonesia	Morwap	300	Animism.	-1 8 1
Mossi	Upper Volta	Mole	3,300,000	Animism	-7 8 6 80
Motilon	Colombia	Motilon	2,000	Animism	-1 8 1
Movima	Bolivia	Movima	1,000	Animism	-1 8 1
Mru	Bangladesh	Murung	50,000	Animism	-1 8 1
Mualthuam	India	Mualthuam	2,000	Animism	5 8 4
Mubi	Chad	Mubi	36,000	Islam-Animist	-1 8 1
Muinane	Colombia	Muinane	150	Animism	-1 8 1
Multani	India	Multani	15,690	Hindu-Animist	-1 8 1
Mumbake	Nigeria	Mumbake	10,000	Islam	-1 8 1
Mumuye	Nigeria	Mumuye	10,000	Animism	-1 8 5
Mun	Burma	Mun	10,000	Buddhist-Animist	-1 8 1
Muna	Indonesia	Muna	200,000	Islam-Animist	-1 8 1
Mundang	Chad	Mundang	100,000	Islam-Animist	-1 8 1
Mundari	India	Mundari	770,920	Hindu-Animist	-1 8 1
**Mundas	India	Munda	25,000	Animism	0 8 4
Munduruku	Brazil	Munduruku	2,000	Animism	-1 8 1
Mungqui	Indonesia	Munqui	650	Animism	-1 8 1
Munji-Yidgha	Afghanistan	Munji-Yidgha	14,000	Islam	1 8 4
Mura-Piraha	Brazil	Mura-Piraha	110	Animism	-1 8 1
Muria	India	Muria	12,900	Hindu-Animist	1 8 4
Murle	Sudan	Murle	40,000	Animism	1 8 4
*Murngin (Wulamba)	Australia	Dhuwal	3,500	Animism	-1 8 4
Mursi	Ethiopia	Mursi	6,000	Animism	-1 8 1
Musei	Chad	Musei	60,000	Islam-Animist	-1 8 1
Musgu	Chad	Musgu	75,000	Islam-Animist	-1 8 1
Muslim Community of Bawku	Ghana	Hausa, Ghana	20,000	Islam	0 8 3
**Muslim Immigrants in U.K.	United Kingdom	not reported	500,000	Islam	-1 8 6 80
Muslim Malays	Malaysia	Bahasa Malaysia	5,500,000	Islam	1 8 6 79
Muslims (West Nile Dist.)	Uganda	Lugbara	45,000	Islam	1 8 4
Muslims in U.A.E.	United Arab Emirates	Arabic	202,000	Islam	-1 8 1
Muslims of Jordan	Jordan	Arabic	1,000,000	Islam	-1 8 1
Muthuvan	India	Muthuvan	7,000	Hindu-Animist	-1 8 1
Muwasi	India	Muwasi	21,120	Hindu-Animist	-1 8 1
Nabi	Indonesia	Nabi	550	Animism	-1 8 1
Nadeb Maku	Brazil	Nadeb Maku	200	Animism	-1 8 1
**Nafaara	Ghana	Mafaara	40,000	Animism	15 8 6 79
Nafri	Iran	Turkish	3,500	Islam	0 8 3
Nafri	Indonesia	Nafri	1,630	Animism	-1 8 1
Naga, Angami	India	Naga, Angami	34,430	Hindu-Animist	-1 8 1
Naga, Ao	India	Naga, Ao	56,390	Hindu-Animist	-1 8 1
Naga, Kalyokengnyu	India	Naga, Kalyokengnyu	14,410	Hindu-Animist	-1 8 1

Group	Country	Population	Religion		
Naga, Konyak	India	72,340	Hindu-Animist	-1%	1
Naga, Kuki	India	30,250	Hindu-Buddhist	-1%	1
Naga, Lotha	India	36,950	Hindu-Buddhist	-1%	1
Naga, Mao	India	19,970	Hindu-Buddhist	-1%	1
Naga, Nruanghmei	India	48,600	Hindu-Buddhist	-1%	1
Naga, Sangtam	India	20,000	Hindu-Buddhist	-1%	1
Naga, Sema	India	65,230	Unknown	-1%	1
Naga, Tangkhul	India	58,170	Hindu-Buddhist	-1%	1
Naga, Wancho	India	28,650	Hindu-Buddhist	-1%	1
Nagar	India	7,090	Hindu-Animist	-1%	1
Nahsi	China	155,750	Traditional Chinese	-1%	1
*Nahua, North Pueblo	Mexico	55,000	Christo-Paganism	9%	4
Naltya	Indonesia	7,000	Animism	-1%	1
Nambikuara	Brazil	400	Animism	3%	5
*Nambya	Rhodesia	40,000	Animism	8%	5
Namshi	Cameroon	30,000	Animism	-1%	1
Nanai	China	1,000	Traditional Chinese	-1%	1
Nancere	Chad	35,000	Islam-Animist	-1%	1
Nandu-Tari	Nigeria	4,000	Islam	-1%	1
Nao	Ethiopia	5,000	Animism	-1%	1
Nara	Ethiopia	25,000	Islam-Animist	-1%	1
Naraguta	Nigeria	3,000	Animism	-1%	1
Nawuri	Ghana	10,000	Animism	1%	5
Nchimburu	Ghana	7,000	Animism	7%	5
Ndao	Indonesia	2,160	Animism	-1%	1
Nde-Nsele-Nta	Nigeria	10,000	Animism	-1%	1
Sindebele	Rhodesia	1,000,000	Animism	7%	6 79
Ndoe	Nigeria	3,000	Animism	-1%	1
Ndom	Indonesia	450	Animism	-1%	1
*Ndoro	Nigeria	10,000	Animism	6%	5
Nduga	Indonesia	10,000	Animism	-1%	1
Ndunpa Duupa	Cameroon	1,000	Islam	1%	4
*Nepali	Nepal	6,060,758	Hinduism	0%	3
Cantonese	Hong Kong	1,400,000	Secularism	2%	4
*Newari	Nepal	500,000	Hinduism	0%	3
Nevo	Ivory Coast	5,000	Animism	0%	3
Ngada	Indonesia	40,000	Christo-Paganism	-1%	1
Ngalik, North	Indonesia	35,000	Animism	-1%	1
Ngalik, Southern	Indonesia	5,000	Animism	-1%	1
Ngalum	Indonesia	10,000	Animism	-1%	1
*Ngamo	Nigeria	18,000	Animism	8%	4
*Ngen	Ivory Coast	20,000	Animism	2%	4
Ngeq	Laos	50,000	Animism	5%	5

Name	Country	Group	Population / Religion	Code
Ngere	Ivory Coast	not reported	150,000 Animism	-18 4
Ngizim	Nigeria	Ngizim	39,200 Islam	-18 1
Ngwoi	Nigeria	Ngwoi	1,000 Islam	-18 1
Nhengatu	Brazil	Nhengatu	3,000 Animism	-18 1
Nias	Indonesia	Nias	230,000 Animism	-18 1
Nielim	Chad	Nielim	2,000 Islam-Animist	-18 1
Nihali	India	Nihali	1,178 Hindu-Animist	-18 1
Nimadi	India	Nimadi	794,250 Hindu-Buddhist	-18 1
Nimboran	Indonesia	Nimboran	3,500 Animism	-18 1
Ninam	Brazil	Ninam	470 Animism	-18 1
*Ningerum	Papua New Guinea	Ningerum	3,000 Animism	-18 4
Ninggrum	Indonesia	Ninggrum	3,500 Animism	-18 1
Ninzam	Nigeria	Ninzam	35,000 Islam	-18 1
Nisa	Indonesia	Nisa	250 Animism	-18 1
Njadu	Indonesia	Njadu	9,000 Animism	-18 1
Nkem-Nkum	Nigeria	Nkem-Nkum	16,700 Animism	-18 4
*Nkoya	Zambia	Shinkoya	nr Animism	58 4
***Nocte	India	Nocte	19,400 Animism	08 3
Norra	Burma	Norra	10,000 Buddhist-Animist	-18 1
North Africans in Belgium	Belgium	Arabic	90,000 Islam	-18 6 80
Northern Cagayan Negrito	Philippines	Northern Cagayan Negrito	1,200 Christo-Paganism	-18 1
Nosu	China	Nosu	556,000 Traditional Chinese	-18 1
Ntrubs	Ghana	Ntrubo	5,000 Animism	-18 5
*Nuer	Ethiopia	Nuer	70,000 Animism	-18 4
Nuer	Sudan	Nuer	844,000 Animism	-18 6 79
Numana-Nunku-Gwantu	Nigeria	Numana-Nunku-Gwantu	15,000 Islam	-18 1
Nung	China	Nung	100,000 Traditional Chinese	-18 1
Nungu	Nigeria	Nungu	25,000 Animism	-18 1
**Nupe	Nigeria	Nupe	600,000 Islam	28 5
Nuristani	Afghanistan	Local dialects	67,000 Islam	08 5 80
Nyabwa-Nyedebwa	Ivory Coast	Nyabwa-Nyedebwa	21,000 Islam-Animist	-18 1
Nyaheun	Laos	Nyaheun	15,000 Animism	28 4
Nyamwezi	Tanzania	Nyamwezi	590,000 Animism	98 6 80
*Nyantruku	Benin	Aledjo	4,000 Animism	08 3
Nyzatom	Sudan	Toposa, Donyiro	80,000 Animism	-18 1
Nzanyi	Nigeria	Nzanyi	14,080 Islam	-18 1
Nzema	Ivory Coast	Nzema	24,080 Islam-Animist	-18 1
Obanliku	Nigeria	Obanliku	19,800 Animism	-18 1
Obolo	Nigeria	Obolo	70,000 Animism	-18 1
Ocaina	Peru	Ocaina	250 Animism	-18 4
Od	Pakistan	Odki	40,000 Hinduism	-18 4
Odual	Nigeria	Odual	9,000 Animism	-18 1
Odut	Nigeria	Odut	700 Animism	-18 1

Name	Country	Listing	Population	Religion	Code
Ogbia	Nigeria	Ogbia	22,000	Animism	-18 1
Oi	Laos	Oi	10,000	Animism	-18 5
Oirat	China	Oirat	60,000	Traditional Chinese	-18 1
Ojhi	India	Ojhi	1,070	Hindu-Animist	-18 1
Okobo	Nigeria	Okobo	11,200	Animism	-18 1
Okpamheri	Nigeria	Okpamheri	30,800	Animism	-18 1
Ollari	India	Ollari	9,250	Hindu-Animist	-18 1
Olulumo-Ikom	Nigeria	Olulumo-Ikom	200	Animism	-18 1
Ong	India	Ong	600	Hindu-Animist	-18 1
Onin	Indonesia	Onin	337,395	Animism	-18 1
**Orang Asli	Malaysia	Native Senoi	300	Animism	2 4
Orejon	Peru	Orejon	300	Animism	-18 1
Oring	Nigeria	Oring	25,000	Animism	-18 1
Oriya	India	Oriya	19,726,750	Hindu-Animist	-18 1
Ormu	Indonesia	Ormu	750	Animism	-18 1
Oron	Nigeria	Oron	48,300	Animism	-18 1
Oronchon	China	Oronchon	2,400	Traditional Chinese	-18 1
Ot Danum	Indonesia	Ot Danum	30,000	Animism	-18 1
Otank	Nigeria	Otank	3,000	Animism	-18 1
Ouaddai	Chad	Maba	320,000	Islam	-18 4
Oubi	Ivory Coast	Oubi	1,340	Islam-Animist	15 8 4
*Overseas Chin. Port.	United States of America	Cantonese	nr	Secularism	-18 1
Oyampipuku	Brazil	Oyampipuku	100	Animism	-18 1
Oyda	Ethiopia	Oyda	3,000	Animism	-18 1
Pacu	Brazil	Tucano	120	Animism	-18 1
***Paez	Colombia	Paez	40,000	Christo-Paganism	11 6 5
Pahari Garhwali	India	Pahari Garhwali	1,277,150	Hindu-Animist	-18 1
Pai	Nigeria	Pai	2,520	Animism	-18 1
Paite, Northern	India	Paite	27,520	Hindu-Animist	-18 1
Paiute, Northern	United States of America	Paiute, Northern	5,000	Peyote Religion	3 8 4
Pakasnovos	Brazil	Pakaasnovos	800	Animism	-18 1
***Pakabeti of Equator	Zaire	Pakabeti	3,000	Animism	3 8 4
Palara	Ivory Coast	Palara	10,000	Animism	-18 5
Palaung	Burma	Palaung	150,000	Buddhism	-18 5 79
Palawano	Philippines	Palawano	3,000	Islam-Animist	-18 1
— Palawano, Central	Philippines	Palawano, Central	3,000	Animism	-18 1
Palembang	Indonesia	Palembang	500,000	Islam	-18 1
Palenquero	Colombia	Spanish	3,000	Animism	-18 1
Palikur	Brazil	Palikur	500	Animism	-18 1
Paliyan	India	Paliyan	590	Hindu-Animist	-18 1
Panika	India	Panika	30,690	Hindu-Animist	-18 1
Paniyan	India	Paniyan	6,330	Hindu-Animist	-18 1
Pankararu	Brazil	Portuguese	2,000	Animism	-18 1

Pankhu	Bangladesh	Pankhu	630 Islam	-18 1
Pantu	Indonesia	Pantu	9,000 Animism	-18 1
Pao	India	Pao	15,860 Hindu-Buddhist	-18 1
Paongan	China	Paongan	8,000 Traditional Chinese	-18 1
Papuma	Indonesia	Papuma	700 Animism	-18 1
Parakanan	Brazil	Parakanan	500 Animism	-18 1
Paranan	Philippines	Paranan	6,000 Christo-Paganism	-18 1
Pardhan	India	Pardhan	450 Hindu-Animist	-18 1
Parengi	India	Parengi	3,000 Hindu-Animist	-18 1
Paresi	Brazil	Paresi	350 Animism	-18 1
Parintintin	Brazil	Parintintin	200 Animism	-18 4
*Parsees	India	Gujarati	120,000 Zoroastrianism	08 4
Pashayi	Afghanistan	Pashayi	96,000 Islam-Animist	-18 1
Pashtuns	Iran	Pashtu	3,000 Islam	-18 1
Patelia	India	Patelia	23,210 Hindu-Animist	09 6 80
Pato Tapuia	Brazil	Pato Tapuia	140 Animism	-18 1
Paumari	Brazil	Paumari	250 Animism	-18 1
Pengo	India	Pengo	1,250 Hindu-Animist	-18 1
Pero	Nigeria	Pero	20,000 Islam	-18 1
Persians of Iran	Iran	Persian	2,000,000 Islam	-18 6 80
Phu Thai	Laos	Phu Thai	100,000 Buddhism	-18 5
Piapoco	Colombia	Piapoco	3,000 Animism	-18 1
**Pila	Benin	Pila-Pila	50,000 Animism	-18 4
Pilaga	Argentina	Pilaga	800 Animism	-18 1
Piratapuyo	Brazil	Tucano	2,500 Animism	-18 1
Piro	Peru	Maniteneri	3,500 Animism	-18 1
Pisa	Indonesia	Pisa	1,000 Islam	-18 1
Pishaqchi	Iran	Pishaqchi	1,600 Islam	-18 1
Piti	Indonesia	Piti	175,000 Animism	-18 1
Pitu Uluna Salu	Nigeria	Pitu Uluna Salu	2,500 Islam	-18 1
Piya	Nigeria	Piya	82,500 Hindu-Animist	-18 1
Pnar	India	Pnar	25,000 Animism	-18 4
Podokwo	Cameroon	Podokwo	6,150 Islam	-18 1
Polci	Nigeria	Polci	1,700 Animism	-18 1
Pom	Indonesia	Pom	3,680 Islam	-18 1
Pongu	Nigeria	Pongu	23,006 Animism	-18 1
Porohanon	Philippines	Porohanon	150,000 Secularism	10 8 4
**Portuguese in France	France	Portuguese	2,000 Islam	-18 1
***Prasuni	Afghanistan	Prasuni	1,311,020 Traditional Chinese	-18 1
Pu-I	China	Pu-I	15,000 Islam	-18 1
Puku-Geeri-Keri-Wipsi	Nigeria	Puku-Geeri-Keri-Wipsi	281,900 not reported	08 3
Pular	Senegal	Fouta Toro		
Punjabis	Pakistan	English	49,000,000 Islam	28 6 80

Name	Country	Language	Population	Religion			
Punu	China	Punu	220,000	Traditional Chinese	-18	1	
Puragi	Indonesia	Puragi	900	Animism	-18	1	
Purum	Burma	Purum	300	Buddhist-Animist	-18	1	
Pye	Ivory Coast	Pye	6,120	Islam-Animist	-18	1	
Pygmy (Binga)	Burundi	Local dialects	30,000	Animism	68	5	
*Pygmy (Mbuti)	Central African Empire	Local dialects	2,000	Animism	08	4	
	Zaire	local languages	40,000	Animism	08	4	
Pyu	Indonesia	Pyu	100	Animism	-18	5	79
Qajars	Iran	Qajar	3,000	Islam	-18	1	
Qara'i	Iran	Qara'i	2,000	Islam	08	3	
Qaragozlu	Iran	Qaragozlu	2,000	Islam	08	3	
Qashqa'i	Iran	Qashqa'i	350,000	Islam	08	3	
Quaiquer	Colombia	Quaiquer	5,000	Islam	78	5	80
Quarequena	Brazil	Tucano	340	Animism	-18	1	
**Quechua	Bolivia	Quechua	1,000,000	Christo-Paganism	-18	1	
	Peru	Quechua	3,000,000	Christo-Paganism	48	4	
**Quechua, Huanco	Peru	Quechua, Huancayo	275,000	Animism	28	5	
**Quiche	Guatemala	Quiche	500,000	Christo-Paganism	58	6	79
Rabha	India	Rabha	10,000	Hinduism	48	4	
Rabinal-Achi	Guatemala	Rabinal Achi	21,000	Christo-Paganism	48	4	
**Racetrack Residents	United States of America	English	50,000	Secularism	68	5	79
*Rai, Danuwar	Nepal	Rai	232,000	Hinduism	08	3	
	Nepal	Danuwar Rai	12,000	Hinduism	08	3	
Rajbansi	Nepal	Rajbansi	15,000	Hinduism	-18	1	
Ralte	Burma	Ralte	17,000	Buddhist-Animist	-18	1	
Ratahan	Indonesia	Ratahan	150,000	Animism	-18	1	
Rataning	Chad	Rataning	10,000	Islam-Animist	-18	1	
*Rava	India	Rava	45,000	Hinduism	-18	5	
Rawang	China	Rawang	60,000	Traditional Chinese	-18	1	
Redjang	Indonesia	Rejang	300,000	Islam	-18	6	80
Reshe	Nigeria	Reshe	30,000	Animism	-18	1	
Reshiat	Ethiopia	not reported	10,000	Animism	-18	3	
Reyesano	Bolivia	Reyesano	1,000	Animism	-18	1	
Riang	India	Riang	74,930	Hindu-Buddhist	-18	1	
Riang-Lang	Burma	Riang-Lang	20,000	Buddhist-Animist	-18	1	
Riantana	Indonesia	Riantana	1,100	Animism	-18	1	
Rikbaktsa	Brazil	Rikbaktsa	200	Animism	-18	1	
Romany	Turkey	Romany	20,000	Folk Religion	-18	1	
Rotti	Indonesia	Rotti	80,000	Animism	-18	1	
Rukuba	Nigeria	Rukuba	50,000	Islam	-18	1	
Rumaya	Nigeria	Rumaya	1,800	Islam	-18	1	
Runga	Chad	Runga	13,000	Islam-Animist	-18	1	
Ruruma	Nigeria	Ruruma	2,200	Islam	-18	1	

Group	Alternate name	Country	Population	Religion		
*Ryukyuan	Ryukyuan	Japan	1,000,000	Traditional Japanese	4%	4
Saberi	Saberi	Indonesia	1,500	Animism	-18	1
Sadan	Sadan	India	807,180	Hindu-Animist	-18	1
Sadang	Sadang	Indonesia	50,000	Animism	-18	1
Safwa	Safwa	Tanzania	102,000	Animism	3%	4
**Saguye	Galla	Kenya	30,000	Islam	-18	3
Saija	Saija	Colombia	2,500	Animism	-18	1
**Saiva Vellala	Tamil	India	1,500,000	Hinduism	-2%	4
Salar	Salar	China	31,000	Traditional Chinese	-18	1
Saliba	Saliba	Colombia	900	Animism	-18	1
Sama Bangingi	Sinama Bangini	Philippines	70,000	Islam	-18 6	80
Sama Pangutaran	Sama Pangutaran	Philippines	15,000	Islam	-18 6	80
Sama, Mapun	Sama, Mapun	Philippines	20,000	Animism	-18	1
Sama, Siasi	Sama, Siasi	Philippines	100,000	Islam-Animist	-18	1
Sama, Sibuku	Sama, Sibuku	Philippines	11,000	Islam-Animist	-18	1
Sama-Badjaw	Samal dialects	Philippines	120,000	Islam	-18 5	79
Samarkena	Samarkena	Indonesia	750	Animism	-18	1
Samburu	Masai, Samburu	Kenya	60,500	Animism	3%	4
*Samo-Kubo	Samo	Papua New Guinea	1,500	Animism	-18	4
Sanga	Sanga	Nigeria	5,000	Islam	-18	1
Sangil	Sangil	Philippines	7,500	Islam	-18	5
Sangir	Sangir	Indonesia	145,000	Animism	-18	1
Sangke	Sangke	Indonesia	250	Animism	-18	1
Santa	Santa	China	155,500	Traditional Chinese	-18	1
**Santhali	Santhali	Nepal	nr	Animism	3%	4
*Sanuma	Sanuma	Brazil	326	Animism	-18	3
Sapo	not reported	Liberia	30,000	Animism	128	4
Sarakole	Soninke	Senegal	67,400	Islam	-0% 6	80
Sarwa	Sarwa	Chad	400	Islam-Animist	-18	1
Sasak	Sasak	Indonesia	1,600,000	Islam	-18 6	80
Sasanis	Sasani	Iran	1,000	Islam	-0%	3
Sasaru-Enwan Igwe	Sasaru-Enwan Igwe	Nigeria	3,780	Animism	-18	1
Satere	Satere	Brazil	3,000	Animism	-18	1
Sau	Sau	Afghanistan	1,000	Islam	-18	1
Sause	Sause	Indonesia	500	Animism	-18	1
**Save	Save (Yoruba)	Benin	15,000	Animism	-18	4
**Sawi	Sawi	Indonesia	2,800	Animism	16%	5
Saya	Saya	Nigeria	50,000	Islam	-18	1
Secoya	Secoya	Ecuador	400	Animism	-18	1
Sekar	Sekar	Indonesia	450	Animism	-18	1
Seko	Seko	Indonesia	275,000	Animism	-78	4
**Selakau of Sarawak	Selakau	Malaysia	5,300	Animism	-18	1
Sempan	Sempan	Indonesia	2,000	Animism		

People	Country	Name	Population	Religion
Senggi	Indonesia	Senggi	120	Animism
Sentani	Indonesia	Sentani	10,000	Animism
Senthang	Burma	Senthang	10,000	Buddhist-Animist
Senufo	Ivory Coast	Senari	300,000	Animism
Serawai	Indonesia	Serawai (Pasemah)	700,000	Islam
Serere	Senegal	Serere	1,000	Animism
Serui-Laut	Indonesia	Serui-Laut		
Seuci	Brazil	Tucano		
Seychellois	Seychelles	Creole	51,000	Secularism
Sha	Nigeria	Sha	500	Animism
Shahsavans	Iran	Azerbaijani (Shahsavani)	180,000	Islam
Shan	Thailand	Shan	300,000	Buddhism
Shanga	Nigeria	Shanga	5,000	Animism
***Shankilla (Kazza)	Ethiopia	Shankilla (Kazza)	20,000	Christo-Paganism
Sharanahua	Peru	Sharanahua	21,500	Animism
Sharchagpakha	Bhutan	Sharchagpakha	400,000	Buddhist-Animist
Shawiya	Algeria	Shawiya	150,000	Islam
Sheko	Ethiopia	Sheko	23,000	Animism
*Sherpa	Nepal	Sherpa	20,000	Buddhism
**Shihu	United Arab Emirates	Shihu	10,000	Islam
Shina	Afghanistan	Shina	50,000	Islam-Animist
Shinasha	Ethiopia	Shinasha	15,000	Animism
Shipibo	Peru	Shipibo	240	Animism
**Shirishana	Brazil	Shirishana		
*Shourastra	India	Shourastra	200,000	Hinduism
Shughni	Afghanistan	Shughni	3,000	Islam
Shuwa Arabic	Nigeria	Shuwa Arabic	100,000	Islam
Siagha-Yenimu	Indonesia	Siagha-Yenimu	3,000	Animism
Sibo	China	Sibo	21,000	Traditional Chinese
Sidamo	Ethiopia	Sidamo	857,000	Islam-Animist
Sikhule	Indonesia	Sikhule	20,000	Animism
Sikka	Indonesia	Sikka	100,000	Animism
Sikkimese	India	Sikkimese	36,580	Hindu-Buddhist
*Sindhis of India	India	Sindhi	3,000,000	Hinduism
Sinhalese	Sri Lanka	Sinhala	9,146,679	Buddhism
Siona	Colombia	Siona	250	Animism
Siri	Nigeria	Siri	2,000	Islam
Siriano	Colombia	Siriano	600	Animism
Siriono	Bolivia	Siriono	500	Animism
**Sisaala	Ghana	Isaalin	60,000	Animism
So	Laos	So	15,000	Animism
*So	Thailand	So	8,000	Animism
Sobei	Indonesia	Sobei	1,400	Animism

Group	Country	People	Population	Religion	Code
Sochi	Pakistan	Sindhi	6,500,000	nr Hinduism	18 3
Soka Gakkai Believers	Japan	Japanese	131,000,000	Buddhism	09 3
Solor	Indonesia	Solor			-08 1
*Somahai	Indonesia	Somagai	3,000	Animism	08 3
Somahai	Indonesia	Somahai	1,500	Animism	18 1
Somali	Ethiopia	Somali	1,000,000	Islam	18 5
Somali	Somalia	Somali	2,500,000	Islam	18 5 79
	Kenya	Somali (Ajuran)	25,374	Islam	18 6 79
Somali, Ajuran	Kenya	Somali	68,667	Islam	18 5
Somali, Degodia	Kenya	Somali	54,165	Islam	18 5
Somali, Gurreh	Kenya	Somali	99,129	Islam	18 5
*Somali, Ogadenya	Kenya	Somali			18 4
**Somba	Benin	Somba (Detammari)	60,000	Animism	18 4
Somrai	Chad	Somrai	50,000	Islam-Animist	-18 1
Sondwari	India	Sondwari	31,490	Hindu-Animist	-18 1
Soninke	Gambia	Soninke	10,000	Islam	-18 1
Sonjo	Tanzania	Sonjo	7,400	Animism	56 5
Sora	India	Sora	221,710	Hinduism	-08 3
Soruba	Benin	Soruba	5,000	Animism	-18 1
Sowanda	Indonesia	Sowanda	1,100	Animism	-18 1
Spiritists	Brazil	Portuguese	9,000,000	Folk Religion	18 3 79
**Stud. Osaka Christ. Coll.	Japan	Japanese	1,100	Traditional Japanese	24 4
Students in Cuiaba	Brazil	Portuguese	20,000	Secularism	28 3
**Subanen (Tuboy)	Philippines	Subanen, Tuboy	20,000	Animism	28 5
**Subanen, Sindangan	Philippines	Subanun	80,000	Animism	-18 6 80
Subanun,Lapuyan	Philippines	Subanun, Lapuyan	25,000	Islam-Animist	-18 4
**Suena	Papua New Guinea	Suena	2,000	Christo-Paganism	48 4
**Sugut	Malaysia	Dusun	160,000	Animism	09 4
Sui	China	Sui	160,310	Traditional Chinese	-18 4
Suk	Kenya	not reported	133,320	Animism	88 5
Sukur	Nigeria	Sukur	10,000	Islam-Animism	-18 1
Sulung	India	Sulung		nr Hindu-Buddhist	-18 1
Sumba	Indonesia	Sumba	400,000	Christo-Paganism	-18 1
Sumbawa	Indonesia	Sumbawa	114,000	Islam	-18 1
**Sundanese	Indonesia	Sundanese	20,000,000	Islam	-18 6 80
Sungor	Chad	Sungor	39,000	Islam-Animist	-18 1
Sura	Nigeria	Sura	40,000	Animism	-18 4
**Suri	Ethiopia	Suri	30,000	Animism	78 4
**Suriguenos	Philippines	Suriqueno	23,000	Secularism	78 4
Surubu	Nigeria	Surubu	1,950	Islam	-18 1
Surui	Brazil	Surui	250	Animism	-18 1
Swatis	Pakistan	Swati	600,000	Islam	-18 1
Ta-Oi	Laos	Ta-Oi	15,000	Animism	08 6 79
Tacana	Bolivia	Tacana	3,500	Animism	-18 1

People	Country	Language	Religion	Population	Source
Tadjio	Indonesia	Tadjio	Animism	100,000	-18 1
Tadyawan, Aborlan	Philippines	Tadyawan	Animism	1,000	18 1
**Tagbanwa, Aborlan	Philippines	Tagbanwa	Animism	10,000	18 5
***Tagbanwa, Kalamian	Philippines	Tagbanwa, Kalamian	Christo-Paganism	4,500	18 5
***Tagin	India	Tagin	Animism	25,000	08 3
Tagwana	Ivory Coast	Tagwana	Islam-Animist	43,000	-18 1
Tahit	Indonesia	Tehit	Animism	6,000	18 1
Taikat	Indonesia	Taikat	Animism	600	18 1
Tajik	Iran	Dari	Islam	15,000	18 5 80
Takankar	India	Takankar	Hindu-Animism	10,960	-18 1
Takestani	Iran	Takestani	Islam	220,000	18 1
Tal	Nigeria	Tal	Islam	10,000	18 1
Talish	Iran	Talish	Islam	20,000	08 3
Tama	Chad	Tama	Islam-Animist	60,000	-18 1
Tamagario	Indonesia	Tamagario	Animism	3,500	18 1
Taman	Burma	Taman	Buddhist-Animist	10,000	08 3
*Tamang	Nepal	Tamang	Hindu-Buddhist	nr	08 3
Tamaria	India	Tamaria	Animism	5,050	-18 1
Tambas	Nigeria	Tambas	Animism	3,000	-18 1
Tamil (Ceylonese)	Sri Lanka	Tamil	Hinduism	1,415,567	58 5
*Tamil Brahmins	India	Tamil	Hinduism	98,112,000	18 4
***Tamil Plantation Workers	Malaysia	Tamil	Hinduism	137,150	78 4
**Tamils (Indian)	Sri Lanka	Tamil	Hinduism	600,000	58 4 79
**Tamils (Indian)	Sri Lanka	Tamil	Hinduism	1,195,368	28 5
Tampulma	Ghana	Tampulensi	Animism	8,000	18 1
Tana	Chad	Tana	Islam-Animist	35,000	08 1
Tanahmerah	Indonesia	Tanahmerah	Animism	3,200	08 3
Tandanke	Senegal	Tandanke	not reported	1,000	-18 1
Tandia	Indonesia	Tandia	Animism	350	18 1
Tangale	Nigeria	Tangale	Islam	100,000	-18 1
Tangchangya	Bangladesh	Tangchangya	Islam	8,310	08 3
Tangsa	India	Tangsa	Animism	10,000	-18 1
**Tanimuca-Retuama	Colombia	Tanimuca-Retuama	Animism	300	08 4
Tao't Bato	Philippines	not reported	Animism	150	-18 1
Taori-Kei	Indonesia	Taori-Kei	Animism	140	18 1
Tara	Indonesia	Tara	Animism	125,000	-18 1
Targum	Israel	Targum	Judaism	5,000	18 1
Tarof	Indonesia	Tarof	Animism	600	-18 1
Tarok	Nigeria	Tarok	Animism	60,000	18 1
Tarpia	Indonesia	Tarpia	Animism	560	-18 1
Tatars	Soviet Russia	Tatar dialects	Islam	6,000,300	18 6 80
Tatuyo	Colombia	Tatuyo	Islam	300	18 5
Taucouleur	Senegal	Tancouleur	Islam	464,700	08 5 80

Group	Country	Subgroup	Population	Religion	Code
Taungyo	Burma	Taungyo	159,200	Buddhist-Animist	-18 1
Taurap	Indonesia	Taurap	160	Animism	-18 1
Tausug	Philippines	Tausug	500,000	Islam	-18 6 80
Tawbuid	Philippines	Tawbuid	6,000	Animism	-18 1
Tawr	Burma	Tawr	700	Buddhist-Animist	-18 5
**Tboli	Philippines	Tboli	67,500	Animism	-18 6 80
Teda	Chad	Teda	10,000	Islam	-18 6
*Teenbu	Ivory Coast	Lorhon	5,000	Animism	-18 3
Teimuri	Iran	Teimuri	10,000	Islam	-18 3
Teimurtash	Iran	Teimurtash	100,000	Islam	-18 4
Tem	Togo	Kotokoli	250,000	Islam	-18 6
Tembe	Brazil	Tembe	250	Animism	-18 6 80
*Temne	Sierra Leone	Temne	1,000,250	Animism	-18 5
Tenger	Indonesia	Tenggerese	20,000	Hinduism	-18 1
Tepo	Ivory Coast	Tepo	46,000	Islam-Animism	-18 1
Tera	Nigeria	Tera	5,000	Islam	-18 5
Terena	Brazil	Terena	1,000	Animism	-18 1
*Teribe	Panama	Teribe	42,000	Christo-Paganism	-18 6 80
Ternate	Indonesia	Ternate	42,340	Islam	-18 4
Thado	India	Thado	1,700,000	Hindu-Buddhist	-18 6 80
Thai Islam (Malay)	Thailand	Mala, Pattani	600,000	Islam	-18 4
*Thai Islam (Thai)	Thailand	Thai, Southern	6,000,000	Islam	-18 4
Thai Northern	Thailand	North Thai Dialect	4,500,000	Buddhism	-18 4
Thai of Bangkok	Thailand	Thai, Central	15,500,000	Buddhism	-18 4
Thai, North East	Thailand	N.E. Thai	4,000,000	Buddhism	-18 4
Thai, Southern	Thailand	Southern Thai	5,000,000	Buddhism	-18 4
*Thailand Farmers (Ctl)	Thailand	Thai		Buddhism	-18 1
Thakur	India	Thakur	99,000	Hindu-Animist	-18 1
Thar	India	Thar	8,790	Hindu-Animist	-18 4
Tharu	Nepal	Bhojpuri	495,000	Hinduism	-18 5
*Tibetan Refugees	India	Tibetan	nr	Buddhism	-18 4
*Tibetans	China	Tibetan	3,000,000	Buddhism	-18 1
Ticuna	Brazil	Ticuna	26,000	Animism	-18 1
Tidore	Indonesia	Tidore	25,000	Islam-Animism	-18 4
Tigon	Cameroon	Tigon	300,000	Animism	-18 1
Timorese	Indonesia	Timorese	25,000	Animism	-18 4
Tin	Thailand	Tin	38,000	Animism	-18 3
Tippera	Bangladesh	Tippera	75,000	Islam	-18 1
Tiro	Indonesia	Tiro	30,000	Animism	-18 1
Tiruray	Philippines	Tiruray	30,000	Animism	-18 1
Toala	Indonesia	Toala	100	Animism	-18 1
Toba	Argentina	Toba	15,000	Animism	-18 1
Toda	India	Toda	770	Hindu-Animist	-18 1

*Tofi	Benin	Tofi	33,000	Animism	3%	4	
Tokkaru	India	Tokkaru	1,298,860	Hindu-Animist	-1%	1	
Tombulu	Indonesia	Tombulu	40,000	Animism	-1%	1	
Tomini	Indonesia	Tomini	50,000	Animism	-1%	1	
Tondanou	Indonesia	Tondanou	35,000	Animism	-1%	1	
*Tonga	Rhodesia	ChiTonga	90,000	Animism	2%	5	
Tonga, Gwembe Valley	Zambia	ChiTonga	86,000	Animism	2%	7	79
Tonsea	Indonesia	Tonsea	90,000	Animism	-1%	1	
Tontemboa	Indonesia	Tontemboa	140,000	Animism	-1%	1	
*Topotha	Sudan	Toposa	60,000	Animism	2%	4	
Toradja	Indonesia	Toradja	250,000	Animism	-1%	1	
Totis	India	Gondi	nr	Hinduism	0%	3	
Towei	Indonesia	Towei	120	Animism	-1%	1	
Trepo	Ivory Coast	Trepo	3,400	Islam-Animist	-1%	1	
**Tripuri	India	Tripuri	400,000	Animism	1%	4	
**Tsachila	Ecuador	Colorado	1,100	Christo-Paganism	8%	5	
Tsamai	Ethiopia	Tsamai	7,000	Animism	-1%	1	
Tsimane	Bolivia	Tsimane	5,500	Animism	-1%	1	
Tuareg	Niger	Tamachek	200,000	Islam	-1%	6	79
Tucano	Brazil	Tucano	2,000	Animism	-1%	1	
Tugara	India	Tugara	43,680	Hindu-Animist	-1%	1	
Tukude	Indonesia	Tukude	45,000	Christo-Paganism	-1%	1	
Tula	Nigeria	Tula	19,000	Islam	-1%	1	
Tulu	India	Tulu	1,156,950	Hindu-Animist	-1%	1	
Tumawo	Indonesia	Tumawo	350	Animism	-1%	1	
Tunebo, Cobaria	Colombia	Tunebo, Cobaria	2,000	Animism	-1%	1	
Tunya	Chad	Tunya	800	Islam-Animist	-1%	1	
Tupuri	Chad	Tupuri	12,000	Islam-Animist	-1%	1	
Tura	Ivory Coast	Tura	19,230	Islam-Animist	-1%	1	
Turkana	Kenya	Turkana	224,000	Animism	4%	5	
**Turkana Fishing Community	Kenya	Turkana	20,000	Animism	4%	5	79
Turkish Immigrant Workers	German Federal Rep.	Turkish	1,200,000	Islam	1%	6	79
Turkish Workers	Belgium	Kurdish	60,000	Islam	1%	6	80
Turkomans	Iran	Turkomani	550,000	Islam	0%	6	80
Turks, Anatolian	Turkey	Turkish, Osmanli	31,000,000	Islam	-1%	6	
Turkwam	Nigeria	Turkwam	6,000	Islam	-1%	1	
Turu	Indonesia	Turu	800	Animism	-1%	1	
	Tanzania	Nyaturu	316,000	Animism	10%	4	
Tuyuca	Brazil	Tuyuca	500	Animism	-1%	1	
Uduk	Sudan	Uduk	7,000	Animism	9%	4	
Uhunduni	Indonesia	Uhunduni	14,000	Animism	-1%	1	
Uighur	Afghanistan	Uighur	3,000	Islam	-1%	1	
Uiqur	China	Uigur	4,800,000	Islam	0%	5	80

Name	Country	Language	Population	Religion	
Ukaan	not reported	Ukaan	18,000	Animism	-18 1
Ukpe-Bayobiri	Nigeria	Ukpe-Bayobiri	12,000	Animism	-18 1
Ukwuani-Aboh	Nigeria	Ukwuani-Aboh	150,000	Animism	-18 1
Ulithi-Mall	Turks and Caicos Islands	Ulithi	2,000	Christo-Paganism	-18 4
Ulatan	India	Ulatan	1,500	Hindu-Animist	-18 1
**Univ. Students of Japan	Japan	Japanese	2,000,000	Traditional Japanese	18 4
*University Students	France	French	800,000	Secularism	28 6 79
	German Federal Rep.	German	850,000	Secularism	10 6 79
Urali	India	Urali	1,080	Hindu-Animist	-18 1
Urarina	Peru	Urarina	3,500	Animism	-18 1
*Urban Workers in Taiwan	Taiwan	Taiwanese	nr	Traditional Chinese	-18 1
Urhobo	Nigeria	Urhobo	340,000	Animism	-18 1
Uria	Indonesia	Uria	1,200	Animism	-18 1
Uruangnirin	Indonesia	Uruangnirin	250	Animism	-18 1
Urubu	Brazil	Urubu	500	Animism	-18 1
Urupa	Brazil	Urupa	250	Animism	-18 1
Utugwang	Nigeria	Utugwang	12,000	Animism	-18 1
Uvbie	Nigeria	Uvbie	6,000	Animism	-18 1
**Uzbeks	Afghanistan	Uzbek, Turkic	1,000,000	Islam	0? 6 79
Uzekwe	Nigeria	Uzekwe	5,000	Animism	-18 1
Vagala	Ghana	Vagala	3,000	Animism	-18 4
Vagari	Pakistan	Gujarati Dialect	30,000	Hinduism	-18 5
Vagla	Ivory Coast	Vagla	6,000	Islam-Animist	-18 1
*Vai	Liberia	Vai	30,000	Islam	-18 6 80
Vaikino	Indonesia	Vaikino	14,000	Animism	-18 1
Vaiphei	India	Vaiphei	20,000	Animism	-18 1
***Vere	Nigeria	Vere	20,000	Buddhism	98 5
**Vietnamese	Laos	Vietnamese	130,000	Buddhism	18 4
**Vietnamese in the USA	United States of America	Vietnamese	7,800	Folk Religion	7% 4
**Vietnamese Refugees	Australia	Vietnamese	2,000	Buddhism	48 4
Vishavan	Thailand	Vishavan	150	Hindu-Animist	-18 4
**Vohras of Yavatmal	India	Gujarati	10,000	Islam	0? 4
Voko	Cameroon	Woko	1,000	Islam	-18 4
Vute	Nigeria	Vute	1,000	Animism	-18 1
Wa	China	Wa	286,160	Traditional Chinese	18 4
Wabo	Indonesia	Wabo	900	Animism	-18 1
Waddar	India	Waddar	35,900	Hindu-Animist	-18 1
Wagdi	India	Wagdi	756,790	Hindu-Animist	-18 1
Waimiri	Brazil	Waimiri	1,000	Animism	-18 1
Waiwai	Brazil	Waiwai	1,000	Animism	-18 1
Waja	Nigeria	Waja	30,000	Islam	-18 1
**Wajita	Tanzania	Kijita	65,000	Animism	18 4

Wala	Wali	Ghana	60,000 Animism	28 5
Walamo	Walamo	Ethiopia	908,000 Animism	-18 1
Wambon	Wambon	Indonesia	2,000 Animism	-18 1
Wan	Wan	Ivory Coast	10,000 Islam-Animist	68 3
**Wanchoo	Wanchoo	India	nr Animism	-18 1
Wandamen	Wandamen	Indonesia	4,000 Animism	-18 1
Wanggom	Wanggom	Indonesia	1,000 Animism	-18 1
Wano	Wano	Indonesia	1,700 Animism	-18 1
Wapishana	Wapishana	Brazil	1,500 Animism	-18 1
Warembori	Warembori	Indonesia	350 Animism	-18 1
Waris	Waris	Indonesia	1,480 Animism	-18 4
*Warjiwa	Warji	Nigeria	70,000 Animism	-18 1
Warkay-Bipim	Warkay-Bipim	Indonesia	250 Animism	-18 1
Waropen	Waropen	Indonesia	6,000 Animism	-18 1
Watchi	Ge	Togo	1,000,000 Animism	58 4
Waura	Waura	Brazil	120 Animism	-18 1
*Wazinza	Kizinza	Tanzania	2,000 Animism	78 4
Weda	Weda	Indonesia	900 Islam	-18 1
Wetawit	Wetawit	Ethiopia	28,000 Animism	-18 1
Wewewa	Wewewa	Indonesia	55,000 Animism	-18 5
**Wimbum	Limbum	Cameroon	50,000 Animism	18 5
Winji-Winji	Winji-Winji	Benin	5,000 Islam	0% 3
Wobe	Wobe	Ivory Coast	40,000 Animism	12% 4
Wodani	Wodani	Indonesia	3,000 Animism	-18 1
Woi	Woi	Indonesia	1,300 Animism	-18 1
Woleat	Woleat	Indonesia	1,000 Christo-Paganism	-18 4
Wolio	Wolio	Turks and Caicos Islands	25,000 Islam	-18 1
Wolof	Wolof	Senegal	1,500,000 Islam	-18 1
Wolof, Gambian	Wolof, Gambian	Gambia	64,800 Islam-Animist	18 6 80
Wom	Wom	Nigeria	10,000 Islam-Animist	-18 1
*Women Laborers	Amoy	Taiwan	1,200,000 Traditional Chinese	28 4
Xavante	Xavante	Brazil	2,000 Animism	-18 1
Xerente	Xerente	Brazil	500 Animism	-18 1
Xokleng	Xokleng	Brazil	250 Animism	-18 1
Yafi	Yafi	Indonesia	180 Animism	-18 1
Yaqua	Yagua	Peru	4,000 Animism	-18 1
Yahadian	Yahadian	Indonesia	700 Animism	-18 1
—Yakan	Yakan	Philippines	97,000 Islam	-18 6 80
**Yala	Yala	Nigeria	60,000 Animism	68 4
*Yalunka	Yalunka	Sierra Leone	25,000 Islam	18 6 80
Yaly	Yaly	Indonesia	12,000 Animism	-18 1
Yaminahua	Yaminahua	Peru	1,200 Animism	-18 1
Yanadi	Yanadi	India	205,380 Hindu-Animist	-18 1

People	Language	Country	Population	Religion	Code
Yandang	Yandang	Nigeria	10,000	Islam-Animist	-18 1
Yangbye	Yangbye (Waica)	Burma	326,650	Buddhist-Animist	-18 1
*Yanomamo in Brazil	Yanomam (Waica)	Brazil	3,000	Animism	18 6 79
Yanomamo in Venezuela	Shamatali	Venezuela	nr	Animism	58 5
*Yanyula	Yanyula (Yanjula)	Australia	150	Other	98 4
**Yao	Chiyao	Malawi	600,000	Islam	28 5
**Yao	Yao (Mien Wa)	Mozambique	220,000	Islam	128 5
Yaoure	Yaoure	Thailand	19,867	Animism	2 6 79
Yaquis	Yaqui	Ivory Coast	12,700	Islam-Animist	-18 1
Yaur	Yaur	Mexico	14,000	Christo-Paganism	-18 1
Yava	Yava	Indonesia	350	Animism	-18 5
**Yei	Yei	Indonesia	4,500	Animism	-18 1
Yei	Yei	Botswana	10,000	Animism	-18 1
Yellow Uighur	Yellow Uighur	Indonesia	1,000	Animism	48 5
Yelmek	Yelmek	China	4,000	Traditional Chinese	-18 1
Yemenis	Arabic (Eastern)	Indonesia	400	Animism	-18 1
Yeretuar	Yerava	Yemen, Arab Republic	5,600,000	Islam	-18 5 79
Yerukala	Yeretuar	India	10,870	Hindu-Animist	-18 1
Yeskwa	Yerukala	Indonesia	250	Animism	-18 1
Yidinit	Yeskwa	India	67,550	Hindu-Animist	-18 1
Yinchia	Yidinit	Nigeria	13,000	Islam	-16 1
Yinga	Yinchia	Ethiopia	600	Animism	-18 1
Yogad	Yinga	Burma	4,000	Buddhist-Animist	-18 4
Yonggom	Yogad	Cameroon	300	Animism	-18 1
Yos	Yonggom	Philippines	7,000	Animism	-18 1
Yotafa	Yos	Indonesia	2,000	Animism	-18 1
*Yucuna	Yotafa	Burma	4,500	Buddhist-Animist	-18 1
Yukpa	Yucuna	Indonesia	2,460	Animism	18 5
Yuku	Yukpa	Colombia	500	Christo-Paganism	-18 1
Yungur	Yuku	Colombia	2,520	Animism	18 5
Yuracare	Yungur	China	4,000	Traditional Chinese	-18 1
Yuruti	Yuracare	Nigeria	44,300	Islam	-18 1
Zaghawa	Yuruti	Bolivia	2,500	Animism	-18 1
Zangskari	Zaghawa	Colombia	150	Animism	-18 1
Zaramo	Zangskari	Chad	61,000	Islam-Animist	-18 1
**Zaranda Hill Peoples	Zaramo	India	5,000	Hindu-Animist	28 5
Zari	local languages	Tanzania	296,000	Islam	28 4
Zayse	Zari	Nigeria	10,000	Islam	-18 1
Zilmamu	Zayse	Nigeria	3,950	Islam	-18 1
Zinacantecos	Zilmamu	Ethiopia	21,020	Animism	-18 1
Zoliang	Tzotzil, Chenalho	Ethiopia	3,000	Animism	18 7 79
	Naga, Zoliang	Mexico	10,000	Christo-Paganism	09 3
		India	50,000	Animism	

256

Zome					
Zowla					
Zuni					

Burma	Zome	30,000	Buddhist-Animist	-1%	1
India	Zome	30,000	Hindu-Buddhist	-1%	1
Ghana	Ewe	800,000	Animism	2%	5
United States of America	Zuni	6,000	Animism	1%	4

INDEX
by
Receptivity

INDEX BY RECEPTIVITY

This index lists groups by their reported attitude toward the Gospel. The judgment of receptivity or resistance to the Gospel is a subjective and difficult question. Often times what appears to be resistance to the Gospel turns out to be a rejection of the Western or foreign cultural trappings with which the Gospel is offered. Or perhaps it is a resistance to the agents who bear witness because they come from a country or people not respected by those who are being asked to hear the Gospel. Nonetheless, this index gives the considered judgment of those who have reported these unreached peoples. Within each category (very receptive, receptive, indifferent, reluctant, very reluctant, and not reported) peoples are listed alphabetically by group name. Their country is also listed.

Very Receptive

Adi, India
Adivasis of Dang, India
Azteca, Mexico (79)
Banaro, Papua New Guinea
Baoule, Ivory Coast
Basotho, Mountain, Lesotho (79)
Bipim, Indonesia
Cebu, Middle-Class, Philippines
Ch'ol Sabanilla, Mexico
Chakossi, Ghana
Chamars of Bundelkhand, India
Citak, Indonesia
Godie, Ivory Coast
Guarani, Bolivia (79)
Higi, Nigeria
Irulas, India
Kond, India
Koreans in Germany, German Federal
    Rep.
Krahn, Liberia
Maguzawa, Nigeria (79)
Mocha, Ethiopia
Nocte, India
Paez, Colombia
Pakabeti of Equator, Zaire
Prasuni, Afghanistan
Shankilla (Kazza), Ethiopia
Tagin, India
Tamil Plantation Workers, Malaysia
Vere, Nigeria

Receptive

Adja, Benin
Afo, Nigeria (80)
African Students in Cairo, Egypt
Ahl-i-Haqq in Iran, Iran (79)
Akha, Thailand (79)
Ampeeli, Papua New Guinea
Apartment Residents-Seoul, Korea,
    Republic of
Apatani, India
Apayao, Philippines
Aymara, Bolivia
Azerbaijani, Afghanistan
Babur Thali, Nigeria (80)
Bakuba, Zaire
Balangao, Philippines
Banai, Bangladesh
Bessa, Nigeria
Bhil, Pakistan
Bhils, India (79)
Bidayuh of Sarawak, Malaysia
Bijogo, Guinea-Bissau
Bilan, Philippines
Black Caribs, Belize, Belize (79)
Black Caribs, Guatemala, Guatemala
Black Caribs, Honduras, Honduras
Bodo Kachari, India
Boko, Benin
Bontoc, Southern, Philippines

Bukidnon, Philippines
Bus Drivers, South Korea, Korea,
    Republic of
Busanse, Ghana
Chayahuita, Peru
Chinese Hakka of Taiwan, Taiwan
    (79)
Chinese in Australia, Australia
Chinese in Brazil, Brazil
Chinese in Hong Kong, Hong Kong
Chinese in Indonesia, Indonesia
Chinese in Sabah, Malaysia
Chinese in Sarawak, Malaysia
Chinese in United Kingdom, United
    Kingdom
Chinese in United States, United
    States of America
Chinese in Vancouver B.C., Canada
Chinese Refugees, France, France
    (79)
Chinese Stud., Australia, Australia
Chinese Students Glasgow, United
    Kingdom
Chiriguano, Argentina
Chrau, Viet Nam
Coreguaje, Colombia
Dagomba, Ghana
Dhodias, India
Doohwaayo, Cameroon
Dubla, India
Duka, Nigeria
Fakai, Nigeria
Falasha, Ethiopia (79)
Fali, Nigeria
Gagre, Pakistan
Ghimeera, Ethiopia
Glavda, Nigeria
Gouro, Ivory Coast
Grebo, Liberia
Hajong, Bangladesh
Hewa, Papua New Guinea (79)
High School Students, Hong Kong
Huave, Mexico
Huila, Angola
Hunzakut, Pakistan (79)
Ifugao (Kalangoya), Philippines
Indians, East, Trinidad and Tobago
    (79)
Izi, Nigeria
Japanese Students In USA, United
    States of America
Jarawa, Nigeria
Javanese (rural), Indonesia (79)
Javanese of Central Java, Indonesia
Javanese of Pejompongan, Indonesia
Jivaro (Achuara), Venezuela
K'anjobal of San Miguel, Guatemala
Kafirs, Pakistan (79)
Kaipeng-Koloi, India
Kalagan, Philippines
Kalinga,Northern, Philippines
Kankanay, Central, Philippines
Karbis, India
Kasena, Ghana
Kashmiri Muslims, India (79)
Khmer Refugees, Thailand
Koch, Bangladesh
Kohli, Kutchi, Pakistan
Kohli, Tharadari, Pakistan

Kohli, Wadiara, Pakistan
Kohlis, Parkari, Pakistan
Kolam, India
Kono, Sierra Leone
Koranko, Sierra Leone
Korean Prisoners, Korea, Republic of
Kowaao, Liberia
Kuluis, India
Kunimaipa, Papua New Guinea
Kusaasi, Ghana
Lahaulis, India
Lepcha, Sikkim
Lepers of N.E. Thailand, Thailand
Loho Loho, Indonesia
Lotuka, Sudan
Maasai, Kenya (79)
Macuxi, Brazil
Magar, Nepal
Mam Indian, Guatemala
Mamanwa (Mamanua), Philippines
Mangyan, Philippines
Manikion, Indonesia
Manjaco, Guinea-Bissau
Manobo, Cotabato, Philippines
Manobo, Salug, Philippines
Manobo, Tigwa, Philippines
Manobo, Western Bukidnon, Philippines
Mansaka, Philippines
Mazahua, Mexico
Meghwar, Pakistan (79)
Mejah, India
Melanau of Sarawak, Malaysia (80)
Meo, Thailand
Miching, India
Minnan Hoklo, Taiwan
Mixes, Mexico
Mopan Maya, Guatemala
Mopan Maya, Belize
Mundas, India
Muslim Immigrants in U.K., United Kingdom
Nafaara, Ghana (79)
Nambya, Rhodesia
Ndebele, Rhodesia (79)
Ndoro, Nigeria
Ngamo, Nigeria
Nupe, Nigeria
Orang Asli, Malaysia
Pila, Benin
Portuguese in France, France
Quechua, Peru
Quechua, Bolivia
Quechua, Huanco, Peru
Quiche, Guatemala (79)
Racetrack Residents, United States of America (79)
Saguye, Kenya
Saiva Vellala, India
Santhali, Nepal
Save, Benin
Sawi, Indonesia
Selakau of Sarawak, Malaysia
Shihu, United Arab Emirates
Shirishana, Brazil
Sisaala, Ghana
Somba, Benin
Stud. Osaka Christ. Coll., Japan

Subanen (Tuboy), Philippines
Subanen, Sindangan, Philippines (80)
Suena, Papua New Guinea
Sugut, Malaysia
Sundanese, Indonesia (80)
Suri, Ethiopia
Suriguenos, Philippines
Tagbanwa, Aborlan, Philippines
Tamils (Indian), Sri Lanka (79)
Tangsa, India
Tatuyo, Colombia
Tboli, Philippines
Temne, Sierra Leone (80)
Teribe, Panama
Tripuri, India
Tsachila, Ecuador
Turkana Fishing Community, Kenya (79)
Univ. Students of Japan, Japan
Uzbeks, Afghanistan (79)
Vietnamese in the USA, United States of America
Vietnamese Refugees, Thailand
Vietnamese Refugees, Australia
Vohras of Yavatmal, India
Wajita, Tanzania
Wanchoo, India
Wimbum, Cameroon
Yala, Nigeria
Yao, Thailand (79)
Yao, Malawi
Yei, Botswana
Zaranda Hill Peoples, Nigeria

Indifferent

Afawa, Nigeria (80)
Alars, India
Alawites, Syria (79)
Albanian Muslims, Albania (80)
Arnatas, India
Asmat, Indonesia (79)
Ata of Davao, Philippines
Atta, Philippines
Bariba, Benin (80)
Bassa, Liberia
Batak, Angkola, Indonesia (80)
Bhojpuri, Nepal
Bontoc, Central, Philippines
Bororo, Brazil
Bosnian, Yugoslavia (80)
Bushmen (Hiechware), Rhodesia
Bushmen (Kung), Namibia (79)
Cambodians, Thailand
Cham (Western), Kampuchea, Democratic (80)
Chinese (Hoklo) in Taiwan, Taiwan
Chinese in Amsterdam, Netherlands
Chinese in Austria, Austria
Chinese in Holland, Netherlands
Chinese in Japan, Japan
Chinese in Korea, Korea, Republic of
Chinese in Laos, Laos

Chinese in Malaysia, Malaysia
Chinese in New Zealand, New Zealand
Chinese in Osaka, Japan, Japan
Chinese in South Africa, South
  Africa
Chinese in Thailand, Thailand
Chinese in West Germany, German
  Federal Rep.
Chinese Mainlanders, Taiwan
Chinese of W. Malaysia, Malaysia
Chinese Refugees in Macau, Macau
Chinese Restaurant Wrkrs., France
College Students in Japan, Japan
Comorians, Comoros (79)
Cuna, Colombia (79)
Daka, Nigeria
Dani, Baliem, Indonesia (79)
Dewein, Liberia
Dghwede, Nigeria
Dogon, Mali (79)
Dumagat , Casiguran, Philippines
Factory Workers, Young, Hong Kong
Fulani, Benin
Fulbe, Ghana
Gabbra, Ethiopia
Galla (Bale), Ethiopia
Gonds, India
Gorkha, India
Guajiro, Colombia
Guanano, Colombia (79)
Gypsies in Spain, Spain (79)
Ifugao, Philippines
Indians In Rhodesia, Rhodesia
Industry Laborers-Japan, Japan
Inland Sea Island Peoples, Japan
Int'l Stud., Los Banos, Philippines
Iwaidja, Austria
Japanese in Korea, Korea, Republic
  of
Jewish Imgrnts.-American, Israel
Jewish Imgrnts.-Argentine, Israel
Jewish Imgrnts.-Australia, Israel
Jewish Imgrnts.-Brazilian, Israel
Jewish Imgrnts.-Mexican, Israel
Jewish Imgrnts.-Uruguayan, Israel
Jewish Immigrants, Other, Israel
Jibu, Nigeria
Jiye, Sudan
Kaffa, Ethiopia (80)
Kalanga, Botswana
Kalinga, Southern, Philippines
Kambari, Nigeria (80)
Kamuku, Nigeria (80)
Kanarese, India
Kepas, Papua New Guinea
Khamu, Thailand
Kimyal, Indonesia
Kissi, Sierra Leone
Kissi, Liberia
Komo, Ethiopia
Konkomba, Togo
Koreans of Japan, Japan
Korku, India
Krahn., Ivory Coast
Kudisai Vagh Makkal, India
Kui, Thailand
Kuknas, India
Kurds of Turkey, Turkey (79)
Labourers of Jhoparpatti, India

Lahu, Thailand
Lango, Ethiopia
Lao, Laos (79)
Lao Refugees, Thailand
Lisu, Thailand
Lokoro, Sudan
Malayalars, India
Manobo, Ilianen, Philippines
Mao Refugees from Laos, Thailand
Masengo, Ethiopia
Meitei, India (79)
Mimika, Indonesia
Mixteco,San Juan Mixtepic, Mexico
Mokole, Benin
Molbog, Philippines
Murngin (Wulamba), Australia
Nahua, North Pueblo, Mexico
Nepali, Nepal
New Terrestories People, Hong Kong
Newari, Nepal
Ngen, Ivory Coast
Ningerum, Papua New Guinea
Nkoya, Zambia
Nuer, Ethiopia
Nuer, Sudan (79)
Nyantruku, Benin
Overseas Chin. Port., United
  States of America
Parsees, India
Pygmy (Mbuti), Zaire (79)
Rai, Danuwar, Nepal
Rava, India
Ryukyuan, Japan
Samo-Kubo, Papua New Guinea
Sanuma, Brazil
Sherpa, Nepal
Shourastra, India
Sindhis of India, India
So, Thailand
Somahai, Indonesia
Tamang, Nepal
Tamil Brahmins, India
Tamils (Indian), Malaysia
Teenbu, Ivory Coast
Thai Islam (Thai), Thailand
Thailand Farmers (Ctl), Thailand
Tibetan Refugees, India
Tibetans, China
Tofi, Benin
Tonga, Rhodesia
Topotha, Sudan
University Students, France (79)
University Students, German Federal
  Rep. (79)
Urban Workers in Taiwan, Taiwan
Vai, Liberia (80)
Warjawa, Nigeria
Wazinza, Tanzania
Women Laborers, Taiwan
Yalunka, Sierra Leone (80)
Yanomamo in Brazil, Brazil (79)
Yanyula, Australia
Yucuna, Colombia

Reluctant

263

REGISTRY OF THE UNREACHED

Afar, Ethiopia (79)
Alaba, Ethiopia
Alago, Nigeria
Arabs of Khuzestan, Iran
Barasano, Southern, Colombia
Busa, Nigeria (80)
Butawa, Nigeria
Bwa, Upper Volta (80)
Chitralis, Pakistan (79)
Chola Naickans, India
Chuj of San Mateo Ixtatan,
    Guatemala
Druzes, Israel (79)
Farmers of Japan, Japan
Fishing Village People, Taiwan
Fra-Fra, Ghana
Fulani, Cameroon (79)
Ga-Dang, Philippines
Galla, Harar, Ethiopia
Gilakis, Iran
Gourency, Upper Volta
Government officials, Thailand
Guarayu, Bolivia
Gujarati, United Kingdom
Hopi, United States of America
Ica, Colombia
Ifugao in Cababuyan, Philippines
Igbira, Nigeria (80)
Indians in Fiji, Fiji (79)
Indust.Workers Yongdungpo, Korea,
    Republic of
Ixil, Guatemala
Jama Mapun, Philippines (80)
Japanese in Brazil, Brazil (79)
Jews of Iran, Iran
Jews of Montreal, Canada
Jews, Sephardic, Canada
Karen, Pwo, Thailand
Kayagar, Indonesia
Kerewe, Tanzania
Kotokoli, Benin
Lamba, Togo
Lawa, Thailand
Maithili, Nepal
Malappanackers, India
Malays of Singapore, Singapore (79)
Mapuche, Chile
Mazandaranis, Iran
Miya, Nigeria
Moken, Burma (79)
Moken of Thailand, Thailand
Monpa, India
Mru, Bangladesh
Mualthuam, India
Nambikuara, Brazil
Palaung, Burma (79)
Rabinal-Achi, Guatemala
Rajbansi, Nepal
Sama Bangingi, Philippines (80)
Sama Pangutaran, Philippines (80)
Sama-Badjaw, Philippines (79)
Sangil, Philippines
Senufo, Ivory Coast (80)
Sinhalese, Sri Lanka
Somali, Ajuran, Kenya (79)
Somali, Degodia, Kenya
Somali, Gurreh, Kenya
Somali, Ogadenya, Kenya
Swatis, Pakistan (79)

Tagbanwa, Kalamian, Philippines
Temil (Ceylonese), Sri Lanka
Tengger, Indonesia
Thai Northern, Thailand
Thai of Bangkok, Thailand
Thai, North East, Thailand
Thai, Southern, Thailand
Tin, Thailand
Tonga, Gwembe Valley, Zambia (79)
Turkana, Kenya
Turkish Immigrant Workers, German
    Federal Rep. (79)
Watchi, Togo
Winji-Winji, Benin
Woleat, Turks and Caicos Islands
Yakan, Philippines (80)
Yanomamo in Venezuela, Venezuela
Zowla, Ghana
Zuni, United States of America

Very Reluctant

Achehnese, Indonesia (80)
Algerian (Arabs), Algeria (80)
Arawa, Nigeria
Azerbaijani Turks, Iran (80)
Balinese, Indonesia
Baluchi, Iran (80)
Bhutias, Bhutan
Bugis, Indonesia (80)
Caste Hindus (Andra Prd), India
Chamula, Mexico (79)
Dawoodi Muslims, India
Dendi, Benin
Divehi, Maldives (80)
Fula, Guinea
Fulah, Upper Volta
Gugu-Yalanji, Australia
Gwandara, Nigeria
Jains, India
Jemez Pueblo, United States of
    America
Kabyle, Algeria (79)
Khojas, Agha Khani, India
Kotta, India
Kreen-Akakore, Brazil
Kurds in Iran, Iran (80)
Libyans, Libya
Macu, Colombia
Madurese, Indonesia (79)
Maguindano, Philippines (80)
Mala Muthas, India
Malayo, Colombia
Mandingo, Liberia (79)
Maranao, Philippines (79)
Maures, Senegal
Minangkabau, Indonesia (80)
Mirung, Bangladesh
Moor Malays, Sri Lanka (79)
Mumuye, Nigeria
Muslim Malays, Malaysia (80)
Muslims (West Nile Dist.), Uganda
Muslims in U.A.E., United Arab
    Emirates (79)
Muslims of Jordan, Jordan

North Africans in Belgium, Belgium (80)
Ouaddai, Chad
Paiute, Northern, United States of America
Redjang, Indonesia (80)
Shan, Thailand
Soka Gakkai Believers, Japan
Somali, Ethiopia
Somali, Somalia (79)
Spiritists, Brazil (79)
Tausug, Philippines (80)
Tem, Togo
Thai Islam (Malay), Thailand (80)
Tuareg, Niger (79)
Turkomans, Iran (80)
Turks, Anatolian, Turkey
Ulithi-Mall, Turks and Caicos Islands
Wolof, Senegal (80)
Yaquis, Mexico
Yemenis, Yemen, Arab Republic (79)
Zinacantecos, Mexico (79)

Not Reported Once

Abaknon, Philippines
Abanyom, Nigeria
Abau, Indonesia
Abe, Ivory Coast
Abidji, Ivory Coast
Abkhaz, Turkey
Abong, Nigeria
Abou Charib, Chad
Abua, Nigeria
Abujmaria, India
Abure, Ivory Coast
Ach'ang, China
Achagua, Colombia
Achipa, Nigeria
Achual, Peru
Adamawa, Cameroon
Adiyan, India
Adyukru, Ivory Coast
Aeta, Philippines
Afshars, Iran
Agajanis, Iran
Agariya, India
Aghu, Indonesia
Agoi, Nigeria
Aguaruna, Peru
Agutaynon, Philippines
Agwagwune, Nigeria
Ahir, India
Aibondeni, Indonesia
Aikwakai, Indonesia
Aimol, India
Airo-Sumaqhaghe, Indonesia
Airoran, Indonesia
Ajmeri, India
Aka, India
Akan, Brong, Ivory Coast
Ake, Nigeria
Akpa-Yache, Nigeria
Aladian, Ivory Coast

Alak, Laos
Alangan, Philippines
Alas, Indonesia
Alege, Nigeria
Algerian Arabs in France, France
Allar, India
Alor, Kolana, Indonesia
Amahuaca, Peru
Amanab, Indonesia
Amar, Ethiopia
Amarakaeri, Peru
Ambai, Indonesia
Amber, Indonesia
Amberbaken, Indonesia
Ambonese, Netherlands
Ambonese, Indonesia
Amo, Nigeria
Amuesha, Peru
Anaang, Nigeria
Anal, India
Andha, India
Andoque, Colombia
Anga, India
Angas, Nigeria
Ankwe, Nigeria
Ansus, Indonesia
Anuak, Ethiopia
Anuak, Sudan
Apalai, Brazil
Apinaye, Brazil
Apurina, Brazil
Ara, Indonesia
Arab-Jabbari (Kamesh), Iran
Arab-Shaibani (Kamesh), Iran
Arabela, Peru
Aranadan, India
Arandai, Indonesia
Arapaco, Brazil
Arbore, Ethiopia
Argobba, Ethiopia
Arguni, Indonesia
Arusha, Tanzania
Arya, India
Asienara, Indonesia
Assamese, Bangladesh
Asuri, India
Aten, Nigeria
Ati, Philippines
Atruahi, Brazil
Attie, Ivory Coast
Avikam, Ivory Coast
Awngi, Ethiopia
Awyi, Indonesia
Awyu, Indonesia
Ayu, Nigeria
Babri, India
Baburiwa, Indonesia
Bachama, Nigeria
Bada, Nigeria
Badagu, India
Bade, Nigeria
Bagelkhandi, India
Baghati, India
Bagirmi, Chad
Bagri, Pakistan
Baham, Indonesia
Baharlu (Kamesh), Iran
Bahawalpuri, India
Baiga, India

REGISTRY OF THE UNREACHED

Bajania, Pakistan (79)
Bajau, Indonesian, Indonesia
Bakairi, Brazil
Bakhtiaris, Iran (80)
Bakwe, Ivory Coast
Balangaw, Philippines
Balanta, Senegal
Balantak, Indonesia
Balante, Guinea-Bissau
Bali, Nigeria
Balmiki, Pakistan
Balti, India
Bambara, Mali
Bambara, Ivory Coast
Bambuka, Nigeria
Bandawa-Minda, Nigeria
Bandi, Liberia
Banga, Nigeria
Bangaru, India
Banggai, Indonesia
Baniwa, Brazil
Bantuanon, Philippines
Banyun, Guinea-Bissau
Barabaig, Tanzania (79)
Barasano, Colombia
Barasano, Northern, Colombia
Barau, Indonesia
Bare'e, Indonesia
Bareli, India
Bariba, Nigeria
Basakomo, Nigeria
Basari, Togo
Basari, Senegal
Bashar, Nigeria
Bashgali, Afghanistan
Bashkir, Soviet Russia (80)
Basketo, Ethiopia
Bata, Nigeria
Batak, Karo, Indonesia
Batak, Palawan, Philippines
Batak, Simalungun, Indonesia
Batak, Toba, Indonesia
Bathudi, India
Batu, Nigeria
Baushi, Nigeria
Bawm, Bangladesh
Bayats, Iran
Bayot, Gambia
Bazigar, India
Bediya, India
Bedoanas, Indonesia
Beja, Ethiopia
Bekwarra, Nigeria
Bencho, Ethiopia
Bengali, Bangladesh (80)
Berik, Indonesia
Berom, Nigeria
Bete, Ivory Coast
Bete, India
Bette-Bende, Nigeria
Bhakta, India
Bharia, India
Bhatneri, India
Bhattri, India
Bhilala, India
Bhoyari, India
Bhuiya, India
Bhumij, India
Bhunjia, India

Biafada, Guinea-Bissau
Biak, Indonesia
Bihari, India
Bijori, India
Biksi, Indonesia
Bilala, Chad
Bile, Nigeria
Bilen, Ethiopia
Bimanese, Indonesia
Binawa, Nigeria
Bingkokak, Indonesia
Binjhwari, India
Bira, Indonesia
Birhor, India
Birifor, Ghana
Bitare, Nigeria
Bodo, India
Boghom, Nigeria
Bokyi, Nigeria
Bole, Nigeria
Bomou, Chad
Bondo, India
Bonerif, Indonesia
Bonggo, Indonesia
Bora, Colombia
Borai, Indonesia
Boran, Ethiopia
Bovir-Ahmadi, Iran
Boya, Sudan
Braj, India
Brao, Laos (79)
Brat, Indonesia
Bua, Chad
Bual, Indonesia
Budugum, Cameroon
Buduma, Nigeria
Buhid, Philippines
Builsa, Ghana
Buli, Indonesia
Bunak, Indonesia
Bunan, India
Bungku, Indonesia
Bunu, Nigeria
Burak, Nigeria
Buriat, China
Burig, India
Burig, China
Burji, Ethiopia
Buru, Indonesia
Burungi, Tanzania
Busami, Indonesia
Bushmen (Heikum), Namibia
Bushmen in Botswana, Botswana
Bussa, Ethiopia
Butung, Indonesia
Cacua, Colombia
Caiwa, Brazil
Caluyanhon, Philippines
Campa, Peru
Camsa, Colombia
Candoshi, Peru
Canela, Brazil
Capanahua, Peru
Carapana, Colombia
Cashibo, Peru
Cayapa, Ecuador
Ch'iang, China
Ch'ol Tila, Mexico
Chacobo, Bolivia

Chaqhatai, Afghanistan
Chakfem-Mushere, Nigeria
Chakma, India
Chakossi, Togo
Cham, Viet Nam
Chamari, India
Chamba Daka, Nigeria
Chamba Leko, Nigeria
Chameali, India
Chami, Colombia
Chamicuro, Peru
Chamorro, Turks and Caicos Islands
Chara, Ethiopia
Chaungtha, Burma
Chawai, Nigeria
Chonchu, India
Chero, India
Chik-Barik, India
Chin, China
Chin, Asho, Burma
Chin, Falam, Burma
Chin, Haka, Burma
Chin, Khumi, Burma
Chin, Ngawn, Burma
Chin, Tiddim, Burma
Chinbok, Burma
Chinese Businessmen, Hong Kong
Chinese Factory Workers, Hong Kong
Chinese in Burma, Burma
Chinese in Costa Rica, Costa Rica
Chinese in Puerto Rico, Puerto Rico
Chinese Merchants, Ghana
Chinese Villagers, Hong Kong
Chingp'o, China
Chip, Nigeria
Chipaya, Bolivia
Chiquitano, Bolivia
Chiru, India
Chodhari, India
Chokobo, Nigeria
Chokwe (Lunda), Angola
Chorote, Argentina
Chuabo, Mozambique
Chungchia, China
Churahi, India
Chwang, China
Cinta Larga, Brazil
Circassian, Turkey
Cirebon, Indonesia
Citak, Indonesia
Cocama, Peru
Cofan, Colombia
Cogui, Colombia
Coreguaje, Colombia
Cubeo, Colombia
Cuiba, Colombia
Cujareno, Peru
Culina, Brazil
Cuna, Colombia
Curipaco, Colombia
Cuyonon, Philippines
Dabra, Indonesia
Dadiya, Nigeria
Dagada, Indonesia
Dagari, Ghana
Daqur, China
Dai, Burma
Daju of Dar Dadju, Chad
Daju of Dar Sila, Chad

Dan, Ivory Coast
Dangaleat, Chad
Dass, Nigeria
Dathanik, Ethiopia
Davaweno, Philippines
Degama, Nigeria
Dem, Indonesia
Demta, Indonesia
Deno, Nigeria
Deori, India
Dera, Nigeria
Desano, Brazil
Dhanka, India
Dhanwar, India
Dida, Ivory Coast
Didinga, Sudan
Dimasa, India
Dime, Ethiopia
Dinka, Sudan
Diola, Senegal
Diola, Guinea-Bissau (80)
Dirim, Nigeria
Dirya, Nigeria
Dompago, Benin
Dorli, India
Dorobo, Kenya
Dorobo, Tanzania
Dorze, Ethiopia
Dubu, Indonesia
Duquir, Nigeria
Duquza, Nigeria
Duru, Cameroon
Duvele, Indonesia
Dyerma, Niger (80)
Dyerma, Nigeria
Dyimini, Ivory Coast
Dyola, Gambia
Ebira, Nigeria
Ebrie, Ivory Coast
Edo, Nigeria
Efik, Nigeria
Efutop, Nigeria
Eggon, Nigeria
Ejagham, Nigeria
Ekagi, Indonesia
Ekajuk, Nigeria
Eket, Nigeria
Ekpeye, Nigeria
El Molo, Kenya
Eleme, Nigeria
Emai-Iuleha-Ora, Nigeria
Embera, Northern, Colombia
Emumu, Indonesia
Endeh, Indonesia
Engenni, Nigeria
Enggano, Indonesia
Eotile, Ivory Coast
Epie, Nigeria
Erokwanas, Indonesia
Esan, Nigeria
Etulo, Nigeria
Evant, Nigeria
Evenki, China
Foau, Indonesia
Fordat, Indonesia
Fula, Cunda, Gambia
Fulnio, Brazil
Fyam, Nigeria
Fyer, Nigeria

REGISTRY OF THE UNREACHED

Gaanda, Nigeria
Gabbra, Kenya
Gabri, Chad
Gadaba, India
Gaddi, India
Gade, Nigeria
Gagu, Ivory Coast
Galambi, Nigeria
Galeshis, Iran
Galla of Bucho, Ethiopia
Galler, Laos
Galong, India
Gambai, Chad
Gamti, India
Gane, Indonesia
Gangte, India
Gawar-Bati, Afghanistan
Gawari, India
Gawwada, Ethiopia
Gayo, Indonesia (80)
Gbande, Guinea
Gbari, Nigeria (80)
Gbaya, Nigeria
Gbazantche, Benin
Gedeo, Ethiopia
Geji, Nigeria
Gera, Nigeria
Geruma, Nigeria
Gesa, Indonesia
Gheko, Burma
Ghotuo, Nigeria
Gidar, Chad
Gidicho, Ethiopia
Gio, Liberia
Giryama, Kenya
Gisei, Cameroon
Gisiga, Cameroon
Gobato, Ethiopia
Gobeze, Ethiopia
Goemai, Nigeria
Gokana, Nigeria
Golo, Chad
Gonja, Ghana
Gorontalo, Indonesia
Goudari, Iran
Goulai, Chad
Grasia, India
Grunshi, Ghana
Guajajara, Brazil
Guajibo, Colombia
Guambiano, Colombia
Guayabero, Colombia
Guayabevo, Colombia
Gude, Cameroon
Gude, Nigeria
Gudu, Nigeria
Guduf, Nigeria
Guere, Ivory Coast
Gujuri, Afghanistan
Gula, Chad
Gumuz, Ethiopia
Gurage, Ethiopia (80)
Gure-Kahugu, Nigeria
Gurensi, Ghana
Gurung, Nepal
Guruntum-Mbaaru, Nigeria
Gwa, Ivory Coast
Gwari Matai, Nigeria
Hadiyya, Ethiopia

Halbi, India
Hallam, Burma
Hani, China
Hanonoo, Philippines
Harari, Ethiopia
Harauti, India
Havunese, Indonesia
Helong, Indonesia
Hezareh, Iran
Hixkaryana, Brazil
Ho, India
Hohodene, Brazil
Holiya, India
Hrangkhol, Burma
Huachipaire, Peru
Huambisa, Peru
Hui, China (80)
Huitoto, Meneca, Colombia
Huitoto, Murui, Peru
Hukwe, Angola
Eupda Maku, Colombia
Hwana, Nigeria
Hwela-Numu, Ivory Coast
Hyam, Nigeria
Ibaji, Nigeria
Ibanag, Philippines
Ibibio, Nigeria
Icen, Nigeria
Idoma, Nigeria
Idoma, North, Nigeria
Ifuago, Antipolo, Philippines
Ifugao, Ambanad, Philippines
Ifugao, Kiangan, Philippines
Igala, Nigeria
Igede, Nigeria
Ignaciano, Bolivia
Igorot, Philippines
Iha, Indonesia
Ihceve, Nigeria
Ijo, Central-Western, Nigeria
Ijo, Northeast, Nigeria
Ijo, Northeast Central, Nigeria
Ikulu, Nigeria
Ikwere, Nigeria
Ilongot, Philippines
Inallu, Iran
Inanwatan, Indonesia
Inga, Colombia
Ingassana, Sudan
Insinai, Philippines
Intha, Burma
Iquito, Peru
Irahutu, Indonesia
Iraqw, Tanzania
Iraya, Philippines
Iresim, Indonesia
Iria, Indonesia
Irigwe, Nigeria
Isekiri, Nigeria
Isneg, Dibagat-Kabugao, Philippines
Isneg, Karagawan, Philippines
Isoko, Nigeria
Itawit, Philippines
Itik, Indonesia
Itneg, Adasen, Philippines
Itneg, Binongan, Philippines
Itneg, Masadiit, Philippines
Itonama, Bolivia
Ivbie North-Okpela-Atte, Nigeria

Iwur, Indonesia
Iyon, Nigeria
Izarek, Nigeria
Jaba, Nigeria
Jagannathi, India
Jamamadi, Brazil
Jamden, Indonesia
Jamshidis, Iran
Janjero, Ethiopia
Janjo, Nigeria
Jaqaru, Peru
Jara, Nigeria
Jatapu, India
Jati, Afghanistan
Jaunsari, India
Jebero, Peru
Jeng, Laos
Jera, Nigeria
Jerawa, Nigeria
Jharia, India
Jimbin, Nigeria
Jiye, Uganda
Jongor, Chad
Juang, India
Jukun, Nigeria
Jyarung, China
Ka'mis, Papua New Guinea
Kaagan, Philippines
Kabixi, Brazil
Kabre, Togo
Kachama, Ethiopia
Kachchi, India
Kadaklan-Barlig Bontoc, Philippines
Kader, India
Kadara, Nigeria
Kadiweu, Brazil
Kaeti, Indonesia
Kagoma, Nigeria
Kagoro, Mali
Kahluri, India
Kaibu, Nigeria
Kaikadi, India
Kaili, Indonesia
Kaingang, Brazil
Kaiwai, Indonesia
Kajang, Indonesia
Kaka, Nigeria
Kalinga, Kalagua, Philippines
Kalinga, Limus-Linan, Philippines
Kalinga, Quinaang, Philippines
Kalmytz, China
Kam, China
Kamantan, Nigeria
Kamar, India
Kamayura, Brazil
Kambera, Indonesia
Kamberataro, Indonesia
Kamo, Nigeria
Kamoro, Indonesia
Kampung Baru, Indonesia
Kamtuk-Gresi, Indonesia
Kana, Nigeria
Kanauri, India
Kanembu, Chad
Kanikkaran, India
Kanjari, India
Kanum, Indonesia
Kanuri, Nigeria (80)
Kao, Ethiopia

Kapori, Indonesia
Karakalpak, Soviet Russia (80)
Karanga, Chad
Karas, Indonesia
Karekare, Nigeria
Karen, Thailand (79)
Kari, Chad
Karipuna Creole, Brazil
Karipuna Do Guapore, Brazil
Kariya, Nigeria
Karmali, India
Karon Dori, Indonesia
Karon Pantai, Indonesia
Kasseng, Laos
Kasuweri, Indonesia
Katab, Nigeria
Katakari, India
Kati, Northern, Indonesia
Kati, Southern, Indonesia
Katukina, Panoan, Brazil
Kaugat, Indonesia
Kaure, Indonesia
Kavwol, Indonesia
Kawar, India
Kawe, Indonesia
Kayabi, Brazil
Kayapo, Brazil
Kaygir, Indonesia
Kayupulau, Indonesia
Kazakhs, Iran (80)
Kebumtamp, Bhutan
Keer, India
Kei, Indonesia
Kelao, China
Kemak, Indonesia
Kembata, Ethiopia
Kenderi, Indonesia
Kenga, Chad
Kenyah, Indonesia
Kera, Chad
Kerinchi, Indonesia
Khalaj, Iran
Khalka, China
Kham, China
Khamti, India
Khana, Nigeria
Khandesi, India
Kharia, India
Khasi, India
Khirwar, India
Khowar, India
Kibet, Chad
Kichepo, Sudan
Kilba, Nigeria
Kim, Chad
Kimaghama, Indonesia
Kinaray-A, Philippines
Kirchiz, China
Kirghiz, Afghanistan
Kirgiz, Soviet Russia (80)
Kirifi, Nigeria
Kisan, India
Kishanganjia, India
Kishtwari, India
Kissi, Guinea
Kita, Mali
Koalib, Sudan (79)
Koda, India
Kodi, Indonesia

REGISTRY OF THE UNREACHED

Koenoem, Nigeria
Kofyar, Nigeria
Kohoroxitari, Brazil
Kohumono, Nigeria
Koke, Chad
Kol, India
Kolbila, Cameroon
Kom, India
Koma, Ghana
Koma, Nigeria
Konda-Dora, India
Koneraw, Indonesia
Konkani, India
Konkomba, Ghana
Kono, Nigeria
Konso, Ethiopia
Koraga, India
Korapun, Indonesia
Koro, Nigeria
Koroma, Sudan
Korop, Nigeria
Korwa, India
Kota, India
Kotia, India
Kotogut, Indonesia
Kotoko, Chad
Kotopo, Cameroon
Kouya, Ivory Coast
Koya, India
Koyra, Ethiopia
Kpelle, Liberia
Krio, Gambia
Krobou, Ivory Coast
Krongo, Sudan
Kuatinema, Brazil
Kubu, Indonesia (80)
Kuda-Chamo, Nigeria
Kudiya, India
Kugbo, Nigeria
Kuikuro, Brazil
Kuka, Chad
Kukele, Nigeria
Kulango, Ivory Coast
Kulele, Ivory Coast
Kulere, Nigeria
Kullo, Ethiopia
Kulung, Nigeria
Kumauni, India
Kunama, Ethiopia
Kupia, India
Kurfei, Niger
Kurichiya, India
Kuruba, India
Kurudu, Indonesia
Kurux, India
Kushi, Nigeria
Kuteb, Nigeria
Kuturmi, Nigeria
Kuvi, India
Kuzamani, Nigeria
Kwa, Nigeria
Kwansu, Indonesia
Kwerba, Indonesia
Kwere, Tanzania
Kwesten, Indonesia
Kyibaku, Nigeria
Laamang, Nigeria
Labans, India
Labhani, India

Ladakhi, India
Ladinos, Lebanon
Lahul, China
Laka, Cameroon
Laka, Chad
Laka, China
Lakka, Nigeria
Lalung, India
Lama, Burma
Lame, Nigeria
Lampung, Indonesia (80)
Langa, Ethiopia
Lara, Indonesia
Laru, Nigeria
Latdwelam, Indonesia
Lati, China
Laudje, Indonesia
Lebgo, Nigeria
Lebong, Indonesia
Leco, Bolivia
Lele, Chad
Letti, Indonesia
Li, China
Ligbi, Ivory Coast
Ligbi, Ghana
Limba, Sierra Leone
Lio, Indonesia
Lo, Nigeria
Lobi, Ivory Coast
Lodhi, India
Lohar, Pakistan
Loinang, Indonesia
Loko, Sierra Leone
Loma, Guinea
Loma, Liberia
Lomwe, Mozambique
Longuda, Nigeria
Lore, Indonesia
Lors, Iran (80)
Lotsu-Piri, Nigeria
Loven, Laos
Lu, China
Lubu, Indonesia
Lugbara, Uganda
Lunau, Nigeria
Lushai, India
Luwu, Indonesia
Maanyan, Indonesia
Maba, Chad
Machiguenga, Peru
Macuna, Colombia
Madda, Nigeria
Madik, Indonesia
Maghi, Burma
Mahali, India
Mahri, Oman
Maiongong, Brazil
Mairasi, Indonesia
Majhwar, India
Maji, Ethiopia
Majingai-Ngama, Chad
Makasai, Indonesia
Makian, West, Indonesia
Maklew, Indonesia
Makonde, Tanzania
Makua, Mozambique
Malankuravan, India
Malapandaram, India
Malaryan, India

Malavedan, India
Malo, Ethiopia
Mali, India
Malki, India
Malpaharia, India
Malvi, India
Mama, Nigeria
Mamseni, Iran
Mambai, Indonesia
Mambila, Cameroon
Mamprusi, Ghana
Mancang, Senegal
Manchu, China
Mandar, Indonesia
Mandara, Nigeria
Mandaya, Philippines
Mandaya, Mansaka, Philippines
Mander, Indonesia
Manding, Senegal
Mandyak, Gambia
Manem, Indonesia
Mangbai, Chad
Manggarai, Indonesia
Mangs, India
Manjack, Senegal
Manna-Dora, India
Mannan, India
Mano, Liberia
Manobo, Agusan, Philippines
Manobo, Ata, Philippines
Manobo, Binokid, Philippines
Manobo, Dibabawon, Philippines
Manobo, Obo, Philippines
Manobo, Sarangani, Philippines
Manobo, Tagabawa, Philippines
Manobos, Pulangi, Philippines
Mantion, Indonesia
Manu Park Panoan, Peru
Mao, Northern, Ethiopia
Maou, Ivory Coast
Mara, India
Maranao, Lanad, Philippines
Mararit, Chad
Marau, Indonesia
Marba, Chad
Marghi Central, Nigeria
Maria, India
Marind, Indonesia
Marind, Bian, Indonesia
Marubo, Brazil
Marwari, India
Masa, Chad
Masalit, Chad
Masenrempulu, Indonesia
Massalat, Chad
Mataco, Argentina
Matakam, Cameroon
Matakam, Nigeria
Matbat, Indonesia
Matipuhy-Nahukua, Brazil
Matumbi, Tanzania
Mauri, Niger
Mavchi, India
Mawes, Indonesia
Maxakali, Brazil
Mayoruna, Peru
Mbai, Chad
Mbe, Nigeria
Mbembe (Tigong), Nigeria

Mboi, Nigeria
Mbukushu, Angola
Mbula-Bwazza, Nigeria
Mbum, Chad
Me'en, Ethiopia
Meax, Indonesia
Meban, Sudan
Mokwaj, Indonesia
Mende, Sierra Leone
Mentawi, Indonesia
Meos of Rajasthan, India (90)
Mesengo, Ethiopia
Mesme, Chad
Mesmedje, Chad
Migili, Nigeria
Mimi, Chad
Mina, India
Minianka, Mali
Mirdha, India
Mishmi, India
Mo, Ghana
Mo, Ivory Coast
Moba, Ghana
Moba, Togo
Mober, Nigeria
Mogholi, Afghanistan
Mogum, Chad
Moi, Indonesia
Molof, Indonesia
Mombum, Indonesia
Mon, Burma
Mona, Ivory Coast
Mongondow, Indonesia
Mongour, China
Moni, Indonesia
Montol, Nigeria
Moqaddam, Iran
Mor, Indonesia
Mori, Indonesia
Moru, Ivory Coast
Morunahua, Peru
Morwap, Indonesia
Mossi, Upper Volta (80)
Motilon, Colombia
Movima, Bolivia
Mubi, Chad
Muinane, Colombia
Multani, India
Mumbake, Nigeria
Mun, Burma
Muna, Indonesia
Mundang, Chad
Mundari, India
Munduruku, Brazil
Munggui, Indonesia
Munji-Yidgha, Afghanistan
Mura-Piraha, Brazil
Muria, India
Murle, Sudan
Mursi, Ethiopia
Musei, Chad
Musgu, Chad
Muslim Community of Bawku, Ghana
Muthuvan, India
Muwasi, India
Nabi, Indonesia
Nadeb Maku, Brazil
Nafar, Iran
Nafri, Indonesia

Naga, Angami, India
Naga, Ao, India
Naga, Kalyokengnyu, India
Naga, Konyak, India
Naga, Kuki, India
Naga, Lotha, India
Naga, Mao, India
Naga, Nruanghmei, India
Naga, Sangtam, India
Naga, Sema, India
Naga, Tangkhul, India
Naga, Wancho, India
Nagar, India
Nahsi, China
Naltya, Indonesia
Namshi, Cameroon
Nanai, China
Nancere, Chad
Nandu-Tari, Nigeria
Nao, Ethiopia
Nara, Ethiopia
Nareguta, Nigeria
Nawuri, Ghana
Nchimburu, Ghana
Ndao, Indonesia
Nde-Nsele-Nta, Nigeria
Ndoe, Nigeria
Ndom, Indonesia
Nduga, Indonesia
Ndunpa Duupa, Cameroon
Neyo, Ivory Coast
Ngada, Indonesia
Ngalik, North, Indonesia
Ngalik, Southern, Indonesia
Ngalum, Indonesia
Ngeq, Laos
Ngere, Ivory Coast
Ngizim, Nigeria
Ngwoi, Nigeria
Nhengatu, Brazil
Nias, Indonesia
Nielim, Chad
Nihali, India
Nimadi, India
Nimboran, Indonesia
Ninam, Brazil
Ninggrum, Indonesia
Ninzam, Nigeria
Nisa, Indonesia
Njadu, Indonesia
Nkem-Nkum, Nigeria
Norra, Burma
Northern Cagayan Negrito,
    Philippines
Nosu, China
Ntrubs, Ghana
Numana-Nunku-Gwantu, Nigeria
Nung, China
Nungu, Nigeria
Nuristani, Afghanistan (80)
Nyabwa-Nyedebwa, Ivory Coast
Nyaheun, Laos
Nyamwezi, Tanzania (80)
Nyzatom, Sudan
Nzanyi, Nigeria
Nzema, Ivory Coast
Obanliku, Nigeria
Obolo, Nigeria
Ocaina, Peru

Od, Pakistan
Odual, Nigeria
Odut, Nigeria
Ogbia, Nigeria
Oi, Laos
Oirat, China
Ojhi, India
Okobo, Nigeria
Okpamheri, Nigeria
Ollari, India
Olulumo-Ikom, Nigeria
Ong, India
Onin, Indonesia
Orejon, Peru
Oring, Nigeria
Oriya, India
Ormu, Indonesia
Oron, Nigeria
Oronchon, China
Ot Danum, Indonesia
Otank, Nigeria
Oubi, Ivory Coast
Oyampipuku, Brazil
Cyda, Ethiopia
Pacu, Brazil
Pahari Garhwali, India
Pai, Nigeria
Paite, India
Pakaasnovos, Brazil
Palara, Ivory Coast
Palawano, Philippines
Palawano, Central, Philippines
Palembang, Indonesia
Palenquero, Colombia
Palikur, Brazil
Paliyan, India
Panika, India
Paniyan, India
Pankararu, Brazil
Pankhu, Bangladesh
Pantu, Indonesia
Pao, India
Paongan, China
Papuma, Indonesia
Perakanan, Brazil
Paranan, Philippines
Pardhan, India
Parengi, India
Paresi, Brazil
Parintintin, Brazil
Pashayi, Afghanistan
Pashtuns, Iran (80)
Patelia, India
Pato Tapuia, Brazil
Paumari, Brazil
Pengo, India
Pero, Nigeria
Persians of Iran, Iran (80)
Phu Thai, Laos
Piapoco, Colombia
Pilaga, Argentina
Piratapuyo, Brazil
Piro, Peru
Pisa, Indonesia
Pishagchi, Iran
Piti, Nigeria
Pitu Uluna Salu, Indonesia
Piya, Nigeria
Pnar, India

Podokwo, Cameroon
Polci, Nigeria
Pom, Indonesia
Pongu, Nigeria
Porohanon, Philippines
Pu-I, China
Puku-Geeri-Keri-Wiosi, Nigeria
Pular, Senegal
Punjabis, Pakistan (80)
Punu, China
Puragi, Indonesia
Purum, Burma
Pye, Ivory Coast
Pygmy (Binga), Burundi
Pygmy (Binga), Central African
  Empire
Pyu, Indonesia
Qajars, Iran
Qara'i, Iran
Qaragozlu, Iran
Qashqa'i, Iran (80)
Quaiquer, Colombia
Quareguena, Brazil
Rabha, India
Rai, Nepal
Ralte, Burma
Ratahan, Indonesia
Rataning, Chad
Rawang, China
Reshe, Nigeria
Reshiat, Ethiopia
Reyesano, Bolivia
Riang, India
Riang-Lang, Burma
Piantana, Indonesia
Rikbaktsa, Brazil
Romany, Turkey
Rotti, Indonesia
Rukuba, Nigeria
Rumaya, Nigeria
Runga, Chad
Ruruma, Nigeria
Saberi, Indonesia
Sadan, India
Sadang, Indonesia
Safwa, Tanzania
Saija, Colombia
Salar, China
Saliba, Colombia
Sama, Mapun, Philippines
Sama, Siasi, Philippines
Sama, Sibuku, Philippines
Samarkena, Indonesia
Samburu, Kenya
Sanga, Nigeria
Sangir, Indonesia
Sangke, Indonesia
Santa, China
Sapo, Liberia
Sarakole, Senegal (80)
Sarwa, Chad
Sasek, Indonesia (80)
Sasanis, Iran
Sasaru-Enwan Igwe, Nigeria
Satere, Brazil
Sau, Afghanistan
Sause, Indonesia
Saya, Nigeria
Secoya, Ecuador

Sekar, Indonesia
Seko, Indonesia
Sempan, Indonesia
Senggi, Indonesia
Sentani, Indonesia
Senthang, Burma
Serawai, Indonesia
Serere, Senegal (79)
Serui-Laut, Indonesia
Seuci, Brazil
Seychellois, Seychelles
Sha, Nigeria
Shahsavans, Iran (80)
Shanga, Nigeria
Sharanahua, Peru
Sharchagpakha, Bhutan
Shawiya, Algeria
Sheko, Ethiopia
Shina, Afghanistan
Shinasha, Ethiopia
Shipibo, Peru
Shughni, Afghanistan
Shuwa Arabic, Nigeria
Siagha-Yenimu, Indonesia
Sibo, China
Sidamo, Ethiopia
Sikhule, Indonesia
Sikka, Indonesia
Sikkimese, India
Siona, Colombia
Siri, Nigeria
Siriano, Colombia
Siriono, Bolivia
So, Laos
Sobei, Indonesia
Sochi, Pakistan
Solor, Indonesia
Somahai, Indonesia
Somrai, Chad
Sondwari, India
Soninke, Gambia
Sonjo, Tanzania
Sora, India
Soruba, Benin
Sowanda, Indonesia
Students in Cuiaba, Brazil
Subanun,Lapuyan, Philippines
Sui, China
Suk, Kenya
Sukur, Nigeria
Sulung, India
Sumba, Indonesia
Sumbawa, Indonesia
Sungor, Chad
Sura, Nigeria
Surubu, Nigeria
Surui, Brazil
Ta-Oi, Laos
Tacana, Bolivia
Tadjio, Indonesia
Tadyawan, Philippines
Tagwana, Ivory Coast
Tahit, Indonesia
Taikat, Indonesia
Tajik, Iran (80)
Takankar, India
Takestani, Iran
Tal, Nigeria
Talish, Iran

REGISTRY OF THE UNREACHED

Tama, Chad
Tamagario, Indonesia
Taman, Burma
Tamaria, India
Tambas, Nigeria
Tampulma, Ghana
Tana, Chad
Tanahmerah, Indonesia
Tandanke, Senegal
Tandia, Indonesia
Tangale, Nigeria
Tangchangya, Bangladesh
Tanimuca-Retuama, Colombia
Tao't Bato, Philippines
Taori-Kei, Indonesia
Tara, Indonesia
Targum, Israel
Tarof, Indonesia
Tarok, Nigeria
Terpia, Indonesia
Tatars, Soviet Russia (80)
Taucouleur, Senegal (80)
Taungyo, Burma
Taurap, Indonesia
Tawbuid, Philippines
Tawr, Burma
Teda, Chad (80)
Teimuri, Iran
Teimurtash, Iran
Tembe, Brazil
Tepo, Ivory Coast
Tera, Nigeria
Terena, Brazil
Ternate, Indonesia
Thado, India
Thakur, India
Thar, India
Tharu, Nepal
Ticuna, Brazil
Tidore, Indonesia
Tigon, Cameroon
Timorese, Indonesia
Tippera, Bangladesh
Tiro, Indonesia
Tiruray, Philippines
Toala, Indonesia
Toba, Argentina
Toda, India
Tokkaru, India
Tombulu, Indonesia
Tomini, Indonesia
Tondanou, Indonesia
Tonsea, Indonesia
Tontemboa, Indonesia
Toradja, Indonesia
Totis, India
Towei, Indonesia
Trepo, Ivory Coast
Tsamai, Ethiopia
Tsimane, Bolivia
Tucano, Brazil
Tugara, India
Tukude, Indonesia
Tula, Nigeria
Tulu, India
Tumawo, Indonesia
Tunebo, Cobaria, Colombia
Tunya, Chad
Tupuri, Chad

Tura, Ivory Coast
Turkish Workers, Belgium (80)
Turkwam, Nigeria
Turu, Tanzania
Turu, Indonesia
Tuyuca, Brazil
Uduk, Sudan
Uhunduni, Indonesia
Uighur, Afghanistan
Uigur, China (80)
Ukaan, not reported
Ukpe-Bayobiri, Nigeria
Ukwuani-Aboh, Nigeria
Ullatan, India
Urali, India
Urarina, Peru
Urhobo, Nigeria
Uria, Indonesia
Uruangnirin, Indonesia
Urubu, Brazil
Urupa, Brazil
Utugwang, Nigeria
Uvbie, Nigeria
Uzekwe, Nigeria
Vagala, Ghana
Vagari, Pakistan
Vagla, Ivory Coast
Vaikino, Indonesia
Vaiphei, India
Vietnamese, Laos
Vishavan, India
Voko, Cameroon
Vute, Nigeria
Wa, China
Wabo, Indonesia
Waddar, India
Wagdi, India
Waimiri, Brazil
Waiwai, Brazil
Waja, Nigeria
Wala, Ghana
Walamo, Ethiopia
Wambon, Indonesia
Wan, Ivory Coast
Wandamen, Indonesia
Wanggom, Indonesia
Wano, Indonesia
Wapishana, Brazil
Warembori, Indonesia
Waris, Indonesia
Warkay-Bipim, Indonesia
Waropen, Indonesia
Waura, Brazil
Weda, Indonesia
Wetawit, Ethiopia
Wewewa, Indonesia
Wobe, Ivory Coast
Wodani, Indonesia
Woi, Indonesia
Wolio, Indonesia
Wolof, Gambian, Gambia
Wom, Nigeria
Xavante, Brazil
Xerente, Brazil
Xokleng, Brazil
Yafi, Indonesia
Yagua, Peru
Yahadian, Indonesia
Yaly, Indonesia

Yaminahua, Peru
Yanadi, India
Yandang, Nigeria
Yangbye, Burma
Yao, Mozambique
Yaoure, Ivory Coast
Yaur, Indonesia
Yava, Indonesia
Yei, Indonesia
Yellow Uighur, China
Yelmek, Indonesia
Yerava, India
Yaretuar, Indonesia
Yerukala, India
Yeskwa, Nigeria
Yidinit, Ethiopia
Yinchia, Burma
Yinga, Cameroon
Yogad, Philippines
Yonggom, Indonesia
Yos, Burma
Yotafa, Indonesia
Yukpa, Colombia
Yuku, China
Yungur, Nigeria
Yuracare, Bolivia
Yuruti, Colombia
Zaghawa, Chad
Zangskari, India
Zaramo, Tanzania
Zari, Nigeria
Zayse, Ethiopia
Zilmamu, Ethiopia
Zoliang, India
Zome, Burma
Zome, India

INDEX
by
Principal
Professed
Religion

INDEX BY PRINCIPAL PROFESSED RELIGION

This list indicates predominant professed religion, whether or not a majority of those who profess the religion are active practitioners. Many of the groups have more than one professed religion present but only the one with the largest percentage of followers is indicated in this section.

ANCESTOR WORSHIP

**Akha, Thailand (79)
**K'anjobal of San Miguel,
   Guatemala

ANIMISM

Abanyom, Nigeria
Abau, Indonesia
Abua, Nigeria
Achagua, Colombia
Achual, Peru
Adamawa, Cameroon
***Adi, India
***Adivasis of Dang, India
**Adja, Benin
*Afawa, Nigeria (80)
**Afo, Nigeria (80)
Aghu, Indonesia
Agoi, Nigeria
Aguaruna, Peru
Agwagwune, Nigeria
Aibondeni, Indonesia
Aikwakai, Indonesia
Airo-Sumaghaghe, Indonesia
Airoran, Indonesia
Aka, India
Ake, Nigeria
Akpa-Yache, Nigeria
Alago, Nigeria
Alak, Laos
Alege, Nigeria
Alor, Kolana, Indonesia
Amahuaca, Peru
Amanab, Indonesia
Amar, Ethiopia
Amarakaeri, Peru
Ambai, Indonesia
Amber, Indonesia
Amberbaken, Indonesia
Ambonese, Netherlands
Ambonese, Indonesia
Amo, Nigeria
Amuesha, Peru
Anaang, Nigeria
Anal, India
Andha, India
Andoque, Colombia
Angas, Nigeria
Ankwe, Nigeria
Ansus, Indonesia
Anuak, Ethiopia
Anuak, Sudan
Apalai, Brazil
**Apatani, India
Apinaye, Brazil
Apurina, Brazil
Arabela, Peru
Arandai, Indonesia
Arapaco, Brazil
Arbore, Ethiopia
Argobba, Ethiopia

Arguni, Indonesia
*Arnatas, India
Arusha, Tanzania
Asienara, Indonesia
*Asmat, Indonesia (79)
Asuri, India
*Ata of Davao, Philippines
Atruahi, Brazil
*Atta, Philippines
Awyi, Indonesia
Awyu, Indonesia
**Aymara, Bolivia
**Babur Thali, Nigeria (80)
Baburiwa, Indonesia
Bada, Nigeria
Badagu, India
Baghati, India
Babam, Indonesia
Bahawalpuri, India
Baiga, India
Bakairi, Brazil
**Bakuba, Zaire
Baiangaw, Philippines
Baiante, Guinea-Bissau
Balti, India
***Banaro, Papua New Guinea
Bandi, Liberia
Baniwa, Brazil
Banyun, Guinea-Bissau
***Baoule, Ivory Coast
Barabaiq, Tanzania (79)
Barasano, Colombia
Barasano, Northern, Colombia
Barasano, Southern, Colombia
Barau, Indonesia
Bare'e, Indonesia
*Bariba, Benin (80)
Basakomo, Nigeria
Basari, Togo
Basari, Senegal
Bashar, Nigeria
Basketo, Ethiopia
***Basotho, Mountain, Lesotho (79)
*Bassa, Liberia
**Bassa, Nigeria
Batak, Karo, Indonesia
Batak, Simalungun, Indonesia
Batak, Toba, Indonesia
Baziqar, India
Bediya, India
Bedoanas, Indonesia
Bekwarra, Nigeria
Bencho, Ethiopia
Berik, Indonesia
Berom, Nigeria
Bete, India
Bette-Bende, Nigeria
Bharia, India
**Bhils, India (79)
Bhuiya, India
Biafada, Guinea-Bissau
Biak, Indonesia
**Bijogo, Guinea-Bissau
Biksi, Indonesia
**Bilan, Philippines
Birifor, Ghana
Bodo, India
Boghom, Nigeria
**Boko, Benin

Bokyi, Nigeria
Bonerif, Indonesia
Bonggo, Indonesia
*Bontoc, Central, Philippines
Bora, Colombia
Borai, Indonesia
*Bororo, Brazil
Boya, Sudan
Braj, India
Brao, Laos (79)
Brat, Indonesia
Bua, Chad
Buduqum, Cameroon
Builsa, Ghana
**Bukidnon, Philippines
Bunak, Indonesia
Bunan, India
Bunqku, Indonesia
Bunu, Nigeria
Buriq, India
Bur i, Ethiopia
Buru, Indonesia
Burungi, Tanzania
Busami, Indonesia
**Busanse, Ghana
Bushmen (Heikum), Namibia
*Bushmen (Hiechware), Rhodesia
*Bushmen (Kung), Namibia (79)
Bushmen in Botswana, Botswana
Bussa, Ethiopia
Bwa, Upper Volta (80)
ᒍacua, Colombia
ᒍaiwa, Brazil
ᒍampa, Peru
ᒍamsa, Colombia
Candoshi, Peru
Canela, Brazil
ᒍapanahua, Peru
Carapana, Colombia
Cashibo, Peru
Cayapa, Ecuador
Ch'ol Tila, Mexico
Chacobo, Bolivia
Chakfem-Mushere, Nigeria
***Chakossi, Gnana
Chakossi, Togo
Chami, Colombia
Chamicuro, Peru
Chara, Ethiopia
Chawai, Nigeria
Chero, India
Chik-Barik, India
Chip, Nigeria
Chipaya, Bolivia
Chiquitano, Bolivia
**Chiriguano, Argentina
Chiru, India
Chokobo, Nigeria
Chokwe (Lunda), Angola
Chola Naickans, India
Chorote, Argentina
**Chrau, Viet Nam
Chuabo, Mozambique
Chuj of San Mateo Ixtatan,
  Guatemala
Cinta Larga, Brazil
***Citak, Indonesia
Citak, Indonesia
Cocama, Peru

Cofan, Colombia
Cogui, Colombia
**Coreguaje, Colombia
Coreguaje, Colombia
Cubeo, Colombia
Cuiba, Colombia
Cujareno, Peru
Culina, Brazil
*Cuna, Colombia (79)
Cuna, Colombia
Curipaco, Colombia
Dabra, Indonesia
Dagada, Indonesia
Dagari, Ghana
*Daka, Nigeria
*Dani, Baliem, Indonesia (79)
Datnanik, Ethiopia
Deqema, Nigeria
Dem, Indonesia
Demta, Indonesia
Deori, India
Desano, Brazil
*Dghwede, Nigeria
Dhanka, India
Dhanwar, India
Didinga, Sudan
Dimasa, India
Dime, Ethiopia
Dinka, Sudan
*Dogon, Mali (79)
Dompago, Benin
**Doohwaayo, Cameroon
Dorobo, Kenya
Dorobo, Tanzania
Dorze, Ethiopia
Dubu, Indonesia
**Duka, Nigeria
*Dumagat , Casiguran, Philippines
Duru, Cameroon
Duvele, Indonesia
Edo, Nigeria
Efik, Nigeria
Efutop, Nigeria
Eggon, Nigeria
Ejagham, Nigeria
Ekagi, Indonesia
Ekajuk, Nigeria
Eket, Nigeria
Ekpeye, Nigeria
El Molo, Kenya
Eleme, Nigeria
Emai-Iuleha-Ora, Nigeria
Embera, Northern, Colombia
Emumu, Indonesia
Engenni, Nigeria
Enggano, Indonesia
Epie, Nigeria
Erokwanas, Indonesia
Esan, Nigeria
Etulo, Nigeria
Evant, Nigeria
**Fakai, Nigeria
**Fali, Nigeria
Foau, Indonesia
Fordat, Indonesia
Fra-Fra, Ghana
Fulnio, Brazil
Fyam, Nigeria
Fyer, Nigeria

Ga-Dang, Philippines
Gade, Nigeria
**Gagre, Pakistan
Gagu, Ivory Coast
Galler, Laos
Gane, Indonesia
Gawwada, Ethiopia
Gbande, Guinea
Gbari, Nigeria (80)
Gedeo, Ethiopia
Gesa, Indonesia
**Ghimeera, Ethiopia
Ghotuo, Nigeria
Gidicho, Ethiopia
Gio, Liberia
Giryama, Kenya
Gisei, Cameroon
Gisiga, Cameroon
**Glavda, Nigeria
Gobato, Ethiopia
Gobeze, Ethiopia
***Godie, Ivory Coast
Goemai, Nigeria
Gokana, Nigeria
*Gonds, India
Gourency, Upper Volta
**Gouro, Ivory Coast
**Grebo, Liberia
Grunshi, Ghana
Guajajara, Brazil
Guajibo, Colombia
*Guajiro, Colombia
Guambiano, Colombia
***Guarani, Bolivia (79)
Guayabero, Colombia
Guayabevo, Colombia
Gude, Cameroon
Gude, Nigeria
Gudu, Nigeria
Guduf, Nigeria
Gugu-Yalanji, Australia
Gumuz, Ethiopia
Gurensi, Ghana
Gwandara, Nigeria
Hadiyya, Ethiopia
Havunese, Indonesia
Helong, Indonesia
**Hewa, Papua New Guinea (79)
***Higi, Nigeria
Hixkaryana, Brazil
Hohodene, Brazil
Hopi, United States of America
Huachipaire, Peru
Huambisa, Peru
**Huila, Angola
Huitoto, Meneca, Colombia
Huitoto, Murui, Peru
Hukwe, Angola
Hupda Maku, Colombia
Ibaji, Nigeria
Ibanag, Philippines
Ibibio, Nigeria
Ica, Colombia
Idoma, Nigeria
Idoma, North, Nigeria
Ifuago, Antipolo, Philippines
*Ifugao, Philippines
**Ifugao (Kalangoya), Philippines
Ifugao in Cababuyan, Philippines

Ifugao, Ambanad, Philippines
Ifugao, Kiangan, Philippines
Igala, Nigeria
Igede, Nigeria
Ignaciano, Bolivia
Igorot, Philippines
Iha, Indonesia
Ihceve, Nigeria
Ijo, Central-Western, Nigeria
Ijo, Northeast, Nigeria
Ijo, Northeast Central, Nigeria
Ikwere, Nigeria
Ilongot, Philippines
Inanwatan, Indonesia
Ingassana, Sudan
Insinai, Philippines
Iquito, Peru
Irahutu, Indonesia
Iraqw, Tanzania
Iresim, Indonesia
Iria, Indonesia
Irigwe, Nigeria
Isekiri, Nigeria
Isneg, Dibagat-Kabugao,
   Philippines
Isneg, Karagawan, Philippines
Isoko, Nigeria
Itik, Indonesia
Itonama, Bolivia
Ivbie North-Okpela-Atte, Nigeria
*Iwaidja, Austria
Iwur, Indonesia
Iyon, Nigeria
Izarek, Nigeria
**Izi, Nigeria
Jaba, Nigeria
Jamamadi, Brazil
Jamden, Indonesia
Janjero, Ethiopia
Janjo, Nigeria
Jagaru, Peru
**Jarawa, Nigeria
Jebero, Peru
Jeng, Laos
Jerawa, Nigeria
*Jibu, Nigeria
Jiye, Uganda
*Jiye, Sudan
Jukun, Nigeria
Kabixi, Brazil
Kabre, Togo
Kachama, Ethiopia
Kadaklan-Barlig Bontoc,
   Philippines
Kadara, Nigeria
Kadiweu, Brazil
Kaeti, Indonesia
**Kafirs, Pakistan (79)
Kagoro, Mali
Kaili, Indonesia
**Kaipeng-Koloi, India
Kaiwai, Indonesia
Kajang, Indonesia
**Kalagan, Philippines
*Kalanga, Botswana
Kalinga, Kalagua, Philippines
Kalinga, Limus-Linan,
   Philippines
Kalinga, Quinaang, Philippines

*Kalinga, Southern, Philippines
Kamantan, Nigeria
Kamayura, Brazil
*Kambari, Nigeria (80)
Kambera, Indonesia
Kamberataro, Indonesia
Kamoro, Indonesia
Kampung Baru, Indonesia
Kamtuk-Gresi, Indonesia
*Kamuku, Nigeria (80)
Kana, Nigeria
**Kankanay, Central, Philippines
Kanum, Indonesia
Kao, Ethiopia
Kapori, Indonesia
Karas, Indonesia
Karen, Thailand 79
Karen, Pwo, Thailand
Karipuna Creole, Brazil
Karipuna Do Guapore, Brazil
Karon Dori, Indonesia
Karon Pantai, Indonesia
**Kasena, Ghana
Kasseng, Laos
Kasuweri, Indonesia
Kati, Northern, Indonesia
Kati, Southern, Indonesia
Katukina, Panoan, Brazil
Kauqat, Indonesia
Kaure, Indonesia
Kavwol, Indonesia
Kawe, Indonesia
Kayabi, Brazil
Kayagar, Indonesia
Kayapo, Brazil
Kaygir, Indonesia
Kayupulau, Indonesia
Kei, Indonesia
Kemak, Indonesia
Kembata, Ethiopia
Kenyah, Indonesia
*Kepas, Papua New Guinea
Kerewe, Tanzania
*Khamu, Thailand
Kichepo, Sudan
Kimaghama, Indonesia
*Kimyal, Indonesia
*Kissi, Sierra Leone
Kissi, Guinea
*Kissi, Liberia
Koalib, Sudan (79)
Kodi, Indonesia
Koenoem, Nigeria
Kofyar, Nigeria
Kohoroxitari, Brazil
Kohumono, Nigeria
Koma, Ghana
Koma, Nigeria
*Komo, Ethiopia
***Kond, India
Koneraw, Indonesia
*Konkomba, Togo
Konkomba, Ghana
**Kono, Sierra Leone
Konso, Ethiopia
Korapun, Indonesia
*Korku, India
Koro, Nigeria
Koroma, Sudan

Korop, Nigeria
Kotogut, Indonesia
Kotopo, Cameroon
Kotta, India
**Kowaao, Liberia
Koyra, Ethiopia
Kpelle, Liberia
***Krahn, Liberia
*Krahn, Ivory Coast
Kreen-Akakore, Brazil
Krongo, Sudan
Kuatinema, Brazil
Kubu, Indonesia (80)
Kugbo, Nigeria
Kuikuro, Brazil
Kukele, Nigeria
Kulango, Ivory Coast
Kulere, Nigeria
Kurfei, Niger
Kurudu, Indonesia
**Kusaasi, Ghana
Kwansu, Indonesia
Kwerba, Indonesia
Kwere, Tanzania
Kwesten, Indonesia
*Lahu, Thailand
Laka, Cameroon
Lamba, Togo
Langa, Ethiopia
*Lango, Ethiopia
Lara, Indonesia
Latdwalam, Indonesia
Laudje, Indonesia
Lebgo, Nigeria
Leco, Bolivia
Letti, Indonesia
Ligbi, Ivory Coast
Limba, Sierra Leone
*Lisu, Thailand
Lo, Nigeria
Lobi, Ivory Coast
**Loho Loho, Indonesia
Loinang, Indonesia
Loko, Sierra Leone
Loma, Guinea
Loma, Liberia
Lomwe, Mozambique
Lore, Indonesia
Lungu, Nigeria
Maanyan, Indonesia
**Maasai, Kenya (79)
Machiguenga, Peru
Macu, Colombia
Macuna, Colombia
**Macuxi, Brazil
Madda, Nigeria
Madik, Indonesia
***Maguzawa, Nigeria (79)
Mahri, Oman
Maiongong, Brazil
Mairasi, Indonesia
Maji, Ethiopia
Makasai, Indonesia
Makian, West, Indonesia
Maklew, Indonesia
Makua, Mozambique
Malappanackers, India
*Malayalars, India
Malayo, Colombia

Male, Ethiopia
Mama, Nigeria
Mambai, Indonesia
Mambila, Cameroon
Mamprusi, Ghana
Mandaya, Philippines
Mandaya, Mansaka, Philippines
Mander, Indonesia
Manem, Indonesia
**Mangyan, Philippines
**Manikion, Indonesia
**Manjaco, Guinea-Bissau
Mano, Liberia
Manobo, Agusan, Philippines
Manobo, Ata, Philippines
Manobo, Binokid, Philippines
**Manobo, Cotabato, Philippines
Manobo, Dibabawon, Philippines
*Manobo, Ilianen, Philippines
Manobo, Obo, Philippines
**Manobo, Salug, Philippines
Manobo, Sarangani, Philippines
Manobo, Tagabawa, Philippines
**Manobo, Tigwa, Philippines
**Manobo, Western Bukidnon,
    Philippines
Manobos, Pulangi, Philippines
Mantion, Indonesia
Manu Park Panoan, Peru
*Mao Refugees from Laos, Thailand
Mao, Northern, Ethiopia
Marau, Indonesia
Marind, Indonesia
Marind, Bian, Indonesia
Marubo, Brazil
Masa, Chad
*Masengo, Ethiopia
Mataco, Argentina
Matakam, Cameroon
Matbat, Indonesia
Matipuhy-Nahukua, Brazil
Mauri, Niger
Mawes, Indonesia
Maxakali, Brazil
Mayoruna, Peru
Mbe, Nigeria
Mbembe (Tigong), Nigeria
Mbukushu, Angola
Me'en, Ethiopia
Meax, Indonesia
Meban, Sudan
**Mejah, India
Mekwei, Indonesia
**Melanau of Sarawak, Malaysia
    (80)
Mende, Sierra Leone
**Meo, Thailand
Migili, Nigeria
Minianka, Mali
Mirung, Bangladesh
Miya, Nigeria
Mo, Ghana
Moba, Ghana
Moba, Togo
***Mocha, Ethiopia
Moi, Indonesia
Moken, Burma (79)
Moken of Thailand, Thailand
*Mokole, Benin

Molof, Indonesia
Mombum, Indonesia
Mongondow, Indonesia
Moni, Indonesia
Mor, Indonesia
Mori, Indonesia
Morunahua, Peru
Morwap, Indonesia
Mossi, Upper Volta (80)
Motilon, Colombia
Movima, Bolivia
Mru, Bangladesh
Mualthuam, India
Muinane, Colombia
Mumuye, Nigeria
**Mundas, India
Munduruku, Brazil
Munggui, Indonesia
Mura-Piraha, Brazil
Murle, Sudan
*Murnqin (Wulamba), Australia
Mursi, Ethiopia
Nabi, Indonesia
Nadeb Maku, Brazil
**Nafaara, Ghana 79)
Nafri, Indonesia
Naltya, Indonesia
Nambikuara, Brazil
**Nambya, Rhodesia
Namshi, Cameroon
Nao, Ethiopia
Naraguta, Nigeria
Nawuri, Ghana
Nchimburu, Ghana
Ndao, Indonesia
Nde-Nsele-Nta, Nigeria
**Ndebele, Rhodesia (79)
Ndoe, Nigeria
Ndom, Indonesia
**Ndoro, Nigeria
Nduga, Indonesia
Neyo, Ivory Coast
Ngalik, North, Indonesia
Ngalik, Southern, Indonesia
Ngalum, Indonesia
**Ngamo, Nigeria
*Ngen, Ivory Coast
Ngeq, Laos
Ngere, Ivory Coast
Nhengatu, Brazil
Nias, Indonesia
Nimboran, Indonesia
Ninam, Brazil
*Ningerum, Papua New Guinea
Ninggrum, Indonesia
Nisa, Indonesia
Njadu, Indonesia
Nkem-Nkum, Nigeria
*Nkoya, Zambia
***Nocte, India
Ntrubs, Ghana
*Nuer, Ethiopia
*Nuer, Sudan (79)
Nungu, Nigeria
Nyaheun, Laos
Nyamwezi, Tanzania (80)
*Nyantruku, Benin
Nyzatom, Sudan
Obanliku, Nigeria

Obolo, Nigeria
Ocaina, Peru
Odual, Nigeria
Odut, Nigeria
Ogbia, Nigeria
Oi, Laos
Okobo, Nigeria
Okpamneri, Nigeria
Olulumo-Ikom, Nigeria
Onin, Indonesia
**Orang Asli, Malaysia
Orejon, Peru
Oring, Nigeria
Ormu, Indonesia
Oron, Nigeria
Ot Danum, Indonesia
Otank, Nigeria
Oyampibuku, Brazil
Oyda, Ethiopia
Pacu, Brazil
Pai, Nigeria
Pakaasnovos, Brazil
***Pakabeti of Equator, Zaire
Palawano, Philippines
Palawano, Central, Philippines
Palenquero, Colombia
Palikur, Brazil
Pankararu, Brazil
Pantu, Indonesia
Papuma, Indonesia
Parakanan, Brazil
Paresi, Brazil
Parintintin, Brazil
Pato Tapuia, Brazil
Paumari, Brazil
Piapoco, Colombia
**Pila, Benin
Pilaga, Argentina
Piratapuyo, Brazil
Piro, Peru
Pisa, Indonesia
Pitu Uluna Salu, Indonesia
Podokwo, Cameroon
Pom, Indonesia
Porohanon, Philippines
Puraqi, Indonesia
Pygmy (Binga), Burundi
Pygmy (Binga), Central African
  Empire
*Pygmy (Mbuti), Zaire (79)
Pyu, Indonesia
Quaiquer, Colombia
Quarequena, Brazil
**Quechua, Huanco, Peru
Ratahan, Indonesia
Reshe, Nigeria
Reshiat, Ethiopia
Reyesano, Bolivia
Riantana, Indonesia
Rikbaktsa, Brazil
Rotti, Indonesia
Saberi, Indonesia
Sadang, Indonesia
Safwa, Tanzania
Saija, Colombia
Saliba, Colombia
Sama, Mapun, Philippines
Samarkena, Indonesia
Samburu, Kenya

*Samo-Kubo, Papua New Guinea
Sangir, Indonesia
Sangke, Indonesia
**Santhali, Nepal
*Sanuma, Brazil
Sapo, Liberia
Sasaru-Enwan Igwe, Nigeria
Satere, Brazil
Sause, Indonesia
**Save, Benin
**Sawi, Indonesia
Secoya, Ecuador
Sekar, Indonesia
Seko, Indonesia
**Selakau of Sarawak, Malaysia
Sempan, Indonesia
Senggi, Indonesia
Sentani, Indonesia
Senufo, Ivory Coast (80)
Serere, Senegal (79)
Serui-Laut, Indonesia
Seuci, Brazil
Sha, Nigeria
Shanga, Nigeria
Sharanahua, Peru
Sheko, Ethiopia
Shinasha, Ethiopia
Shipibo, Peru
**Shirishana, Brazil
Siagha-Yenimu, Indonesia
Sikhule, Indonesia
Sikka, Indonesia
Siona, Colombia
Siriano, Colombia
Siriono, Bolivia
*Sisaala, Ghana
So, Laos
*So, Thailand
Sobei, Indonesia
*Somahai, Indonesia
Somahai, Indonesia
**Somba, Benin
Sonjo, Tanzania
Soruba, Benin
Sowanda, Indonesia
**Subanen (Tuboy), Philippines
**Subanen, Sindangan, Philippines
  (80)
**Sugut, Malaysia
Suk, Kenya
**Suri, Ethiopia
Surui, Brazil
Ta-Oi, Laos
Tacana, Bolivia
Tadjio, Indonesia
Tadyawan, Philippines
**Tagbanwa, Aborlan, Philippines
***Tagin, India
Tahit, Indonesia
Taikat, Indonesia
Tamagario, Indonesia
Tambas, Nigeria
Tampulma, Ghana
Tanahmerah, Indonesia
Tandia, Indonesia
**Tangsa, India
Tanimuca-Retuama, Colombia
Tao't Bato, Philippines
Taori-Kei, Indonesia

Tara, Indonesia
Tarof, Indonesia
Tarok, Nigeria
Tarpia, Indonesia
**Tatuyo, Colombia
Taurap, Indonesia
Tawbuid, Philippines
**Tboli, Philippines
*Teenbu, Ivory Coast
Tembe, Brazil
**Temne, Sierra Leone (80)
Terena, Brazil
Ticuna, Brazil
Tigon, Cameroon
Timorese, Indonesia
Tin, Thailand
Tiro, Indonesia
Tiruray, Philippines
Toala, Indonesia
Toba, Argentina
*Tofi, Benin
Tombulu, Indonesia
Tomini, Indonesia
Tondanou, Indonesia
*Tonga, Rhodesia
Tonga, Gwembe Valley, Zambia
   (79)
Tonsea, Indonesia
Tontemboa, Indonesia
*Topotha, Sudan
Toradja, Indonesia
Towei, Indonesia
**Tripuri, India
Tsamai, Ethiopia
Tsimane, Bolivia
Tucano, Brazil
Tumawo, Indonesia
Tunebo, Cobaria, Colombia
Turkana, Kenya
**Turkana Fishing Community, Kenya
   (79)
Turu, Tanzania
Turu, Indonesia
Tuyuca, Brazil
Uduk, Sudan
Uhunduni, Indonesia
Ukaan, not reported
Ukpe-Bayobiri, Nigeria
Ukwuani-Aboh, Nigeria
Urarina, Peru
Urhobo, Nigeria
Uria, Indonesia
Uruangnirin, Indonesia
Urubu, Brazil
Urupa, Brazil
Utugwang, Nigeria
Uvbie, Nigeria
Uzekwe, Nigeria
Vagala, Ghana
Vaikino, Indonesia
***Vere, Nigeria
Vute, Nigeria
Wabo, Indonesia
Waimiri, Brazil
Waiwai, Brazil
**Wajita, Tanzania
Wala, Ghana
Walamo, Ethiopia
Wambon, Indonesia

**Wanchoo, India
Wandamen, Indonesia
Wanggom, Indonesia
Wano, Indonesia
Wapishana, Brazil
Warembori, Indonesia
Waris, Indonesia
*Warjawa, Nigeria
Warkay-Bipim, Indonesia
Waropen, Indonesia
Watchi, Togo
Waura, Brazil
*Wazinza, Tanzania
Wetawit, Ethiopia
Wewewa, Indonesia
**Wimbum, Cameroon
Wobe, Ivory Coast
Wodani, Indonesia
Woi, Indonesia
Xavante, Brazil
Xerente, Brazil
Xokleng, Brazil
Yafi, Indonesia
Yagua, Peru
Yahadian, Indonesia
**Yala, Nigeria
Yaly, Indonesia
Yaminahua, Peru
*Yanomamo in Brazil, Brazil (79)
Yanomamo in Venezuela, Venezuela
**Yao, Thailand (79)
Yaur, Indonesia
Yava, Indonesia
**Yei, Botswana
Yei, Indonesia
Yelmek, Indonesia
Yeretuar, Indonesia
Yidinit, Ethiopia
Yinga, Cameroon
Yogad, Philippines
Yonggom, Indonesia
Yotafa, Indonesia
Yukpa, Colombia
Yuracare, Bolivia
Yuruti, Colombia
**Zaranda Hill Peoples, Nigeria
Zayse, Ethiopia
Zilmamu, Ethiopia
Zoliang, India
Zowla, Ghana
Zuni, United States of America

BUDDHISM

**Banai, Bangladesh
Bhutias, Bhutan
*Cambodians, Thailand
*Chinese in Thailand, Thailand
Government officials, Thailand
Japanese in Brazil, Brazil (79)
**Khmer Refugees, Thailand
*Kui, Thailand
**Lahaulis, India
*Lao, Laos (79)
*Lao Refugees, Thailand

Lawa, Thailand
**Lepers of N.E. Thailand, Thailand
Loven, Laos
**Minnan Hoklo, Taiwan
Monpa, India
Palaung, Burma (79)
Phu Thai, Laos
Shan, Thailand
*Sherpa, Nepal
Sinhalese, Sri Lanka
Soka Gakkai Believers, Japan
Thai Northern, Thailand
Thai of Bangkok, Thailand
Thai, North East, Thailand
Thai, Southern, Thailand
*Thailand Farmers (Ctl), Thailand
*Tibetan Refugees, India
*Tibetans, China
Vietnamese, Laos
**Vietnamese in the USA, United
    States of America
**Vietnamese Refugees, Thailand

BUDDHIST-ANIMIST

Chaungtha, Burma
Chin, Asho, Burma
Chin, Falam, Burma
Chin, Haka, Burma
Chin, Khumi, Burma
Chin, Ngawn, Burma
Chin, Tiddim, Burma
Chinbok, Burma
Dai, Burma
Gheko, Burma
Hallam, Burma
Hrangkhol, Burma
Intha, Burma
Kebumtamp, Bhutan
Lama, Burma
Lu, China
Maghi, Burma
Mon, Burma
Mun, Burma
Norra, Burma
Purum, Burma
Ralte, Burma
Riang-Lang, Burma
Senthang, Burma
Sharchagpakha, Bhutan
Taman, Burma
Taungyo, Burma
Tawr, Burma
Yangbye, Burma
Yinchia, Burma
Yos, Burma
Zome, Burma

CHRISTO-PAGANISM

Abaknon, Philippines
Aeta, Philippines
Alangan, Philippines
**Ampeeli, Papua New Guinea
**Apayao, Philippines
Ati, Philippines
***Azteca, Mexico (79)
**Balangao, Philippines
Bantuanon, Philippines
Batak, Palawan, Philippines
**Bidayuh of Sarawak, Malaysia
***Bipim, Indonesia
**Black Caribs, Belize, Belize
    (79)
**Black Caribs, Guatemala,
    Guatemala
**Black Caribs, Honduras, Honduras
**Bontoc, Southern, Philippines
Buhid, Philippines
Caluyanhon, Philippines
***Cebu, Middle-Class, Philippines
***Ch'ol Sabanilla, Mexico
Chamorro, Turks and Caicos
    Islands
Chamula, Mexico (79)
**Chayahuita, Peru
Cuyonon, Philippines
Davaweno, Philippines
Endeh, Indonesia
Galla of Bucho, Ethiopia
*Guanano, Colombia (79)
Guarayu, Bolivia
Hanonoo, Philippines
**Huave, Mexico
Inga, Colombia
Iraya, Philippines
Itawit, Philippines
Itneg, Adasen, Philippines
Itneg, Binongan, Philippines
Itneg, Masadiit, Philippines
Ixil, Guatemala
Jemez Pueblo, United States of
    America
**Jivaro (Achuara), Venezuela
Ka'mis, Papua New Guinea
Kaagan, Philippines
*Kaffa, Ethiopia (80)
Kaingang, Brazil
**Kalinga,Northern, Philippines
Kinaray-A, Philippines
**Kunimaipa, Papua New Guinea
Lio, Indonesia
*Lokoro, Sudan
*Mam Indian, Guatemala
**Mamanwa (Mamanua), Philippines
**Mansaka, Philippines
Mapuche, Chile
**Mazahua, Mexico
*Mimika, Indonesia
**Mixes, Mexico
*Mixteco,San Juan Mixtepic,
    Mexico
**Mopan Maya, Guatemala
**Mopan Maya, Belize
*Nahua, North Pueblo, Mexico
Ngada, Indonesia
Northern Cagayan Negrito,
    Philippines
***Paez, Colombia

Paranan, Philippines
**Quechua, Peru
**Quechua, Bolivia
**Quiche, Guatemala (79)
Rabinal-Achi, Guatemala
***Shankilla (Kazza), Ethiopia
**Suena, Papua New Guinea
Sumba, Indonesia
Tagbanwa, Kalamian, Philippines
**Teribe, Panama
**Tsachila, Ecuador
Tukude, Indonesia
Ulithi-Mall, Turks and Caicos
Islands
Woleat, Turks and Caicos Islands
Yaquis, Mexico
*Yucuna, Colombia
Zinacantecos, Mexico (79)

FOLK RELIGION

*Alars, India
**Apartment Residents-Seoul,
Korea, Republic of
Druzes, Israel (79)
*Gabbra, Ethiopia
Gabbra, Kenya
*Gypsies in Spain, Spain (79)
Indust.Workers Yongdungpo,
Korea, Republic of
*Koreans of Japan, Japan
Romany, Turkey
Spiritists, Brazil (79)
**Vietnamese Refugees, Australia

HINDU-ANIMIST

Abujmaria, India
Aimol, India
Ajmeri, India
Aranadan, India
Bagelkhandi, India
Bangaru, India
Bhakta, India
Bhattri, India
Bhilala, India
Bhoyari, India
Bnumij, India
Bhunjia, India
Bihari, India
Bijori, India
Binjhwari, India
Birhor, India
Chakma, India
Chamari, India
Chameali, India
Chenchu, India
Chodhari, India
Churahi, India
Dorli, India
Gadaba, India

Gaddi, India
Galong, India
Gamti, India
Gangte, India
Gawari, India
Grasia, India
Halbi, India
Harauti, India
Ho, India
Holiya, India
Jagannathi, India
Jatapu, India
Jaunsari, India
Kadar, India
Kahluri, India
Kaikadi, India
Kamar, India
Kanikkaran, India
Kanjari, India
Karmali, India
Katakari, India
Kawar, India
Keer, India
Khandesi, India
Kharia, India
Khirwar, India
Khowar, India
Kisan, India
Kishanganjia, India
Kishtwari, India
Koda, India
Kol, India
Kom, India
Konda-Dora, India
Konkani, India
Koraga, India
Korwa, India
Kota, India
Kotia, India
Koya, India
Kudiya, India
Kumauni, India
Kupia, India
Kurichiya, India
Kuruba, India
Kurux, India
Kuvi, India
Lodhi, India
Lushai, India
Mahali, India
Majhwar, India
Malankuravan, India
Malapandaram, India
Malaryan, India
Mali, India
Malki, India
Malpaharia, India
Malvi, India
Manna-Dora, India
Mannan, India
Mara, India
Maria, India
Marwari, India
Mavchi, India
Mina, India
Mirdha, India
Mishmi, India
Multani, India
Mundari, India

Muria, India
Muthuvan, India
Muwasi, India
Naga, Angami, India
Naga, Ao, India
Naga, Kalyokengnyu, India
Naga, Konyak, India
Nagar, India
Nihali, India
Ojhi, India
Ollari, India
Ong, India
Oriya, India
Pahari Garhwali, India
Paite, India
Paliyan, India
Panika, India
Paniyan, India
Pardhan, India
Parengi, India
Patelia, India
Pengo, India
Pnar, India
Sadan, India
Sondwari, India
Takankar, India
Thakur, India
Thar, India
Toda, India
Tokkaru, India
Tugara, India
Tulu, India
Ullatan, India
Urali, India
Vishavan, India
Waddar, India
Wagdi, India
Yanadi, India
Yerava, India
Yerukala, India
Zangskari, India

HINDU-BUDDHIST

Kanauri, India
Khamti, India
Labhani, India
Ladakhi, India
Lalung, India
Naga, Kuki, India
Naga, Lotha, India
Naga, Mao, India
Naga, Nruanghmei, India
Naga, Sangtam, India
Naga, Tangkhul, India
Naga, Wancho, India
Nimadi, India
Pao, India
Riang, India
Sikkimese, India
Sulung, India
Tamaria, India
Thado, India
Vaiphei, India
Zome, India

HINDUISM

Adiyan, India
Agariya, India
Allar, India
Anga, India
Arya, India
Babri, India
Bagri, Pakistan
Bajania, Pakistan (79)
Balinese, Indonesia
Balmiki, Pakistan
Bareli, India
Bathudi, India
**Bhil, Pakistan
*Bhojpuri, Nepal
**Bodo Kachari, India
Bondo, India
Caste Hindus (Andra Prd), India
Cham, Viet Nam
***Chamars of Bundelkhand, India
**Dhodias, India
*Dubla, India
*Gorkha, India
Gujarati, United Kingdom
Gurung, Nepal
**Hajong, Bangladesh
Indians in Fiji, Fiji (79)
*Indians In Rhodesia, Rhodesia
**Indians, East, Trinidad and
Tobago (79)
***Irulas, India
Jharia, India
Juang, India
Kachchi, India
*Kanarese, India
**Karbis, India
Khasi, India
**Koch, Bangladesh
**Kohli, Kutchi, Pakistan
**Kohli, Tharadari, Pakistan
**Kohli, Wadiara, Pakistan
**Kohlis, Parkari, Pakistan
**Kolam, India
*Kudisai Vagh Makkal, India
*Kuknas, India
**Kuluis, India
Labans, India
*Labourers of Jhoparpatti, India
**Lepcha, Sikkim
Lohar, Pakistan
*Magar, Nepal
Maithili, Nepal
Mala Muthas, India
Malavedan, India
Mangs, India
**Meghwar, Pakistan (79)
*Meitei, India (79)
**Miching, India
*Nepali, Nepal
*Newari, Nepal
Od, Pakistan
Rabha, India
Rai, Nepal
*Rai, Danuwar, Nepal
Rajbansi, Nepal
*Rava, India

**Saiva Vellala, India
*Shourastra, India
*Sindhis of India, India
 Sochi, Pakistan
 Sora, India
*Tamang, Nepal
 Tamil (Ceylonese), Sri Lanka
*Tamil Brahmins, India
***Tamil Plantation Workers,
    Malaysia
*Tamils (Indian), Malaysia
**Tamils (Indian), Sri Lanka (79)
 Tengger, Indonesia
 Tharu, Nepal
 Totis, India
 Vagari, Pakistan

ISLAM

 Abkhaz, Turkey
 Abong, Nigeria
 Achehnese, Indonesia (80)
 Achipa, Nigeria
 Afar, Ethiopia (79)
**African Students in Cairo, Egypt
 Afshars, Iran
 Agajanis, Iran
 Ahir, India
**Ahl-i-Haqq in Iran, Iran (79)
 Alaba, Ethiopia
 Alas, Indonesia
*Alawites, Syria (79)
*Albanian Muslims, Albania (80)
 Algerian (Arabs), Algeria (80)
 Algerian Arabs in France, France
 Ara, Indonesia
 Arab-Jabbari (Kamesh), Iran
 Arab-Shaibani (Kamesh), Iran
 Arabs of Khuzestan, Iran
 Arawa, Nigeria
 Assamese, Bangladesh
 Aten, Nigeria
 Awngi, Ethiopia
 Ayu, Nigeria
**Azerbaijani, Afghanistan
 Azerbaijani Turks, Iran (80)
 Bachama, Nigeria
 Bade, Nigeria
 Baharlu (Kamesh), Iran
 Bajau, Indonesian, Indonesia
 Bakhtiaris, Iran (80)
 Baluchi, Iran (80)
 Bambara, Mali
 Bambuka, Nigeria
 Bandawa-Minda, Nigeria
 Banga, Nigeria
 Banggai, Indonesia
 Bashgali, Afghanistan
 Bashkir, Soviet Russia (80)
*Batak, Angkola, Indonesia (80)
 Batu, Nigeria
 Baushi, Nigeria
 Bawm, Bangladesh
 Bayats, Iran
 Beja, Ethiopia

 Bengali, Bangladesh (80)
 Bhatneri, India
 Bilen, Ethiopia
 Bimanese, Indonesia
 Binawa, Nigeria
 Bingkokak, Indonesia
 Bole, Nigeria
*Bosnian, Yugoslavia (80)
 Bovir-Ahmadi, Iran
 Bual, Indonesia
 Buduma, Nigeria
 Bugis, Indonesia (80)
 Burak, Nigeria
 Busa, Nigeria (80)
 Butawa, Nigeria
 Chaghatai, Afghanistan
*Cham (Western), Kampuchea,
    Democratic (80)
 Chitralis, Pakistan (79)
 Circassian, Turkey
 Cirebon, Indonesia
*Comorians, Comoros (79)
 Dadiya, Nigeria
**Dagomba, Ghana
 Dawoodi Muslims, India
 Dendi, Benin
 Deno, Nigeria
 Dera, Nigeria
*Dewein, Liberia
 Diola, Senegal
 Diola, Guinea-Bissau (80)
 Dirya, Nigeria
 Divehi, Maldives (80)
 Duguir, Nigeria
 Duguza, Nigeria
 Dyerma, Niger (80)
 Dyerma, Nigeria
 Fula, Guinea
 Fulah, Upper Volta
 Fulani, Cameroon (79)
*Fulani, Benin
*Fulbe, Ghana
 Galambi, Nigeria
 Galeshis, Iran
*Galla (Bale), Ethiopia
 Galla, Harar, Ethiopia
 Gawar-Bati, Afghanistan
 Gayo, Indonesia (80)
 Gbaya, Nigeria
 Gbazantche, Benin
 Geji, Nigeria
 Gera, Nigeria
 Geruma, Nigeria
 Gilakis, Iran
 Gonja, Ghana
 Gorontalo, Indonesia
 Goudari, Iran
 Gujuri, Afghanistan
 Gurage, Ethiopia (80)
 Gure-Kahugu, Nigeria
 Guruntum-Mbaaru, Nigeria
 Gwari Matai, Nigeria
 Harari, Ethiopia
 Hezareh, Iran
 Hui, China (80)
**Hunzakut, Pakistan (79)
 Hwana, Nigeria
 Hyam, Nigeria
 Igbira, Nigeria (80)

Ikulu, Nigeria
Inallu, Iran
*Int'l Stud., Los Banos,
  Philippines
Jama Mapun, Philippines (80)
Jamshidis, Iran
Jara, Nigeria
Jati, Afghanistan
**Javanese (rural), Indonesia (79)
**Javanese of Central Java,
  Indonesia
**Javanese of Pejompongan,
  Indonesia
Jera, Nigeria
Jimbin, Nigeria
Kabyle, Algeria (79)
Kagoma, Nigeria
Kaibu, Nigeria
Kaka, Nigeria
Kamo, Nigeria
Kanuri, Nigeria (80)
Karakalpak, Soviet Russia (80)
Karekare, Nigeria
Kariya, Nigeria
**Kashmiri Muslims, India (79)
Katab, Nigeria
Kazakhs, Iran (80)
Khalaj, Iran
Khojas, Agha Khani, India
Kilba, Nigeria
Kirghiz, Afghanistan
Kirgiz, Soviet Russia (80)
Kirifi, Nigeria
Kita, Mali
Kolbila, Cameroon
Kono, Nigeria
**Koranko, Sierra Leone
Kotokoli, Benin
Kuda-Chamo, Nigeria
Kunama, Ethiopia
Kurds in Iran, Iran (80)
*Kurds of Turkey, Turkey (79)
Kushi, Nigeria
Kuteb, Nigeria
Kuturmi, Nigeria
Kuzamani, Nigeria
Kwa, Nigeria
Kyibaku, Nigeria
Laamang, Nigeria
Lakka, Nigeria
Lame, Nigeria
Lampung, Indonesia (80)
Laru, Nigeria
Lebong, Indonesia
Libyans, Libya
Ligbi, Ghana
Longuda, Nigeria
Lors, Iran (80)
Lotsu-Piri, Nigeria
Lubu, Indonesia
Luwu, Indonesia
Madurese, Indonesia (79)
Maguindano, Philippines (80)
Makonde, Tanzania
Malays of Singapore, Singapore
  (79)
Mamasani, Iran
Mandar, Indonesia
Mandara, Nigeria

Mandingo, Liberia (79)
Maranao, Philippines (79)
Marghi Central, Nigeria
Masenrempulu, Indonesia
Matakam, Nigeria
Matumbi, Tanzania
Maures, Senegal
Mazandaranis, Iran
Mboi, Nigeria
Mbula-Bwazza, Nigeria
Meos of Rajasthan, India (80)
Minangkabau, Indonesia (80)
Mober, Nigeria
Mogholi, Afghanistan
*Molbog, Philippines
Montol, Nigeria
Moor Malays, Sri Lanka (79)
Moqaddam, Iran
Mumbake, Nigeria
Munji-Yidgha, Afghanistan
Muslim Community of Bawku, Ghana
**Muslim Immigrants in U.K.,
  United Kingdom
Muslim Malays, Malaysia (80)
Muslims (West Nile Dist.),
  Uganda
Muslims in U.A.E., United Arab
  Emirates (79)
Muslims of Jordan, Jordan
Nafar, Iran
Nandu-Tari, Nigeria
Ndunpa Duupa, Cameroon
Ngizim, Nigeria
Ngwoi, Nigeria
Ninzam, Nigeria
North Africans in Belgium,
  Belgium (80)
Numana-Nunku-Gwantu, Nigeria
**Nupe, Nigeria
Nuristani, Afghanistan (80)
Nzanyi, Nigeria
Ouaddai, Chad
Palembang, Indonesia
Pankhu, Bangladesh
Pashtuns, Iran (80)
Pero, Nigeria
Persians of Iran, Iran (80)
Pishagchi, Iran
Piti, Nigeria
Piya, Nigeria
Polci, Nigeria
Pongu, Nigeria
***Prasuni, Afghanistan
Puku-Geeri-Keri-Wipsi, Nigeria
Punjabis, Pakistan (80)
Qajars, Iran
Qara'i, Iran
Qaragozlu, Iran
Qashqa'i, Iran (80)
Redjang, Indonesia (80)
Rukuba, Nigeria
Rumaya, Nigeria
Ruruma, Nigeria
**Saguye, Kenya
Sama Bangingi, Philippines (80)
Sama Pangutaran, Philippines
  (80)
Sama-Badjaw, Philippines (79)
Sanga, Nigeria

Sangil, Philippines
Sarakole, Senegal (80)
Sasak, Indonesia (80)
Sasanis, Iran
Sau, Afghanistan
Saya, Nigeria
Serawai, Indonesia
Shahsavans, Iran (80)
Shawiya, Algeria
**Shihu, United Arab Emirates
Shughni, Afghanistan
Shuwa Arabic, Nigeria
Siri, Nigeria
Solor, Indonesia
Somali, Ethiopia
Somali, Somalia (79)
Somali, Ajuran, Kenya (79)
Somali, Degodia, Kenya
Somali, Gurreh, Kenya
Somali, Ogadenya, Kenya
Soninke, Gambia
Sukur, Nigeria
Sumbawa, Indonesia
**Sundanese, Indonesia (80)
Sura, Nigeria
Surubu, Nigeria
Swatis, Pakistan (79)
Tajik, Iran (80)
Takestani, Iran
Tal, Nigeria
Talish, Iran
Tangale, Nigeria
Tangchangya, Bangladesh
Tatars, Soviet Russia (80)
Taucouleur, Senegal (80)
Tausug, Philippines (80)
Teda, Chad (80)
Teimuri, Iran
Teimurtash, Iran
Tem, Togo
Tera, Nigeria
Ternate, Indonesia
Thai Islam (Malay), Thailand
  (80)
 *Thai Islam (Thai), Thailand
Tippera, Bangladesh
Tuareg, Niger (79)
Tula, Nigeria
Turkish Immigrant Workers,
  German Federal Rep. (79)
Turkish Workers, Belgium (80)
Turkomans, Iran (80)
Turks, Anatolian, Turkey
Turkwam, Nigeria
Uighur, Afghanistan
Uigur, China (80)
**Uzbeks, Afghanistan (79)
 *Vai, Liberia (80)
**Vohras of Yavatmal, India
Voko, Cameroon
Waja, Nigeria
Weda, Indonesia
Winji-Winji, Benin
Wolof, Senegal (80)
Yakan, Philippines (80)
 *Yalunka, Sierra Leone (80)
Yao, Mozambique
**Yao, Malawi
Yemenis, Yemen, Arab Republic
  (79)

Yeskwa, Nigeria
Yungur, Nigeria
Zaramo, Tanzania
Zari, Nigeria

ISLAM-ANIMIST

Abe, Ivory Coast
Abidji, Ivory Coast
Abou Charib, Chad
Abure, Ivory Coast
Adyukru, Ivory Coast
Agataynon, Philippines
Akan, Brong, Ivory Coast
Aladian, Ivory Coast
Attie, Ivory Coast
Avikam, Ivory Coast
Bagirmi, Chad
Bakwe, Ivory Coast
Balantak, Indonesia
Bali, Nigeria
Bambara, Ivory Coast
Bariba, Nigeria
Bata, Nigeria
Bayot, Gambia
Bete, Ivory Coast
Bilala, Chad
Bile, Nigeria
Bira, Indonesia
Bitare, Nigeria
Bomou, Chad
Boran, Ethiopia
Buli, Indonesia
Butunq, Indonesia
Chamba Daka, Nigeria
Chamba Leko, Nigeria
Daju of Dar Dadju, Chad
Daju of Dar Sila, Chad
Dan, Ivory Coast
Dangaleat, Chad
Dass, Nigeria
Dida, Ivory Coast
Dirim, Nigeria
Dyimini, Ivory Coast
Dyola, Gambia
Ebira, Nigeria
Ebrie, Ivory Coast
Eotile, Ivory Coast
Fula, Cunda, Gambia
Gaanda, Nigeria
Gabri, Chad
Gambai, Chad
Gidar, Chad
Golo, Chad
Goulai, Chad
Guere, Ivory Coast
Gula, Chad
Gwa, Ivory Coast
Hwela-Numu, Ivory Coast
Icen, Nigeria
Jongor, Chad
Kanembu, Chad
Karanga, Chad
Kari, Chad
Kendari, Indonesia

Konga, Chad
Kera, Chad
Kerinchi, Indonesia
Kibet, Chad
Kim, Chad
Koke, Chad
Kotoko, Chad
Kouya, Ivory Coast
Krio, Gambia
Krobou, Ivory Coast
Kuka, Chad
Kulele, Ivory Coast
Kullo, Ethiopia
Kurung, Nigeria
Laka, Chad
Lele, Chad
Maba, Chad
Majingai-Ngama, Chad
Mandyak, Gambia
Mangbai, Chad
Manggarai, Indonesia
Maou, Ivory Coast
Maranao, Lanad, Philippines
Mararit, Chad
Marba, Chad
Masalit, Chad
Massalat, Chad
Mbai, Chad
Mbum, Chad
Mentawi, Indonesia
Mesengo, Ethiopia
Mesme, Chad
Mesmedje, Chad
Mimi, Chad
Mo, Ivory Coast
Mogum, Chad
Mona, Ivory Coast
Moru, Ivory Coast
Mubi, Chad
Muna, Indonesia
Mundang, Chad
Musei, Chad
Musgu, Chad
Nancere, Chad
Nara, Ethiopia
Nielim, Chad
Nyabwa-Nyedebwa, Ivory Coast
Nzema, Ivory Coast
Oubi, Ivory Coast
Palara, Ivory Coast
Pashayi, Afghanistan
Pye, Ivory Coast
Rataning, Chad
Runga, Chad
Sama, Siasi, Philippines
Sama, Sibuku, Philippines
Sarwa, Chad
Shina, Afghanistan
Sidamo, Ethiopia
Somrai, Chad
Subanun,Lapuyan, Philippines
Sungor, Chad
Tagwana, Ivory Coast
Tama, Chad
Tana, Chad
Tepo, Ivory Coast
Tidore, Indonesia
Trepo, Ivory Coast
Tunya, Chad

Tupuri, Chad
Tura, Ivory Coast
Vagla, Ivory Coast
Wan, Ivory Coast
Wolio, Indonesia
Wolof, Gambian, Gambia
Wom, Nigeria
Yandang, Nigeria
Yaoure, Ivory Coast
Zaghawa, Chad

JAIN

Jains, India

JUDAISM

**Falasha, Ethiopia (79)
*Jewish Imgrnts.-American, Israel
*Jewish Imgrnts.-Argentine,
   Israel
*Jewish Imgrnts.-Australia,
   Israel
*Jewish Imgrnts.-Brazilian,
   Israel
*Jewish Imgrnts.-Mexican, Israel
*Jewish Imgrnts.-Uruguayan,
   Israel
*Jewish Immigrants, Other, Israel
Jews of Iran, Iran
Jews of Montreal, Canada
Jews, Sephardic, Canada
Ladinos, Lebanon
Targum, Israel

PEYOTE RELIGION

Paiute, Northern, United States
   of America

SECULARISM

*Chinese in Korea, Korea,
   Republic of
*Chinese in West Germany, German
   Federal Rep.
*Chinese Mainlanders, Taiwan
**Chinese Stud., Australia,
   Australia
*College Students in Japan, Japan
**Japanese Students In USA, United
   States of America
**Korean Prisoners, Korea,
   Republic of

*New Terrestories People, Hong Kong
*Overseas Chin. Port., United States of America
**Portuguese in France, France
**Racetrack Residents, United States of America (79)
Seychellois, Seychelles
Students in Cuiaba, Brazil
**Suriguenos, Philippines
*University Students, France (79)
*University Students, German Federal Rep. (79)

TRADITIONAL CHINESE

Ach'ang, China
Buriat, China
Burig, China
Ch'iang, China
Chin, China
*Chinese (Hoklo) in Taiwan, Taiwan
Chinese Businessmen, Hong Kong
Chinese Factory Workers, Hong Kong
**Chinese Hakka of Taiwan, Taiwan 79)
**Chinese in Australia, Australia
*Chinese in Austria, Austria
**Chinese in Brazil, Brazil
Chinese in Burma, Burma
**Chinese in Hong Kong, Hong Kong
**Chinese in Indonesia, Indonesia
*Chinese in Japan, Japan
*Chinese in Laos, Laos
*Chinese in Malaysia, Malaysia
*Chinese in New Zealand, New Zealand
Chinese in Puerto Rico, Puerto Rico
**Chinese in Sabah, Malaysia
**Chinese in Sarawak, Malaysia
*Chinese in South Africa, South Africa
**Chinese in United Kingdom, United Kingdom
**Chinese in United States, United States of America
**Chinese in Vancouver B.C., Canada
*Chinese of W. Malaysia, Malaysia
*Chinese Refugees in Macau, Macau
**Chinese Refugees, France, France 79
*Chinese Restaurant Wrkrs., France
**Chinese Students Glasgow, United Kingdom
Chinese Villagers, Hong Kong
Chingp'o, China
Chungchia, China
Chwang, China
Dagur, China

Evenki, China
Fishing Village People, Taiwan
Hani, China
**High School Students, Hong Kong
Jyarung, China
Kalmytz, China
Kam, China
Kelao, China
Khalka, China
Kham, China
Kirchiz, China
Lahul, China
Laka, China
Lati, China
Li, China
Manchu, China
Mongour, China
Nahsi, China
Nanai, China
Nosu, China
Nung, China
Oirat, China
Oronchon, China
Paongan, China
Pu-I, China
Punu, China
Rawang, China
Salar, China
Santa, China
Sibo, China
Sui, China
*Urban Workers in Taiwan, Taiwan
Wa, China
*Women Laborers, Taiwan
Yellow Uighur, China
Yuku, China

TRADITIONAL JAPANESE

Farmers of Japan, Japan
*Industry Laborers-Japan, Japan
*Inland Sea Island Peoples, Japan
*Japanese in Korea, Korea, Republic of
*Ryukyuan, Japan
**Stud. Osaka Christ. Coll., Japan
**Univ. Students of Japan, Japan

ZOROASTRIANISM

*Parsees, India

OTHER

**Lotuka, Sudan
*Yanyula, Australia

REGISTRY OF THE UNREACHED

UNKNOWN

    **Bus Drivers, South Korea, Korea,
        Republic of
    *Chinese in Amsterdam,
        Netherlands
     Chinese in Costa Rica, Costa
        Rica
    *Chinese in Holland, Netherlands
    *Chinese in Osaka, Japan, Japan
     Chinese Merchants, Ghana
    *Factory Workers, Young, Hong
        Kong
     Khana, Nigeria
    ***Koreans in Germany, German
        Federal Rep.
     Lugbara, Uganda
     Naga, Soma, India

NOT REPORTED

     Balanta, Senegal
     Mancang, Senegal
     Manding, Senegal
     Manjack, Senegal
     Pular, Senegal
     Tandanke, Senegal

INDEX
by
Language

INDEX BY LANGUAGE

Groups are listed according to their primary vernacular language. In many cases, groups are bilingual or trilingual, speaking several languages including a more commonly known trade language.

Abaknon	Abaknon, Philippines
Abanyom	Abanyom, Nigeria
Abau	Abau, Indonesia
Abe	Abe, Ivory Coast
Abkhaz	Abkhaz, Turkey
Abong	Abong, Nigeria
Abou Charib	Abou Charib, Chad
Abua	Abua, Nigeria
Abujmaria	Abujmaria, India
Abure	Abure, Ivory Coast
Ach'ang	Ach'ang, China
Acnagua	Achagua, Colombia
Achehnese	Achehnese, Indonesia (80)
Achipa	Achipa, Nigeria
Achual	Achual, Peru
Adi	***Adi, India
Adidji	Abidji, Ivory Coast
Adiyan	Adiyan, India
Adyukru	Adyukru, Ivory Coast
Aeta	Aeta, Philippines
Afanci	*Afawa, Nigeria (80)
Afar	Afar, Ethiopia (79)
Afshari	Afshars, Iran
	Inallu, Iran
Agajanis	Agajanis, Iran
Agariya	Agariya, India
Agau	**Falasha, Ethiopia (79)
Aghu	Aghu, Indonesia
Agoi	Agoi, Nigeria
Aguaruna	Aguaruna, Peru
Agutaynon	Agutaynon, Philippines
Agwagwune	Agwagwune, Nigeria
Ahir	Ahir, India
Aibondeni	Aibondeni, Indonesia
Aikwakai	Aikwakai, Indonesia
Aimol	Aimol, India
Airo-Sumaghaghe	Airo-Sumaghaghe, Indonesia
Airoran	Airoran, Indonesia
Ajmeri	Ajmeri, India
Aka	Aka, India
Akan, Brong	Akan, Brong, Ivory Coast
Ake	Ake, Nigeria
Akha	**Akha, Thailand (79)
Akpa-Yache	Akpa-Yache, Nigeria
Alaban	Alaba, Ethiopia
Aladian	Aladian, Ivory Coast
Alago	Alago, Nigeria
Alak	Alak, Laos
Alangan	Alangan, Philippines
Albanian Tosk	*Albanian Muslims, Albania (80)
Aledjo	*Nyantruku, Benin
Alege	Alege, Nigeria
Allar	*Alars, India
	Allar, India
Alor, Kolana	Alor, Kolana, Indonesia
Amahuaca	Amahuaca, Peru
Amanab	Amanab, Indonesia
Amar	Amar, Ethiopia
Amarakaeri	Amarakaeri, Peru
Ambai	Ambai, Indonesia
Amber	Amber, Indonesia
Amberbaken	Amberbaken, Indonesia
Ambonese	Ambonese, Netherlands
	Ambonese, Indonesia
Amo	Amo, Nigeria
Amoy	Fishing Village People, Taiwan
	*Women Laborers, Taiwan
Amoy Dialect	**Minnan Hoklo, Taiwan
Ampale	**Ampeeli, Papua New Guinea

297

Amuesha	Amuesha, Peru
Anaang	Anaang, Nigeria
Anal	Anal, India
Andha	Andha, India
Andoque	Andoque, Colombia
Anga	Anga, India
Angas	Angas, Nigeria
Ankwai	Ankwe, Nigeria
Ansus	Ansus, Indonesia
Anuak	Anuak, Ethiopia
	Anuak, Sudan
Apalai	Apalai, Brazil
Apartani	**Apatani, India
Apinaye	Apinaye, Brazil
Apurina	Apurina, Brazil
Ara	Ara, Indonesia
Arabela	Arabela, Peru
Arabic	*Alawites, Syria (79)
	Algerian (Arabs), Algeria (80)
	Algerian Arabs in France, France
	Arab-Jabbari (Kamesh), Iran
	Arab-Shaibani (Kamesh), Iran
	Arabs of Khuzestan, Iran
	Druzes, Israel (79)
	Libyans, Libya
	Maures, Senegal
	Muslims in U.A.E., United Arab Emirates (79)
	Muslims of Jordan, Jordan
	North Africans in Belgium, Belgium (80)
Arabic (Eastern)	Yemenis, Yemen, Arab Republic (79)
Aranadan	Aranadan, India
Aranatan	*Arnatas, India
Arandai	Arandai, Indonesia
Arbore	Arbore, Ethiopia
Argobba	Argobba, Ethiopia
Arguni	Arguni, Indonesia
Arusha	Arusha, Tanzania
Arya	Arya, India
Asienara	Asienara, Indonesia
Asmat	*Asmat, Indonesia (79)
Assamese	Assamese, Bangladesh
Asuri	Asuri, India
Asurini	Kuatinema, Brazil
Aten	Aten, Nigeria
Ati	Ati, Philippines
Atruahi	Atruahi, Brazil
Atta	*Atta, Philippines
Attie	Attie, Ivory Coast
Avikam	Avikam, Ivory Coast
Awngi	Awngi, Ethiopia
Awyi	Awyi, Indonesia
Awyu	Awyu, Indonesia
Aymara	**Aymara, Bolivia
Ayu	Ayu, Nigeria
Azerbaijani	**Azerbaijani, Afghanistan
Azerbaijani (Shahsavani)	Shahsavans, Iran (80)
Azerbaijani Turkish	Azerbaijani Turks, Iran (80)
Babri	Babri, India
Baburiwa	Baburiwa, Indonesia
Bachama	Bachama, Nigeria
Bada	Bada, Nigeria
Badagu	Badagu, India
Bade	Bade, Nigeria
Bagelkhandi	Bagelkhandi, India
Baghati	Baghati, India
Bagirmi	Bagirmi, Chad
Bagri	Bagri, Pakistan
Baham	Baham, Indonesia

Bahasa Jawa	**Javanese of Pejompongan, Indonesia
Bahasa Malaysia	Muslim Malays, Malaysia (80)
Bahawalpuri	Bahawalpuri, India
Baiga	Baiga, India
Bajau, Indonesian	Bajau, Indonesian, Indonesia
Bakairi	Bakairi, Brazil
Bakhtiaris	Bakhtiaris, Iran (80)
Bakwe	Bakwe, Ivory Coast
Balangao	**Balangao, Philippines
Balangaw	Balangaw, Philippines
Balanta	Balanta, Senegal
	Balante, Guinea-Bissau
Balantak	Balantak, Indonesia
Bali	Bali, Nigeria
Balinese	Balinese, Indonesia
Balti	Balti, India
Baluchi	Baluchi, Iran (80)
Bambara	Bambara, Mali
	Bambara, Ivory Coast
Bambuka	Bambuka, Nigeria
Banaro	***Banaro, Papua New Guinea
Bandawa-Minda	Bandawa-Minda, Nigeria
Bandi	Bandi, Liberia
	Gbande, Guinea
Banga	Banga, Nigeria
Banggai	Banggai, Indonesia
Bangri	Bangaru, India
Baniwa	Baniwa, Brazil
Bantuanon	Bantuanon, Philippines
Banyun	Banyun, Guinea-Bissau
Barasano	Barasano, Colombia
Barasano, Northern	Barasano, Northern, Colombia
Barau	Barau, Indonesia
Bare'e	Bare'e, Indonesia
Bareli	Bareli, India
Bariba	*Bariba, Benin (80)
	Bariba, Nigeria
Basari	Basari, Togo
Bashar	Bashar, Nigeria
Bashgali	Bashgali, Afghanistan
Basketo	Basketo, Ethiopia
Bassa	*Bassa, Liberia
	**Bassa, Nigeria
Bata	Bata, Nigeria
Batak, Angkola	*Batak, Angkola, Indonesia (80)
Batak, Karo	Batak, Karo, Indonesia
Batak, Palawan	Batak, Palawan, Philippines
Batak, Simalungun	Batak, Simalungun, Indonesia
Batak, Toba	Batak, Toba, Indonesia
Bathudi	Bathudi, India
Batu	Batu, Nigeria
Baule	***Baoule, Ivory Coast
Baushi	Baushi, Nigeria
Bawm	Bawm, Bangladesh
Bayat	Bayats, Iran
Bayot	Bayot, Gambia
Bazigar	Bazigar, India
Bediya	Bediya, India
Bedoanas	Bedoanas, Indonesia
Beja	Beja, Ethiopia
Bekwarra	Bekwarra, Nigeria
Bencho	Bencho, Ethiopia
Bengali	**Banai, Bangladesh
	Bengali, Bangladesh (80)
	**Hajong, Bangladesh
	**Koch, Bangladesh
Berik	Berik, Indonesia
Berom	Berom, Nigeria
Bete	Bete, Ivory Coast

Bette-Bende	Bete, India
	Bette-Bende, Nigeria
Bhakta	Bhakta, India
Bharia	Bharia, India
Bhatneri	Bhatneri, India
Bhattri	Bhattri, India
Bhilala	Bhilala, India
Bhojpuri	*Bhojpuri, Nepal
	Tharu, Nepal
Bhoyari	Bhoyari, India
Bhuiya	Bhuiya, India
Bhumij	Bhumij, India
Bhunjia	Bhunjia, India
Biafada	Biafada, Guinea-Bissau
Biak	Biak, Indonesia
Biatah	**Bidayuh of Sarawak, Malaysia
Bidyogo	**Bijogo, Guinea-Bissau
Bihari	Bihari, India
Bijori	Bijori, India
Biksi	Biksi, Indonesia
Bilaan	**Bilan, Philippines
Bilala	Bilala, Chad
Bile	Bile, Nigeria
Bilen	Bilen, Ethiopia
Bima	Bimanese, Indonesia
Bimoba	Moba, Ghana
	Moba, Togo
Binawa	Binawa, Nigeria
Bingkokak	Bingkokak, Indonesia
Binjhwari	Binjhwari, India
Bipim	***Bipim, Indonesia
Bira	Bira, Indonesia
Birhor	Birhor, India
Birifor	Birifor, Ghana
Bisa (Busanga)	**Busanse, Ghana
Bitare	Bitare, Nigeria
Bodo	Bodo, India
	**Bodo Kachari, India
Boghom	Boghom, Nigeria
Boko (Busa)	**Boko, Benin
Bokyi	Bokyi, Nigeria
Bole	Bole, Nigeria
Bomou	Bomou, Chad
Bondo	Bondo, India
Bonerif	Bonerif, Indonesia
Bonggo	Bonggo, Indonesia
Bontoc, Central	*Bontoc, Central, Philippines
Bora	Bora, Colombia
Borai	Borai, Indonesia
Boran	Boran, Ethiopia
Bororo	*Bororo, Brazil
Boya	Boya, Sudan
Braj	Braj, India
Brao	Brao, Laos (79)
Brat	Brat, Indonesia
Bua	Bua, Chad
Bual	Bual, Indonesia
Buamu (Bobo Wule)	Bwa, Upper Volta (80)
Buduma	Buduma, Nigeria
Bugis	Bugis, Indonesia (80)
Buhid	Buhid, Philippines
Buka-khwe	Bushmen in Botswana, Botswana
Buli	Builsa, Ghana
	Buli, Indonesia
Bunak	Bunak, Indonesia
Bunan	Bunan, India
Bundelkhandi	***Chamars of Bundelkhand, India
Bungku	Bungku, Indonesia
Bunu	Bunu, Nigeria

Bura (Babur)	**Babur Thali, Nigeria (80)
Burak	Burak, Nigeria
Buriat	Buriat, China
Burig	Burig, India
	Burig, China
Burji	Burji, Ethiopia
Burmese	*Chinese Refugees in Macau, Macau
Buru	Buru, Indonesia
Burungi	Burungi, Tanzania
Burushaski	**Hunzakut, Pakistan (79)
Busa (Bokobarn Akiba)	Busa, Nigeria (80)
Busami	Busami, Indonesia
Bussa	Bussa, Ethiopia
Buta	Butawa, Nigeria
Butung	Butung, Indonesia
Cacua	Cacua, Colombia
Cagayan	Jama Mapun, Philippines (80)
Caiwa	Caiwa, Brazil
Caluyanhon	Caluyanhon, Philippines
Cambodia	**Khmer Refugees, Thailand
Campa	Campa, Peru
Camsa	Camsa, Colombia
Canarese	Chola Naickans, India
Candoshi	Candoshi, Peru
Canela	Canela, Brazil
Cantonese	Chinese Businessmen, Hong Kong
	Chinese Factory Workers, Hong Kong
	*Chinese in Amsterdam, Netherlands
	**Chinese in Australia, Australia
	Chinese in Costa Rica, Costa Rica
	**Chinese in Hong Kong, Hong Kong
	*Chinese in New Zealand, New Zealand
	*Chinese in South Africa, South Africa
	**Chinese in Vancouver B.C., Canada
	*Chinese of W. Malaysia, Malaysia
	Chinese Villagers, Hong Kong
	*Factory Workers, Young, Hong Kong
	**High School Students, Hong Kong
	*New Terrestories People, Hong Kong
	*Overseas Chin. Port., United States of America
Capanahua	Capanahua, Peru
Carapana	Carapana, Colombia
Cashibo	Cashibo, Peru
Cayapa	Cayapa, Ecuador
Cebuano	***Cebu, Middle-Class, Philippines
Ch'iang	Ch'iang, China
Ch'ol	***Ch'ol Sabanilla, Mexico
Chacobo	Chacobo, Bolivia
Chaghatai	Chaghatai, Afghanistan
Chakfem-Mushere	Chakfem-Mushere, Nigeria
Chakma	Chakma, India
Chakossi	***Chakossi, Ghana
	Chakossi, Togo
Cham	Cham, Viet Nam
	*Cham (Western), Kampuchea, Democratic (80)
Chamari	Chamari, India
Chamba Daka	Chamba Daka, Nigeria
Chamba Leko	Chamba Leko, Nigeria
Chameali	Chameali, India
Chami	Chami, Colombia
Chamicuro	Chamicuro, Peru
Chamorro	Chamorro, Turks and Caicos Islands
Chara	Chara, Ethiopia
Chaungtha	Chaungtha, Burma
Chawai	Chawai, Nigeria
Chayawita	**Chayahuita, Peru
Chenchu	Chenchu, India
Chero	Chero, India

REGISTRY OF THE UNREACHED

Chik-Barik	Chik-Barik, India
ChiKalanga	*Kalanga, Botswana
Chin	Chin, China
Chin, Asho	Chin, Asho, Burma
Chin, Falam	Chin, Falam, Burma
Chin, Haka	Chin, Haka, Burma
Chin, Khumi	Chin, Khumi, Burma
Chin, Ngawn	Chin, Ngawn, Burma
Chin, Tiddim	Chin, Tiddim, Burma
Chinbok	Chinbok, Burma
Chinese	*Chinese in Korea, Korea, Republic of
Chinese dialects	*Chinese in Malaysia, Malaysia
	Chinese Merchants, Ghana
	**Chinese Stud., Australia, Australia
Chingp'o	Chingp'o, China
Chip	Chip, Nigeria
Chipaya	Chipaya, Bolivia
Chiquitano	Chiquitano, Bolivia
Chiru	Chiru, India
ChiTonga	*Tonga, Rhodesia
	Tonga, Gwembe Valley, Zambia (79)
Chiyao	**Yao, Malawi
Chodhari	Chodhari, India
Chokobo	Chokobo, Nigeria
Chokwe	Chokwe (Lunda), Angola
Chorote	Chorote, Argentina
Chuj	Chuj of San Mateo Ixtatan, Guatemala
Chungchia	Chungchia, China
Churahi	Churahi, India
Chwabo	Chuabo, Mozambique
Chwang	Chwang, China
Cinta Larga	Cinta Larga, Brazil
Circassian	Circassian, Turkey
Citak	Citak, Indonesia
Citak (Asmat)	***Citak, Indonesia
Cocama	Cocama, Peru
Cofan	Cofan, Colombia
Cogui	Cogui, Colombia
Colorado	**Tsachila, Ecuador
Comorian (Shingazidja)	*Comorians, Comoros (79)
Coreguaje	**Coreguaje, Colombia
	Coreguaje, Colombia
Cotabato Manobo	**Manobo, Cotabato, Philippines
Creole	Seychellois, Seychelles
Cubeo	Cubeo, Colombia
Cuiba	Cuiba, Colombia
Cujareno	Cujareno, Peru
Culina	Culina, Brazil
Cuna	*Cuna, Colombia (79)
	Cuna, Colombia
Curipaco	Curipaco, Colombia
Cuyolbal	Ixil, Guatemala
Cuyonon	Cuyonon, Philippines
Dabra	Dabra, Indonesia
Dadiya	Dadiya, Nigeria
Dagada	Dagada, Indonesia
Dagari	Dagari, Ghana
Dagbanli	**Dagomba, Ghana
Dagur	Dagur, China
Dai	Dai, Burma
Daju of Dar Dadju	Daju of Dar Dadju, Chad
Daju of Dar Sila	Daju of Dar Sila, Chad
Dakanci	*Daka, Nigeria
Dan	Dan, Ivory Coast
Dan (Yacouba)	Gio, Liberia
Dangaleat	Dangaleat, Chad
Dangi	***Adivasis of Dang, India
	**Bhils, India (79)
Dani, Grand Valley	*Dani, Baliem, Indonesia (79)

Danuwar Rai	*Rai, Danuwar, Nepal
Dari	Tajik, Iran (80)
Dass	Dass, Nigeria
Dathanik	Dathanik, Ethiopia
Davaweno	Davaweno, Philippines
De	*Dewoin, Liberia
Degeme	Degema, Nigeria
Dem	Dem, Indonesia
Demta	Demta, Indonesia
Dendi	Dendi, Benin
Deno	Deno, Nigeria
Deori	Deori, India
Dera	Dera, Nigeria
Desano	Desano, Brazil
Dhanka	Dhanka, India
Dhanwar	Dhanwar, India
Dhodia Dialects	**Dhodias, India
Dhuwal	*Murngin (Wulamba), Australia
Dida	Dida, Ivory Coast
Didinga	Didinga, Sudan
Dimasa	Dimasa, India
Dime	Dime, Ethiopia
Dinka	Dinka, Sudan
Diola	Diola, Senegal
	Diola, Guinea-Bissau (80)
Dirim	Dirim, Nigeria
Dirya	Dirya, Nigeria
Divehi	Divehi, Maldives (80)
Dogon	*Dogon, Mali (79)
Dompago	Dompago, Benin
Doohyaayo	**Doohwaayo, Cameroon
Dorli	Dorli, India
Dorze	Dorze, Ethiopia
Dubu	Dubu, Indonesia
Duguri	Duguir, Nigeria
Duguza	Duguza, Nigeria
Dukanci	**Duka, Nigeria
Dumagat	*Dumagat , Casiguran, Philippines
Duru	Duru, Cameroon
Dusun	**Sugut, Malaysia
Duvele	Duvele, Indonesia
Dyerma	Dyerma, Niger (80)
	Dyerma, Nigeria
Dyimini	Dyimini, Ivory Coast
Dyola	Dyola, Gambia
Ebira	Ebira, Nigeria
Ebrie	Ebrie, Ivory Coast
Edo	Edo, Nigeria
Efik	Efik, Nigeria
Efutop	Efutop, Nigeria
Eggon	Eggon, Nigeria
Ejagham	Ejagham, Nigeria
Ekagi	Ekagi, Indonesia
Ekajuk	Ekajuk, Nigeria
Eket	Eket, Nigeria
Ekpeye	Ekpeye, Nigeria
Eleme	Eleme, Nigeria
Eloyi	**Afo, Nigeria (80)
Emai-Iuleha-Ora	Emai-Iuleha-Ora, Nigeria
Embera	Embera, Northern, Colombia
Emumu	Emumu, Indonesia
Endeh	Endeh, Indonesia
Engenni	Engenni, Nigeria
Enggano	Enggano, Indonesia
English	Jews of Montreal, Canada
	Punjabis, Pakistan (80)
	**Racetrack Residents, United States of America (79)
English with Hindi	**Indians, East, Trinidad and Tobago (79)

Eotile	Eotile, Ivory Coast
Epie	Epie, Nigeria
Erokwanas	Erokwanas, Indonesia
Esan	Esan, Nigeria
Etulo	Etulo, Nigeria
Evant	Evant, Nigeria
Evenki	Evenki, China
Ewe	Zowla, Ghana
Faka	**Fakai, Nigeria
Fali	**Fali, Nigeria
Farsi	Jews of Iran, Iran
Foau	Foau, Indonesia
Fordat	Fordat, Indonesia
Fouta Toro	Pular, Senegal
Fra-Fra	Fra-Fra, Ghana
French	Jews, Sephardic, Canada
	*University Students, France (79)
Fula	Fula, Guinea
	Fula, Cunda, Gambia
Fulani	Adamawa, Cameroon
	Fulah, Upper Volta
	Fulani, Cameroon (79)
	*Fulani, Benin
	*Pulbe, Ghana
Fulnio	Fulnio, Brazil
Fyam	Fyam, Nigeria
Fyer	Fyer, Nigeria
Ga-Dang	Ga-Dang, Philippines
Gaanda	Gaanda, Nigeria
Gabri	Gabri, Chad
Gabrinja	*Gabbra, Ethiopia
Gadaba	Gadaba, India
Gaddi	Gaddi, India
Gade	Gade, Nigeria
Gagou	Gagu, Ivory Coast
Galambi	Galambi, Nigeria
Galeshi	Galeshis, Iran
Galla	Gabbra, Kenya
	*Galla (Bale), Ethiopia
	**Saguye, Kenya
Galler	Galler, Laos
Gallinya	Galla, Harar, Ethiopia
Gallinya (Oromo)	Galla of Bucho, Ethiopia
Galong	Galong, India
Gambai	Gambai, Chad
Gamti	Gamti, India
Gane	Gane, Indonesia
Gangte	Gangte, India
Gasari	Basari, Senegal
Gawar-Bati	Gawar-Bati, Afghanistan
Gawari	Gawari, India
Gawwada	Gawwada, Ethiopia
Gayo	Alas, Indonesia
	Gayo, Indonesia (80)
Gbari	Gbari, Nigeria (80)
Gbaya	Gbaya, Nigeria
Gbazantche	Gbazantche, Benin
Ge	**Adja, Benin
	Watchi, Togo
Gedeo	Gedeo, Ethiopia
Geji	Geji, Nigeria
Gera	Gera, Nigeria
German	*University Students, German Federal Rep. (79)
Geruma	Geruma, Nigeria
Gesa	Gesa, Indonesia
Gheko	Gheko, Burma
Ghotuo	Ghotuo, Nigeria
Gidar	Gidar, Chad

Gidicho	Gidicho, Ethiopia
Gilaki	Gilakis, Iran
Gimira	**Ghimeera, Ethiopia
Giryama	Giryama, Kenya
Gisiga	Gisiga, Cameroon
Glavda	**Glavda, Nigeria
Gobato	Gobato, Ethiopia
Gobeze	Gobeze, Ethiopia
Godie	***Godie, Ivory Coast
Goemai	Goemai, Nigeria
Gokana	Gokana, Nigeria
Golo	Golo, Chad
Gondi	*Gonds, India
	Totis, India
Gonja	Gonja, Ghana
Gorontalo	Gorontalo, Indonesia
Goudari	Goudari, Iran
Goulai	Goulai, Chad
Gourendi	Gourency, Upper Volta
Gouro	**Gouro, Ivory Coast
Grasia	Grasia, India
Grebo Dialects	**Grebo, Liberia
Guajajara	Guajajara, Brazil
Guajibo	Guajibo, Colombia
Guajiro	*Guajiro, Colombia
Guambiano	Guambiano, Colombia
Guanano	*Guanano, Colombia (79)
Guarani	***Guarani, Bolivia (79)
Guarani (Bolivian)	**Chiriguano, Argentina
Guarayu	Guarayu, Bolivia
Guayabero	Guayabero, Colombia
	Guayabevo, Colombia
Gude	Gude, Cameroon
	Gude, Nigeria
Gudu	Gudu, Nigeria
Guduf	Guduf, Nigeria
Guere	Guere, Ivory Coast
	*Krahn, Ivory Coast
Gugu-Yalanji	Gugu-Yalanji, Australia
Gujarati	Dawoodi Muslims, India
	**Dubla, India
	Gujarati, United Kingdom
	*Indians In Rhodesia, Rhodesia
	Khojas, Agha Khani, India
	*Parsees, India
	**Vohras of Yavatmal, India
Gujarati Dialect	Bajania, Pakistan (79)
	Lohar, Pakistan
	Vagari, Pakistan
Gujarati, Koli	**Kohli, Kutchi, Pakistan
	**Kohli, Tharadari, Pakistan
	**Kohli, Wadiara, Pakistan
	**Kohlis, Parkari, Pakistan
Gujuri	Gujuri, Afghanistan
Gula	Gula, Chad
Gumuz	Gumuz, Ethiopia
Gurage Dialects	Gurage, Ethiopia (80)
Gure-Kahugu	Gure-Kahugu, Nigeria
Gurenne	Gurensi, Ghana
Gurung	Gurung, Nepal
Guruntum-Mbaaru	Guruntum-Mbaaru, Nigeria
Gwa	Gwa, Ivory Coast
Gwandara	Gwandara, Nigeria
Gwari Matai	Gwari Matai, Nigeria
Hadiyya	Hadiyya, Ethiopia
Hadza	Dorobo, Tanzania
Hakka	**Chinese Hakka of Taiwan, Taiwan (79)
	**Chinese in Brazil, Brazil
	Chinese in Puerto Rico, Puerto Rico

	**Chinese in Sabah, Malaysia
	*Chinese in Thailand, Thailand
Halbi	Halbi, India
Hallam	Hallam, Burma
Hani	Hani, China
Hanonoo	Hanonoo, Philippines
Harari	Harari, Ethiopia
Harauti	Harauti, India
Hausa	Arawa, Nigeria
	Kurfei, Niger
	***Maguzawa, Nigeria (79)
	Mauri, Niger
Hausa, Ghana	Muslim Community of Bawku, Ghana
Havunese	Havunese, Indonesia
Hebrew	*Jewish Imgrnts.-American, Israel
	*Jewish Imgrnts.-Argentine, Israel
	*Jewish Imgrnts.-Australia, Israel
	*Jewish Imgrnts.-Brazilian, Israel
	*Jewish Imgrnts.-Mexican, Israel
	*Jewish Imgrnts.-Uruguayan, Israel
	*Jewish Immigrants, Other, Israel
Heikum	Bushmen (Heikum), Namibia
Helong	Helong, Indonesia
Hewa	**Hewa, Papua New Guinea (79)
Hezara'i	Hezareh, Iran
Higi	***Higi, Nigeria
Hindi	Jains, India
Hindustani	Balmiki, Pakistan
	Indians in Fiji, Fiji (79)
Hixkaryana	Hixkaryana, Brazil
Ho	Ho, India
Hohodene	Hohodene, Brazil
Holiya	Holiya, India
Hopi	Hopi, United States of America
Hrangkhol	Hrangkhol, Burma
Huachipaire	Huachipaire, Peru
Huambisa	Huambisa, Peru
Huave	**Huave, Mexico
Hui-hui-yu	Hui, China (80)
Huila	**Huila, Angola
Huitoto, Meneca	Huitoto, Meneca, Colombia
Huitoto, Murui	Huitoto, Murui, Peru
Hukwe	Hukwe, Angola
Hupda Maku	Hupda Maku, Colombia
Hwana	Hwana, Nigeria
Hwela-Numu	Hwela-Numu, Ivory Coast
Hyam	Hyam, Nigeria
Ibaji	Ibaji, Nigeria
Ibanag	Ibanag, Philippines
Ibibio	Ibibio, Nigeria
Ica	Ica, Colombia
Icen	Icen, Nigeria
Icheve	Ihceve, Nigeria
Idoma	Idoma, Nigeria
Idoma, North	Idoma, North, Nigeria
Ifugao	*Ifugao, Philippines
	Ifugao in Cababuyan, Philippines
Ifugao, Ambanad	Ifugao, Ambanad, Philippines
Ifugao, Kiangan	Ifugao, Kiangan, Philippines
Igala	Igala, Nigeria
Igbirra	Igbira, Nigeria (80)
Igede	Igede, Nigeria
Ignaciano	Ignaciano, Bolivia
Igorot	Igorot, Philippines
Iha	Iha, Indonesia
Ijo	Ijo, Central-Western, Nigeria
	Ijo, Northeast, Nigeria
	Ijo, Northeast Central, Nigeria
Ikulu	Ikulu, Nigeria

Ikwere	Ikwere, Nigeria
Ilianen Manobo	*Manobo, Ilianen, Philippines
Ilongot	Ilongot, Philippines
Inanwatan	Inanwatan, Indonesia
Indonesian	**Chinese in Indonesia, Indonesia
Inga	Inga, Colombia
Insinai	Insinai, Philippines
Intha	Intha, Burma
Irahutu	Irahutu, Indonesia
Iraqw	Iraqw, Tanzania
Iraya	Iraya, Philippines
Iresim	Iresim, Indonesia
Iria	Iria, Indonesia
Irigwe	Irigwe, Nigeria
Irula	***Irulas, India
Isaalin	**Sisaala, Ghana
Isekiri	Isekiri, Nigeria
Isneg	**Apayao, Philippines
Isneg, Dibagat-Kabugao	Isneg, Dibagat-Kabugao, Philippines
Isneg, Karagawan	Isneg, Karagawan, Philippines
Isoko	Isoko, Nigeria
Itawit	Itawit, Philippines
Itik	Itik, Indonesia
Itneg, Adasen	Itneg, Adasen, Philippines
Itneg, Binongan	Itneg, Binongan, Philippines
Itneg, Masadiit	Itneg, Masadiit, Philippines
Itonama	Itonama, Bolivia
Ivbie North-Okpela-Atte	Ivbie North-Okpela-Atte, Nigeria
Iwaidja	*Iwaidja, Austria
Iwur	Iwur, Indonesia
Iyon	Iyon, Nigeria
Izarek	Izarek, Nigeria
Izi	**Izi, Nigeria
Jaba	Jaba, Nigeria
Jagannathi	Jagannathi, India
Jamamadi	Jamamadi, Brazil
Jamden	Jamden, Indonesia
Jamshidi	Jamshidis, Iran
Janena	Barasano, Southern, Colombia
Janjero	Janjero, Ethiopia
Janjo	Janjo, Nigeria
Japanese	*Chinese in Osaka, Japan, Japan
	*College Students in Japan, Japan
	Farmers of Japan, Japan
	*Industry Laborers-Japan, Japan
	*Inland Sea Island Peoples, Japan
	Japanese in Brazil, Brazil (79)
	*Japanese in Korea, Korea, Republic of
	**Japanese Students In USA, United States of America
	Soka Gakkai Believers, Japan
	**Stud. Osaka Christ. Coll., Japan
	**Univ. Students of Japan, Japan
Jaqaru	Jaqaru, Peru
Jara	Jara, Nigeria
Jaranchi	**Jarawa, Nigeria
Jatapu	Jatapu, India
Jati	Jati, Afghanistan
Jaunsari	Jaunsari, India
Javanese	*Javanese (rural), Indonesia (79)
	**Javanese of Central Java, Indonesia
Javanese, Tjirebon	Cirebon, Indonesia
Jeng	Jeng, Laos
Jera	Jera, Nigeria
Jharia	Jharia, India
Jibu, Jibanci	*Jibu, Nigeria
Jimbin	Jimbin, Nigeria
Jivaro	**Jivaro (Achuara), Venezuela
Jiye	Jiye, Uganda

Jiye (Karamojong)	*Jiye, Sudan
Jongor	Jongor, Chad
Jro	**Chrau, Viet Nam
Juang	Juang, India
Jyarung	Jyarung, China
K'anjobal	**K'anjobal of San Miguel, Guatemala
Kaagan	Kaagan, Philippines
Kabixi	Kabixi, Brazil
Kabre	Kabre, Togo
Kabyle	Kabyle, Algeria (79)
Kachama	Kachama, Ethiopia
Kachchi	Kachchi, India
Kadaklan-Barlig Bontoc	Kadaklan-Barlig Bontoc, Philippines
Kadar	Kadar, India
Kadara	Kadara, Nigeria
	Kamantan, Nigeria
Kadiweu	Kadiweu, Brazil
Kaeti	Kaeti, Indonesia
Kaffenya (Kefa)	*Kaffa, Ethiopia (80)
Kafiristani (Bashgali)	**Kafirs, Pakistan (79)
Kagoma	Kagoma, Nigeria
Kahluri	Kahluri, India
Kaibu	Kaibu, Nigeria
Kaikadi	Kaikadi, India
Kaili	Kaili, Indonesia
Kaingang	Kaingang, Brazil
Kaipeng	**Kaipeng-Koloi, India
Kaiwai	Kaiwai, Indonesia
Kajang	Kajang, Indonesia
Kaka	Kaka, Nigeria
Kalagan	**Kalagan, Philippine's
Kalangoya	**Ifugao (Kalangoya), Philippines
Kalimga,Sumadel-Tinglayan	*Kalinga, Southern, Philippines
Kalinga	**Kalinga,Northern, Philippines
Kalinga, Kalagua	Kalinga, Kalagua, Philippines
Kalinga, Limus-Linan	Kalinga, Limus-Linan, Philippines
Kalinga, Quinaang	Kalinga, Quinaang, Philippines
Kalmytz	Kalmytz, China
Kam	Kam, China
Kamar	Kamar, India
Kamayura	Kamayura, Brazil
Kambarci	*Kambari, Nigeria (80)
Kambera	Kambera, Indonesia
Kamberataro	Kamberataro, Indonesia
Kamo	Kamo, Nigeria
Kamoro	Kamoro, Indonesia
Kampung Baru	Kampung Baru, Indonesia
Kamtuk-Gresi	Kamtuk-Gresi, Indonesia
Kamuku	*Kamuku, Nigeria (80)
Kana	Kana, Nigeria
Kanauri	Kanauri, India
Kanembu	Kanembu, Chad
Kanikkaran	Kanikkaran, India
Kanjari	Kanjari, India
Kankanay	**Kankanay, Central, Philippines
Kannada	*Kanarese, India
Kanum	Kanum, Indonesia
Kanuri Dialects	Kanuri, Nigeria (80)
Kapori	Kapori, Indonesia
Karakalpak	Karakalpak, Soviet Russia (80)
Karanga	Karanga, Chad
Karas	Karas, Indonesia
Karekare	Karekare, Nigeria
Kari	Kari, Chad
Karipuna Creole	Karipuna Creole, Brazil
Karipuna Do Guapore	Karipuna Do Guapore, Brazil
Kariya	Kariya, Nigeria
Karmali	Karmali, India
Karo	Kao, Ethiopia

Karon Dori	Karon Dori, Indonesia
Karon Pantai	Karon Pantai, Indonesia
Kasem	**Kasena, Ghana
Kashmiri	**Kashmiri Muslims, India (79)
Kasseng	Kasseng, Laos
Kasuweri	Kasuweri, Indonesia
Katab	Katab, Nigeria
Katakari	Katakari, India
Kati, Northern	Kati, Northern, Indonesia
Kati, Southern	Kati, Southern, Indonesia
Katukina, Panoan	Katukina, Panoan, Brazil
Kaugat	Kaugat, Indonesia
Kaure	Kaure, Indonesia
Kavwol	Kavwol, Indonesia
Kawar	Kawar, India
Kawe	Kawe, Indonesia
Kayabi	Kayabi, Brazil
Kayagar	Kayagar, Indonesia
Kayapo	Kayapo, Brazil
Kaygir	Kaygir, Indonesia
Kayupulau	Kayupulau, Indonesia
Kazakhi	Kazakhs, Iran (80)
Kebumtamp	Kebumtamp, Bhutan
Keer	Keer, India
Kei	Kei, Indonesia
Kelao	Kelao, China
Keley-i	Ifuago, Antipolo, Philippines
Kemak	Kemak, Indonesia
Kembata	Kembata, Ethiopia
Kendari	Kendari, Indonesia
Kenga	Kenga, Chad
Kenyah	Kenyah, Indonesia
Kera	Kera, Chad
Kerinchi	Kerinchi, Indonesia
Kewa	*Kepas, Papua New Guinea
Khalaj	Khalaj, Iran
Khalka	Khalka, China
Kham	Kham, China
Khamti	Khamti, India
Khamu	*Khamu, Thailand
Khana	Khana, Nigeria
Khandesi	Khandesi, India
Kharia	Kharia, India
Khasi	Khasi, India
Khirwar	Khirwar, India
Khowar	Khowar, India
Khuwar	Chitralis, Pakistan (79)
Kibet	Kibet, Chad
Kichepo	Kichepo, Sudan
Kijita	**Wajita, Tanzania
Kikerewe	Kerewe, Tanzania
Kilba	Kilba, Nigeria
Kim	Kim, Chad
Kimaghama	Kimaghama, Indonesia
Kimyal	*Kimyal, Indonesia
Kinaray-A	Kinaray-A, Philippines
Kirghiz	Kirchiz, China
	Kirghiz, Afghanistan
Kirgiz	Kirgiz, Soviet Russia (80)
Kisan	Kisan, India
Kishanganjia	Kishanganjia, India
Kishtwari	Kishtwari, India
Kissi	Kissi, Guinea
	*Kissi, Liberia
Kissi, Southern	*Kissi, Sierra Leone
Kizinza	*Wazinza, Tanzania
Koalib (Nuba)	Koalib, Sudan (79)
Koda	Koda, India
Kodi	Kodi, Indonesia

Koenoem	Koenoem, Nigeria
Kofyar	Kofyar, Nigeria
Kohoroxitari	Kohoroxitari, Brazil
Kohumono	Kohumono, Nigeria
Koke	Koke, Chad
Kol	Kol, India
Kolaka	**Loho Loho, Indonesia
Kolami	**Kolam, India
Kolbila	Kolbila, Cameroon
Kom	Kom, India
Kom Komba	*Konkomba, Togo
Koma	Koma, Ghana
	Koma, Nigeria
Komering	Lampung, Indonesia (80)
Komo	*Komo, Ethiopia
Konda-Dora	Konda-Dora, India
Koneraw	Koneraw, Indonesia
Konkani	Konkani, India
Konkomba	Konkomba, Ghana
Kono	**Kono, Sierra Leone
	Kono, Nigeria
Konso	Konso, Ethiopia
Koraga	Koraga, India
Korapun	Korapun, Indonesia
Korean	**Apartment Residents-Seoul, Korea, Rep of
	**Bus Drivers, South Korea, Korea, Repu of
	Indust.Workers Yongdungpo, Korea, Rep of
	**Korean Prisoners, Korea, Republic of
	***Koreans in Germany, German Federal Re
	*Koreans of Japan, Japan
Korku	*Korku, India
Koro	Koro, Nigeria
Koroma	Koroma, Sudan
Korop	Korop, Nigeria
Korwa	Korwa, India
Kota	Kota, India
	Kotta, India
Kotia	Kotia, India
Kotogut	Kotogut, Indonesia
Kotoko	Kotoko, Chad
Kotokoli	Kotokoli, Benin
	Tem, Togo
Kotopo	Kotopo, Cameroon
Kouya	Kouya, Ivory Coast
Kowaao	**Kowaao, Liberia
Koya	Koya, India
Koyra	Koyra, Ethiopia
Kpelle	Kpelle, Liberia
Krahn	***Krahn, Liberia
Kreen-Akakore	Kreen-Akakore, Brazil
Krifi	Kirifi, Nigeria
Krio	Krio, Gambia
Krobou	Krobou, Ivory Coast
Krongo	Krongo, Sudan
Kuda-Chamo	Kuda-Chamo, Nigeria
Kudiya	Kudiya, India
Kugbo	Kugbo, Nigeria
Kui	***Kond, India
	*Kui, Thailand
Kuikuro	Kuikuro, Brazil
Kuka	Kuka, Chad
Kukele	Kukele, Nigeria
Kukni	*Kuknas, India
Kulango	Kulango, Ivory Coast
Kulele	Kulele, Ivory Coast
Kulere	Kulere, Nigeria

Kullo	Kullo, Ethiopia
Kului	**Kuluis, India
Kulung	Kulung, Nigeria
Kumauni	Kumauni, India
Kunama	Kunama, Ethiopia
Kunimaipa	**Kunimaipa, Papua New Guinea
Kupia	Kupia, India
Kuranko (Maninka)	**Koranko, Sierra Leone
Kurdish	Turkish Workers, Belgium (80)
Kurdish (Kirmancho)	*Kurds of Turkey, Turkey (79)
Kurdish dialects	**Ahl-i-Hagq in Iran, Iran (79)
	Kurds in Iran, Iran (80)
Kurichiya	Kurichiya, India
Kuruba	Kuruba, India
Kurudu	Kurudu, Indonesia
Kurux	Kurux, India
Kusaal	**Kusaasi, Ghana
Kushi	Kushi, Nigeria
Kusso	Mbukushu, Angola
Kuteb	Kuteb, Nigeria
Kuturmi	Kuturmi, Nigeria
Kuvi	Kuvi, India
Kuzamani	Kuzamani, Nigeria
Kwa	Kwa, Nigeria
Kwansu	Kwansu, Indonesia
Kwe-Etshari	*Bushmen (Hiechware), Rhodesia
Kwerba	Kwerba, Indonesia
Kwere	Kwere, Tanzania
Kwesten	Kwesten, Indonesia
Kyibaku	Kyibaku, Nigeria
Laamang	Laamang, Nigeria
Labaani	Labans, India
Labhani	Labhani, India
Ladakhi	Ladakhi, India
Ladinos	Ladinos, Lebanon
Lahouli	**Lahaulis, India
Lahu	*Lahu, Thailand
Lahul	Lahul, China
Laka	Laka, Cameroon
	Laka, China
Lakal	Laka, Chad
Lakka	Lakka, Nigeria
Lalung	Lalung, India
Lama	Lama, Burma
Lamba	Lamba, Togo
Lame	Lame, Nigeria
Langa	Langa, Ethiopia
Lango	*Lango, Ethiopia
Lao	*Lao, Laos (79)
	*Lao Refugees, Thailand
Lara	Lara, Indonesia
Laru	Laru, Nigeria
Latdwalam	Latdwalam, Indonesia
Lati	Lati, China
Latuka	**Lotuka, Sudan
Laudje	Laudje, Indonesia
Lawa	Lawa, Thailand
Lebgo	Lebgo, Nigeria
Leco	Leco, Bolivia
Lele	Lele, Chad
Lepcha	**Lepcha, Sikkim
Letti	Letti, Indonesia
Li	Li, China
Ligbi	Ligbi, Ivory Coast
	Ligbi, Ghana
Limba	Limba, Sierra Leone
Limbum	**Wimbum, Cameroon
Lio	Lio, Indonesia
Lisu	*Lisu, Thailand

Lo	Lo, Nigeria
Lobi	Lobi, Ivory Coast
Local dialects	Kubu, Indonesia (80)
	Moken of Thailand, Thailand
	Nuristani, Afghanistan (80)
	Pygmy (Binga), Burundi
	Pygmy (Binga), Central African Empire
local languages	*Pygmy (Mbuti), Zaire (79)
	**Zaranda Hill Peoples, Nigeria
Lodhi	Lodhi, India
Logoro (Bambara)	Kagoro, Mali
Loinang	Loinang, Indonesia
Loko	Loko, Sierra Leone
Lokoro	*Lokoro, Sudan
Loma	Loma, Guinea
	Loma, Liberia
Longuda	Longuda, Nigeria
Lore	Lore, Indonesia
Lorhon	*Teenbu, Ivory Coast
Lori	Bovir-Ahmadi, Iran
Lotsu-Piri	Lotsu-Piri, Nigeria
Loven	Loven, Laos
Lu	Lu, China
Lubu	Lubu, Indonesia
Lugbara	Lugbara, Uganda
	Muslims (West Nile Dist.), Uganda
Lungu	Lungu, Nigeria
Luri	Lors, Iran (80)
	Mamasani, Iran
Lushai	Lushai, India
Luwu	Luwu, Indonesia
Maanyan	Maanyan, Indonesia
Maba	Maba, Chad
	Ouaddai, Chad
Maban-Jumjum	Meban, Sudan
Machiguenga	Machiguenga, Peru
Macu	Macu, Colombia
Macuna	Macuna, Colombia
Macuxi	**Macuxi, Brazil
Madda	Madda, Nigeria
Madik	Madik, Indonesia
Madurese	Madurese, Indonesia (79)
Nafaara	**Nafaara, Ghana (79)
Magar	**Magar, Nepal
Maghi	Maghi, Burma
Maguindano	Maguindano, Philippines (80)
Mahali	Mahali, India
Mahri	Mahri, Oman
Maiongong	Maiongong, Brazil
Mairasi	Mairasi, Indonesia
Maithili	Maithili, Nepal
Majangiir	*Masengo, Ethiopia
Majhwar	Majhwar, India
Maji	Maji, Ethiopia
Majingai-Ngama	Majingai-Ngama, Chad
Makasai	Makasai, Indonesia
Makian, West	Makian, West, Indonesia
Maklew	Maklew, Indonesia
Makua	Makua, Mozambique
Mala, Pattani	Thai Islam (Malay), Thailand (80)
Malamutha	Mala Muthas, India
Malankuravan	Malankuravan, India
Malapandaram	Malapandaram, India
Malappanackan	Malappanackers, India
Malaryan	Malaryan, India
Malavedan	Malavedan, India
Malay	Malays of Singapore, Singapore (79)
Malayalam	*Malayalars, India
Malayo	Malayo, Colombia

Male	Male, Ethiopia
Mali	Mali, India
Malinke, Senegalese	Manding, Senegal
Malki	Malki, India
Malpaharia	Malpaharia, India
Malvi	Malvi, India
Mam	**Mam Indian, Guatemala
Mama	Mama, Nigeria
Mambai	Mambai, Indonesia
Mambila	Mambila, Cameroon
Manchu	Manchu, China
Mandar	Mandar, Indonesia
Mandara	Mandara, Nigeria
Mandarin	*Chinese in Austria, Austria
	Chinese in Burma, Burma
	*Chinese in Holland, Netherlands
	*Chinese in Japan, Japan
	*Chinese in Laos, Laos
	**Chinese in Sarawak, Malaysia
	**Chinese in United Kingdom, United Kingdom
	**Chinese in United States, United States of America
	*Chinese in West Germany, German Federal Rep.
	*Chinese Mainlanders, Taiwan
	**Chinese Students Glasgow, United Kingdom
Mandaya	Mandaya, Philippines
Mandaya, Mansaka	Mandaya, Mansaka, Philippines
Mander	Mander, Indonesia
Mandingo	Mandingo, Liberia (79)
Mandyak	Mandyak, Gambia
Mandyako	**Manjaco, Guinea-Bissau
Mandyale	Manjack, Senegal
Manem	Manem, Indonesia
Mangbai	Mangbai, Chad
Manggarai	Manggarai, Indonesia
Manipuri	*Meitei, India (79)
Maniteneri	Piro, Peru
Mankanya	Mancang, Senegal
Manna-Dora	Manna-Dora, India
Mannan	Mannan, India
Mano	Mano, Liberia
Manobo	*Ata of Davao, Philippines
Manobo, Agusan	Manobo, Agusan, Philippines
Manobo, Ata	Manobo, Ata, Philippines
Manobo, Binokid	Manobo, Binokid, Philippines
	**Manobo, Western Bukidnon, Philippines
Manobo, Binukid	**Bukidnon, Philippines
Manobo, Dibabawon	Manobo, Dibabawon, Philippines
Manobo, Obo	Manobo, Obo, Philippines
Manobo, Pulangi	Manobos, Pulangi, Philippines
Manobo, Sarangani	Manobo, Sarangani, Philippines
Manobo, Tagabawa	Manobo, Tagabawa, Philippines
Manobo, Tigwa	**Manobo, Salug, Philippines
	**Manobo, Tigwa, Philippines
Mansaka	**Mansaka, Philippines
Mantion	Mantion, Indonesia
Manu Park Panoan	Manu Park Panoan, Peru
Mao, Northern	Mao, Northern, Ethiopia
Maou	Maou, Ivory Coast
Mapuche	Mapuche, Chile
Mara	Mara, India
Maranao	Maranao, Philippines (79)
Maranao, Lanad	Maranao, Lanad, Philippines
Mararit	Mararit, Chad
Marathi	*Labourers of Jhoparpatti, India
	Mangs, India
Marau	Marau, Indonesia
Marba	Marba, Chad

Marghi Central	Marghi Central, Nigeria
Maria	Maria, India
Marind	Marind, Indonesia
Marind, Bian	Marind, Bian, Indonesia
Marubo	Marubo, Brazil
Marwari	**Bhil, Pakistan
	Marwari, India
	**Mcghwar, Pakistan (79)
Masa	Budugum, Cameroon
	Gisei, Cameroon
	Masa, Chad
Masai	**Maasai, Kenya (79)
Masai, Samburu	Samburu, Kenya
Masalit	Masalit, Chad
Masenrempulu	Masenrempulu, Indonesia
Massalat	Massalat, Chad
Mataco	Mataco, Argentina
Matakam	Matakam, Cameroon
	Matakam, Nigeria
Matbat	Matbat, Indonesia
Matipuhy-Nahukua	Matipuhy-Nahukua, Brazil
Matumbi	Matumbi, Tanzania
Mavchi	Mavchi, India
Mawes	Mawes, Indonesia
Maxakali	Maxakali, Brazil
Mayoruna	Mayoruna, Peru
Mazahua	**Mazahua, Mexico
Mazandarani	Mazandaranis, Iran
Mbai	Mbai, Chad
Mbe	Mbe, Nigeria
Mbembe	Mbembe (Tigong), Nigeria
Mboi	Mboi, Nigeria
Mbula-Bwazza	Mbula-Bwazza, Nigeria
Mbum	Mbum, Chad
Me'en	Me'en, Ethiopia
Meax	Meax, Indonesia
Mejah	**Mejah, India
Mekwei	Mekwei, Indonesia
Melanau	**Melanau of Sarawak, Malaysia (80)
Mende	Mende, Sierra Leone
Mentawi	Mentawi, Indonesia
Meo	**Meo, Thailand
Mesengo	Mesengo, Ethiopia
Mesme	Mesme, Chad
Mesmedje	Mesmedje, Chad
Miching	**Miching, India
Migili	Migili, Nigeria
Mikir	**Karbis, India
Mimi	Mimi, Chad
Mimika	*Mimika, Indonesia
Mina	Mina, India
Minamanwa	**Mamanwa (Mamanua), Philippines
Minangkabau	Minangkabau, Indonesia (80)
Mirdha	Mirdha, India
Mirung	Mirung, Bangladesh
Mishmi	Mishmi, India
Mixe	**Mixes, Mexico
Mixteco	*Mixteco,San Juan Mixtepic, Mexico
Miya	Miya, Nigeria
Mo	Mo, Ivory Coast
Mo (Degha)	Mo, Ghana
Mober	Mober, Nigeria
Mocha	***Mocha, Ethiopia
Mogholi	Mogholi, Afghanistan
Mogum	Mogum, Chad
Moi	Moi, Indonesia
Moken	Moken, Burma (79)
Mokole	*Mokole, Benin
Molbog	*Molbog, Philippines

Mole	Mossi, Upper Volta (80)
Molof	Molof, Indonesia
Mombum	Mombum, Indonesia
Mon	Mon, Burma
Mona	Mona, Ivory Coast
Mongondow	Mongondow, Indonesia
Mongour	Mongour, China
Moni	Moni, Indonesia
Monpa	Monpa, India
Montol	Montol, Nigeria
Mopan Maya	**Mopan Maya, Guatemala
	**Mopan Maya, Belize
Moqaddam	Moqaddam, Iran
Mor	Mor, Indonesia
Moreno	**Black Caribs, Belize, Belize (79)
	**Black Caribs, Guatemala, Guatemala
	**Black Caribs, Honduras, Honduras
Mori	Mori, Indonesia
Moru	Moru, Ivory Coast
Morunahua	Morunahua, Peru
Morwap	Morwap, Indonesia
Motilon	Motilon, Colombia
Movima	Movima, Bolivia
Mualthuam	Mualthuam, India
Mubi	Mubi, Chad
Muinane	Muinane, Colombia
Multani	Multani, India
Mumbake	Mumbake, Nigeria
Mumuye	Mumuye, Nigeria
Mun	Mun, Burma
Muna	Muna, Indonesia
Munda	**Mundas, India
Mundang	Mundang, Chad
Mundari	Mundari, India
Munduruku	Munduruku, Brazil
Munggui	Munggui, Indonesia
Munji-Yidgha	Munji-Yidgha, Afghanistan
Mura-Piraha	Mura-Piraha, Brazil
Muria	Muria, India
Murle	Murle, Sudan
Mursi	Mursi, Ethiopia
Murung	Mru, Bangladesh
Musei	Musei, Chad
Musgu	Musgu, Chad
Muthuvan	Muthuvan, India
Muwasi	Muwasi, India
N.E. Thai	Thai, North East, Thailand
Nabi	Nabi, Indonesia
Nadeb Maku	Nadeb Maku, Brazil
Nafri	Nafri, Indonesia
Naga, Angami	Naga, Angami, India
Naga, Ao	Naga, Ao, India
Naga, Kalyokengnyu	Naga, Kalyokengnyu, India
Naga, Konyak	Naga, Konyak, India
Naga, Kuki	Naga, Kuki, India
Naga, Lotha	Naga, Lotha, India
Naga, Mao	Naga, Mao, India
Naga, Nruanghmei	Naga, Nruanghmei, India
Naga, Sangtam	Naga, Sangtam, India
Naga, Sema	Naga, Sema, India
Naga, Tangkhul	Naga, Tangkhul, India
Naga, Wancho	Naga, Wancho, India
Naga, Zoliang	Zoliang, India
Nagar	Nagar, India
Nahsi	Nahsi, China
Nahua	*Nahua, North Pueblo, Mexico
Nahuatl, Hidalgo	***Azteca, Mexico (79)
Naltya	Naltya, Indonesia
Nambikuara	Nambikuara, Brazil

Nambya	**Nambya, Rhodesia
Namshi	Namshi, Cameroon
Nanai	Nanai, China
Nancere	Nancere, Chad
Nandi	Dorobo, Kenya
Nandu-Tari	Nandu-Tari, Nigeria
Nao	Nao, Ethiopia
Napali	*Gorkha, India
Nara	Nara, Ethiopia
Naraguta	Naraguta, Nigeria
Native Senoi	**Orang Asli, Malaysia
Nawuri	Nawuri, Ghana
Nchumburu	Nchimburu, Ghana
Ndao	Ndao, Indonesia
Nde-Nsele-Nta	Nde-Nsele-Nta, Nigeria
Ndoe	Ndoe, Nigeria
Ndom	Ndom, Indonesia
Ndoro	**Ndoro, Nigeria
Nduga	Nduga, Indonesia
Ndunpa Duupa	Ndunpa Duupa, Cameroon
Nepali	*Nepali, Nepal
Nevo	Neyo, Ivory Coast
Newari	*Newari, Nepal
Ngada	Ngada, Indonesia
Ngalik, North	Ngalik, North, Indonesia
Ngalik, Southern	Ngalik, Southern, Indonesia
Ngalum	Ngalum, Indonesia
Ngamo	**Ngamo, Nigeria
Ngen	*Ngen, Ivory Coast
Ngeq	Ngeq, Laos
Ngizim	Ngizim, Nigeria
Ngwoi	Ngwoi, Nigeria
Nhengatu	Nhengatu, Brazil
Nias	Nias, Indonesia
Nielim	Nielim, Chad
Nihali	Nihali, India
Nimadi	Nimadi, India
Nimboran	Nimboran, Indonesia
Ninam	Ninam, Brazil
Ningerum	*Ningerum, Papua New Guinea
Ninggrum	Ninggrum, Indonesia
Ninzam	Ninzam, Nigeria
Nisa	Nisa, Indonesia
Njadu	Njadu, Indonesia
Nkem-Nkum	Nkem-Nkum, Nigeria
Nocte	***Nocte, India
Norra	Norra, Burma
North Thai Dialect	Thai Northern, Thailand
Northeast Thai	**Lepers of N.E. Thailand, Thailand
Northern Cagayan Negrito	Northern Cagayan Negrito, Philippines
Northern Kamer	*Cambodians, Thailand
Nosu	Nosu, China
Ntrubo	Ntrubs, Ghana
Nuer	*Nuer, Ethiopia
	*Nuer, Sudan (79)
Numana-Nunku-Gwantu	Numana-Nunku-Gwantu, Nigeria
Nung	Nung, China
Nungu	Nungu, Nigeria
Nupe	**Nupe, Nigeria
Nyabwa-Nyedebwa	Nyabwa-Nyedebwa, Ivory Coast
Nyaheun	Nyaheun, Laos
Nyamwezi	Nyamwezi, Tanzania (80)
Nyaturu	Turu, Tanzania
Nzanyi	Nzanyi, Nigeria
Nzema	Nzema, Ivory Coast
Obanliku	Obanliku, Nigeria
Obolo	Obolo, Nigeria
Ocaina	Ocaina, Peru
Odki	Od, Pakistan

Odual	Odual, Nigeria
Odut	Odut, Nigeria
Ogbia	Ogbia, Nigeria
Oi	Oi, Laos
Oirat	Oirat, China
Ojhi	Ojhi, India
Okobo	Okobo, Nigeria
Okpamheri	Okpamheri, Nigeria
Ollari	Ollari, India
Olulumo-Ikom	Olulumo-Ikom, Nigeria
Ong	Ong, India
Onin	Onin, Indonesia
Orejon	Orejon, Peru
Oring	Oring, Nigeria
Oriya	Oriya, India
Ormu	Ormu, Indonesia
Oron	Oron, Nigeria
Oronchon	Oronchon, China
Ot Danum	Ot Danum, Indonesia
Otank	Otank, Nigeria
Oubi	Oubi, Ivory Coast
Oyampipuku	Oyampipuku, Brazil
Oyda	Oyda, Ethiopia
Paez	***Paez, Colombia
Pahari Garhwali	Pahari Garhwali, India
Pai	Pai, Nigeria
Paite	Paite, India
Paiute, Northern	Paiute, Northern, United States of America
Pakaasnovos	Pakaasnovos, Brazil
Pakabeti	***Pakabeti of Equator, Zaire
Palara	- Palara, Ivory Coast
Palaung	Palaung, Burma (79)
Palawano	Palawano, Philippines
Palawano, Central	Palawano, Central, Philippines
Palembang	Palembang, Indonesia
Palikur	Palikur, Brazil
Paliyan	Paliyan, India
Panika	Panika, India
Paniyan	Paniyan, India
Pankhu	Pankhu, Bangladesh
Pantu	Pantu, Indonesia
Pao	Pao, India
Paongan	Paongan, China
Papuma	Papuma, Indonesia
Parakanan	Parakanan, Brazil
Paranan	Paranan, Philippines
Pardhan	Pardhan, India
Parengi	Parengi, India
Paresi	Paresi, Brazil
Parintintin	Parintintin, Brazil
Pashayi	Pashayi, Afghanistan
Pashtu	Pashtuns, Iran (80)
Patelia	Patelia, India
Pato Tapuia	Pato Tapuia, Brazil
Paumari	Paumari, Brazil
Pengo	Pengo, India
Pero	Pero, Nigeria
Persian	Persians of Iran, Iran (80)
Phu Thai	Phu Thai, Laos
Piapoco	Piapoco, Colombia
Pila-Pila	**Pila, Benin
Pilaga	Pilaga, Argentina
Pisa	Pisa, Indonesia
Pishagchi	Pishagchi, Iran
Piti	Piti, Nigeria
Pitu Uluna Salu	Pitu Uluna Salu, Indonesia
Piya	Piya, Nigeria
Pnar	Pnar, India
Podokwo	Podokwo, Cameroon

Polci	Polci, Nigeria
Pom	Pom, Indonesia
Pongu	Pongu, Nigeria
Porohanon	Porohanon, Philippines
Portuguese	Pankararu, Brazil
	**Portuguese in France, France
	Spiritists, Brazil (79)
	Students in Cuiaba, Brazil
Prasuni	***Prasuni, Afghanistan
Pu-I	Pu-I, China
Puku-Geeri-Keri-Wipsi	Puku-Geeri-Keri-Wipsi, Nigeria
Punjabi	**Gagre, Pakistan
Punu	Punu, China
Puragi	Puragi, Indonesia
Purum	Purum, Burma
Pwo Karen	Karen, Pwo, Thailand
Pye	Pye, Ivory Coast
Pyu	Pyu, Indonesia
Qajar	Qajars, Iran
Qara'i	Qara'i, Iran
Qaragozlu	Qaragozlu, Iran
Qashqa'i	Qashqa'i, Iran (80)
Quaiquer	Quaiquer, Colombia
Quechua	**Quechua, Peru
	**Quechua, Bolivia
Quechua, Huancayo	**Quechua, Huanco, Peru
Quiche	**Quiche, Guatemala (79)
Rabha	Rabha, India
Rabinal Achi	Rabinal-Achi, Guatemala
Rai	Rai, Nepal
Rajasthani	Meos of Rajasthan, India (80)
Rajbansi	Rajbansi, Nepal
Ralte	Ralte, Burma
Ratahan	Ratahan, Indonesia
Rataning	Rataning, Chad
Rava	*Rava, India
Rawang	Rawang, China
Redjang-Lebong	Lebong, Indonesia
Rejang	Redjang, Indonesia (80)
Reshe	Reshe, Nigeria
Reyesano	Reyesano, Bolivia
Riang	Riang, India
Riang-Lang	Riang-Lang, Burma
Riantana	Riantana, Indonesia
Rikbaktsa	Rikbaktsa, Brazil
Rom	*Gypsies in Spain, Spain (79)
Romany	Romany, Turkey
Rotti	Rotti, Indonesia
Rukuba	Rukuba, Nigeria
Rumaya	Rumaya, Nigeria
Runga	Runga, Chad
Ruruma	Ruruma, Nigeria
Ryukyuan	*Ryukyuan, Japan
Saberi	Saberi, Indonesia
Sadan	Sadan, India
Sadang	Sadang, Indonesia
Safwa	Safwa, Tanzania
Saija	Saija, Colombia
Salar	Salar, China
Saliba	Saliba, Colombia
Sama Pangutaran	Sama Pangutaran, Philippines (80)
Sama, Mapun	Sama, Mapun, Philippines
Sama, Siasi	Sama, Siasi, Philippines
Sama, Sibuku	Sama, Sibuku, Philippines
Samal dialects	Sama-Badjaw, Philippines (79)
Samarkena	Samarkena, Indonesia
Samburu	El Molo, Kenya
Samo	*Samo-Kubo, Papua New Guinea
Sanga	Sanga, Nigeria

Sangil	Sangil, Philippines
Sangir	Sangir, Indonesia
Sangke	Sangke, Indonesia
Santa	Santa, China
Santhali	**Santhali, Nepal
Sanuma	*Sanuma, Brazil
Sarwa	Sarwa, Chad
Sasak	Sasak, Indonesia (80)
Sasani	Sasanis, Iran
Sasaru-Enwan Igwe	Sasaru-Enwan Igwe, Nigeria
Satere	Satere, Brazil
Sau	Sau, Afghanistan
Sause	Sause, Indonesia
Save (Yoruba)	**Save, Benin
Sawi	**Sawi, Indonesia
Saya	Saya, Nigeria
Secoya	Secoya, Ecuador
Sekar	Sekar, Indonesia
Seko	Seko, Indonesia
Selakau	**Selakau of Sarawak, Malaysia
Sempan	Sempan, Indonesia
Senari	Senufo, Ivory Coast (80)
Senggi	Senggi, Indonesia
Sentani	Sentani, Indonesia
Senthang	Senthang, Burma
Serawai (Pasemah)	Serawai, Indonesia
Serbo-Croation	*Bosnian, Yugoslavia (80)
Serere	Serere, Senegal (79)
Serui-Laut	Serui-Laut, Indonesia
Sgaw Karen	Karen, Thailand (79)
Sha	Sha, Nigeria
Shamatali	Yanomamo in Venezuela, Venezuela
Shan	Shan, Thailand
Shanga	Shanga, Nigeria
Shankilla (Kazza)	***Shankilla (Kazza), Ethiopia
Sharanahua	Sharanahua, Peru
Sharchagpakha	Bhutias, Bhutan
	Sharchagpakha, Bhutan
Shawiya	Shawiya, Algeria
Sheko	Sheko, Ethiopia
Sherpa	*Sherpa, Nepal
Shihu	**Shihu, United Arab Emirates
Shina	Shina, Afghanistan
Shinasha	Shinasha, Ethiopia
Shinkoya	*Nkoya, Zambia
Shipibo	Shipibo, Peru
Shirishana	**Shirishana, Brazil
Shourastra	*Shourastra, India
Shughni	Shughni, Afghanistan
Shuwa Arabic	Shuwa Arabic, Nigeria
Siagha-Yenimu	Siagha-Yenimu, Indonesia
Sibo	Sibo, China
Sidamo	Sidamo, Ethiopia
Sikhule	Sikhule, Indonesia
Sikka	Sikka, Indonesia
Sikkimese	Sikkimese, India
Sinama Bangini	Sama Bangingi, Philippines (80)
Sindebele	**Ndebele, Rhodesia (79)
Sindhi	*Sindhis of India, India
	Sochi, Pakistan
Sinhala	Sinhalese, Sri Lanka
Siona	Siona, Colombia
Siri	Siri, Nigeria
Siriano	Siriano, Colombia
Siriono	Siriono, Bolivia
So	So, Laos
	*So, Thailand
Sobei	Sobei, Indonesia
Solor	Solor, Indonesia

Somagai	*Somahai, Indonesia
Somahai	Somahai, Indonesia
Somali	Somali, Ethiopia
	Somali, Somalia (79)
	Somali, Degodia, Kenya
	Somali, Gurreh, Kenya
	Somali, Ogadenya, Kenya
Somali (Ajuran)	Somali, Ajuran, Kenya (79)
Somba (Detammari)	**Somba, Benin
Somrai	Somrai, Chad
Sondwari	Sondwari, India
Soninke	Sarakole, Senegal (80)
	Soninke, Gambia
Sonjo	Sonjo, Tanzania
Sora	Sora, India
Soruba	Soruba, Benin
Sough	**Manikion, Indonesia
Southern Bontoc	**Bontoc, Southern, Philippines
Southern Sesotho	***Basotho, Mountain, Lesotho (79)
Southern Thai	Thai, Southern, Thailand
Sowanda	Sowanda, Indonesia
Spanish	Iquito, Peru
	Jebero, Peru
	Palenquero, Colombia
Subanen, Tuboy	**Subanen (Tuboy), Philippines
Subanun	**Subanen, Sindangan, Philippines (80)
Subanun, Lapuyan	Subanun, Lapuyan, Philippines
Suena	**Suena, Papua New Guinea
Sui	Sui, China
Sukur	Sukur, Nigeria
Sulung	Sulung, India
Sumba	Sumba, Indonesia
Sumbawa	Sumbawa, Indonesia
Sundanese	**Sundanese, Indonesia (80)
Sungor	Sungor, Chad
Suppire	Minianka, Mali
Sura	Sura, Nigeria
Suri	**Suri, Ethiopia
Surigueno	**Suriguenos, Philippines
Surubu	Surubu, Nigeria
Surui	Surui, Brazil
Swati	Swatis, Pakistan (79)
Ta-Oi	Ta-Oi, Laos
Tabi	Ingassana, Sudan
Tacana	Tacana, Bolivia
Tadjio	Tadjio, Indonesia
Tadyawan	Tadyawan, Philippines
Tagbanwa	**Tagbanwa, Aborlan, Philippines
Tagbanwa, Kalamian	Tagbanwa, Kalamian, Philippines
Tagin	***Tagin, India
Tagwana	Tagwana, Ivory Coast
Taikat	Taikat, Indonesia
Taiwanese	*Urban Workers in Taiwan, Taiwan
Taiwanese (Minnan)	*Chinese (Hoklo) in Taiwan, Taiwan
Takankar	Takankar, India
Takestani	Takestani, Iran
Tal	Tal, Nigeria
Talish	Talish, Iran
Tama	Tama, Chad
Tamachek	Tuareg, Niger (79)
Tamagario	Tamagario, Indonesia
Taman	Taman, Burma
Tamang	*Tamang, Nepal
Tamaria	Tamaria, India
Tambas	Tambas, Nigeria
Tamil	*Kudisai Vagh Makkal, India
	Moor Malays, Sri Lanka (79)
	**Saiva Vellala, India
	Tamil (Ceylonese), Sri Lanka

	*Tamil Brahmins, India
	***Tamil Plantation Workers, Malaysia
	*Tamils (Indian), Malaysia
	**Tamils (Indian), Sri Lanka (79)
Tampulensi	Tampulma, Ghana
Tana	Tana, Chad
Tanahmerah	Tanahmerah, Indonesia
Tancouleur	Taucouleur, Senegal (80)
Tandanke	Tandanke, Senegal
Tandia	Tandia, Indonesia
Tangale	Tangale, Nigeria
Tangchangya	Tangchangya, Bangladesh
Tangsa	**Tangsa, India
Tanimuca-Retuama	Tanimuca-Retuama, Colombia
Taori-Kei	Taori-Kei, Indonesia
Tara	Tara, Indonesia
Targum	Targum, Israel
Tarof	Tarof, Indonesia
Tarok	Tarok, Nigeria
Tarpia	Tarpia, Indonesia
Tatar	Bashkir, Soviet Russia (80)
Tatar dialects	Tatars, Soviet Russia (80)
Tatoga	Barabaig, Tanzania (79)
Tatuyo	**Tatuyo, Colombia
Taungyo	Taungyo, Burma
Taurap	Taurap, Indonesia
Tausug	Tausug, Philippines (80)
Tawbuid	Tawbuid, Philippines
Tawr	Tawr, Burma
Tboli	**Tboli, Philippines
Teda	Teda, Chad (80)
Tehit	Tahit, Indonesia
Teimuri	Teimuri, Iran
Teimurtash	Teimurtash, Iran
Telugu	Caste Hindus (Andra Prd), India
Tembe	Tembe, Brazil
Temne	**Temne, Sierra Leone (80)
Tenggerese	Tengger, Indonesia
Tepo	Tepo, Ivory Coast
Tera	Tera, Nigeria
Terena	Terena, Brazil
Teribe	**Teribe, Panama
Ternate	Ternate, Indonesia
Tewa (Jemez)	Jemez Pueblo, United States of America
Thado	Thado, India
Thai	Government officials, Thailand
	*Thailand Farmers (Ctl), Thailand
Thai, Central	Thai of Bangkok, Thailand
Thai, Southern	*Thai Islam (Thai), Thailand
Thakur	Thakur, India
Thar	Thar, India
Tibetan	*Tibetan Refugees, India
	*Tibetans, China
Ticuna	Ticuna, Brazil
Tidore	Tidore, Indonesia
Tien-Chiu	**Chinese Refugees, France, France (79)
Tigon	Tigon, Cameroon
Tila Chol	Ch'ol Tila, Mexico
Timorese	Timorese, Indonesia
Tin	Tin, Thailand
Tippera	Tippera, Bangladesh
Tiro	Tiro, Indonesia
Tiruray	Tiruray, Philippines
Toala	Toala, Indonesia
Toba	Toba, Argentina
Toda	Toda, India
Tofi	*Tofi, Benin
Tokkaru	Tokkaru, India
Tombulu	Tombulu, Indonesia

REGISTRY OF THE UNREACHED

Tomini	Tomini, Indonesia
Tondanou	Tondanou, Indonesia
Tonsea	Tonsea, Indonesia
Tontemboa	Tontemboa, Indonesia
Toposa	*Topotha, Sudan
Toposa, Donyiro	Nyzatom, Sudan
Toradja	Toradja, Indonesia
Towei	Towei, Indonesia
Trepo	Trepo, Ivory Coast
Tripuri	**Tripuri, India
Tsamai	Tsamai, Ethiopia
Tshiluba	**Bakuba, Zaire
Tsimane	Tsimane, Bolivia
Tucano	Pacu, Brazil
	Piratapuyo, Brazil
	Quarequena, Brazil
	Seuci, Brazil
	Tucano, Brazil
Tucanoan	Arapaco, Brazil
Tugara	Tugara, India
Tukude	Tukude, Indonesia
Tula	Tula, Nigeria
Tulu	Tulu, India
Tumawo	Tumawo, Indonesia
Tunebo, Cobaria	Tunebo, Cobaria, Colombia
Tunya	Tunya, Chad
Tupuri	Tupuri, Chad
Tura	Tura, Ivory Coast
Turkana	Turkana, Kenya
	**Turkana Fishing Community, Kenya (79)
Turkish	Baharlu (Kamesh), Iran
	Nafar, Iran
	Turkish Immigrant Workers, German Federal
	Rep. (79)
Turkish, Osmanli	Turks, Anatolian, Turkey
Turkomani	Turkomans, Iran (80)
Turkwam	Turkwam, Nigeria
Turu	Turu, Indonesia
Tuyuca	Tuyuca, Brazil
Tzotzil (Chamula)	Chamula, Mexico (79)
Tzotzil, Chenalho	Zinacentecos, Mexico (79)
Uduk	Uduk, Sudan
Uhunduni	Uhunduni, Indonesia
Uighur	Uighur, Afghanistan
Uigur	Uigur, China (80)
Ukaan	Ukaan, not reported
Ukpe-Bayobiri	Ukpe-Bayobiri, Nigeria
Ukwuani-Aboh	Ukwuani-Aboh, Nigeria
Ulithi	Ulithi-Mall, Turks and Caicos Islands
Ullatan	Ullatan, India
Urali	Urali, India
Urarina	Urarina, Peru
Urhobo	Urhobo, Nigeria
Uria	Uria, Indonesia
Uruangnirin	Uruangnirin, Indonesia
Urubu	Urubu, Brazil
Urupa	Urupa, Brazil
Utugwang	Utugwang, Nigeria
Uvbie	Uvbie, Nigeria
Uzbeki, Turkic	**Uzbeks, Afghanistan (79)
Uzekwe	Uzekwe, Nigeria
Vagala	Vagala, Ghana
Vagla	Vagla, Ivory Coast
Vai	*Vai, Liberia (80)
Vaikino	Vaikino, Indonesia
Vaiphei	Vaiphei, India
Various dialects	**African Students in Cairo, Egypt
	**Mangyan, Philippines
Vere	***Vere, Nigeria

Vietnamese	*Int'l Stud., Los Banos, Philippines
	Vietnamese, Laos
	**Vietnamese in the USA, United States of America
	**Vietnamese Refugees, Thailand
	**Vietnamese Refugees, Australia
Vishavan	Vishavan, India
Vute	Vute, Nigeria
Wa	Wa, China
Wabo	Wabo, Indonesia
Waddar	Waddar, India
Waffa Dialect	Ka'mis, Papua New Guinea
Wagdi	Wagdi, India
Waimiri	Waimiri, Brazil
Waiwai	Waiwai, Brazil
Waja	Waja, Nigeria
Walamo	Walamo, Ethiopia
Wali	Wala, Ghana
Wambon	Wambon, Indonesia
Wan	Wan, Ivory Coast
Wanchoo	**Wanchoo, India
Wandamen	Wandamen, Indonesia
Wanggom	Wanggom, Indonesia
Wano	Wano, Indonesia
Wapishana	Wapishana, Brazil
Warembori	Warembori, Indonesia
Waris	Waris, Indonesia
Warji	*Warjawa, Nigeria
Warkay-Bipim	Warkay-Bipim, Indonesia
Waropen	Waropen, Indonesia
Waura	Waura, Brazil
Weda	Weda, Indonesia
Wetawit	Wetawit, Ethiopia
Wewewa	Wewewa, Indonesia
Winji-Winji	Winji-Winji, Benin
Wobe	Wobe, Ivory Coast
Wodani	Wodani, Indonesia
Woi	Woi, Indonesia
Woko	Voko, Cameroon
Woleat	Woleat, Turks and Caicos Islands
Wolio	Wolio, Indonesia
Wolof	Wolof, Senegal (80)
Wolof, Gambian	Wolof, Gambian, Gambia
Wom	Wom, Nigeria
Won Chow	*Chinese Restaurant Wrkrs., France
Xavante	Xavante, Brazil
Xerente	Xerente, Brazil
Xokleng	Xokleng, Brazil
Xu	*Bushmen (Kung), Namibia (79)
Yafi	Yafi, Indonesia
Yagua	Yagua, Peru
Yahadian	Yahadian, Indonesia
Yakan	Yakan, Philippines (80)
Yala	**Yala, Nigeria
Yalunka	*Yalunka, Sierra Leone (80)
Yaly	Yaly, Indonesia
Yaminahua	Yaminahua, Peru
Yanadi	Yanadi, India
Yandang	Yandang, Nigeria
Yangbye	Yangbye, Burma
Yanomam (Waica)	*Yanomamo in Brazil, Brazil (79)
Yanyula (Yanjula)	*Yanyula, Australia
Yao	*Mao Refugees from Laos, Thailand
	Yao, Mozambique
Yao (Mien Wa)	**Yao, Thailand (79)
Yaoure	Yaoure, Ivory Coast
Yaqui	Yaquis, Mexico
Yaur	Yaur, Indonesia
Yava	Yava, Indonesia

Yei	**Yei, Botswana
	Yei, Indonesia
Yellow Uighur	Yellow Uighur, China
Yelmek	Yelmek, Indonesia
Yerava	Yerava, India
Yeretuar	Yeretuar, Indonesia
Yerukala	Yerukala, India
Yeskwa	Yeskwa, Nigeria
Yidinit	Yidinit, Ethiopia
Yinchia	Yinchia, Burma
Yinga	Yinga, Cameroon
Yogad	Yogad, Philippines
Yonggom	Yonggom, Indonesia
Yos	Yos, Burma
Yotafa	Yotafa, Indonesia
Yucuna	*Yucuna, Colombia
Yukpa	Yukpa, Colombia
Yuku	Yuku, China
Yungur	Yungur, Nigeria
Yuracare	Yuracare, Bolivia
Yuruti	Yuruti, Colombia
Zaghawa	Zaghawa, Chad
Zangskari	Zangskari, India
Zaramo	Zaramo, Tanzania
Zari	Zari, Nigeria
Zayse	Zayse, Ethiopia
Zighvana(Dghwede)	*Dghwede, Nigeria
Zilmamu	Zilmamu, Ethiopia
Zome	Zome, Burma
	Zome, India
Zuni	Zuni, United States of America

INDEX
by
Country

INDEX BY COUNTRY

Groups are listed by the countries for which information has been reported by questionnaires. In most cases, this means they are listed in the country where they are primarily located. Many peoples are found in several countries. This listing is limited to the country for which the MARC files have information. Groups are listed alphabetically under each country listed. Please note that not all countries will be found in this index. Peoples have not been reported from every country. Cambodia is listed under its new name Kampuchea. The Republic of China is listed as Taiwan. Dahomey is listed under its current name, Benin. The population estimate given is an indication of the size of that people in that one country. In some cases, it is only a part of a large people to be found in several other countries as well.

Afghanistan	**Azerbaijani	5,000
	Bashgali	10,000
	Chaghatai	300,000
	Gawar-Bati	8,900
	Gujuri	10,000
	Jati	1,000
	Kirghiz	45,000
	Mogholi	2,000
	Munji-Yidgha	14,000
	Nuristani (80)	67,000
	Pashayi	96,000
	***Prasuni	2,000
	Sau	1,000
	Shina	50,000
	Shughni	3,000
	Uighur	3,000
	**Uzbeks (79)	1,000,000
Albania	*Albanian Muslims (80)	1,700,000
Algeria	Algerian (Arabs) (80)	8,000,000
	Kabyle (79)	1,000,000
	Shawiya	150,000
Angola	Chokwe (Lunda)	400,000
	**Huila	200,000
	Hukwe	9,000
	Mbukushu	6,000
Argentina	**Chiriguano	15,000
	Chorote	500
	Mataco	10,000
	Pilaga	4,000
	Toba	15,000
Australia	**Chinese in Australia	30,000
	**Chinese Stud., Australia	5,500
	Gugu-Yalanji	5,400
	*Murngin (Wulamba)	3,500
	**Vietnamese Refugees	7,800
	*Yanyula	150
Austria	*Chinese in Austria	1,000
	*Iwaidja	150
Bangladesh	Assamese	10,000,000
	**Banai	2,000
	Bawm	7,000
	Bengali (80)	80,000,000
	**Hajong	17,000
	**Koch	35,000
	Mirung	12,000
	Mru	50,000
	Pankhu	630
	Tangchangya	8,310
	Tippera	38,000
Belgium	North Africans in Belgium (80)	90,000
	Turkish Workers (80)	60,000
Belize	**Black Caribs, Belize (79)	10,000
	**Mopan Maya	4,000
Benin	**Adja	250,000
	*Bariba (80)	400,000
	**Boko	40,000
	Dendi	40,000
	Dompago	19,000
	*Fulani	70,000
	Gbazantche	9,000
	Kotokoli	75,000
	*Mokole	7,000
	*Nyantruku	4,000
	**Pila	50,000
	**Save	15,000
	**Somba	60,000
	Soruba	5,000
	*Tofi	33,000
	Winji-Winji	5,000

327

REGISTRY OF THE UNREACHED

Bhutan	Bhutias	780,000
	Kebumtamp	400,000
	Sharchagpakha	400,000
Bolivia	**Aymara	850,000
	Chacobo	250
	Chipaya	850
	Chiquitano	20,000
	***Guarani (79)	15,000
	Guarayu	5,000
	Ignaciano	5,000
	Itonama	110
	Leco	200
	Movima	1,000
	**Quechua	1,600,000
	Reyesano	1,000
	Siriono	500
	Tacana	3,500
	Tsimane	5,500
	Yuracare	2,500
Botswana	Bushmen in Botswana	30,000
	*Kalanga	150,000
	**Yei	10,000
Brazil	Apalai	100
	Apinaye	210
	Apurina	1,000
	Arapaco	310
	Atruahi	500
	Bakairi	300
	Baniwa	2,440
	*Bororo	500
	Caiwa	7,000
	Canela	1,400
	**Chinese in Brazil	45,000
	Cinta Larga	500
	Culina	900
	Desano	1,040
	Fulnio	1,500
	Guajajara	5,000
	Hixkaryana	150
	Hohodene	1,000
	Jamamadi	1,200
	Japanese in Brazil (79)	750,000
	Kabixi	160
	Kadiweu	550
	Kaingang	7,000
	Kamayura	110
	Karipuna Creole	500
	Karipuna Do Guapore	150
	Katukina, Panoan	180
	Kayabi	300
	Kayapo	600
	Kohoroxitari	620
	Kreen-Akakore	90
	Kuatinema	70
	Kuikuro	120
	**Macuxi	6,000
	Maiongong	85
	Marubo	400
	Matipuhy-Nahukua	100
	Maxakali	400
	Munduruku	2,000
	Mura-Piraha	110
	Nadeb Maku	200
	Nambikuara	400
	Nhengatu	3,000
	Ninam	470
	Oyampipuku	100
	Pacu	120
	Pakaasnovos	800

	Palikur	500
	Pankararu	2,000
	Parakanan	500
	Paresi	350
	Parintintin	200
	Pato Tapuia	140
	Paumari	250
	Piratapuyo	800
	Quarequena	340
	Rikbaktsa	200
	*Sanuma	325
	Satere	3,000
	Seuci	400
	**Shirishana	240
	Spiritists (79)	9,000,000
	Students in Cuiaba	20,000
	Surui	250
	Tembe	250
	Terena	5,000
	Ticuna	8,000
	Tucano	2,000
	Tuyuca	500
	Urubu	500
	Urupa	250
	Waimiri	1,000
	Waiwai	1,000
	Wapishana	1,500
	Waura	120
	Xavante	2,000
	Xerente	500
	Xokleng	250
	*Yanomamo in Brazil (79)	2,000
Burma	Chaungtha	34,600
	Chin, Asho	11,000
	Chin, Falam	92,000
	Chin, Haka	85,000
	Chin, Khumi	30,000
	Chin, Ngawn	5,000
	Chin, Tiddim	38,000
	Chinbok	21,000
	Chinese in Burma	600,000
	Dai	10,000
	Gheko	4,000
	Hallam	11,000
	Hrangkhol	8,500
	Intha	80,000
	Lama	3,000
	Maghi	300,000
	Moken (79)	5,000
	Mon	350,000
	Mun	10,000
	Norra	10,000
	Palaung (79)	150,000
	Purum	300
	Ralte	17,000
	Riang-Lang	20,000
	Senthang	10,000
	Taman	10,000
	Taungyo	159,200
	Tawr	700
	Yangbye	326,650
	Yinchia	4,000
	Yos	4,500
	Zome	30,000
Burundi	Pygmy (Binga)	30,000
Cameroon	Adamawa	380,000
	Budugum	10,000
	**Doohwaayo	15,000
	Duru	20,000

	Fulani (79)	250,000
	Gisei	10,000
	Gisiga	30,000
	Gude	100,000
	Kolbila	1,000
	Kotopo	10,000
	Laka	10,000
	Mambila	40,000
	Matakam	140,000
	Namshi	30,000
	Ndunpa Duupa	1,000
	Podokwo	25,000
	Tigon	25,000
	Voko	1,000
	**Wimbum	50,000
	Yinga	300
Canada	**Chinese in Vancouver B.C.	80,000
	Jews of Montreal	120,300
	Jews, Sephardic	26,600
Central African Empire	Pygmy (Binga)	2,000
Chad	Abou Charib	25,000
	Bagirmi	40,000
	Bilala	42,000
	Bomou	15,000
	Bua	20,000
	Daju of Dar Dadju	27,000
	Daju of Dar Sila	33,000
	Danqaleat	20,000
	Gabri	20,000
	Gambai	200,000
	Gidar	50,000
	Golo	3,400
	Goulai	30,000
	Gula	2,500
	Jongor	16,000
	Kanembu	2,250
	Karanga	57,000
	Kari	40,000
	Kenga	25,000
	Kera	5,000
	Kibet	22,000
	Kim	5,000
	Koke	1,000
	Kotoko	31,000
	Kuka	38,000
	Laka	40,000
	Lele	30,000
	Maba	56,000
	Majingai-Ngama	47,000
	Mangbai	2,000
	Mararit	42,000
	Marba	30,000
	Masa	80,000
	Masalit	73,500
	Massalat	23,000
	Mbai	73,000
	Mbum	20,000
	Mesme	28,000
	Mesmedje	11,000
	Mimi	15,000
	Mogum	6,000
	Mubi	36,000
	Mundang	100,000
	Musei	60,000
	Musgu	75,000
	Nancere	35,000
	Nielim	2,000
	Ouaddai	320,000
	Rataning	10,000

	Fungo	13,068
	Sarwa	400
	Somrai	50,000
	Sungor	39,000
	Tama	60,000
	Tana	35,600
	Teda (80)	10,000
	Tunya	880
	Tupuri	12,000
	Zaghawa	61,000
Chile	Mapuche	300,000
China	Ach'ang	10,300
	Buriat	26,500
	Burig	148,000
	Ch'iang	77,000
	Chin	95,500
	Chingp'o	101,850
	Chungchia	1,500,000
	C'wang	7,785,410
	Dagur	22,600
	Evenki	7,200
	Hani	138,000
	Hui (80)	5,200,000
	Jyarung	70,000
	Kalmytz	70,000
	Kam	825,320
	Kelao	23,000
	Khalka	68,000
	Kham	11,400
	Kirchiz	68,000
	Lahul	1,600
	Laka	6,000
	Lati	450
	Li	1,000,000
	Lu	400,000
	Manchu	200,000
	Mongour	50,000
	Nahsi	155,750
	Nanai	1,000
	Nosu	556,000
	Nung	100,000
	Oirat	60,000
	Oronchon	2,400
	Paongan	8,000
	Pu-I	1,311,020
	Punu	220,000
	Rawang	60,000
	Salar	31,000
	Santa	155,500
	Sibo	21,000
	Sui	160,310
	*Tibetans	3,000,000
	Uigur (80)	4,800,000
	Wa	286,160
	Yellow Uighur	4,000
	Yuku	4,000
Colombia	Achagua	100
	Andoque	100
	Barasano	400
	Barasano, Northern	450
	Barasano, Southern	400
	Bora	400
	Cacua	150
	Camsa	2,000
	Carapana	200
	Chami	3,000
	Cofan	250
	Cogui	4,000
	**Coreguaje	500

	Coreguaje	500
	Cubeo	2,000
	Cuiba	2,000
	*Cuna (79)	600
	Cuna	600
	Curipaco	2,500
	Embera, Northern	2,000
	Guajibo	15,000
	*Guajiro	60,000
	Guambiano	9,000
	*Guanano (79)	800
	Guayabero	700
	Guayabevo	600
	Huitoto, Meneca	600
	Hupda Maku	150
	Ica	3,000
	Inga	6,000
	Macu	1,000
	Macuna	300
	Malayo	1,000
	Motilon	2,000
	Muinane	150
	***Paez	40,000
	Palenquero	3,000
	Piapoco	3,000
	Quaiquer	5,000
	Saija	2,500
	Saliba	900
	Siona	250
	Siriano	600
	Tanimuca-Retuama	300
	**Tatuyo	300
	Tunebo, Cobaria	2,000
	*Yucuna	500
	Yukpa	2,500
	Yuruti	150
Comoros	*Comorians (79)	300,000
Costa Rica	Chinese in Costa Rica	5,000
Ecuador	Cayapa	3,000
	Secoya	460
	**Tsachila	1,100
Egypt	**African Students in Cairo	700
Ethiopia	Afar (79)	300,000
	Alaba	50,000
	Amar	22,500
	Anuak	52,000
	Arbore	2,000
	Argobba	3,000
	Awngi	50,000
	Basketo	9,000
	Beja	39,000
	Bencho	5,000
	Bilen	32,000
	Boran	132,600
	Burji	20,000
	Bussa	1,000
	Chara	1,000
	Dathanik	18,000
	Dime	2,000
	Dorze	3,000
	**Falasha (79)	30,000
	*Gabbra	nr
	*Galla (Bale)	750,000
	Galla of Bucho	1,500
	Galla, Harar	1,305,400
	Gawwada	4,000
	Gedeo	250,000
	**Ghimeera	50,000
	Gidicho	500

	Gobato	1,000
	Gobeze	22,000
	Gumuz	53,000
	Gurage (80)	750,000
	Hadiyya	700,000
	Harari	13,000
	Janjero	1,000
	Kachama	500
	*Kaffa (80)	320,000
	Kao	600
	Kembata	250,000
	*Komo	20,000
	Konso	30,000
	Koyra	5,000
	Kullo	82,000
	Kunama	70,000
	Langa	2,000
	*Lango	8,000
	Maji	15,000
	Male	12,000
	Mao, Northern	13,000
	*Masengo	7,000
	Me'en	38,000
	Mesengo	28,000
	***Mocha	170,000
	Mursi	6,000
	Nao	5,000
	Nara	25,000
	*Nuer	70,000
	Oyda	3,000
	Reshiat	10,000
	***Shankilla (Kazza)	20,000
	Sheko	23,000
	Shinasha	4,000
	Sidamo	857,000
	Somali	1,000,000
	**Suri	30,000
	Tsamai	7,000
	Walamo	908,000
	Wetawit	28,000
	Yidinit	600
	Zayse	21,000
	Zilmamu	3,000
Fiji	Indians in Fiji (79)	265,000
France	Algerian Arabs in France	804,000
	**Chinese Refugees, France (79)	100,000
	*Chinese Restaurant Wrkrs.	50,000
	**Portuguese in France	150,000
	*University Students (79)	800,000
Gambia	Bayot	4,000
	Dyola	216,000
	Fula, Cunda	70,200
	Krio	3,000
	Mandyak	85,000
	Soninke	10,000
	Wolof, Gambian	64,800
German Federal Rep.	*Chinese in West Germany	5,200
	***Koreans in Germany	10,000
	Turkish Immigrant Workers (79)	1,200,000
	*University Students (79)	850,000
Ghana	Birifor	40,000
	Builsa	97,000
	**Busanse	50,000
	***Chakossi	22,000
	Chinese Merchants	40
	Dagari	200,000
	**Dagomba	350,000
	Fra-Fra	230,000
	*Fulbe	5,500

	Gonja	108,000
	Grunshi	200,000
	Gurensi	250,000
	**Kasena	70,000
	Koma	1,000
	Konkomba	175,000
	**Kusaasi	150,000
	Ligbi	6,000
	Mamprusi	80,000
	Mo	13,000
	Moba	80,000
	Muslim Community of Bawku	20,000
	**Nafaara (79)	40,000
	Nawuri	10,000
	Nchimburu	7,000
	Ntrubs	5,000
	**Sisaala	60,000
	Tampulma	8,000
	Vagala	3,000
	Wala	60,000
	Zowla	800,000
Guatemala	**Black Caribs, Guatemala	1,500
	Chuj of San Mateo Ixtatan	17,000
	Ixil	45,000
	**K'anjobal of San Miguel	18,000
	**Mam Indian	470,000
	**Mopan Maya	2,000
	**Quiche (79)	500,000
	Rabinal-Achi	21,000
Guinea	Fula	1,500,000
	Gbande	66,000
	Kissi	266,000
	Loma	180,000
Guinea-Bissau	Balante	100,000
	Banyun	15,000
	Biafada	15,000
	**Bijogo	25,000
	Diola (80)	15,000
	**Manjaco	80,000
Honduras	**Black Caribs, Honduras	20,000
Hong Kong	Chinese Businessmen	10,000
	Chinese Factory Workers	500,000
	**Chinese in Hong Kong	4,135,000
	Chinese Villagers	500,000
	*Factory Workers, Young	40,000
	**High School Students	453,000
	*New Terrestories People	1,400,000
India	Abujmaria	11,000
	***Adi	80,300
	***Adivasis of Dang	95,000
	Adiyan	2,500
	Agariya	11,790
	Ahir	132,520
	Aimol	110
	Ajmeri	580
	Aka	2,257
	*Alars	400
	Allar	350
	Anal	6,590
	Andha	64,650
	Anga	423,500
	**Apatani	11,900
	Aranadan	600
	*Arnatas	700
	Arya	2,590
	Asuri	4,540
	Babri	9,700
	Badagu	104,920
	Bagelkhandi	231,230

Baghati	3,980
Bahawalpuri	640
Baiga	11,110
Balti	40,140
Bangaru	4,000,000
Bareli	230,030
Bathudi	73,890
Bazigar	100
Bediya	32,200
Bete	2,960
Bhakta	55,150
Bharia	5,380
Bhatneri	190
Bhattri	103,770
Bhilala	246,720
**Bhils (79)	800,000
Bhoyari	5,390
Bhuiya	4,430
Bhumij	48,240
Bhunjia	5,240
Bihari	23,220
Bijori	2,390
Binjhwari	48,800
Birhor	590
Bodo	509,010
**Bodo Kachari	610,000
Bondo	2,370
Braj	6,000,000
Bunan	2,000
Burig	132,200
Caste Hindus (Andra Prd)	44,000,000
Chakma	68,710
Chamari	5,320
***Chamars of Bundelkhand	nr
Chameali	52,970
Chenchu	17,610
Chero	28,370
Chik-Barik	30,040
Chiru	3,060
Chodhari	138,980
Chola Naickans	100
Churahi	34,670
Dawoodi Muslims	225,000
Deori	14,940
Dhanka	10,230
Dhanwar	21,140
**Dhodias	300,000
Dimasa	37,900
Dorli	24,320
**Dubla	202,218
Gadaba	20,410
Gaddi	70,220
Galong	36,860
Gamti	136,210
Gangte	6,030
Gawari	21,100
*Gonds	4,000,000
*Gorkha	180,000
Grasia	27,160
Halbi	349,260
Harauti	334,380
Ho	749,800
Holiya	3,090
***Irulas	10,000
Jagannathi	1,310
Jains	2,000,000
Jatapu	36,450
Jaunsari	56,560
Jharia	2,060

Juang	12,170
Kachchi	470,990
Kadar	800
Kahluri	66,190
Kaikadi	11,850
**Kaipeng-Koloi	30,000
Kamar	10,110
*Kanarese	21,707,000
Kanauri	28,500
Kanikkaran	10,000
Kanjari	55,390
**Karbis	300,000
Karmali	69,620
**Kashmiri Muslims (79)	3,060,000
Katakari	4,950
Kawar	33,770
Keer	2,890
Khamti	300
Khandesi	14,700
Kharia	88,900
Khasi	384,010
Khirwar	34,250
Khojas, Agha Khani	175,000
Khowar	6,960
Kisan	73,850
Kishanganjia	56,920
Kishtwari	12,170
Koda	14,140
Kol	82,900
**Kolam	60,000
Kom	6,970
***Kond	900,000
Konda-Dora	15,650
Konkani	1,522,680
Koraga	1,500
*Korku	250,000
Korwa	14,250
Kota	860
Kotia	15,000
Kotta	1,200
Koya	211,880
*Kudisai Vagh Makkal	1,000,000
Kudiya	100
*Kuknas	125,000
**Kuluis	200,000
Kumauni	1,234,940
Kupia	4,000
Kurichiya	12,130
Kuruba	7,900
Kurux	1,240,400
Kuvi	190,000
Labans	nr
Labhani	1,203,340
*Labourers of Jhoparpatti	1,500
Ladakhi	56,740
**Lahaulis	18,000
Lalung	10,650
Lodhi	44,070
Lushai	270,310
Mahali	14,300
Majhwar	27,960
Mala Muthas	1,000
Malankuravan	5,000
Malapandaram	500
Malappanackers	1,000
Malaryan	5,000
Malavedan	2,000
*Malayalars	nr
Mali	970

Malki	88,650
Malpaharia	9,080
Malvi	644,030
Mangs	nr
Manna-Dora	8,480
Mannan	4,980
Mara	11,870
Maria	78,500
Marwari	6,807,650
Mavchi	44,240
*Meitei (79)	700,000
**Mejah	5,500
Meos of Rajasthan (80)	500,000
**Miching	259,551
Mina	764,850
Mirdha	5,820
Mishmi	5,230
Monpa	22,000
Mualthuam	2,000
Multani	15,690
Mundari	770,920
**Mundas	25,000
Muria	12,900
Muthuvan	7,000
Muwasi	21,120
Naga, Angami	34,430
Naga, Ao	56,390
Naga, Kalyokengnyu	14,410
Naga, Konyak	72,340
Naga, Kuki	30,250
Naga, Lotha	36,950
Naga, Mao	19,970
Naga, Nruanghmei	48,600
Naga, Sangtam	20,000
Naga, Sema	65,230
Naga, Tangkhul	58,170
Naga, Wancho	28,650
Nagar	7,090
Nihali	1,170
Nimadi	794,250
***Nocte	19,400
Ojhi	1,070
Ollari	800
Ong	200
Oriya	19,726,750
Pahari Garhwali	1,277,150
Paite	27,520
Paliyan	590
Panika	30,690
Paniyan	6,330
Pao	15,860
Pardhan	450
Parengi	3,000
*Parsees	120,000
Patelia	23,210
Pengo	1,250
Pnar	82,500
Rabha	10,000
*Rava	45,000
Riang	74,930
Sadan	807,180
**Saiva Vellala	1,500,000
*Shourastra	200,000
Sikkimese	36,580
*Sindhis of India	3,000,000
Sondwari	31,490
Sora	221,710
Sulung	nr
***Tagin	25,000

Takankar	10,960
Tamaria	5,050
*Tamil Brahmins	98,112,000
**Tangsa	10,700
Thado	42,340
Thakur	99,000
Thar	8,790
*Tibetan Refugees	nr
Toda	770
Tokkaru	1,298,860
Totis	nr
**Tripuri	400,000
Tugara	43,680
Tulu	1,156,950
Ullatan	1,500
Urali	1,080
Vaiphei	12,210
Vishavan	150
**Vohras of Yavatmal	10,000
Waddar	35,900
Wagdi	756,790
**Wanchoo	nr
Yanadi	205,380
Yerava	10,870
Yerukala	67,550
Zangskari	5,000
Zoliang	50,000
Zome	30,000

Indonesia

Abau	3,390
Achehnese (80)	2,200,000
Aghu	3,000
Aibondeni	150
Aikwakai	400
Airo-Sumaghaghe	2,000
Airoran	350
Alas	30,000
Alor, Kolana	90,000
Amanab	2,800
Ambai	6,000
Amber	300
Amberbaken	5,000
Ambonese	80,000
Ansus	3,000
Ara	75,000
Arandai	2,000
Arguni	200
Asienara	700
*Asmat (79)	30,000
Awyi	400
Awyu	18,000
Baburiwa	160
Baham	500
Bajau, Indonesian	50,000
Balantak	125,000
Balinese	2,000,000
Banggai	200,000
Barau	150
Bare'e	325,000
*Batak, Angkola (80)	nr
Batak, Karo	400,000
Batak, Simalungun	800,000
Batak, Toba	1,600,000
Bedoanas	250
Berik	800
Biak	40,000
Biksi	200
Bimanese	300,000
Bingkokak	150,000
***Bipim	450

Bira	75,000
Bonerif	100
Bonggo	430
Borai	1,000
Brat	20,000
Bual	150,000
Bugis (80)	3,500,000
Buli	1,000
Bunak	50,000
Bungku	180,000
Buru	6,000
Busami	350
Butung	200,000
**Chinese in Indonesia	3,600,000
Cirebon	2,500,000
***Citak	6,500
Citak	6,000
Dabra	100
Dagada	30,000
*Dani, Baliem (79)	50,000
Dem	2,000
Demta	840
Dubu	130
Duvele	500
Ekagi	100,000
Emumu	1,100
Endeh	34,000
Enggano	400
Erokwanas	250
Foau	230
Fordat	9,770
Gane	1,500
Gayo (80)	200,000
Gesa	200
Gorontalo	500,000
Havunese	40,000
Helong	5,000
Iha	5,500
Inanwatan	1,100
Irahutu	4,000
Iresim	100
Iria	850
Itik	100
Iwur	1,000
Jamden	14,330
**Javanese (rural) (79)	60,000,000
**Javanese of Central Java	20,000,000
**Javanese of Pejompongan	5,000
Kaeti	4,000
Kaili	300,000
Kaiwai	600
Kajang	50,000
Kambera	200,000
Kamberataro	970
Kamoro	8,000
Kampung Baru	400
Kamtuk-Gresi	5,000
Kanum	320
Kapori	60
Karas	200
Karon Dori	5,000
Karon Pantai	2,500
Kasuweri	1,200
Kati, Northern	8,000
Kati, Southern	4,000
Kaugat	1,000
Kaure	800
Kavwol	500
Kawe	300

Kayagar	9,000
Kaygir	4,000
Kayupulau	570
Kei	30,000
Kemak	50,000
Kendari	500,000
Kenyah	37,500
Kerinchi	170,000
Kimaghama	3,000
*Kimyal	7,000
Kodi	25,000
Koneraw	300
Korapun	4,000
Kotogut	1,000
Kubu (80)	6,000
Kurudu	1,100
Kwansu	350
Kwerba	2,000
Kwesten	2,480
Lampung (80)	1,500,000
Lara	12,000
Latdwalam	860
Laudje	125,000
Lebong	nr
Letti	6,000
Lio	100,000
**Loho Loho	10,000
Loinang	100,000
Lore	140,000
Lubu	1,000,000
Luwu	500,000
Maanyan	15,000
Madik	1,000
Madurese (79)	7,000,000
Mairasi	1,000
Makasai	70,000
Makian, West	12,000
Maklew	120
Mambai	80,000
Mandar	302,000
Mander	100
Manem	400
Manggarai	251,000
**Manikion	8,000
Mantion	12,000
Marau	1,200
Marind	7,000
Marind, Bian	900
Masenrempulu	250,000
Matbat	550
Mawes	690
Meax	10,000
Mekwei	1,200
Mentawi	50,000
*Mimika	10,000
Minangkabau (80)	5,000,000
Moi	4,000
Molof	200
Mombum	250
Mongondow	400,000
Moni	20,000
Mor	1,000
Mori	200,000
Morwap	300
Muna	200,000
Munggui	650
Nabi	550
Nafri	1,630
Naltya	7,000

Ndao	2,160
Ndom	450
Nduga	10,000
Ngada	40,000
Ngalik, North	35,000
Ngalik, Southern	5,000
Ngalum	10,000
Nias	230,000
Nimboran	3,500
Ninggrum	3,500
Nisa	250
Njadu	9,000
Onin	600
Ormu	750
Ot Danum	30,000
Palembang	500,000
Pantu	9,000
Papuma	700
Pisa	3,500
Pitu Uluna Salu	175,000
Pom	1,700
Puragi	900
Pyu	100
Ratahan	150,000
Redjang (80)	300,000
Riantana	1,100
Rotti	80,000
Saberi	1,500
Sadang	50,000
Samarkena	750
Sangir	145,000
Sangke	250
Sasak (80)	1,600,000
Sause	500
**Sawi	2,800
Sekar	450
Seko	275,000
Sempan	2,000
Senggi	120
Sentani	10,000
Serawai	60,000
Serui-Laut	1,000
Siagha-Yenimu	3,000
Sikhule	20,000
Sikka	100,000
Sobei	1,400
Solor	131,000
*Somahai	3,000
Somahai	1,500
Sowanda	1,100
Sumba	400,000
Sumbawa	114,000
**Sundanese (80)	20,000,000
Tadjio	100,000
Tahit	6,000
Taikat	600
Tamagario	3,500
Tanahmerah	3,200
Tandia	350
Taori-Kei	140
Tara	125,000
Tarof	600
Tarpia	560
Taurap	160
Tengger	400,000
Ternate	42,000
Tidore	26,000
Timorese	300,000
Tiro	75,000

Toala	100
Tombulu	40,000
Tomini	50,000
Tondanou	35,000
Tonsea	90,000
Tontemboa	140,000
Toradja	250,000
Towei	120
Tukude	45,000
Tumawo	350
Turu	800
Uhunduni	14,000
Uria	1,200
Uruangnirin	250
Vaikino	14,000
Wabo	900
Wambon	2,000
Wandamen	4,000
Wanggom	1,000
Wano	1,700
Warembori	350
Waris	1,480
Warkay-Bipim	250
Waropen	6,000
Weda	900
Wewewa	55,000
Wodani	3,000
Woi	1,300
Wolio	25,000
Yafi	180
Yahadian	700
Yaly	12,000
Yaur	350
Yava	4,500
Yei	1,000
Yelmek	400
Yeretuar	250
Yonggom	2,000
Yotafa	2,460

Iran	
Afshars	290,000
Agajanis	1,000
**Ahl-i-Haqq in Iran (79)	500,000
Arab-Jabbari (Kamesh)	13,000
Arab-Shaibani (Kamesh)	16,000
Arabs of Khuzestan	520,000
Azerbaijani Turks (80)	6,000,000
Baharlu (Kamesh)	7,500
Bakhtiaris (80)	590,000
Baluchi (80)	1,100,000
Bayats	nr
Bovir-Ahmadi	110,000
Galeshis	2,000
Gilakis	1,950,000
Goudari	2,000
Hezareh	nr
Inallu	5,000
Jamshidis	1,000
Jews of Iran	93,000
Kazakhs (80)	3,000
Khalaj	20,000
Kurds in Iran (80)	2,000,000
Lors (80)	600,000
Mamasani	110,000
Mazandaranis	1,620,000
Moqaddam	1,000
Nafar	3,500
Pashtuns (80)	3,000
Persians of Iran (80)	2,000,000
Pishagchi	1,000

	Qajars	3,000
	Qara'i	2,000
	Qaragozlu	2,000
	Qashqa'i (80)	350,000
	Sasanis	1,000
	Shahsavans (80)	180,000
	Tajik (80)	15,000
	Takestani	220,000
	Talish	20,000
	Teimuri	10,000
	Teimurtash	7,000
	Turkomans (80)	550,000
Israel	Druzes (79)	33,000
	*Jewish Imgrnts.-American	25,797
	*Jewish Imgrnts.-Argentine	17,686
	*Jewish Imgrnts.-Australia	1,257
	*Jewish Imgrnts.-Brazilian	4,005
	*Jewish Imgrnts.-Mexican	1,065
	*Jewish Imgrnts.-Uruguayan	2,720
	*Jewish Immigrants, Other	5,520
	Targum	5,000
Ivory Coast	Abe	28,500
	Abidji	23,000
	Abure	25,000
	Adyukru	50,450
	Akan, Brong	50,000
	Aladian	14,770
	Attie	160,000
	Avikam	7,940
	Bakwe	5,060
	Bambara	1,000,000
***Baoule		1,200,000
	Bete	350,000
	Dan	245,000
	Dida	115,000
	Dyimini	42,000
	Ebrie	50,000
	Eotile	4,000
	Gagu	25,000
***Godie		20,000
**Gouro		200,000
	Guere	117,870
	.Gwa	8,300
	Hwela-Numu	50,000
	Kouya	5,690
	*Krahn	250,000
	Krobou	3,400
	Kulango	60,000
	Kulele	15,000
	Ligbi	20,000
	Lobi	40,000
	Maou	80,000
	Mo	800
	Mona	5,570
	Moru	10,000
	Neyo	5,000
	*Ngen	20,000
	Ngere	150,000
	Nyabwa-Nyedebwa	21,000
	Nzema	24,080
	Oubi	1,340
	Palara	10,000
	Pye	6,120
	Senufo (80)	300,000
	Tagwana	43,000
	*Teenbu	5,000
	Tepo	20,000
	Trepo	3,400
	Tura	19,230

	Vagla	6,000
	Wan	10,000
	Wobe	40,000
	Yaoure	12,700
Japan	*Chinese in Japan	50,000
	*Chinese in Osaka, Japan	9,000
	*College Students in Japan	350,000
	Farmers of Japan	24,988,740
	*Industry Laborers-Japan	21,000,000
	*Inland Sea Island Peoples	1,000,000
	*Koreans of Japan	600,000
	*Ryukyuan	1,000,000
	Soka Gakkai Believers	6,500,000
	**Stud. Osaka Christ. Coll.	1,100
	**Univ. Students of Japan	2,000,000
Jordan	Muslims of Jordan	1,000,000
Kampuchea, Democratic	*Cham (Western) (80)	90,000
Kenya	Dorobo	22,000
	El Molo	1,000
	Gabbra	12,000
	Giryama	335,900
	**Maasai (79)	100,000
	**Saguye	30,000
	Samburu	60,500
	Somali, Ajuran (79)	25,374
	Somali, Degodia	68,667
	Somali, Gurreh	54,165
	Somali, Ogadenya	99,129
	Suk	133,200
	Turkana	224,000
	**Turkana Fishing Community (79)	20,000
Korea, Republic of	**Apartment Residents-Seoul	87,000
	**Bus Drivers, South Korea	26,000
	*Chinese in Korea	35,000
	Indust.Workers Yongdungpo	140,000
	*Japanese in Korea	5,000
	**Korean Prisoners	45,000
Laos	Alak	8,000
	Brao (79)	18,000
	*Chinese in Laos	25,000
	Galler	50,000
	Jeng	500
	Kasseng	15,000
	*Lao (79)	1,908,600
	Loven	25,000
	Ngeq	50,000
	Nyaheun	15,000
	Oi	10,000
	Phu Thai	100,000
	So	15,000
	Ta-Oi	15,000
	Vietnamese	20,000
Lebanon	Ladinos	7,300
Lesotho	***Basotho, Mountain (79)	70,000
Liberia	Bandi	32,000
	*Bassa	200,000
	*Dewein	5,000
	Gio	92,000
	**Grebo	65,000
	*Kissi	35,000
	**Kowaao	7,000
	Kpelle	200,000
	***Krahn	55,000
	Loma	60,000
	Mandingo (79)	30,000
	Mano	65,000
	Sapo	30,000
	*Vai (80)	30,000
Libya	Libyans	2,300,000

Macau	*Chinese Refugees in Macau	10,000
Malawi	**Yao	600,000
Malaysia	**Bidayuh of Sarawak	110,000
	*Chinese in Malaysia	3,555,879
	**Chinese in Sabah	180,000
	**Chinese in Sarawak	330,000
	*Chinese of W. Malaysia	3,500,000
	**Melanau of Sarawak (80)	61,000
	Musl_m Malays (80)	5,500,000
	**Orang Asli	337,395
	**Selakau of Sarawak	5,300
	**Sugut	10,000
	***Tamil Plantation Workers	137,150
	*Tamils (Indian)	600,000
Maldives	Divehi (80)	120,000
Mali	Bambara	1,000,000
	*Dogon (79)	312,000
	Kagoro	30,000
	Kita	150,000
	Minianka	300,000
Mexico	***Azteca (79)	250,000
	***Ch'ol Sabanilla	20,000
	Ch'ol Tila	38,000
	Chamula (79)	50,000
	**Huave	18,000
	**Mazahua	150,000
	**Mixes	60,000
	*Mixteco,San Juan Mixtepic	15,000
	*Nahua, North Pueblo	55,000
	Yaquis	14,000
	Zinacantecos (79)	10,000
Mozambique	Chuabo	250,000
	Lomwe	1,000,000
	Makua	1,200,000
	Yao	220,000
Namibia	Bushmen (Heikum)	16,000
	*Bushmen (Kung) (79)	10,000
Nepal	*Bhojpuri	806,480
	Gurung	172,000
	**Magar	300,000
	Maithili	1,000,000
	*Nepali	6,060,758
	*Newari	500,000
	Rai	232,000
	*Rai, Danuwar	12,000
	Rajbansi	15,000
	**Santhali	nr
	*Sherpa	20,000
	*Tamang	nr
	Tharu	495,000
Netherlands	Ambonese	30,000
	*Chinese in Amsterdam	15,000
	*Chinese in Holland	35,000
New Zealand	*Chinese in New Zealand	9,500
Niger	Dyerma (80)	1,000,000
	Kurfei	50,000
	Mauri	100,000
	Tuareg (79)	200,000
Nigeria	Abanyom	3,850
	Abong	1,000
	Abua	24,000
	Achipa	3,600
	*Afawa (80)	10,000
	**Afo (80)	25,000
	Agoi	3,650
	Agwagwune	20,000
	Ake	300
	Akpa-Yache	15,000
	Alago	35,000

Alege	1,200
Amo	3,550
Anaang	246,000
Angas	100,000
Ankwe	10,000
Arawa	200,000
Aten	4,000
Ayu	4,000
**Babur Thalı (80)	75,000
Bachama	20,000
Bada	10,000
Bade	100,000
Bali	1,000
Bambuka	10,000
Bandawa-Minda	10,000
Banga	8,000
Bariba	55,000
Basakomo	60,000
Bashar	20,000
**Bassa	100,000
Bata	26,400
Batu	25,000
Baushi	2,650
Bekwarra	34,000
Berom	116,000
Bette-Bende	36,800
Bile	1,000
Binawa	2,000
Bitare	3,000
Boghom	50,000
Bokyi	87,000
Bole	32,000
Buduma	80,000
Bunu	150,000
Burak	2,000
Busa (80)	50,000
Butawa	20,000
Chakfem-Mushere	5,000
Chamba Daka	66,000
Chamba Leko	30,000
Chawai	30,000
Chip	6,000
Chokobo	425
Dadiya	2,300
*Daka	10,000
Dass	8,830
Degema	10,000
Deno	10,000
Dera	20,000
*Dghwede	13,000
Dirim	11,000
Dirya	3,750
Duguir	12,000
Duguza	2,000
**Duka	10,000
Dyerma	50,000
Ebira	325,000
Edo	430,000
Efik	26,300
Efutop	10,000
Eggon	80,000
Ejagham	100,000
Ekajuk	15,000
Eket	22,000
Ekpeye	30,000
Eleme	16,000
Emai-Iuleha-Ora	48,000
Engenni	10,000
Epie	12,000

Esan	200,000
Etulo	2,900
Evant	5,000
**Fakai	15,000
**Fali	25,000
Fyam	14,000
Fyer	3,000
Gaanda	10,000
Gade	25,000
Galambi	1,000
Gbari (80)	500,000
Gbaya	350,000
Geji	2,650
Gera	13,300
Geruma	4,700
Ghotuo	9,000
**Glavda	19,000
Goemai	80,000
Gokana	54,000
Gude	40,000
Gudu	1,200
Guduf	21,300
Gure-Kahugu	5,000
Guruntum-Mbaaru	10,000
Gwandara	25,000
Gwari Matai	200,000
***Higi	150,000
Hwana	20,000
Hyam	60,000
Ibaji	20,000
Ibibio	2,000,000
Icen	7,000
Idoma	300,000
Idoma, North	56,000
Igala	350,000
Igbira (80)	400,000
Igede	70,000
Ihceve	5,000
Ijo, Central-Western	338,700
Ijo, Northeast	395,300
Ijo, Northeast Central	8,400
Ikulu	6,000
Ikwere	200,000
Irigwe	15,000
Isekiri	33,000
Isoko	20,000
Ivbie North-Okpela-Atte	20,000
Iyon	2,000
Izarek	30,000
**Izi	200,000
Jaba	60,000
Janjo	6,100
Jara	40,000
**Jarawa	150,000
Jera	23,000
Jerawa	70,000
*Jibu	20,000
Jimbin	1,500
Jukun	20,000
Kadara	40,000
Kagoma	6,250
Kaibu	650
Kaka	2,000
Kamantan	5,000
*Kambari (80)	100,000
Kamo	3,000
*Kamuku (80)	20,000
Kana	90,000
Kanuri (80)	3,000,000

Karekare	39,000
Kariya	2,200
Katab	32,370
Khana	90,000
Kilba	80,000
Kirifi	14,000
Koenoem	3,000
Kofyar	40,000
Kohumono	11,870
Koma	15,000
Kono	1,550
Koro	35,000
Korop	10,000
Kuda-Chamo	4,000
Kugbo	2,000
Kukele	31,700
Kulere	8,000
Kulung	15,000
Kushi	4,000
Kuteb	26,000
Kuturmi	2,950
Kuzamani	1,000
Kwa	1,000
Kyibaku	20,000
Laamang	40,000
Lakka	500
Lame	2,000
Laru	1,000
Lebgo	30,000
Lo	2,000
Longuda	32,000
Lotsu-Piri	2,000
Lungu	10,000
Madda	30,000
***Maguzawa (79)	100,000
Mama	20,000
Mandara	19,300
Marghi Central	135,000
Matakam	2,000
Mbe	14,300
Mbembe (Tigong)	2,900
Mboi	3,200
Mbula-Bwazza	7,900
Migili	10,000
Miya	5,200
Mober	44,800
Montol	20,000
Mumbake	10,000
Mumuye	200,000
Nandu-Tari	4,000
Naraguta	3,000
Nde-Nsele-Nta	10,000
Ndoe	3,000
**Ndoro	10,000
**Ngamo	18,000
Ngizim	39,200
Ngwoi	1,000
Ninzam	35,000
Nkem-Nkum	16,700
Numana-Nunku Gwantu	15,000
Nungu	25,000
**Nupe	600,000
Nzanyi	14,000
Obanliku	19,800
Obolo	70,000
Odual	9,000
Odut	700
Ogbia	22,000
Okobo	11,200

Okpamheri	30,000	
Olulumo-Ikom	9,250	
Oring	25,000	
Oron	48,300	
Otank	3,000	
Pai	2,000	
Pero	20,000	
Piti	1,600	
Piya	2,500	
Polci	6,150	
Pongu	3,680	
Puku-Geeri-Keri-Wipsi	15,000	
Reshe	30,000	
Rukuba	50,000	
Rumaya	1,800	
Ruruma	2,200	
Sanga	5,000	
Sasaru-Enwan Igwe	3,780	
Saya	50,000	
Sha	500	
Shanga	5,000	
Shuwa Arabic	100,000	
Siri	2,000	
Sukur	10,000	
Sura	40,000	
Surubu	1,950	
Tal	10,000	
Tambas	3,000	
Tangale	100,000	
Tarok	60,000	
Tera	46,000	
Tula	19,000	
Turkwam	6,000	
Ukpe-Bayobiri	12,000	
Ukwuani-Aboh	150,000	
Urhobo	340,000	
Utugwang	12,000	
Uvbie	6,000	
Uzekwe	5,000	
***Vere	20,000	
Vute	1,000	
Waja	30,000	
*Warjawa	70,000	
Wom	10,000	
**Yala	60,000	
Yandang	10,000	
Yeskwa	13,000	
Yungur	44,300	
**Zaranda Hill Peoples	10,000	
Zari	3,950	
not reported	Ukaan	18,000
Oman	Mahri	50,000
Pakistan	Bagri	20,000
	Bajania (79)	20,000
	Balmiki	20,000
	**Bhil	800,000
	Chitralis (79)	120,000
	**Gagre	40,000
	**Hunzakut (79)	10,000
	**Kafirs (79)	3,000
	**Kohli, Kutchi	50,000
	**Kohli, Tharadari	40,000
	**Kohli, Wadiara	40,000
	**Kohlis, Parkari	100,000
	Lohar	nr
	**Meghwar (79)	100,000
	Od	40,000
	Punjabis (80)	49,000,000
	Sochi	nr

	Swatis (79)	600,000
	Vagari	30,000
Panama	**Teribe	1,000
Papua New Guinea	**Ampeeli	1,000
	***Banaro	2,500
	**Hewa (79)	1,500
	Ka'mis	50
	*Kepas	5,000
	**Kunimaipa	9,000
	*Ningerum	3,000
	*Samo-Kubo	1,500
	**Suena	2,000
Peru	Achual	5,000
	Aguaruna	22,000
	Amahuaca	1,500
	Amarakaeri	500
	Amuesha	5,000
	Arabela	200
	Campa	5,000
	Candoshi	3,000
	Capanahua	500
	Cashibo	1,500
	Chamicuro	150
	**Chayahuita	6,000
	Cocama	18,000
	Cujareno	100
	Huachipaire	215
	Huambisa	5,000
	Huitoto, Murui	800
	Iquito	150
	Jaqaru	2,000
	Jebero	3,000
	Machiguenga	10,000
	Manu Park Panoan	200
	Mayoruna	1,000
	Morunahua	150
	Ocaina	250
	Orejon	300
	Piro	2,500
	**Quechua	3,000,000
	**Quechua, Huanco	275,000
	Sharanahua	1,500
	Shipibo	15,000
	Urarina	3,500
	Yagua	4,000
	Yaminahua	1,200
Philippines	Abaknon	10,000
	Aeta	500
	Agutaynon	7,000
	Alangan	6,000
	**Apayao	12,000
	*Ata of Davao	10,000
	Ati	1,500
	*Atta	1,000
	**Balangao	4,500
	Balangaw	5,000
	Bantuanon	50,000
	Batak, Palawan	390
	**Bilan	75,000
	*Bontoc, Central	20,000
	**Bontoc, Southern	12,000
	Buhid	6,000
	**Bukidnon	100,000
	Caluyanhon	30,000
	***Cebu, Middle-Class	500,000
	Cuyonon	49,000
	Davaweno	13,000
	*Dumagat , Casiguran	1,000
	Ga-Dang	5,500

Hanonoo	6,000
Ibanag	319
Ifuago, Antipolo	5,000
*Ifugao	95,000
**Ifugao (Kalangoya)	35,000
Ifugao in Cababuyan	4,000
Ifugao, Ambanad	15,000
Ifugao, Kiangan	25,000
Igorot	20,000
Ilongot	7,640
Insinai	10,000
*Int'l Stud., Los Banos	nr
Iraya	6,000
Isneg, Dibagat-Kabugao	10,000
Isneg, Karagawan	8,000
Itawit	15,000
-Itneg, Adasen	4,000
Itneg, Binongan	7,000
Itneg, Masadiit	7,500
Jama Mapun (80)	15,000
Kaagan	20,000
Kadaklan-Barlig Bontoc	4,000
**Kalagan	19,000
Kalinga, Kalagua	3,600
Kalinga, Limus-Linan	20,000
Kalinga, Quinaang	41,000
*Kalinga, Southern	11,000
**Kalinga,Northern	20,000
**Kankanay, Central	40,000
Kinaray-A	288,000
Maguindano (80)	700,000
**Mamanwa (Mamanua)	1,000
Mandaya	3,000
Mandaya, Mansaka	35,400
**Mangyan	60,000
Manobo, Agusan	15,000
Manobo, Ata	7,000
Manobo, Binokid	40,550
**Manobo, Cotabato	10,000
Manobo, Dibabawon	1,790
*Manobo, Ilianen	5,000
Manobo, Obo	4,000
**Manobo, Salug	4,000
Manobo, Sarangani	15,000
Manobo, Tagabawa	9,900
**Manobo, Tigwa	4,000
**Manobo, Western Bukidnon	12,000
Manobos, Pulangi	5,000
**Mansaka	25,000
Maranao (79)	500,000
Maranao, Lanad	500,000
*Molbog	5,000
Northern Cagayan Negrito	1,200
Palawano	3,000
Palawano, Central	3,000
Paranan	6,000
Porohanon	23,000
Sama Bangingi (80)	70,000
Sama Pangutaran (80)	15,000
Sama, Mapun	20,000
Sama, Siasi	100,000
Sama, Sibuku	11,000
Sama-Badjaw (79)	120,000
Sangil	7,500
**Subanen (Tuboy)	20,000
**Subanen, Sindangan (80)	80,000
Subanun,Lapuyan	25,000
**Suriguenos	23,000
Tadyawan	1,000

	**Tagbanwa, Aborlan	10,000
	Tagbanwa, Kalamian	4,500
	Tao't Bato	150
	Tausug (80)	500,000
	Tawbuid	6,000
	**Tboli	67,500
	Tiruray	30,000
	Yakan (80)	97,000
	Yogad	7,000
Puerto Rico	Chinese in Puerto Rico	200
Rhodesia	*Bushmen (Hiechware)	1,600
	*Indians In Rhodesia	9,600
	**Nambya	40,000
	**Ndebele (79)	1,000,000
	*Tonga	90,000
Senegal	Balanta	49,200
	Basari	8,000
	Diola	266,000
	Mancang	35,200
	Manding	208,400
	Manjack	44,200
	Maures	57,000
	Pular	281,900
	Sarakole (80)	67,600
	Serere (79)	700,000
	Tandanke	1,000
	Taucouleur (80)	464,700
	Wolof (80)	1,500,000
Seychelles	Seychellois	51,000
Sierra Leone	*Kissi	48,000
	**Kono	133,000
	**Koranko	103,000
	Limba	233,000
	Loko	80,000
	Mende	600,000
	**Temne (80)	1,000,000
	*Yalunka (80)	25,000
Sikkim	**Lepcha	18,000
Singapore	Malays of Singapore (79)	300,000
Somalia	Somali (79)	2,500,000
South Africa	*Chinese in South Africa	10,000
Soviet Russia	Bashkir (80)	1,200,000
	Karakalpak (80)	277,000
	Kirgiz (80)	1,700,000
	Tatars (80)	6,000,000
Spain	*Gypsies in Spain (79)	200,000
Sri Lanka	Moor Malays (79)	895,322
	Sinhalese	9,146,679
	Tamil (Ceylonese)	1,415,567
	**Tamils (Indian) (79)	1,195,368
Sudan	Anuak	30,000
	Boya	15,000
	Didinga	30,000
	Dinka	1,940,000
	Ingassana	35,000
	*Jiye	7,000
	Kichepo	16,000
	Koalib (79)	320,000
	Koroma	30,000
	Krongo	121,000
	*Lokoro	22,000
	**Lotuka	150,000
	Meban	130,000
	Murle	40,000
	*Nuer (79)	844,000
	Nyzatom	80,000
	*Topotha	60,000
	Uduk	7,000
Syria	*Alawites (79)	600,000

Taiwan	*Chinese (Hoklo) in Taiwan	11,470,000
	**Chinese Hakka of Taiwan (79)	1,750,000
	*Chinese Mainlanders	2,010,000
	Fishing Village People	150,000
	**Minnan Hoklo	11,625,000
	*Urban Workers in Taiwan	nr
	*Women Laborers	1,200,000
Tanzania	Arusha	110,000
	Barabaig (79)	49,000
	Burungi	20,000
	Dorobo	3,000
	Iraqw	218,000
	Kerewe	35,000
	Kwere	63,000
	Makonde	550,000
	Matumbi	72,000
	Nyamwezi (80)	590,000
	Safwa	102,000
	Sonjo	7,400
	Turu	316,000
	**Wajita	65,000
	*Wazinza	2,000
	Zaramo	296,000
Thailand	**Akha (79)	9,916
	*Cambodians	1,000,000
	*Chinese in Thailand	3,600,000
	Government officials	100,000
	Karen (79)	80,000
	Karen, Pwo	40,000
	*Khamu	6,300
	**Khmer Refugees	15,000
	*Kui	160,000
	*Lahu	22,500
	*Lao Refugees	20,000
	Lawa	10,000
	**Lepers of N.E. Thailand	390,000
	*Lisu	12,500
	*Mao Refugees from Laos	7,000
	**Meo	29,173
	Moken of Thailand	3,000
	Shan	300,000
	*So	8,000
	Thai Islam (Malay) (80)	1,700,000
	*Thai Islam (Thai)	600,000
	Thai Northern	6,000,000
	Thai of Bangkok	4,500,000
	Thai, North East	15,500,000
	Thai, Southern	4,000,000
	*Thailand Farmers (Ctl)	5,000,000
	Tin	25,000
	**Vietnamese Refugees	2,000
	**Yao (79)	19,867
Togo	Basari	100,000
	Chakossi	29,000
	Kabre	273,000
	*Konkomba	25,000
	Lamba	29,000
	Moba	70,000
	Tem	100,000
	Watchi	1,000,000
Trinidad and Tobago	**Indians, East (79)	400,000
Turkey	Abkhaz	12,400
	Circassian	113,370
	*Kurds of Turkey (79)	1,900,000
	Romany	20,000
	Turks, Anatolian	31,000,000
Turks and Caicos Islands	Chamorro	15,000
	Ulithi-Mall	2,000
	Woleat	1,000

REGISTRY OF THE UNREACHED

Uganda	Jiye	34,000
	Lugbara	260,000
	Muslims (West Nile Dist.)	45,000
United Arab Emirates	Muslims in U.A.E. (79)	202,000
	**Shihu	10,000
United Kingdom	**Chinese in United Kingdom	105,000
	**Chinese Students Glasgow	1,000
	Gujarati	300,000
	**Muslim Immigrants in U.K.	500,000
United States of America	**Chinese in United States	550,000
	Hopi	6,000
	**Japanese Students In USA	nr
	Jemez Pueblo	1,800
	*Overseas Chin. Port.	nr
	Paiute, Northern	5,000
	**Racetrack Residents (79)	50,000
	**Vietnamese in the USA	130,000
	Zuni	6,000
Upper Volta	Bwa (80)	140,000
	Fulah	300,000
	Gourency	300,000
	Mossi (80)	3,300,000
Venezuela	**Jivaro (Achuara)	20,000
	Yanomamo in Venezuela	nr
Viet Nam	Cham	45,000
	**Chrau	15,000
Yemen, Arab Republic	Yemenis (79)	5,600,000
Yugoslavia	*Bosnian (80)	1,740,000
Zaire	**Bakuba	75,000
	***Pakabeti of Equator	3,000
	*Pygmy (Mbuti) (79)	40,000
Zambia	*Nkoya	nr
	Tonga, Gwembe Valley (79)	86,000

Appendices

Appendices

APPENDIX A

GLOSSARY OF ISLAMIC TERMS

abangan
the name used to describe the less orthodox of soft-line Muslims of Indonesia.

adat
the name applied to the indigenous system of customary law in Indonesia.

Ahmadi, Ahmadiah
a heretical sect of Islam. The name is taken from the founder, Ghulam Ahmad Mirza, who claimed to have superseded Muhammad.

Ali

the son-in-law of the prophet Muhammad. He became the rallying point for the Shiah branch of Islam who believe Ali and his family were the rightful rulers of the Islamic world.

Allah

literally it means "The God," the name of the Supreme Being of the Muslims.

baraka

the blessing of God; that charisma that characterizes a person with special religious power.

Bektashi

a Sufi order (tariqa) which originated in Turkey stemming in its present forms from the 16th century. The brotherhood is to be found principally in the Balkans.

chador

a head-to-foot covering worn by Islamic women when in public in many Islamic countries.

Chistiya

a Sufi order (tariqa) active today in India and Pakistan.

dawah

the act of calling men to the path of Allah; the Islamic equivalent of missionary activity.

dervishes

a common Persian term for Sufis of any persuasion but referring especially to the poor or wandering Sufi who belongs to no established brotherhood (tariqa). Also known as fakirs. Associated with various ritual acts of ascetic nature such as whirling or mutilation that induce ecstatic states as part of a search for union with Allah.

din
the term for religion in Islam; it is applied to such religious duties as the five basic obligations of the Muslim.

dhikr
Sufi practices designed to foster the remembrance of Allah

dhimmis
protected minorities in Islamic lands who follow tolerated religions such as Judaism and Christianity.

Five Pillars of Islam
1. the witness or recitation of the creed.
2. the saying of prayers at the five specified times of day
3. the keeping of the fast during the month of Ramadan.
4. the giving of 1/40th of one's income to the poor, or for religious causes.
5. the pilgrimage to Mecca and its environs.

hadith
"tradition" in Islam, with regard to the reporting and recording of it; that which is transmitted is called the sunnah.

hajj
pilgrimage to Mecca and its environs during the sacred month of Ramadan; required of a Muslim once in his lifetime.

Hammal
a "deviationist" Sufi sect found in Mauritania practicing many extravagant dhikrs with convulsive movements and including women in many ceremonies.

Hanafi
a Sunni legal school of interpretation founded by Abu Hanifa (d. 767). It is considered relatively liberal and the most favorable to modern economic development. The most widespread school of Sunni Islam, predominating in Turkey and Asia.

Hanbali

a Sunni legal school founded by Ahmad b. Hanbal (d. 855). Considered the most conservative school of thought, being hostile to both speculative theology and Sufi mysticism. Rejects all innovation beyond the literal Quran and the sunna. Found only in central Arabia.

hijrah

the emigration of Muhammad and the Muslim community from Mecca to Medina in 622 A.D. The Muslim calendar commences from this date.

'id al adha

the major festival in Islam during which sheep, camels, or cattle are sacrificed; it is obligatory of any Muslim who can afford it.

'id al fitr

a major feast heralding the end of the month of the fast (Ramadan).

imam

the leader of the mosque prayers.

Imami

the school of law followed by the Twelver Shiah; it rejects jihad and the legal declarations of the Ummayyad caliphs, but is otherwise similar to the Sunni Hanafi school.

iman

the articles of faith in Islam; the act of faith as distinguished from the practice of faith or din.

Injil

the quranic term applied to the New Testament, incorrectly understood by Muslims to mean the book that God revealed to and through Jesus.

Isa
the Arabic term for the name of Jesus.

Ishmaeli, Ismaeli, Ismaili
a person belonging to a branch of Shiite Islam; taken from the name of the son of Abraham, Ishmael.

Islam
literally, submission or surrender; understood to mean surrender to Allah; the faith and practice of Muslim people.

Ithna Ashari
the majority Twelver sect of Shiah Islam in Iran. Believes the Divine Light given by God passed through a succession of 12 sinless imams beginning with Ali. The last disappeared in 878 but will return as the Mahdi (messiah) to institute the divine rule on earth.

jihad
exertion or militancy in the cause of Islam; holy war.

jinn
supernatural or angelic type beings, thought to be made of fire; generally understood to be more evil than good.

Kaabah
a cubic construction at Mecca considered the most sacred site of Islam. Prayers are directed toward the Kaabah and circumambulation about it is the culminating point of pilgrimage.

kadhi, qadhi
an Islamic religious judge.

kafir
the person who blasphemes, who says "no" to God, hence, one who rejects revelation in the Islamic sense.

Mahdi
> the rightly guided one; Muslims believe that such a one shall return or appear, particularly in Shiah Islam, to lead the whole world to embrace Islam.

Maliki
> a Sunni legal school founded by Malik ibn Anas (d. 795). Based on the hadith and only a limited use of the ijma (consensus of knowledgeable Islamic scholars). Concentrated in North and West Africa, upper Egypt and the Sudan.

marabout
> North African religious saint; a charismatic leader of a Muslim religious order.

mihrab
> the niche or slab in a prayer building indicating the direction of Mecca.

minbar
> the pulpit in the mosque.

mosque
> the anglicized word for *masjid,* the Muslim place of worship.

Mouric
> a Sufi order (tariqa), located principally in North and West Africa and the Sudan.

Muhammad
> the Arabian prophet (570-632) whose "recitations" serve as the basis for Islam as found in the Quran.

mullah
> a term applied to a Muslim religious leader.

Muslim
> one who has surrendered to God; a follower of the Islamic faith.

Naqshabandiya
a Sufi order (tariqa), found throughout the Muslim world

pir
a Sufi master or saint, able to lead disciples on the mystical way. Devotion to dead pirs is common in many parts of the Muslim world in connection with Sufi orders.

purdah
the practice of secluding women.

Qadiriya
a Sufi order (tariqa) found throughout the Muslim world.

Quran
the name of the sacred Scriptures of Islam; the book of the revelations which Muhammad understood he was to recite.

Ramadan, Ramadhan
the name of the sacred month in the Islamic (lunar) calendar during which a Muslim is supposed to fast from sunrise to sunset.

salat
ritual or liturgical prayer, performed five times a day.

santri
applied to orthodox Muslims in Indonesia.

Shafi
a Sunni legal school founded by Imam al-Shafi (d. 820). Stresses a liberal interpretation, consensus, and the prerogative of the community. Found in lower Egypt, western and southern Arabia, East Africa, and Indonesia.

sharia, shariah
the sacred law in Islam.

shaykh, sheik

the head of a religious brotherhood in Islam.

shia, shiah

literally, "the sect," a minority sect of Islam that arose over the question of who should succeed Muhammad; the followers of Ali.

shirk

association of anything with God; idolatry; the worst sin in Islam.

sufi

Muslim mystics; the word originally came from the word for "wool," because of the woolen garments worn by members of these orders.

sunnah

the path of tradition; the traditions of Muhammad and the community of Islam.

sunni

the major sect of Islam; those who follow the sunnah and the Quran.

sura, surah

the word applied to describe a chapter of the Quran.

tariqa

mystical and ascetic brotherhoods of aspirants who join together to follow the way (tariqa) of a saint (pir) who devises means to seek union with Allah. Over 70 major active brotherhoods are to be found today.

Tijaniya

a Sufi order (tariqa) found principally in North and West Africa and the Sudan.

Towrah
  the law which God gave to Moses.

ulama, ulamah
  the learned and scholarly men of Islam; those who define and
  protect Islamic orthodoxy.

Wahabi
  a conservative sect founded on the teachings of Muhammad
  Abd al-Wahab, stressing the absoluteness of the Sharia,
  opposing syncretistic Sufi pirism, and insisting on a strongly
  "purified" form of Islamic practice. Strongest contemporary
  representation is found in Saudi Arabia and India.

Zabur
  the name applied to the Scriptures or the book God gave to
  David the prophet.

zakat
  the word for alms, or the religious tax.

ACHING THE UNREACHED

t of a program being carried out jointly by the Strategy Working Group of the
sanne Committee for World Evangelization and MARC, the Missions Advanced
earch and Communication Center, which is a ministry of World Vision International.

919 West Huntington Drive, Monrovia, California, USA

MARC

There are over 3 billion people in the world who do not know Jesus Christ as Lord and Savior. Large numbers of these people are not being reached by the gospel because they are hidden among larger populations or because the gospel message has not been expressed in ways that they can understand and respond to.

They are unreached people.

It has been estimated that there are at least 15,000 major unreached people groups, the vast majority of which have not been identified as to where they are and how they can be reached. This is a task for Christ's Church throughout the world. This is your task.

In order to understand and locate these unreached people the Strategy Working Group of the Lausanne Committee for World Evangelization has been working with the Missions Advanced Research and Communication Center (MARC). The early results of this research were presented at the Lausanne Congress on World Evangelization in 1974. Since then this worldwide effort has continued.

The on-going results are published annually in a directory entitled *Unreached Peoples*. As new information comes in from around the world, basic data about each group is listed and some 80 to 100 groups are described in detail. Information on each group is available for your use from MARC.

By publishing whatever information is available, the *Unreached Peoples* directory acts as a bridge between those who are discovering new unreached people, and those whom God has chosen to seek them out with the good news. Your contribution is important!

This questionnaire has been designed to make that task as simple as possible. We ask that you supply whatever information you can, trusting that the Lord of the Harvest has others who will supply what is missing.

Thank you for being a part of this grand vision that every person in the world may have an opportunity to know Jesus Christ.

52479A

FINDING THE UNREACHED: YOU CAN HELP!

You can help locate unreached people groups

You are part of a worldwide network of concerned Christians. There are millions upon millions of people in the world who have had little or no contact with the gospel of Jesus Christ. Because of this, we are asking you to help the Church locate and identify these peoples so it can reach them.

Within each country, there are distinct and unique groups of people who may be unreached. This questionnaire is designed to help you describe such groups so that Christians everywhere may pray and consider how these groups might be reached with the gospel. This information will be continuously compiled and made available to the Church and her mission agencies. It appears each year in an annual directory, *Unreached Peoples*, produced by David C. Cook.

There are many different groups of people in the world. How varied they are! Consequently, this questionnaire may not always ask the best questions for understanding a particular people. The questions have been asked in a way that will give comparative information to as large a number of Christians as possible. Where you feel another form of question would better suit your situation, please feel free to comment.

What is a "people group"?

A people group is a part of a society that has some basic characteristics in common that cause it to feel a sense of oneness, and set it apart from other groups. It may be unified by language, religion, economic status, occupation, ethnic origin, geographic location or social position. For example, a distinct group based on ethnic, language and geographic characteristics might be the Quechua of Bolivia, a sociological group might be the urban university and college students of Colombia, or the urban industrial workers of France. It is important to see that groups may share a common way of life and sense of oneness because of social, occupational or economic characteristics, as well as because of language or ethnic origin. Therefore, whenever possible, *describe the smallest number of persons who make up a distinct group*; that is, don't say that all persons in a region or province are a group, rather describe the specific subgroups within that region or province.

Who are the "unreached and unevangelized people"?

Christians have different definitions of the terms "unreached" or "unevangelized." For the purposes of this worldwide effort, we describe an unreached or unevangelized people as a people who has not received or responded to the gospel. This unresponsiveness may be due to lack of opportunity, to lack of understanding, or because the people has not received enough information about the gospel message in its own language through the eyes of its own culture so that it can truly respond to Christ.

We consider a people "unreached" when less than 20 percent of the members of the group are practicing Christians, that is, are active members of the Christian community. By "Christian" we mean adherents (church members, families and followers) of the historic Christian communions, Protestant, Anglican, Roman Catholic, Orthodox and such independent groups as may claim the Bible as the basis of faith and Jesus Christ as Lord and Savior. A group less than 20 percent Christian may yet need Christians from outside the group to help with the evangelism task.

How you can provide information

The attached questionnaire has two parts. If you only have information for the first part, send that in now.

Please fill in one questionnaire for each people group with which you are familiar. Do not put several groups on one questionnaire. (If you need more questionnaires, ask for extra copies or photocopy this one, or typewrite the questions you are answering on a separate sheet of paper.) We realize that one person may not have all the answers to these questions. Just answer what you can. PLEASE DO NOT WAIT UNTIL YOU HAVE ALL THE INFORMATION REQUESTED ON THIS QUESTIONNAIRE. SEND WHAT YOU HAVE. Other people may provide information that you do not have. Thank you for your help!

When you have completed this questionnaire, please return it to

Unreached Peoples Program Director
c/o MARC, 919 W. Huntington Drive, Monrovia, CA 91016 USA

SURVEY QUESTIONNAIRE FOR UNEVANGELIZED AND UNREACHED PEOPLES

Do you see a group of people who are unreached or unevangelized? Identify them! As the Lord spoke to Ezekiel of old, so He speaks to us today. "Son of man. What do you see"?

Answers to the questions on these two pages will provide the minimum information needed to list this people group in the *Unreached Peoples* annual.

After you have read the directions, type or print your answers so they can be easily read. It is unlikely that you will have all the information requested. Do the best you can. What information you are lacking others may supply. If your information is a best guess or estimate, merely place an "E" after it. Send in what you have as soon as possible. Please ignore the small numbers next to the answers. They help others prepare your answers for the *Unreached Peoples* annual.

*his reason I bow·
knees before the
ther, from whom
family in heaven
and on earth is
named . . ."
ans 3:14-15 (RSV)*

1. Name of the group or people:_____

2. Alternate name(s) or spelling: _____

3. Country where located: _____

4. Approximate size of the group in this country: _____

5. Vernacular or common language: _____

6. Lingua franca or trade language: _____

7. Name of religious groups found among this people:

	¹⁸ who are adherents of this religion	¹⁹ who practice this religion
CHRISTIAN GROUPS:		
Protestant	_____ ⁹⁹	_____ ⁹⁹
Roman Catholic	_____ ⁹⁹	_____ ⁹⁹
Eastern Orthodox	_____ ⁹⁹	_____ ⁹⁹
Other Christian: _____ (name)	_____ ⁹⁹	_____ ⁹⁹
NON-CHRISTIAN GROUPS OR SECULARISM:		
_____	_____ ⁹⁹	_____ ⁹⁹
_____	_____ ⁹⁹	_____ ⁹⁹
_____	_____ ⁹⁹	_____ ⁹⁹
_____	_____ ⁹⁹	_____ ⁹⁹
TOTAL FOR ALL GROUPS:	100 ⁹⁹	

*hren, My heart's
e and prayer to
r them is that
may be saved."
Romans 10:1
(RSV)*

8. In your opinion, what is the attitude of this people toward Christianity?

(01)☐ Strongly favorable (02)☐ Somewhat favorable (03)☐ Indifferent (04)☐ Somewhat opposed (05)☐ Strongly opposed

52479B

369

9. Questionnaire completed by:

Name: _____ Date: __ __

Organization: _____

Address: _____

_____

10. Who else might be able to provide information about this people?

Name   Organization (if any)   Address

_____

_____

_____

11. If you are aware of any publications describing this people, please give title and author.

_____

12. What other information do you have that could help others to understand this people better? What do you would help in evangelizing them?   *(Use additional sheet if necessary.)*

*"And how are they to
believe in him of whom
they have never heard?
And how are they to
hear without a
preacher?"
Romans 10:14 (RSV)*

13. Are you also sending in pages 3 and 4? ☐ Yes   ☐ No

Please send whatever information you have immediately. Do not wait until you have every answer.

Mail to:

Unreached Peoples Program Director
c o MARC, 919 W. Huntington Drive, Monrovia, CA 91016 USA

Name of people group described_____ Your name _____ Date ___

If you have any more information about this people group, please complete the following two pages as best you can. If not, please send in pages one and two now. If you can obtain more information later, send it in as soon as possible.

PEOPLE DISTINCTIVES—What makes them different? Why are they a people group?

14. A number of different things contribute to create a distinctive people or group, one that in some way shares a common way of life, sees itself as a particular group having an affinity toward one another, and differs to some extent from other groups or peoples. What would you say makes the people you are describing distinctive? Check the appropriate box of as many of the following descriptions as are important in making this people distinctive. Use the following scale: "High" importance, "Medium" importance, "Low" importance. For example, if you thought that the fact that they had a common political loyalty was of medium importance in unifying and making a group distinctive, you would place an "X" in the middle box under "Medium".

Importance

High Medium Low

(10)☐ ☐ ☐ Same language
(16)☐ ☐ ☐ Common political loyalty
(18)☐ ☐ ☐ Similar occupation
(19)☐ ☐ ☐ Racial or ethnic similarity
(17)☐ ☐ ☐ Shared religious customs
(20)☐ ☐ ☐ Common kinship ties
(22)☐ ☐ ☐ Strong sense of unity
(14)☐ ☐ ☐ Similar education level
(20)☐ ☐ ☐ Other(s) .. _____
(please write in)

Importance

High Medium Low

(10)☐ ☐ ☐ Common residential area
(33)☐ ☐ ☐ Similar social class or caste
(42)☐ ☐ ☐ Similar economic status
(40)☐ ☐ ☐ Shared hobby or special interest
(31)☐ ☐ ☐ Discrimination from other groups
(43)☐ ☐ ☐ Unique health situation
(36)☐ ☐ ☐ Distinctive legal status
(5)☐ ☐ ☐ Similar age
(38)☐ ☐ ☐ Common significant problems

15. How rapidly would you say the lifestyle of this people is changing? (check one)

(10)☐Very Slow Change   (49)☐ Slow Change   (46)☐ Moderate Change   (44)☐ Rapid Change   (40)☐ Very Rapid Change

---

PEOPLE LANGUAGES—What do they speak?

Please list the various languages used by the members of this people:

LANGUAGE TYPE	Primary name(s) of their language(s)	Approximate % who speak this language	Approximate % of people over 15 years of age who read this language
16. Vernacular or common language:	_____	___%	___%
17. Lingua franca or trade language:	_____	___%	___%
18. Language used for instruction in schools:	_____	___%	___%
19. Language suitable for presentation of the gospel:	_____	___%	___%

20. If there is Christian witness at present, what language(s) is being used? _____

21. Place an "x" in the boxes that indicate the status of Scripture translation in the language you consider most suitable for communicating the gospel (question 19):

	CURRENT STATUS			AVAILABLE		
	Not available	In process	Completed	In oral form	In print	On cassette or records
(POR)New Testament portions	☐	☐	☐	☐	☐	☐
(NT)Complete New Testament	☐	☐	☐	☐	☐	☐
(OT)Complete Old Testament	☐	☐	☐	☐	☐	☐

22. Of the Christians present among this people, what percent over 15 years of age can and do read any language?
_____%

to him was given *dominion and glory and* *kingdom, that all* *peoples, nations, and* *...Daniel 7:14 (RSV)*

CHRISTIAN WITNESS TO THIS PEOPLE—Who is trying to reach them?

23. If there are Christian churches or missions (national or foreign) now active *within the area or region where the people is concentrated*, please give the following information:

(If there are none, check here: ☐)

CHURCH OR MISSION Name of church, denomination	YEAR Year work began in this area	MEMBERS Approximate number of full members from this people	ADHERENTS Approximate number of adherents (community including children)	WORKERS Approximate numbers of trained pastors and evangelists from this people
_____	_____	_____	_____	_____
_____	_____	_____	_____	_____
_____	_____	_____	_____	_____

"... with an eternal gospel to proclaim to those who dwell on earth, to every nation and tribe and tongue, and people."
Revelation 14:6 (RSV)

24. What is the growth rate of the total Christian community among this people group?

(01)☐ Rapid growth   (02)☐ Slow growth   (03)☐ Stable   (04)☐ Slow decline   (05)☐ Rapid decline

25. In your opinion, what is the attitude of this people to religious change of any kind?

(01)☐ Very open   (02)☐ Somewhat open   (03)☐ Indifferent   (04)☐ Somewhat closed   (05)☐ Very closed

26. In your opinion, what is the attitude of this people toward Christianity?

(01)☐ Strongly favorable   (02)☐ Somewhat favorable   (03)☐ Indifferent   (04)☐ Somewhat opposed   (05)☐ Strongly opposed

---

27. Most people move through a series of more or less well-defined stages in their attitude toward Christianity. Parts of a people group will be further along than other parts. Here are ten categories that attempt to show this progression. However, locating people in some of these categories can be difficult, so to make things simpler some categories are combined in the questions that follow.

In your estimation, what percentage of this people can be described as those who: (These percentages are exclusive. Do not include people more than once. Your total should add up to 100%.)

"And you he made alive when you were dead, through the trespasses and sins in which you once walked ..."
Ephesians 2:1-2 (RSV)

Have no awareness of Christianity.................................... _____

Have awareness of the existence of Christianity .... _____

Have some knowledge of the gospel .... _____

Understand the message of the gospel .... _____

See the personal implications of the gospel .... _____

Recognize a personal need that the gospel can meet .... }
Are being challenged to receive Christ .... } _____

Have decided for Christ, but are not incorporated into a fellowship (may be evaluating their decision) .... _____

Are incorporated into a fellowship of Christians .... _____

Are active propagators of the gospel................................. _____

TOTAL 100

28. On the whole, how accurate is the information you have given us?

(V)☐ Very accurate   (F)☐ Fairly accurate   (E)☐ Good estimate   (G)☐ Mainly guesses

29. Are you willing to have your name publically associated with this information?

☐ No   ☐ Yes   ☐ Yes, with qualifications: _____

APPENDIX C

RECOMMENDED BIBLIOGRAPHY

Background Notes, U.S. Government Printing Office.

Beaver, R. Pierce, ed. *The Gospel and Frontier Peoples.* Pasadena: William Carey Library, 1973.

Dayton, Edward R., ed. *Mission Handbook: North American Protestant Ministries Overseas.* Monrovia: MARC, 1976.

Dayton, Edward R., *That Everyone May Hear.* Monrovia: MARC, 1979.

Douglas, J., ed. *Let the Earth Hear His Voice.* Minneapolis: World Wide Publications, 1975.

Europa World Year Book. London: Europa Publications, Ltd.

Grimes, Barbara, ed. *Ethnologue*. Huntington Beach: Wycliffe Bible Translators, 1978.

Johnstone, Patrick St. G., *World Handbook for the World Christian*. Pasadena: World Christian Book Shelf.

Kane, Herbert, Jr. *Global View of Christian Mission*. Grand Rapids: Baker Book Co., 1971.

Lebar, Frank M., ed. *Ethnic Groups of Insular Southeast Asia. (Vols. 1 & 2)*. New Haven: Human Relations Area Files Press, 1972.

Lebar, Frank M., G. C. Hickey and J. K. Musgrave, *Ethnic Groups of Mainland Southeast Asia*. New Haven: Human Relations Area Files Press, 1964.

Liao, David C.E., ed. *World Christianity: Eastern Asia*. Monrovia: MARC, 1979.

Luzbetak, Louis J., *The Church and Cultures*. Illinois: Divine Word Publications, 1963.

Maloney, Clarence, *People of South Asia*. New York: Holt, Reinhart and Wilson, 1974.

McCurry, Don M., ed. *The Gospel and Islam: A 1978 Compendium*. Monrovia: MARC, 1979.

McCurry, Don M., ed. *World Christianity: Middle East*. Monrovia: MARC, 1979.

Murdock, George P., *Africa: Its Peoples and Their Culture History*. New York: McGraw-Hill, 1959.

Nida, Eugene A., ed. *The Book of a Thousand Tongues*. New

York: United Bible Societies, 1972.

Pentecost, Edward C., *Reaching the Unreached.* Pasadena: William Carey Library, 1974.

Read, William R. and Frank A. Ineson, *Brazil 1980: The Protestant Handbook.* Monrovia: MARC, 1973.

Steward, Julian H., *Handbook of South American Indians.* New York: Cooper Square Pub., 1959.

Tindale, Norman B., *Aboriginal Tribes of Australia.* Berkeley: Univ. of Calif. Press, 1975.

Wagner, C. Peter., *Frontiers in Missionary Strategy.* Chicago: Moody Press, 1971.

Wagner, C. Peter and Edward R. Dayton, eds. *Unreached Peoples '79: The Challenge of the Church's Unfinished Business.* Elgin, Illinois: David C. Cook Publishing Co., 1978.

Wauchope, Robert, ed. *Handbook of Middle American Indians: Guide to Ethnohistorical Sources. Vols. 1-15.* Austin: Univ. of Texas Press, 1964.

Weekes, Richard V., *Muslim Peoples: A World Ethnographic Survey.* Westport, Connecticut: Greenwood Press, 1978.

Wong, James, Peter Larson and Edward Pentecost. *Missions from the Third World.* Singapore: Church Growth Study Center, 1973.

Audiovisual

Dayton, Edward R., *That Everyone May Hear.* Audiovisual. Monrovia: MARC, 1979.

Notes

NOTES

INTRODUCTION

1. E-1 and E-2 represent degrees of difference from the evangelist's culture, which in shorthand is called an E-1 culture. E-1, or "monocultural evangelism," is contrasted to "cross-cultural evangelism," for which the symbols E-2 and E-3 stand.

2. These data are gleaned from R. Max Kershaw, "Islam in the Western World," *Muslim World Pulse* (Wheaton, Ill.: EMIS), April 1978.

3. "Soviet Central Asia: A Ripening Field," *Sparks* (Slavic Gospel Association), February 1979, pp. 4-5.

4. "The Glen Eyrie Report—Muslim Evangelization," *Lausanne Occasional Papers No. 4.* Available from LCWE, P.O. Box 1100, Wheaton, IL 60187, at $1.00 each.

5. Available from MARC, World Vision International, 919 W. Huntington Dr., Monrovia, CA 91016, at $6.00 each.

PART ONE: THE UNREACHED AND HOW TO REACH THEM

PLANNING STRATEGIES FOR EVANGELISM

1. MARC, Monrovia, Calif., 1978.

2. The workbook is available from MARC, 919 W. Huntington Drive, Monrovia, CA 91016.

3. I have written a simplified version of the workbook, *That Everyone May Hear* (MARC, 1979). It is the basic study guide for the Consultation on World Evangelism, sponsored by the LCWE, to be held in Pattaya, Thailand, on June 1980.

4. See James F. Engel and H. Wilbert Norton, *What's Gone Wrong with the Harvest?* (Grand Rapids: Zondervan, 1975), and Viggo B. Søgaard, *Everything You Need to Know for a Cassette Ministry* (Minneapolis: Bethany Fellowship, 1975).

5. The Theology and Education Group of LCWE has developed a basic study in their *Occasional Paper No. 2*, "The Willowbank Report," 1978.

MUSLIM EVANGELISM IN THE 1980s

1. C. Peter Wagner, *What Are We Missing?* (Carol Stream, Ill.: Creation House, 1973, 1978), p. 66.

2. Norman Horner, "Present-Day Christianity in the Gulf States of the Arabian Peninsula," *Occasional Bulletin of Missionary Research,* April 1978.

PART TWO: CASE STUDIES

THE SUNDANESE OF INDONESIA

1. C. Peter Wagner and Edward R. Dayton, eds., *Unreached Peoples '79* (Elgin, Ill. and Weston, Ontario: David C. Cook Publishing Co., 1978), pp. 257-89.

2. Materials received during February 1979 in a letter from Roger Dixon, my missionary colleague in West Java; these sources (hereinafter referred to as "Dixon") greatly helped in preparing this case study.

3. Ibid.

4. Koernia Atje Soejana, ed., *A Seed That Grew II: A Survey of the Pasundan Christian Church* (Jakarta and Bandung: The Pasundan Christian Church and the Study and Research Agency of the Indonesian Council of Churches, 1974), p. 57. (Indonesian terms and titles translated by the writer of this case study.)

5. Ibid., pp. 11-14.

6. Hendrik Kraemer, *From Missionfield to Independent Church* (The Hague: Boekencentrum, 1958 reprint ed.), p. 113. Originally published in 1930.

7. Materials received during February 1979 in a letter from George Trotter, my missionary colleague in West Java; these sources (hereinafter referred to as "Trotter") were based mainly on a conversation with Dr. Wesley Mintardja Rikin and were very helpful in preparing this case study.

8. Soejana, p. 257.

9. K.A.H. Hidding, *Sundanese Tradition* (Bandung: Pajajaran State University, 1972), p. 21. (Indonesian terms and titles translated by the writer.)

10. Kraemer, p. 115.

11. Dixon materials.

12. Frank L. Cooley, *Indonesia: Church and Society* (New York: Friendship Press, 1968), p. 93.

13. Kraemer, p. 97.

14. Cooley, pp. 6-7.

15. See, for instance, Avery T. Willis, Jr., *Indonesian Revival: Why Two Million Came to Christ* (South Pasadena: William

Carey Library, 1978), and Ebbie C. Smith, *God's Miracles: Indonesian Church Growth* (South Pasadena: William Carey Library, 1970).

16. Dixon materials. See also Th. Muller Krugger, *Church History in Indonesia* (Jakarta: Christian Publishing House, 1959), pp. 191-95. (Indonesian terms and titles translated by the writer.)

17. Dixon materials.

18. Trotter materials.

19. Dixon materials.

20. Ibid.

21. Soejana, p. 195.

22. Dixon materials.

23. Ibid.

24. Trotter materials.

25. Dixon materials.

26. Trotter materials.

27. Kraemer, p. 131.

A UNIQUE EFFORT TO REACH JAMMU-KASHMIR FOR CHRIST

1. Richard V. Weekes, ed., *Muslim Peoples, A World Ethnographic Survey* (Westport, Conn.: Greenwood Press, 1978), pp. 207-8.

It appears that there is the following error/omission on page
_____ of *Unreached Peoples '80:* _____

_____

_____

_____

_____

_____

I would like to receive more information on the _____

_____(name of people group).

Additional Comments: _____

_____

_____

Name _____Date _____

Address _____

Please detach, insert in an envelope, and mail to:

Missions Advanced Research and
Communication Center
919 West Huntington Drive
Monrovia, CA 91016
U.S.A.

What reviewers said about UNREACHED PEOPLES '79...

"Much more than just tables of statistics and regional clas[si]cations. Some of the best minds in missions have b[een] tapped." **Alliance Witness**

"...belongs in the library of every missionary-minded ch[urch] and home." **Christian Herald**

"Approach is significant." **Eternity**

UNREACHED PEOPLES '79, the first volume in this ann[ual] series, was honored by *Occasional Bulletin of Mission Research* as one of the fifteen outstanding books in the fiel[d of] missiology for the year 1978.

UNREACHED PEOPLES '80, focusing on the Muslim wo[rld] continues this distinguished tradition. It is a source book [of] missions you will want to own and use.

THE EDITORS

EDWARD R. DAYTON is the founder of Missions Advanc[ed] Research and Communication Center (MARC), a ministry [of] World Vision International. He currently heads the Evangeli[sm] and Research Division of World Vision and has written exte[n]sively on management and mission strategy.

C. PETER WAGNER is chairman of the Strategy Work[ing] Group of the Lausanne Committee for World Evangeliz[ation]. He is also associate professor of church growth at the Ful[ler] Theological Seminary School of World Mission. W[a]gn[er] served as a missionary to Bolivia for sixteen years and h[as] authored fourteen books on missions and ch[urch]

Special Consultant

DON M. McCURRY is the founding director [of the] Zwemer Institute, a coordinating agenc[y for] evangelism. Previously he served for eighte[en years as a] Presbyterian missionary to Pakistan.

The UNREACHED PEOPLES series is a joint proje[ct of the] Strategy Working Group of the Lausanne Com[mittee for] World Evangelization and the MARC ministry of [World Vision] International.

28373 A2759 ISBN